Entrepreneurship, Small and Medium-Sized Enterprises and the Macroeconomy

The U.S. economy has restructured itself, moving away from an industrial economy towards one based on information, while the European Union and Japan have been left to worry about rising government deficits, inflexible businesses, persistent unemployment, and workers inadequately trained for the information age. Why has the U.S. economy successfully moved beyond its chief competitors?

This collection, edited by Zoltan J. Acs, Bo Carlsson and Charlie Karlsson, suggests that at least some of the answers to the pattern of divergent development can be found in the role of the entrepreneur. By examining the functions of new firms and entrepreneurs in the economy, the essays in this volume make a fundamental contribution to our understanding of the macroeconomy. Each chapter clarifies the role of entrepreneurs in economic theory, the function of small and medium-sized enterprises that they found and build and the impact of the innovations introduced on employment, productivity and economic growth.

The public policy implications of this process are clear. Countries that encourage entrepreneurship and free entry will have better macroeconomic performance than those that retard it. And a dynamic small and medium-sized enterprise sector requires addressing the issue of inadequate management competence and bridging the gap between large and small firms.

T0328846

Entrepreneurship, Small and Medium-Sized Enterprises and the Macroeconomy

Edited by

ZOLTAN J. ACS   BO CARLSSON   CHARLIE KARLSSON

CAMBRIDGE
UNIVERSITY PRESS

CAMBRIDGE UNIVERSITY PRESS
Cambridge, New York, Melbourne, Madrid, Cape Town, Singapore,
São Paulo, Delhi, Dubai, Tokyo, Mexico City

Cambridge University Press
The Edinburgh Building, Cambridge CB2 8RU, UK

Published in the United States of America by Cambridge University Press, New York

www.cambridge.org
Information on this title: www.cambridge.org/9780521629256

First published 1999
First paperback edition 2010

A catalogue record for this publication is available from the British Library

Library of Congress Cataloguing in Publication Data

Entrepreneurship, small and medium-sized enterprises and the
macroeconomy / edited by Zoltan J. Acs, Bo Carlsson, Charlie
Karlsson.
    p.   cm.
  "The selections in this volume are edited versions of papers
presented at an international conference ... at Jönköping
International Business School, Jönköping, Sweden on June 13-15" –
Pref.
  Includes bibliographical references and index.
  ISBN 0-521-62105-4
  1. Entrepreneurship - Congresses. 2. Small business - Congresses.
3. Industries - Size - Congresses. 4. Competition - Congresses.
5. Macroeconomics - Congresses. 6. Comparative economics -
Congresses. I. Acs, Zoltan J. II. Carlsson, Bo, 1942- .
III. Karlsson, Charlie, 1945- .
HB615.E63465   1998   98-17417
338'.04 - dc21   CIP

ISBN 978-0-521-62105-2 Hardback
ISBN 978-0-521-62925-6 Paperback

Contents

Preface

The selections in this volume are edited versions of papers presented at the international conference Entrepreneurship, Small and Medium-Sized Enterprises and the Macroeconomy, at Jönköping International Business School, Jönköping University, Jönköping, Sweden, on June 13–15, 1996. The idea for this conference came over four years ago when we realized that there was a need to integrate recent research on small and medium-sized firms and the macroeconomy. Many macroeconomic topics were being discussed in the small firm literature, including productivity and economic growth, innovation and technological change, employment, income distribution and finance. The conference was host to some of the leading scholars from Europe and the U.S., many of whom have been studying the small firm for years. Chapters represent a careful mix of theoretical and empirical research in large and small advanced economies. The conference was organized by Zoltan J. Acs in collaboration with David J. Storey, Bo Carlsson and Charlie Karlsson. Financial support for the workshop was provided by the Carl-Olof and Jenz Hamrin's Foundation, the Free Media Foundation, the county administration in the county of Jönköping, Jönköping International Business School, and the Harry Y. Wright Chair at the University of Baltimore. We would like to thank Katarina Harryson, who provided for local arrangements, and Benjamine Gahari, who helped to organize the conference. We are particularly grateful to three anonymous referees, who played an important role shaping this book through their helpful suggestions and comments, and to Scott V. Parris of Cambridge University Press, who enabled us to move from conference to publication of this volume with a minimum of impediments.

Contributors

Zoltan J. Acs, University of Baltimore

David B. Audretsch, University of Indiana

Pontus Braunerhjelm, Industrial Institute for Economic and Social Research

Bo Carlsson, Case Western Reserve University

Mark Casson, University of Reading

Andy Cosh, University of Cambridge

Robert Cressy, University of Warwick

Per Davidsson, Jönköping International Business School

Paul A. Gompers, Harvard University

John Haltiwanger, University of Maryland

Alan Hughes, University of Cambridge

Charlie Karlsson, Jönköping International Business School

Luuk Klomp, Erasmus University

Leif Lindmark, Jönköping International Business School

Randall Morck, University of Alberta

Christer Olofsson, The Swedish University of Agricultural Sciences

Gavin C. Reid, University of St. Andrews

Paul D. Reynolds, Babson College

Roy Thurik, Erasmus University

Eric Wood, University of Cambridge

Bernard Yeung, University of Michigan

Introduction and Overview

CHAPTER 1

The Linkages Among Entrepreneurship, SMEs and the Macroeconomy

Zoltan J. Acs, Bo Carlsson and Charlie Karlsson

1   The Macroeconomy in the 1990s

When William Jefferson Clinton was first elected President of the United States in 1992, one of the main issues in the public debate was *competitiveness*. A common perception was that U.S. industry was losing the global economic race. If government didn't respond, living standards would suffer. During that recession year, economic thinking was summed up by Jeffrey E. Garten (1992, p. 221), Under Secretary of Commerce in the first Clinton administration: "Relative to Japan and Germany, our economic prospects are poor and our political influence is waning. Their economic underpinnings – trends in investment, productivity, market share in high technology, education and training – are stronger. Their banks and industry are in better shape; their social problems are far less severe than ours."[1]

As the United States reelected President Clinton in 1996, the economic anxiety of four years earlier was no longer to be found in the electorate. After a quarter century of painful ups and downs, the U.S. economy appeared to be doing extraordinarily well. According to Lawrence H. Summers, Deputy Treasury Secretary, "The economy seems better balanced than at any time in my professional lifetime."[2] In 1997 unemployment was just over 5 percent, the economy was growing at 3 percent a year, inflation was at bay, manufacturing productivity was rising by 4 percent a year, the dollar was strong, and the Dow Jones Industrial Average was breaking records almost as a matter of course. It seemed clear that the U.S. economy had restructured, moving from an industrial economy to an information one, and made the transition to the twenty-first century.

The impressive performance of the U.S. in the last few years may be contrasted with the rather lackluster performance in both Europe and

4   Zoltan J. Acs, Bo Carlsson and Charlie Karlsson

Japan, where gross national product (GNP) has grown at less than 1.5 percent per annum in the last five years. In the European Union (EU) the unemployment rate has remained stubbornly in double digits, and in Japan the stock market has been stagnant since the early 1990s at half of its previous level.

But a comparison of only the last few years may be heavily influenced by cyclical elements which may distort more long-term developments. It is instructive, therefore, to compare the macroeconomic experience in Europe and the United States over the last few decades. In the period 1960–84, GNP grew at almost identical rates in Europe and the U.S.: it rose by 3.3 percent annually in the EC and 3.1 percent in the U.S. But beneath this superficial similarity lie some fundamental differences. While the total employment in the EC was virtually unchanged, it increased by 33 million (from 65 to 98 million, i.e., by 1.7 percent per annum) in the United States. (Another 25 million were added between 1983 and 1996.) At the same time, the capital stock increased by 3.5 percent per year in the EC and by 2.4 percent in the U.S. (de Jong, 1989). As a result, labor productivity rose much more rapidly in Europe than in the U.S. – but so did unemployment. The unemployment rate hovered around 5 percent in the U.S. from 1960 to 1975 while it stayed below 3 percent in the EC. It then rose rapidly on both sides of the Atlantic to around 10 percent in 1982 but subsequently diverged: the unemployment rate has remained around 10 percent in Europe while it has been cut in half, to less than 5 percent, in the United States.

What explains this divergent macroeconomic behavior? Among the contributing factors are certainly differences in competition and entrepreneurship. Between 1960 and 1983, the number of corporations and partnerships in the United States more than doubled (from 2.0 million to 4.5 million) while the number of companies in Europe stagnated. It declined in Sweden, Denmark, the Netherlands, and Britain and increased only slightly in West Germany, France, Switzerland, and Italy (de Jong, 1989). The difference in business formation rates, in turn, reflects a number of other economic factors, such as consistently higher return on investment in the U.S. than in Europe, higher productivity, and lower unit labor costs, as well as some institutional factors such as less rigid labor and capital markets, freer competition, and lower industrial subsidies.

There are at least two entrepreneurial stories to the U.S. success. First, large firms that existed in mature industries have adapted during the 1980s and 1990s and are now thriving. Even though they have shed thousands of jobs, these large firms still employ millions of workers. However, as they have become "leaner," their sales and profits have increased sharply. For example, General Electric cut its work force by 40 percent, from over 400,000 twenty years ago to less than 240,000 in 1996, while sales increased fourfold, from less than $20 billion to nearly $80 billion. Second, while these large companies have been holding their own, new and small start-up companies have been blossoming. Twenty years ago, Nucor Steel was a small steel manufacturer who embraced a new technology called thin slab casting, allowing it to thrive while other steel companies were stumbling. In 1995, Nucor had 59,000 employees, sales of $3.4 billion, and a net income of $274 million. In fact, according to Lynch and Rothchild (1996) 25 companies, some of which did not exist in 1975, created 1.4 million jobs between 1975 and 1995.

The purpose of this volume is to examine the macroeconomic implications of an evolving small firm sector. Underneath the smooth path of macroeconomic aggregates there is a very active microeconomic world. Massive reshuffling of factors of production is constantly taking place. Market economies seem to handle this overwhelming "churn" with remarkable success. It follows that the eventual failure of economies that repress private initiative is perhaps unavoidable (Caballero and Hammour, 1996). Our focus is not on the vast majority of firms which remain small but rather on the dynamic behavior of new and growing small and medium-sized enterprises and of the entrepreneurs that guide them, and their impact on the macroeconomy.

The chapters are arranged in four groups: entrepreneurship and its role in industry dynamics and in the macroeconomy; financing entrepreneurship and small and medium-sized enterprises (SMEs); job creation and destruction; and innovation, productivity, and growth. Together, the chapters that follow bring us a little closer to understanding the fundamental economic, social, and political changes that are continuing to affect the global economy and the ways economic policy might cope with these changes.[3]

2   The Historical Background

With a few notable exceptions, for the better part of the history of the profession, economists have not spent much time studying small firms.[4] However, this has begun to change in the last twenty years. The "twin oil" shocks triggered an unexpected reappraisal of the role and importance of small and medium-sized enterprises. A surprising finding has been that small firms and entrepreneurship play a much more important role in economic growth than had been acknowledged previously.[5] It has been shown, for example, that contrary to Chandler's thesis (Chandler, 1990), the differences in performance of the U.S., British, and German

6   Zoltan J. Acs, Bo Carlsson and Charlie Karlsson

economies in the first half of the 20th century cannot be explained entirely by differences in the behavior of the largest firms but also by the different degrees to which these economies became reliant on large firms alone, with Britain exhibiting the greatest dependence and also the worst macroeconomic performance (Hannah, 1996).

2.1   The Conventional Wisdom

The view that the cornerstone of the modern economy is the large firm dates back to the onset of the industrial revolution. The belief in the inherent potential of scale economies was proposed by Adam Smith (1776) with the famous passage on the pin factory. The domination of the economy by large firms was observed by Karl Marx, who held the view that the corporate form of organization would lead to a "... constantly diminishing number of the magnates of capital, who usurp and monopolize all advantages of transformation." The ultimate state is one in which "... the entire social capital would be united, either in the hands of one single capitalist, or in those of one single corporation" (Marx, 1912, p. 836).

In this view, which has prevailed for the better part of this century, small firms do not play an important role in the economy, and their role should be expected to diminish in the future (Galbraith, 1956). This has been the case especially in the manufacturing sector, where large and even giant firms dominated Western economies throughout most of the 20th century. As E. F. Schumacher pointed out (1973, p. 64): "I was brought up on the theory of 'economies of scale ...'" In country after country, official policies favored large units of production and mechanisms of ownership. These goals were pursued in free market and planned economies alike, as well as in developed and developing countries. *Thus, for the better part of two centuries, there was a convergence of opinion on the relevance of firm size, and its importance for economic growth.*[6]

Readers interested in documenting the importance of small firms in the 1970s found much talk and few facts. For years the small firm sector remained ignored and poorly understood. However, all that has begun to change as powerful computers and large data sets have enabled researchers to assemble a far better understanding of the economic role of small firms.

In the first authoritative book on small businesses, Brock and Evans (1986) examined the changes in small businesses over time. Between 1958 and 1980 the number of businesses in the U.S. economy increased

Table 1.1. *Changes in the Small Business Share of Employment,*
Sales, and Gross Product Originating

	Employment[1] (1958-1977)	Business Receipts (1958-1979)	Gross Product Originating (1958-1977)
Total Change	-6	-23	-4
Change due to shifts in industry composition[2]	+4	-2	+3
Change due to shifts in small business share within industries[3]	-9	-21	-7

Source: W. A. Brock and D. S. Evans, 1986, *The Economics of Small Firms* (New York: Holmes & Meier), Table 2.11, p. 21. Used with permission.
Note: Small businesses are those with fewer than 500 employees for the employment and value added (gross product originating) measures and those with sales of under $5 million in 1958 dollars for the business receipts measure.
[1] Excludes the construction industry.
[2] Calculated under the assumption that each industry's share of total employment, sales, or value added, respectively, remained constant over time period under consideration.
[3] Calculated under the assumption that small businesses' share of employment, sales, or value added, respectively, remained constant for each industry over time period under consideration.

from 10.7 million to 16.8 million. But the relative economic importance of small business in the overall economy declined over this period. Between 1958 and 1977 the share of employment accounted for by firms with fewer than 500 employees decreased from 55.5 percent to 52.5 percent. Between 1958 and 1979 the share of business receipts obtained by companies with less than $5 million in receipts declined from 51.5 percent to 28.7 percent. Between 1958 and 1977 the share of value added contributed by firms with 500 or fewer employees decreased from 57 percent to 52 percent. These trends are summarized in Table 1.1. The decline in the small business share of value added was due to a shift in small business share of value added within industries. In other words, firms were getting bigger, and therefore the share of small firms was being reduced. The small business share of value added is the best measure of the relative importance of small business in the economy. Sales tend to understate the importance of small business, and employment tends to overstate the importance of small businesses because they are more labor-intensive than large businesses.

8   Zoltan J. Acs, Bo Carlsson and Charlie Karlsson

2.2   New Trends in the 1970s

However, by the early 1970s "cracks" had begun to appear in the structure of the manufacturing sector in some developed countries, including
some of the most important firms and industries. At the same time, casual
evidence began to suggest that small firms in several countries were out-
performing their larger counterparts. One example of this was the U.S.
steel industry, where new firms entered in the form of "minimills" (for
example, Nucor) and small firm employment expanded, while the incumbent large companies shut down plants and reduced employment in a
number of countries. Other examples are found in industries characterized by rapid product innovation, such as electronics and software. This
development following the "twin oil shocks" triggered an unexpected
reappraisal of the role and importance of small manufacturing firms,
resulting in a divergence of opinion on the importance of firm size (Acs,
1984).[7]

In fact, several lines of research have found that something happened
to the centuries-old trend towards larger business: depending upon the
measure of business size examined, the trend sometimes decelerated,
ceased, or reversed itself between the late 1960s and late 1970s. Contrary
to the conventional wisdom at the time, Birch (1981, p. 8) found that
". . . whatever else they are doing, large firms are no longer the major
providers of new jobs for Americans." Davis (1990) showed that the
typical nonfarm private-sector employee worked at increasingly larger
establishments during the 1950s and 1960s but at increasingly smaller
establishments in the late 1960s and 1970s. Brock and Evans (1989)
showed that the average gross national product per firm increased from
$150,000 in 1947 to $245,000 in 1980 but then decreased to $210,000 in
1986. Loveman and Sengenberger (1991) reported that average firm
and establishment size began to decrease in most of the countries they
examined in the 1970s after having increased from at least the end of
World War II. Acs and Audretsch (1993b) showed that the small firm
share of manufacturing employment increased in most Organization
for Economic Cooperation and Development (OECD) countries in
the 1980s. Acs and Evans (1995) found that the increase in the self-
employment rate after 1975 in most OECD countries was due to
structural change.

Between 1982 and 1992 the small firm share of value added in the U.S.
economy stabilized at 51 percent, peaking at 52 percent between 1985
and 1987, as shown in Table 1.2. This result is quite remarkable in light
of the mega mergers and consolidation in retail trade during the 1980s,
and the growth of giant global business service firms during the 1990s.

Table 1.2. *Small Business Share of Private Nonfarm Gross Product, 1982–1992*

	Total Private Business	Mining and Manufacturing	Construction	TCPU	Trade	FIRE	Services
1982	51	23	78	22	70	62	81
1983	51	23	81	21	69	60	81
1984	51	24	83	22	68	60	80
1985	52	25	84	23	67	58	79
1986	52	25	86	23	66	56	78
1987	52	25	87	23	65	55	77
1988	51	24	88	23	64	54	76
1989	51	24	88	23	64	52	76
1990	51	24	88	24	63	51	75
1991	51	25	88	24	61	50	74
1992	51	25	88	24	62	51	74

Source: Joel Popkin and Company, 1997, "Small Business Share of Private, Nonfarm Gross Product," prepared under contract for the U.S. Small Business Administration, Office of Advocacy, SBAHQ-95-C-0021, Table 1, p. 2.

The significant expansion of the service sector – and the role of growing small firms in it – helped end the decline in the small firm share of value added. If the industrial makeup of the U.S. economy had remained constant at its 1982 distribution, the small business share of value added would have declined from 51 percent in 1982 to 48 percent in 1992. Therefore, small service firms – many of them new start-ups – contributed to maintaining the aggregate small business output share during the 1980s and early 1990s. The output share gains in some sectors during the past ten years were counterbalanced by relative declines in other sectors. In construction, for example, small business value added rose from 78 percent to 88 percent of the industry total during the 1982–1992 period. Meanwhile, the small firm share of value added in manufacturing and mining rose from 23 percent to 25 percent.

The picture is somewhat different if one looks at employment shares instead of output shares. As shown in Table 1.3, between 1958 and 1977 the small firm share of employment in the United States *decreased* in

Table 1.3. *Change in Small Firms' Share of Employment, by Industry, 1958–1992*

Industry	Change in percent of employment in firms with fewer than 500 employees		
	1958 - 77 (%)	1977 - 87 (%)	1987-92 (%)
Mining	-16.8	15.8	-6.90
Construction	-4.4[1]	6.2	0.81
Manufacturing	-8.2	4.0	1.90
Wholesale trade	-10.3	-4.3	-1.50
Retail trade	-10.3	-5.8	-1.60
Services	-8.4	-5.9	-10.8

Source: 1958–1977: U.S. Census Bureau, U.S. Enterprise Statistics for 1958 through 1977, as reported in U.S. Small Business Administration, *The State of Small Business*, 1984, Table A2-24; 1977–1987 U.S. Census Bureau, U.S. Enterprise Statistics, for 1977 through 1987, as reported in U.S. Small Business Administration, *The State of Small Business*, 1992, Table 2.3, p. 60; 1987–1992 U.S. Census Bureau, U.S. Enterprise Statistics for 1987 and 1992. Calculated by the author.
[1] 1967–1977 only.

every sector of the economy. However, between 1977 and 1987 the small firm share of employment *increased* in the goods-producing sectors – mining, construction, and manufacturing – while it continued to decrease in the non-goods-producing sectors. The small firm employment share increased by 15.8 percent in construction, by 6.2 percent in mining, and by 4.0 percent in manufacturing. This trend continued between 1987 and 1992.[8]

This shift in the share of employment has not been confined to the U.S. In a recent study, Acs and Audretsch (1993b) showed that a distinct and consistent shift away from large firms and towards small enterprises has occurred within the manufacturing sector of every developed Western country. While the magnitude of the shift varies considerably among nations, the direction does not. As shown in Table 1.4, the shift in the firm-size distribution ranged from an increase of 3.1 percent in the Federal Republic of Germany between 1970 and 1987 to an increase of 10.9 percentage points between 1981 and 1987 in the North of Italy, and an increase of 9.8 percentage points between 1979 and 1986 in the United

Table 1.4. *Summary from Country Studies of Small Firm Share of Manufacturing Employment and Their Rates of Change[1]*

Country	Year	Small firm employment share (%)	Year	Small firm employment share (%)	Share change
United Kingdom	1986	39.9	1979	30.1	+9.8
Federal Republic of Germany	1987	57.9	1970	54.8	+3.1
United States	1987	33.0	1977	29.1	+3.9
Netherlands[2]	1986	39.9	1978	36.1	+3.8
Portugal	1986	71.8	1982	68.3	+3.5
Italy[3]					
North	1987	55.2	1981	44.3	+10.9
South	1987	68.4	1981	61.4	+7.0
Czechoslovakia	1988	1.4	1954	13.0	-11.6
East Germany	1986	1.1	-	-	-
Poland[2]	1985	10.0	1937	33.0	-23.0

Source: Z. J. Acs and D. B. Audretsch, 1993[b], *Small Firms and Entrepreneurship: An East–West Perspective* (Cambridge: Cambridge University Press), Table 12.1, p. 228. Used with permission.
[1] A "small firm" is defined as an enterprise with fewer than 500 employees, unless designated otherwise.
[2] A "small firm" is defined as an enterprise with fewer than 100 employees.
[3] A "small firm" is defined as an enterprise with fewer than 200 employees.

Kingdom. By contrast, small firms were practically wiped out in Eastern Europe after the Communist takeover.

In sum, small and medium-sized firms represent a large, diverse, and important part of the economy. In 1994, firms with fewer than 500 employees accounted for 53 percent of private sector employment, 47 percent of sales, and 51 percent of value added in the United States (U.S. Small Business Administration, 1995).

2.3   The Role of Small Firms

Historically, small firms have played an important role in industrial evolution. Alfred Marshall (1920, p. 263) described this process of industry evolution by analogy, where one can observe "[t]he young trees of the forest as they struggle upwards through the benumbing shade of their older rivals." The 1971 Bolton Committee in the United Kingdom argued that new firms in an industry would promote new products and ultimately shape the evolutionary path of the industry, as well as constrain any market power exercised by the entrenched firms. This "seedbed" function appears to be a vital contribution of the small firm sector to the long-run health of the economy. Similar concerns led to the creation of the U.S. Small Business Administration and the Office of Advocacy.[9]

According to Piore and Sabel (1984), the economic crisis of the 1970s resulted from the inability of firms and policymakers to maintain the conditions necessary to preserve mass production, i.e., the stability of markets. Their claim is that the deterioration in economic performance in the 1980s resulted from the limits of the model of industrial development that is found in mass production: the use of special-purpose machines and of semiskilled workers to produce standardized products. In fact, if the Great Depression represented a macroeconomic crisis, the economic problems of the 1970s–1990s were essentially microeconomic in that the focus was on the choice of technologies, organization of firms and industries, and markets. As we move toward the 21st century, the emerging conventional wisdom seems to suggest that small firms and entrepreneurship are both necessary for long-run macroeconomic prosperity (OECD, 1997).[10]

3   Small Firms in Economic Theory

Economic theory has not kept up with the strong public policy interest in small firms (You, 1995). The microeconomic theory of the firm has been mostly devoted to analyzing the single representative firm, and the industrial organization literature has been mostly concerned with large dominant firms (apparently out of concern about their monopoly power).

In the diverse literature on the theory of the firm, four approaches to the size distribution of firms may be distinguished. The first is the conventional microeconomic approach (or the technological approach), in which firm size is determined by technical and allocative efficiency. Long-run average cost is minimized in this model (Viner, 1932). However, the theory does not explain the size distribution of firms in an industry. Lucas (1978) develops a model of the size distribution of firms in which individuals have different endowments of what might be called business acumen or managerial ability.[11] The greater the talent of an agent, the greater the size of the firm (number of employees). Those with talent below that of the marginal manager, who is indifferent between being a manager and an employee, will be employees. The size distribution of firms depends on the given distribution of such inputs.

The second approach is the transactions cost approach (or the institutional approach), in which firm size is determined by transactions cost efficiency (Coase, 1937). Here the firm is viewed as an alternative to the market as a mechanism of resource allocation. The basic insight is that all transactions entail costs, e.g., searching for prices, writing and monitoring contracts. In this view, transactions for which the market is a highly costly form of governance are withdrawn from market competition and internalized within the firm. The assumption that there is a clear boundary between purely market transactions and purely administrative interfirm allocations implies that firms interact with each other only through anonymous arm's-length market transactions which are governed by the law of competition. While convenient for some purposes, this assumption masks the reality of the dense networks of cooperation and affiliation by which firms are related (Williamson, 1991). The Japanese subcontracting system and the Italian industrial districts illustrate cooperative interfirm relationships. Both the linkages between large and small firms and the networks among small firms can substitute for, *and even outperform*, integration as a nonmarket coordination in the presence of complementarities (Lazerson, 1988; Saxenian, 1991; Gomes-Casseres, 1996).

The third is the industrial organization approach, in which firm size and its distribution (market structure) are related to market power in a relationship of mutual causality. It is customary to classify the imperfectly competitive markets into monopoly, oligopoly, and monopolistic competition.

The final set of theories are the dynamic models of size distribution. Gibrat's Law states that the growth rate of a firm is independent of its current size and its past growth history. Starting from any size distribution of a population of firms, if every firm experiences the same growth rate subject to random variation year after year, the size distribution will tend to a log normal distribution.

While Marshall's story of the life cycle of firms is based largely on sociological observations about the personal differences among different generations of the entrepreneur's lineage, Jovanovic (1982 and 1994) develops a model of the firm life cycle based on learning. He suggests that the learning process of entrepreneurs determines intraindustry dynamics. He assumes that individuals are unsure about their abilities to manage a business, but that they can assess themselves by observing how well they perform in the rough and tumble of the business world. Pakes and Ericson (1998) build on Jovanovic's model by arguing that firms can actively accelerate the learning process by investing in R&D. These models are especially useful for understanding firm dynamics in new industries. Large and small firms coexist in this model because better managers run bigger firms, and firms start out small but grow over time as their owners learn and become better managers.

Empirical work by Evans (1987), Dunne, Roberts, and Samuelson (1989), and Davis and Haltiwanger (1992) using large samples of manufacturing firms has found evidence supporting Jovanovic's conclusions. The following regularities among firm growth, firm size, and firm age are found: First, firm growth decreases with firm size for firms of the same age and decreases with firm age for firms of the same size. Second, the variability of firm growth decreases with firm age for firms of the same size. Third, the probability that a firm will fail over a given period of time decreases with firm size for firms of the same age and decreases with firm age for firms of the same size. The extent to which a change in the rate of new firm creation affects the size distribution of firms will, of course, depend on its impact on survival, and on which firms, if any, give up market share to the new entrants (Audretsch, 1991; Bates, 1990).

4   The Dynamics of Competition

Words in common usage tend to take on a variety of meanings. *Competition* is no exception. Although many nuances are attached to the term, most writers tend to view competition as either a dynamic process or a state of affairs. When competition is described as a process, it is the competitive struggle that receives attention (Reid, 1987). However, "... it [is] inevitable that models built according to the orthodox blueprint miss completely, or deal awkwardly with, these features of change" (Nelson and Winter, 1982, p. 400).

The academic microeconomics of the post–World War II era, which grew out of Hicks' *Value and Capital* and Samuelson's *Foundations*, starts out with given production sets or functions. Based on general equilibrium models, where markets are characterized by perfect competition, these standard tools are not fashioned to deal with dynamics. In *The Theory of Economic Development* (1934), first published in German in 1911, Schumpeter unveiled his concept of economic development. He looked upon economic development not as a mere adjunct to the central body of orthodox economic theory, but as the basis for reinterpreting a vital process that had been crowded out of neoclassical economic analysis by static general equilibrium theory. Schumpeter viewed the competitive struggle as one that revolved around innovation and economic progress. He drew attention to the role of the entrepreneur, who is a key figure and plays a central role in his analysis of capitalist evolution. "[Q]uite simply, he is the *persona causa* of economic development" (Hebert and Link, 1989, p. 43). He was a proponent of the view that who becomes an entrepreneur is determined by function and not personality (Knight, 1921; Holmes and Schmidts, 1990; Gifford, 1992; Baumol, 1993).

5   Overview of the Book

The first section in this volume deals with the role of the entrepreneur in the theory of the firm, in industry dynamics, and in the macroeconomy. In Chapter 2, Mark Casson examines entrepreneurship and the theory of the firm. While there have been important developments in the theory of the firm, even in these new theories the role of the entrepreneur has not been featured prominently. Casson argues that a comprehensive theory of the firm requires an intellectual synthesis of existing theories in which entrepreneurship plays the leading role. Contrary to Schumpeter's view, the firm is essentially an institutionalized extension of the personality of an entrepreneur. The role of the entrepreneur is to monitor a volatile environment for shocks of two types – transitory and persistent – and then take appropriate action. Shocks emanate from both supply and demand, and information on both needs to be synthesized in a special way in order to optimize the firm's response to them. Shocks that generate opportunities for establishing new markets tend to persist for a considerable time, while shocks to already existing markets tend to be more transitory. The latter are handled by routine procedures typically set up by large firms, while small entrepreneurial firms are often better at responding to new market opportunities, especially if they require new organizational forms and if established firms exhibit a high degree of managerial inertia. Casson finds that it is the quality of entrepreneurial judgment which holds the key to long-term success, not specific business strategies or technologies. The ability to synthesize information is the hallmark of the successful entrepreneur.

In Chapter 3, David B. Audretsch examines the role of entrepreneurship and new firms in economic restructuring. He begins by observing two phenomena which need to be explained. The first is that most industries are characterized by a firm size distribution which has remained remarkably stable over time and across industries. This size distribution is highly skewed with a large number of small firms coexisting with a few large ones; as a result, the bulk of firms operate at an apparently suboptimal scale of output. The second phenomenon is that the entry of new firms does not seem to be deterred substantially even in industries in which scale economies and innovative activity are important.

Audretsch then posits an evolutionary theory focusing on the role of new firms in generating diversity and in selecting among diverse alternatives. The key is that markets are in perpetual motion with a lot of firms entering and exiting the industry. On the exit side, the question is whether the exiting firms are made up of firms that entered recently (last in–first out) or of long-established incumbents (first in–first out). The answer seems to be that the technological regime has a lot to do with the process of firm selection and therefore the type of firm which is likely to exit. In the entrepreneurial regime (in which innovations are primarily associated with entry of new firms), new entrants have a greater likelihood of innovating and are therefore less likely to exit. In the routinized regime (in which innovations are typically carried out by established firms) the incumbents have the innovative advantage, so that exiting firms tend to be new entrants. On the entry side, the question is which entering firms will survive. The postentry growth of surviving entrants depends on the size of the gap between the entry level of output and the minimum efficient level, with lower likelihood of survival the greater the gap is. Only firms who offer a viable product and ultimately approach or attain minimum efficient scale survive. Others stagnate and/or exit. The conclusion is that the persistence of a firm-size distribution skewed towards small-scale enterprise is a result of a continuing process of entry of new firms and not necessarily the existence of a permanent set of small and suboptimal firms.

The extent to which firms enter, grow, decline, and exit an industry has been termed "mobility," "turnover," "dynamic evolution," and "turbulence," depending upon the author. We adopt the term *turbulence* (Beesley and Hamilton, 1984; Audretsch and Acs, 1990) which we define as the extent of movement of firms within as well as into and out of an industry. Despite the recognition that *firm and job turbulence is a necessary feature of economic growth*, there have been only a few empirical studies actually attempting to measure the effect of industry turbulence on economic growth.

In Chapter 4, Paul D. Reynolds uses diverse measures of establishment and job turbulence in 362 U.S. labor market areas over an eight year period (1980–88) to determine the relative impact of creative destruction on concurrent, subsequent, and short-term regional economic growth. The study utilizes unique data on the birth and death of U.S. business establishments and business jobs to consider the relationship to economic growth, as measured by annual job growth. Two different sets of measures of creative destruction (turbulence) are developed and utilized in analysis of relations to economic growth, defined as regional job growth. Substantial evidence is developed to indicate that turbulence is an important feature accompanying economic growth. Reynolds finds that no matter what measure of business volatility is used, the higher the volatility, the higher the economic growth rate. On the other hand, he finds little evidence for the view that turbulence alone is an independent factor causing or even affecting future economic growth. In other words, turbulence is a necessary but not sufficient condition for growth.[12]

While Audretsch focuses on the role of entrepreneurship in restructuring within industries and Reynolds on the contribution of entry and exit of firms (turbulence) to economic growth, Pontus Braunerhjelm and Bo Carlsson study the interdependence among existing industry structure, entrepreneurship, and macroeconomic performance. In Chapter 5, they compare two regions, similar in size and industrial development, Ohio and Sweden, in terms of gross domestic product (GDP) growth, manufacturing output, development of employment and unemployment, and change in the number of establishments throughout the economy over the last two decades. They find that both regions have performed considerably worse than the United States as a whole and the OECD countries as a group with respect to economic growth but that Ohio has been much more successful than Sweden in creating new jobs and somewhat better in creating growth in the number of establishments. The authors then examine the industry composition of employment and the distribution of establishments, as well as changes therein over the last twenty years. They also look at the main clusters of economic activity and find that in both regions the biggest clusters are all in mature industries, most of which are declining in employment. Thus, the lack (relative to the U.S. as a whole) of entrepreneurship seems at least in part due to path dependence. The industries which once led Ohio and Sweden to leading positions in industrial development now seem to be retarding the transition to a more modern structure. A lack of vigorous entrepreneurship has also contributed to the relatively slow transformation of the economy. On the other hand, there is also evidence that new clusters that are forming, e.g., in biomedicine and polymers, are strongly related to "old" industrial know-how in industrial machinery, measurement devices, etc., suggesting that a transformation process has started but has yet to show up in the statistical accounts.[13]

6   Financing Entrepreneurship and SMEs

The role of finance in promoting entrepreneurship and small business growth is the subject of a large literature. One of the main questions in this literature is whether or not the financial markets are biased against entrepreneurs and small firms in the sense that small firms suffer from lack of information about and/or lack of access to financial markets. A rich theoretical literature has emerged in the last decade, flowing from the early papers of Jaffee and Russell (1976) and Stiglitz and Weiss (1981).[14] Whilst the underpinnings of the notion of a "debt gap" and the "asymmetric information" thesis have been questioned (de Meza and Webb, 1987), their broad implications seem to have been accepted by policymakers around the world. The belief that capital markets do not provide adequate funds for new business is one of the rationales for government-assisted programs for small business (European Network for SME Research, 1993; U.S. Small Business Administration, 1996; Besley and Levenson, 1996).

Table 1.5 shows that the small business share of the $8.5 trillion in measurable financing of all business was only about $550 billion (about 6 percent) in 1995. It is well known that small firms are less capital intensive than large firms, therefore requiring less finance. However, when these results are compared with the fact that small firms provide 47 percent of sales, 51 percent of private sector output, and 53 percent of employment, it is easy to draw the conclusion that there are imbalances and a need for policy action to improve both the capital and credit markets for small business.

In support of the debt-gap thesis are the findings of Evans and Jovanovic (1989) and more recently Blanchflower and Oswald (1996), Holtz-Eakin, Joulfaian, and Rosen (1994) and Black, de Meza, and Jeffreys (1996). They show that the probability of survival is a function of the individual's assets. For example, Holtz-Eakin et al. (1994) show that a $150,000 inheritance in 1985 increases the probability that an individual will continue as a sole proprietor by 1.3 percentage points. Also, an inheritance has a substantial impact on firm growth: receipt of any surviving enterprise increases by almost 20 percent.

Although pioneering works, these studies include only a relatively small set of human and financial capital variables in the survival function, thus excluding the "people" factors that are often regarded by practitioners as critical to small business success. If, as some recent studies have suggested (Cressy, 1996a), assets are in fact explained by human capital, an observed correlation of financial capital and survival may instead indicate the human deficiencies of the business. This alternative

Table 1.5. *Measurable Financing of Business (Billions of Dollars)*

Small Business		Large Business	
Bank Loans[1]	$98	Bank Loans[1]	$418
Commercial Mortgages[2]	66	Commercial Mortgages[2]	224
Trade Debt[3]	233	Trade Debt[3]	638
Finance Companies	91	Finance companies[3]	272
IPO[4]	10	IPO[4]	117
Bond Market[5]	12	Bond Market[5]	1,280
Venture Capital[6]	34	Stock Market[5]	5,241
SBA Disaster Loans[7]	2	Commercial Paper[5]	163
		International Borrowing[5]	250
Totals	$546	Totals	$8,486

Source: U.S. Small Business Administration, Office of Advocacy, 1996, *White Paper on the Financing of Small Business,* Table 2.

Note: The grand total is $9.0 trillion, of which the small business share is only 6.0 percent.

[1] Small firm loans are C&I loans of less than $250,000. Large firm loans are all other C&I loans. Call Reports, June 1995.

[2] Small firm mortgages are mortgages of less than $250,000. Large firm loans are all other mortgages. Call Reports, June 1995.

[3] The State of Small Business: A Report of the President, 1995, Table B.1.

[4] IPO for the last seven years, 1988–1994, valued at their selling price, The State of Small Business: A Report of the President, 1995, Table B.13. IPOs for large business are assumed to be in the stock market value. They are included for large business for comparison reasons only.

[5] Flow of funds accounts, 2nd quarter 1995. Data are for nonfinancial corporations.

[6] Venture Capital Journal, 1994.

[7] SBA's portfolio as of 10/31/94 was $21.5 billion, of which $19 billion is included in bank loans and commercial mortgages.

view, presented in Cressy (1996b), argues from United Kingdom start-up data that funds, and the assets that underpin them, are determined entirely by the human capital engaged in the business: the bank selects businesses, or businesses self-select for finance to yield maximum returns. Thus, in this view credit rationing does not necessarily play a role in small business start-ups.

Part II consists of three chapters focusing on various financial aspects of entrepreneurship and small business. Robert Cressy examines the role of finance in explaining why small firms fail; Gavin C. Reid looks at the role of capital structure in determining the performance of very young microfirms; and Paul A. Gompers studies the importance of venture capital in financing entrepreneurial firms.

In Chapter 6, Robert Cressy explores empirically the shape (inverted U-shape, with a negative skew indicating that most business failures occur in the first two years of existence) and underlying stability of the UK firm failure distribution using a large start-up database. The hypothesis tested is that the shape of the failure distribution is determined not by the amount of financial capital available but by a division of the population of entrepreneurs into those with and those without significant initial human capital. This, combined with a learning process that occurs through time, determines success or failure. Human capital, which changes relatively slowly, is what keeps the business failure rate and its distribution by firm age constant over time, even though macroeconomic conditions vary considerably.

The results of the estimation suggest that financial and human capital together reduce the variance of sales and the firm failure rate, as predicted by Cressy's model. Aggregate failure rates have an inverted U-shaped relation to the age of the firm. Specifically, current and mean past sales both reduce the failure rate (holding firm age constant), while low current human capital increases the failure rate. The higher the growth rate of GDP, the lower the failure rate of small businesses, suggesting that the failure distribution is not invariant to macrofactors. Cressy concludes that access to financial capital is determined both by learning that takes place within firms and by different human capital endowments at start-up. They reduce the variance of sales, thereby reducing the need for contingency finance to cope with business judgment "errors."

In Chapter 7, Reid examines the financial structure and performance of young microfirms and reaches results similar to those of Cressy.[15] As regards age, their average time from financial inception is one and a half years; as regards size, their average number of employees is just three full-time and two part-time workers. The key issue explored is the extent to which financial structure close to inception has a bearing on early performance of the microfirm. The approach taken is empirical. The general finding is that financial structure is not a major determinant of performance in the earliest phase of the life cycle of the microfirm. While firms that continued to trade were about twice the size of those which ceased trading, other features, financial as well as nonfinancial, were similar in both categories of firms. The distinctive features of surviving firms, in addition to their greater size, include the following: they were found to pay higher wages, suggesting that the abilities of economic agents are unequally distributed and that the agents of higher ability receive greater rewards. Other distinctive features are that the firms which continued trading had significantly longer planning horizons and greater access to trade credit; they also avoided extended purchase agreements and overcommitment of resources to innovation at an early age. However, it was also found that purely microeconomic factors provide an incomplete account of survivability. Macroeconomic factors such as business cycle fluctuations in pricing, production, employment, and innovation must also be taken into account.

Table 1.5 also shows that the single most important source of finance for small businesses in the United States is trade debt, which makes up over 40 percent of small business finance. Bank loans, commercial mortgages, and finance companies together make up only slightly more. The remaining 15–20 percent is made up of venture capital, bonds, initial public offerings (IPOs), and U.S. Small Business Administration (SBA) Disaster Loans. The total pool of venture capital in the U.S. is about $34 billion – vastly larger than that in any other country, but only a small fraction of total small business finance. Also, only a small fraction of new business start-ups receive venture capital. Each year there are about 800,000 start-ups in the United States; of these, only 1,000 to 2,000 receive venture capital financing. But the firms that receive venture capital are primarily high-growth, high-potential companies that have the opportunity to become dominant players in their industries. The importance of venture capital is indicated by the fact that such fast-growing and well-known companies as Microsoft, Netscape, Sun Microsystems, Apple, Genentech, Starbucks, Staples, and Federal Express all received venture capital financing in their early stages.

In Chapter 8, Paul A. Gompers surveys the U.S. venture capital market over the last two decades. He argues that the important element in the U.S. model of venture capital is not just the access to capital but also the contributions to corporate governance that venture capitalists provide. Whether the project is in a high- or low-technology industry, venture capitalists are active investors, supplying new firms with important competence. They monitor the progress of firms, sit on boards of directors, structure compensation packages, and help in hiring management talent. Venture capitalists retain important control rights including the ability to appoint key managers and remove members of the entrepreneurial team. Venture capitalists also provide entrepreneurs with access to consultants, investment bankers, lawyers, and accountants.

Entrepreneurial start-ups are fraught with numerous agency conflicts and asymmetric information that may lead to capital rationing. Gompers analyzes the various mechanisms employed by venture capitalists to minimize potential losses due to such conflicts. These mechanisms are staged capital infusions, syndication of investment, and the use of convertible financing instruments.

The staging of capital infusions allows venture capitalists to gather information and monitor the progress of firms, maintaining the option to periodically abandon projects. Most venture capital investments are made in syndicates. One venture firm will originate the deal and look to bring in other venture capital firms. This syndication of investment serves multiple purposes. One is that it allows the venture capital firm to diversify in more investments than would be possible if the venture capitalist had to invest the entire amount in all its companies. Because the total risk of any particular investment is so high compared to the systematic risk, diversification is also beneficial. Finally, the contractual relationship between venture capitalists and entrepreneurs makes it necessary to align entrepreneurs' incentives with venture capitalists' goals. Convertible debt is a financial instrument that alleviates the adverse selection problem (arising from the fact that it is difficult to distinguish between good and bad entrepreneurs) and leads to better allocation of control rights. If self-finance or other financing is available, high-ability entrepreneurs may otherwise opt out of the venture capital market, leaving only low-ability entrepreneurs seeking venture capital financing. The role of each of these mechanisms is examined and a control theory of venture capital is suggested.[16]

7   Job Creation and Destruction

In the late 1970s small businesses burst into the news, in large part because of the research of David Birch, formerly at M.I.T. Birch (1979) made two seminal contributions, which have, unfortunately, often been overlooked in the subsequent controversy over his methods and conclusions. First, he pieced together an extremely rich and powerful data set that allowed researchers, for the first time, to study business dynamics for the full spectrum of businesses and industries in the U.S. Second, he initiated the systematic study of small businesses. Few economists had studied small businesses in the U.S. economy before Birch, even though these businesses constituted a large fraction of employment and sales.

Until Birch it was virtually impossible to measure economic activity for small firms as well as for large firms and to make comparisons over time. In 1981 Birch revealed the startling findings from his long-term study of U.S. job generation. Contrary to the conventional wisdom at the time, Birch (1981, p. 8) found that ". . . whatever else they are doing, large firms are no longer the major providers of new jobs for Americans." Instead, he discovered that most new jobs were created by small firms.

Birch's methodology as well as his application of the underlying data have been sources of considerable controversy,[17] as have his quantitative estimates. His qualitative conclusion that the bulk of new jobs have been generated by small and medium-sized enterprises has also been criticized.[18] For example, Brown, Hamilton, and Medoff (1990) in *Employers Large and Small* challenged the finding that small firms are becoming more important over time and that small firms are the primary job creators in the economy.[19] They also showed that small firms pay less than large firms, offer fewer benefits, and provide poorer working conditions.[20] This has been substantiated in several studies, but the gap appears to be closing.[21] More recently, an OECD study (1996) has largely confirmed Birch's original result that the bulk of new jobs are in fact generated by SMEs.

Table 1.6 shows longitudinal data for employment changes from births, deaths, and existing establishments for the U.S. economy for the years 1992–1993. Between March 1992 and March 1993 employment increased by 1,948,253 or 2.1 percent. Over 75 percent of the employment gains were in the service sector, followed by 15 percent in retail trade. There are three interesting statistical regularities in Table 1.6. First, the U.S. economy is characterized by high annual rates of job reallocation, 31.5 percent for the whole economy, with similar rates in services and retail trade. Reallocation rates are lower in manufacturing, 22.2 percent, and higher in finance, 37.2 percent. Second, job reallocation rates are a decreasing function of firm size, indicating that births and deaths play an important role in reallocation. Third, in an expanding high-technology economy, job creation is greater than job destruction in all sectors of the economy, as well as in most firm size classes (Acs and Armington, 1998).

In a new book that has important implications for labor economics, industrial organization, and macroeconomics, Davis, Haltiwanger, and Schuh (1996a) have produced the most comprehensive treatment of the subject of employment dynamics to date. Using the Longitudinal Research Database constructed by the U.S. Census Bureau, *Job Creation*

Table 1.6. *United States: Employment Changes from Births, Deaths, and Existing Establishments, 1992–1993*

Industry	Data Type	Total	Beginning Year U.S., All Industries Employment Size of Firm					
			1-4	5-9	10-19	20-99	100-499	500+
U.S. Totals								
	Employment in 1992	92,791,532	5,171,122	6,195,603	7,383,380	17,111,967	13,304,504	43,624,956
	Net Change	1,948,253	1,081,375	288,193	106,260	68,760	242,648	161,017
	Percent Change, Total	2.1	20.9	4.7	1.4	0.4	1.8	0.4
	Percent Change, Job Creation	16.8	41.5	23.1	18.6	16	16.4	13.1
	Percent Change, Job Destruction	14.7	20.7	18.5	17.2	15.6	14.5	12.7
	Percent Change, Job Reallocation	31.5	62.2	41.6	35.8	31.6	30.9	25.8
Manufacturing								
	Employment in 1992	18,164,463	230,695	409,597	710,205	2,658,843	2,935,137	11,219,986
	Net Change	33,815	67,094	34,616	24,441	15,053	35,685	-143,074
	Percent Change, Total	0.2	29.1	8.5	3.4	0.6	1.2	-1.3
	Percent Change, Job Creation	11.2	51.3	26.4	18.9	14.2	12.9	8.1
	Percent Change, Job Destruction	11	22.2	18	15.5	13.6	11.7	9.4
	Percent Change, Job Reallocation	22.2	73.5	44.4	34.4	27.8	24.6	17.5
Retail Trade								
	Employment in 1992	19,674,534	1,055,935	1,492,043	1,882,283	4,130,884	2,061,504	9,051,885
	Net Change	313,604	162,531	34,267	842	-23,182	-3,894	143,040
	Percent Change, Total	1.6	15.4	2.3	0	-0.6	-0.2	1.6
	Percent Change, Job Creation	17.2	38.2	22.3	18.5	15.7	15.7	14.6
	Percent Change, Job Destruction	15.6	22.8	20	18.5	16.3	15.9	13.1
	Percent Change, Job Reallocation	32.8	61	42.3	37	32	31.6	27.7

Finance, Insurance, and Real Estate

Employment in 1992	6,904,252	473,768	359,094	370,412	927,447	832,119	3,941,412
Net Change	-39,462	69,675	14,147	7,396	16,724	-7,042	-140,362
Percent Change, Total	-0.6	14.7	3.9	2	1.8	-0.8	-3.6
Percent Change, Job Creation	18.3	32.7	21.3	18.1	16	16.4	17.2
Percent Change, Job Destruction	18.9	18	17.4	16.1	14.1	17.3	20.8
Percent Change, Job Reallocation	37.2	50.7	38.7	34.2	30.1	33.7	38

Services

Employment in 1992	30,659,327	2,148,079	2,406,307	2,524,986	5,470,404	5,269,834	12,839,717
Net Change	1,482,298	407,598	120,924	70,453	184,402	288,814	410,107
Percent Change, Total	4.8	19	5	2.8	3.4	5.5	3.2
Percent Change, Job Creation	18.5	36.9	21.1	18.1	17.9	19.5	15
Percent Change, Job Destruction	13.7	17.9	16	15.3	14.6	14	11.8
Percent Change, Job Reallocation	32.2	54.8	37.1	33.4	32.5	33.5	26.8

Source: U.S. Small Business Administration, Office of Advocacy, from data provided by the U.S. Department of Commerce, Bureau of the Census.
Notes: Longitudinal data for establishments active (payroll) in first quarter of the year (establishments with 0 employment in the first quarter were excluded).
New firm births are classified by their employment size at the first quarter.
Represents private establishments excluding railroad, domestic, and farms.

and Destruction focuses on the manufacturing sector from 1972 to 1988 and develops a statistical portrait of microeconomic adjustments. The authors paint a picture in which large gross job flows characterize the economy with job destruction dominating the cyclical features of the economy. With respect to firm size they find that job creation is roughly proportional to employment share.

The idea that long-term job creation is closely linked to gross flows of entry and exit taking place over the business cycle is fundamental to understanding the economic growth process. As mentioned already (also see Reynolds, Chapter 4 in this volume), turbulence is necessary (although not sufficient) for economic growth. The greater flexibility of U.S. labor markets relative to those in Europe and Japan is increasingly viewed as an important factor explaining superior American economic performance in recent years. The basic idea is that U.S. firms can fire, so they hire. By contrast, European firms can't fire, so they don't hire. The net long-term result is slower net job creation in Europe.

The first two chapters in Part III of this volume deal with job creation and destruction over the business cycle. The authors rely on better and more sophisticated databases than available earlier. In Chapter 9, John Haltiwanger examines the cyclical dynamics of job creation and destruction by employer size and age for the period 1973–1988. Much of the recent focus on job creation by employer size has emphasized the respective contributions of small vs. large employers to net job creation. Here the focus is on the cyclical dynamics of gross job creation and destruction by employer size and age. The objective is to document the cyclical patterns by employer size and age and, in turn, account for the differential cyclical patterns in terms of the responses to alternative driving forces. The latter include common and reallocation shocks including specific shocks such as oil prices and credit market shocks.

Haltiwanger's main conclusions are that small and young plants exhibit much higher average rates of job creation and destruction than larger and more mature plants in U.S. manufacturing and that the cyclical patterns of job creation and destruction differ substantially across employer size and age groups. The cyclical volatility of job destruction is much greater than that for job creation. This volatility is driven entirely by the behavior of mature plants (both large and small); young plants, regardless of whether they are large or small, exhibit about the same cyclical volatility in job creation as in job destruction. Macroeconomic shocks such as oil price shocks and abrupt changes in monetary or credit policy affect job destruction more than job creation, since they are more important for mature plants.

In Chapter 10, Per Davidsson, Leif Lindmark, and Christer Olofsson use a unique database that tracks all births, deaths, expansions, and contractions among commercially active business establishments in Sweden in the 1989–94 period. During the years 1990–93, Sweden experienced the deepest recession since the 1930s, while a dramatic recovery occurred in 1994.

The authors address the following main issues: (1) What is the role of SMEs in job creation under different business cycle conditions? (2) What are the constituent parts of SME job creation in terms of different types of SME establishments and different forms of business dynamics?

The main findings are the following: during the deep recession of 1990–93, SMEs were an important source of new jobs in Sweden. In both gross and net terms, SMEs performed better as job creators than did large firms, even though both groups suffered net job losses during the recession. The same result holds also when the data are disaggregated into manufacturing, professional services, retailing/hospitality services, and "miscellaneous industries": the SME shares of job gains and losses were found to be larger than the SME share of the existing job stock; the SME share of job gains is larger than the SME share of job losses; as a result, SMEs are overrepresented as job creators in both gross and net terms. The SME share of the job stock increases was found to increase over time in all four industries.

When the distinction was made between establishments which are part of multiestablishment enterprises and those which are single establishment firms, it was found that it was not the larger, multiestablishment SMEs which kept up SME employment and job creation during the recession. Rather, the development of multiestablishment SMEs was similar to and only marginally better than that of large firms. It was primarily the development among the many small, single site firms that made the SMEs as a group come out better as job creators than large firms.

In Chapter 11, Luuk Klop and Roy Thurik examine job flows in two traditional service sectors (retail trade and hospitality industries) in the Netherlands. Similarly to Haltiwanger and Davidsson, Lindmark, and Olofsson, they analyze job creation and destruction with respect to both firm age and firm size. The period studied is 1985–88. They find that the annual gross job reallocation rates (the sum of creation and destruction) are in excess of 20 percent for the retail trade and in excess of 30 percent for the hospitality industries. This may be compared with quarterly rates ranging from 8 to 15 percent (19.7 percent annual rates) calculated by Haltiwanger for U.S. manufacturing (see Chapter 9 in this volume). Thus, the numbers reported by Haltiwanger imply much lower annual rates than those obtained by Klop and Thurik.

Also in contrast to the previous chapters, Klop and Thurik find that small firms do not outperform their larger counterparts with respect to net job creation. Instead, they find that the net job reallocation rate even increases with firm size in retail trade. However, it should be noted that the largest size class is 20 or more employees. But consistently with the results in the previous chapters, the gross job reallocation rates are found to be substantially higher for the youngest firms than for their elder counterparts.

8   Innovation, Productivity, and Growth

The systematic relationship between output and productivity growth rates suggests that technological progress is not a random process but rather one guided by market forces. Schmookler (1966) argued in great detail that it is the expected profitability of inventive activity, reflecting conditions in the relevant factor and product markets, that determines the pace and direction of industrial innovation. Schumpeter (1942, p. 110) had expressed a similar view more than twenty years earlier when he wrote, "It is quite wrong . . . to say, as so many economists do, that capitalist enterprise was one, and technological progress a second, distinct factor in the observed development of output; they were essentially one and the same thing." We focus on technological progress that results from intentional industrial innovation, that is, from the allocation of resources and other information-generating activities in response to perceived profit opportunities.

At the heart of the conventional wisdom regarding technological change has been the belief that large enterprises able to exploit at least some market power are the engine of technological change. This view dates back at least to Schumpeter, who argued, "The monopolistic firm will generate a larger supply of innovations because there are advantages which though not strictly unattainable on the competitive level of enterprise, are as a matter of fact secured only at the monopoly level" (Schumpeter, 1942, p. 101).

Just as there are persuasive theories defending the Schumpeterian Hypothesis that large corporations are a prerequisite for technological change (Comanor, 1967; Kamien and Schwartz, 1975; Cohen et al., 1987), there are also substantial theories predicting that small enterprises also have an important role to play in that change. Scherer (1991, and works cited therein) argued that the bureaucratic organization of large firms is not conducive to undertaking risky R&D. The decision to innovate must survive layers of bureaucratic resistance, where any inertia regarding risk results in a bias against undertaking new projects. In small firms the decision to innovate is made by relatively few people; therefore, bureaucratic inertia and resistance to new R&D projects are reduced.

The development and application of direct measures of technological change have led to new learning about the sources of innovative activity (Acs and Audretsch, 1990b; 1993a). Central to the new learning is that *small firms, as well as large enterprises*, play an important role in innovative activity. The greater the extent to which an industry is composed of large firms, the greater will be the innovative activity, but, ceteris paribus, the increased innovative activity will tend to emanate more from the small firms than from the large firms (Acs and Audretsch, 1988). There does not appear to be much evidence of increasing returns to R&D expenditures in producing innovative output. With just a few exceptions, diminishing returns to R&D are the rule (Acs and Audretsch, 1991). However, as noted later, the evidence does suggest that large firms have an advantage in appropriating the returns to R&D.

The new learning about technological change has raised a number of questions about why smaller enterprises may, in fact, have an innovative advantage over their larger counterparts, at least in certain industries. One answer was suggested by Link and Rees (1990), who concluded that there are diseconomies of scale in the production of innovations due to the "inherent bureaucratization process which inhibits both innovative activity and the speed with which new inventions move through the corporate system towards the market." Cohen and Klepper (1996) and Klepper (1996) suggest that while small firms are more innovative, large firms are in a better position to appropriate the results, particularly of process innovation. This is consistent with observed patterns of industry evolution as well as the product life cycle. As a new industry emerges, many new and small firms enter initially, but eventually the rate of entry declines and large firms come to dominate. New industries are characterized by a high rate of product innovation, carried out mostly by small firms. As the entry rate declines over time, so does the rate of product innovation. The firms remaining in the industry devote an increasing share of their R&D efforts to process innovation, in which large firms may have an advantage due to their ability to spread costs over a larger output.

The two chapters in the last part examine the relationships among innovation, productivity, and growth. In Chapter 12, Andy Cosh, Alan Hughes, and Eric Wood describe the extent and nature of innovative activity amongst small and medium-sized businesses in the UK in the 1990s. They also provide an analysis of the way in which it is influenced by past performance and affects future performance. With regard to the former, innovative activity in one period is expressed as a function of innovative activity in a previous period, past growth performance, and the competitive environment facing the firm. In the latter case, they model business failure and acquisition on past innovative activity, controlling for firm age, size, and industry. The analysis makes use of a specially constructed longitudinal database compiled by the authors and their colleagues at the Centre for Business Research at the University of Cambridge. Since 1990, the Centre has conducted three separate postal and telephone surveys covering a sample of over 2,000 small and medium-sized UK firms.

The results provide valuable new insights into the role which technological innovation plays in firm performance and which factors determine the extent of innovative activity. Poor relative growth performance does not appear to be a major factor motivating firms to innovate. However, the motivation to innovate is closely linked with a firm's perception of its competitive environment and, in particular, the existence of overseas competition. In contrast to previous research, which points to a link between product innovation activity and the probability of firm failure, the study by Cosh, Hughes, and Wood has found that the probability of failure is strongly influenced by process innovations but not product innovations. The introduction of process innovations significantly *reduces* the probability of firm failure. However, the introduction of product innovations significantly *increases* the probability that a firm will be acquired.

It seems generally to be agreed that the key to economic growth is the degree of success of an economy in enhancing productivity. If the role of small firms in the economy has been increasing, what contribution have they made to productivity and growth? According to Baily, Bartlesman, and Haltiwanger (1996), plants that increased and/or decreased employment made the same contribution to productivity growth, and Baily, Hulten, and Campbell (1992) found that entry and exit are relatively unimportant in aggregate productivity growth. In the United States, between 1967 and 1992, value added per worker rose just 2.1 percent per year on average at small and medium-sized manufacturing establishments compared to 2.9 percent at large plants. Partly as a result of this, the value added per worker at small and midsize plants in 1992 stood at $66,170, just 65.7 percent of the $100,640 in value added per worker for larger manufacturers.[22]

Chapter 13 tries to shed some light on this question. Zoltan J. Acs, Randal Morck, and Bernard Yeung examine the relationship between productivity growth and the firm-size distribution. The study is based on cross section industry data pooled from two sources: the National Bureau of Economic Research (NBER) manufacturing and productivity database and the new Census-based Statistics of U.S. Businesses (SUSB) from the U.S. Small Business Administration (SBA). They find that productivity growth is positively associated with the level and growth of larger firms' market shares. This does not mean that smaller firms do not make substantial contributions to productivity growth; after all, many radical and fruitful innovations are brought into the marketplace by small firms. However, most small firms are noninnovating, do not grow very much, and eventually exit. Therefore, the average contribution of smaller firms to productivity growth is quite small. Radical innovations brought about by truly innovative small firms will take time to manifest their influence on productivity, and the firms are likely to have become large, either by growth or by acquisition, before their innovations measurably impact productivity.

9   Concluding Remarks

Given the theme of this volume – the role of entrepreneurship and SMEs in the macroeconomy – what can we conclude, and what are the implications for public policy?

As noted, large enterprises have historically been viewed as the most important source of jobs, innovation and growth. In recent years, policymakers, economists, and business leaders have increasingly come to recognize the contributions that small and medium-sized enterprises make to these objectives.

The main theme that underlies all the chapters in this volume is that there is a strong connection between changes that occur at the microlevel and macroeconomic performance (as measured, e.g., in terms of economic growth, job creation, unemployment, price stability, and productivity). Economic growth occurs not because of broad improvements in technology, productivity, and resources available but because some economic agents (i.e., firms) improve their technology, management, or organization; become more productive; innovate; and force other firms out of business. As this ongoing creative destruction occurs, more and better jobs are created than the ones lost, the overall level of productivity rises, and the standard of living rises as well.

To sum up briefly, the conclusions from the section on entrepreneurship, industrial dynamics, and the macroeconomy are (1) that the observed persistence of a firm-size distribution skewed towards SMEs is a result of a continuing process of entry and exit of firms (with the implication that if entry is stymied, the result is greater dominance of large firms and a more rigid industry structure); (2) that turbulence (gross flows of entry and exit of firms and jobs) is a necessary but not sufficient condition for economic growth; and (3) that lack of entrepreneurship contributes to a slow transformation of the economy.

The conclusions from the section on financing entrepreneurship and SMEs may be summarized as follows: small businesses make up half of the economy but represent only about 6 percent of total business finance in the United States. The fact that SMEs are less capital intensive than larger firms provides only a small part of the explanation. The conventional wisdom is that SMEs are unable to obtain credit because of lack of information and/or lack of access. An additional explanation is that small firms lack management competence and other human capital and thus are less attractive fund recipients. The financial gap is filled through personal or individual resources. Over 40 percent of the external financing SMEs do receive is made up of short-term trade debt, while over 75 percent of large business finance consists of stocks and bonds. The studies of small business failures in this volume emphasize the importance of competence (human capital, especially management capability, as reflected, e.g., in good planning and prudent risk taking) as the distinctive feature of surviving firms and those that get access to financial capital. Even though venture capital plays only a small role as a source of finance for small businesses generally, it is crucial to the growth of companies with high growth potential. But the most important aspect of venture capital is not finance but rather its contribution to corporate governance (i.e., a form of management competence).

With regard to job creation and destruction, it is now reasonably well established that the bulk of new jobs are generated by SMEs. The focus of recent research has been on the large magnitude of gross job flows through entry and exit and job reallocation relative to the net employment changes. The results here show (1) that small and young plants in U.S. manufacturing exhibit much higher rates of job creation and destruction than larger and more mature plants over the business cycle and (2) that the cyclical volatility of job destruction is much higher than that of job creation as a result of greater cyclical variability of job destruction in mature plants (both large and small). A similar study for Sweden indicates that SMEs are overrepresented in both job creation and job destruction but more so in job creation, thus making them better job creators than large firms, and that the multitude of small, single-site firms are better job generators than large, or small, multiestablishment firms. A study of service industries in the Netherlands shows that the gross job flows are greater in hospitality industries than in retail trade but that the rates in both are higher than reported for U.S. manufacturing. Thus, the overall picture that emerges is that new and small firms provide the most dynamic element in the economy.

The last section, on innovation, productivity, and growth, shows that, contrary to the conventional wisdom, small firms as well as large play an important role in innovative activity. Large firms dominate in process innovation because they have an advantage in appropriating the returns to R&D, while small firms are more innovative when it comes to generating new products. This is particularly evident in new industries, which are characterized by a high rate of product innovation, carried out mostly by small firms. A study of innovative activity among SMEs in the UK shows that the motivation to innovate is closely linked to the firms' perception of their competitive environment, especially in terms of its openness to foreign competition. In another chapter it was found that productivity growth is higher, the higher the level and growth rate of firms' market shares. This is consistent with the fact that large firms dominate in process innovation, which has a direct impact on productivity. In the longer run, it may well be argued, it is product innovation which expands the range of business opportunities and hence creates new growth; this is where SMEs excel.

The issues for public policy which arise from the present volume fall into two categories. The first relates to the importance of creative destruction and is based on three of the four groups of chapters. A dynamic economy requires a high level of innovative activity, which, in turn, requires vigorous entry of new firms, most of which are necessarily small. This causes a high degree of turbulence: it is the *gross* flows of entry and exit, of newly created jobs and jobs destroyed, which are important, not the net changes. Therefore, if one wants to stimulate economic growth, the most important policy objective is not to retard this process of change and displacement but to facilitate it, particularly by encouraging entrepreneurship and free entry and tolerating failure.

The second issue for public policy involves financing of SMEs. The broader issue, which is only touched upon in this volume, is how to bridge the financial gap arising from the fact that SMEs represent nearly half of the economy but less than 10 percent of total business finance. The main conclusion from the chapters on finance here is that one of the main reasons for lack of access to external finance for SMEs is that they have inadequate management competence and other forms of human capital. This is of particular importance in the small subset of firms with high growth potential, typically supported by venture capital. Thus, the main policy issue is how to raise the level of competence in small (and particularly in entrepreneurial) firms. It is primarily a question of competence and only secondarily one of availability of finance. It is therefore also important to have multiple and diverse sources of finance, with different capabilities, viewpoints, risk assessments and willingness to absorb risk, working closely with entrepreneurs and SMEs.

In both of these policy areas it is striking that the choices made and the institutions built in the United States differ dramatically from those in Europe and Japan. Differences in the size of the national economy and the degree of decentralization play an important role, as do differences in culture, history, and geography. Japan's current economic woes, like those of its neighbors, have been due in part to its unique form of capitalism, in which government bureaucrats removed or controlled a substantial part of the risk inherent in a market economy. In market capitalism reward corresponds to risk (Mandel, 1997). Japanese industrial policy tried to give the private sector the full benefit of rewards without having to pay the government for minimizing the risks (Morck et al., 1988). Japan paid a huge economic price for prolonged controlled-risk capitalism.[23]

For a variety of reasons, Americans tend to embrace change, sometimes even for its own sake, while Europeans and Japanese tend to mistrust it. There is little doubt that the dramatic increase in the number of business incorporations (and business failures) in the United States in the late 1970s and early 1980s, then maintained at a high level, has contributed significantly to the relatively vigorous U.S. economy in recent years. While the Americans allow entrepreneurs continually to change the economic system, the French, for example, "are fighting to preserve what is to them one of the most successful societies and most agreeable ways of life in the world – one that other Europeans esteem and Americans still flock to, admire and even envy" (Trueheart, 1997). History suggests that differences of this sort are deeply rooted and therefore extremely difficult to change. They represent fundamentally different preferences and choices. The role of the economist is to help clarify what the tradeoffs of various choices are.

Notes

[1] Also see Tyson (1992) and Thurow (1992).
[2] "U.S. Sails on Tranquil Economic Seas," *The Washington Post*, December 2, 1996, p. 1.
[3] This volume does not deal with questions of globalization. Those questions are examined in Preston and Heller (1997).
[4] A notable early exception was the work of J. Steindl (1945).
[5] For a review of the literature see Whittaker (1997), Acs (1996), Admiraal (1996), OECD (1996), and Storey (1994b).
[6] For a discussion of scale economies in small firms see Pratten (1991).
[7] Many of the issues raised by Acs (1984) were examined by David B. Audretsch

and Zoltan J. Acs at the Wissenschaftszentrum (WZB) in Berlin in the late 1980s. These findings are to be found in the inaugural issue of *Small Business Economics*, 1989, 1(1), and in Acs and Audretsch (1990a), proceedings from the first Global Workshop on Small Business Economics in Berlin. Subsequent issues of *Small Business Economics* (1994, 6[2]; 1996, 8[3] and 8[5]) have reported more recent research findings from the second and third Global Workshops.

[8] The comparison between 1987 and 1992 Enterprise Statistics (ES) should be interpreted with some caution. In 1987 ES excluded all establishments in Agriculture, Financial Services, Public Administration, and Unclassified. Its coverage of Transportation, Communication, and Public Utilities and Services was partial. This partly explains the large decline in the small business share of services between 1987 and 1992. Also as a result of these apparently minor differences in industry classification, the small business shares of various industries in the 1992 ES are considerably different from the 1992 distribution in Statistics of U.S. Business (SUSB) static tables (Armington, 1997).

[9] Public Law 94–305, 90 Stat.668, 4 (June 1976).

[10] The shift in the firm size distribution in the manufacturing sector has been examined by Carlsson, Audretsch, and Acs (1994); Dosi (1988); and Carlsson (1989a; 1989b; 1992), among others, who have argued that the implementation of flexible manufacturing technology has led to a reduction in the importance of scale economies and subsequently to a decrease in plant and firm size in the metalworking industries.

[11] This is also true of the models of Oi (1983) and Jovanovic (1982).

[12] The issues of innovation and R&D spillovers are examined in Jaffe (1989); Acs, Audretsch, and Feldman (1994); Almeida and Kogut (1997); Feldman (1994); Anselin, Varga, and Acs (1997).

[13] Also see Stohr (1986), Storper and Walker (1989), Suarez-Villa and Karlsson (1996).

[14] For a review of the literature on credit rationing see Hillier and Ibrahimo (1993).

[15] Also see Reid (1991) for an earlier treatment.

[16] Access to "patient capital" emerged from the 1995 White House Conference on Small Business as the most critical obstacle to the vitality of early-stage, innovative high-growth ventures. The need was defined more precisely as seed and start-up capital on the order of $250,000 to $1,000,000, well below the interest thresholds of most venture capital funds, but well within the range of typical private equity investor financing (Freear et al., 1996). For a discussion of the government as venture capitalist see Lerner (1996) and Acs and Tarpley (1998).

[17] Also see Storey and Johnson (1987); Storey (1994b, ch. 6); Kirchhoff (1994); Harrison (1994, ch. 3); and Davis et al. (1996).

[18] The 1996 International Award for Entrepreneurship and Small Business Research was awarded Dr. David L. Birch by the Swedish Foundation for Industrial and Technical Development (NUTEK) and the Swedish Foundation for Small Business in recognition of his work on the job generation process.

[19] For a review see Kirchhoff (1991).

[20] For health care coverage by firm size see U.S. Small Business Administration (1994).

[21] When one controls for industry differences and geographic areas, as well as worker characteristics – education and experience – two-thirds of the large

36   **Zoltan J. Acs, Bo Carlsson and Charlie Karlsson**

firm wage premium disappears (Evans and Leighton, 1989b). If unobservable
characteristics could be controlled, the large firm premium might disappear
altogether.

[22] "Modernization Matters," The Modernization Forum, Dearborn, Michigan,
May 1996, p. 6.

[23] Total asset value suffered a loss of close to $10 trillion during the first half of
the 1990s (Amano and Blohm, 1997).

References

Acs, Z. J., 1984, *The Changing Structure of the U.S. Economy*, New York: Praeger.
Acs, Z. J., ed, 1996, *Small Firms and Economic Growth*, Vol. I and II, Cheltenham:
Edward Elgar.
Acs, Z. J., and C. Armington, 1998, "Longitudinal Establishment and Enterprise
Microdata (LEEM) Documentation, Center for Economic Studies, U.S.
Bureau of the Census.
Acs, Z. J., and D. B. Audretsch, 1988, "Innovation in Large and Small Firms," *The
American Economic Review*, 78, 678–690.
Acs, Z. J., and D. B. Audretsch, eds, 1990a, *The Economics of Small Firms: A Euro-
pean Challenge*, Boston: Kluwer.
Acs, Z. J., and D. B. Audretsch, 1990b, *Innovation and Small Firms*, Cambridge,
Mass.: MIT Press.
Acs, Z. J., and D. B. Audretsch, eds, 1991, R&D, Firm Size and Innovative Activ-
ity, in Z. J. Acs and D. B. Audretsch, eds, *Innovation and Technological
Change*, Ann Arbor: The University of Michigan Press, 39–59.
Acs, Z. J., and D. B. Audretsch, 1993a, "Innovation and Firm Size: The New Learn-
ing," in M. Dodgson and R. Rothwell, eds, *International Journal of Tech-
nology Management*, Special Publication on Small Firms and Innovation,
23–35.
Acs, Z. J., and D. B. Audretsch, 1993b, *Small Firms and Entrepreneurship: An
East–West Perspective*, Cambridge: Cambridge University Press.
Acs, Z. J., D. B. Audretsch, and M. Feldman, 1994, "R&D Spillovers and Recipi-
ent Firm Size," *Review of Economics and Statistics*, 336–340.
Acs, Z. J., and D. S. Evans, 1995, "The Determinants of Variation in Self-
Employment Rates Across Countries and Over Time," University of
Maryland working paper.
Acs, Z. J., and F. A. Tarpley, 1998, "The Angel Capital Electronic Network (Ace-
Net)," *Journal of Banking and Finance*, special issue on "The Economics
of Small Business Finance," eds. A. N. Berger and G. F. Udel.
Admiraal, P. H., ed, 1996, *Small Business in the Modern Economy*, Oxford: Basil
Blackwell.
Almeida P., and B. Kogut, 1997, "The Exploration of Technological Diversity and
Geographic Localization in Innovation: Start-up Firms in the Semicon-
ductor Industry," *Small Business Economics*, 9(1).
Amano, T., and R. Blohm, 1997, "Japan's Economic Miracle Is Still to Come,"
The Wall Street Journal, June 24, editorial page.
Anselin, L., A. Varga, and Z. J. Acs, 1997, "Local Geographic Spillovers Between
University Research and High Technology Innovations," *Journal of Urban
Economics*, 42, 422–448.

Armington, C., 1997, "Statistics & U.S. Business – Microdata and Tables SBA/ Census: Data on Establishments by Firm Size, December 31, 1997," Office of Advocacy, U.S. Small Business Administration, Washington, D.C.

Audretsch, D. B., 1991, "New-Firm Survival and the Technological Regime," *Review of Economics and Statistics*, 73, 441–450.

Audretsch, D. B., and Z. J. Acs, 1990, "The Entrepreneurial Regime, Learning, and Industry Turbulence," *Small Business Economics*, 2, 119–128.

Baily, M. N., E. J. Bartelsman, and J. Haltiwanger, 1996, "Downsizing and Productivity Growth: Myth or Reality?" *Small Business Economics*, 8(4), 259–298.

Baily, M. N., C. Hulten, and D. Campbell, 1992, "Productivity Dynamics in U. S. Manufacturing Plants," *Brookings Papers on Economic Activity*, 187–267.

Baldwin, J., 1995, *The Dynamics of Industrial Competition*, Cambridge: Cambridge University Press.

Bates, T., 1990, "Entrepreneurial Human Capital Inputs and Small Business Longevity," *Review of Economics and Statistics*, 72, 64–80.

Baumol, W. J., 1993, *Entrepreneurship, Management, and the Structure of Payoffs*, Cambridge, Mass.: The MIT Press.

Beesley, M. E., and R. T. Hamilton, 1984, "Small Firms' Seedbed Role and the Concept of Turbulence," *Journal of Industrial Economics*, 33, 217–232.

Besley, T., and A. R. Levenson, 1996, "The Role of Informal Finance in Household Capital Accumulation: Evidence from Taiwan," *Economic Journal*, 106(January), 39–60.

Birch, D., 1979, *The Job Generation Process*, Program on Regional Studies, MIT.

Birch, D., 1981, "Who Creates Jobs?" *The Public Interest*, 65, 3–14.

Black, J., D. de Meza, and D. Jeffreys, 1996, "House Prices, The Supply of Collateral and the Enterprise Economy," *Economic Journal*, 106(Janaury), 60–75.

Blanchflower, D., and A. Oswald, 1996, "What Makes a Young Entrepreneur?" *Journal of Labor Economics*.

Board of Governors of the Federal Reserve System, 1995, *Consolidated Reports of Condition and Income* (Call Reports), Washington, D.C.

Bolton Report, 1971, Committee of Inquiry on Small Firms, Cmnd 4811, London: HMSO.

Brock, W. A., and D. S. Evans, 1986, *The Economics of Small Firms*, New York: Holmes & Meier.

Brock, W. A., and D. S. Evans, 1989, "Small Business Economics," *Small Business Economics*, 1(1), 7–20.

Brown, C., J. Hamilton, and J. Medoff, 1990, *Employers: Large and Small*, Cambridge, Mass.: Harvard University Press.

Caballero, R. J., and L. Hammour, 1996, "On the Timing and Efficiency of Creative Destruction," *Quarterly Journal of Economics*, 446(3), 805–852.

Carlsson, B., 1989a, "The Evolution of Manufacturing Technology and Its Impact on Industrial Structure: An International Study," *Small Business Economics*, 1(1), 21–38.

Carlsson, B., 1989b, "Flexibility and the Theory of the Firm," *International Journal of Industrial Organization*, 7, 179–203.

Carlsson, B., 1992, "The Rise of Small Business: Causes and Consequences," in W. J. Adams, ed, *Singular Europe: Economy and Polity of the European Community After 1992*. Ann Arbor: The University of Michigan Press.

Carlsson, B., D. B. Audretsch, and Z. J. Acs, 1994, "Flexible Technology and Plant Size: US Manufacturing and Metalworking Industries," *International Journal of Industrial Organization*, 12(3), 359–372.

Chandler, A., 1990, *Scale and Scope: The Dynamics of Industrial Capitalism*, Cambridge: The Bellknap Press of Harvard University Press.

Coase, R., 1937, The Nature of the Firm," *Economica*, 4, 386–405.

Cohen, W. M., and S. Klepper, 1996, "A Reprise of Size and R&D," *Economic Journal*, 106(July), 925–951.

Cohen, W. M., R. C. Levin, and D. C. Mowery, 1987, "Firm Size and R&D Intensity: A Re-examination," *Journal of Industrial Economics*, 35, 543–565.

Comanor, W. S., 1967, "Market Structure, Product Differentiation and Industrial Research," *Quarterly Journal of Economics*, 81, 639–657.

Cressy, R. C., 1996a, "Commitment Lending Under Asymmetric Information: Theory and Test on U.K. Startup Data," *Small Business Economics*, 8(5), 397–408.

Cressy, R. C., 1996b, "Are Business Startups Debt-Rationed?" *The Economic Journal*, 106(438), 1253–1270.

Davis, S., 1990, "The Distribution of Employees by Establishment Size: Patterns of Change and Co-Movement in the United States, 1962–1985," Working Paper, University of Chicago.

Davis, S., and J. Haltiwanger, 1992, "Gross Job Creation, Gross Job Destruction and Employment Reallocation," *Quarterly Journal of Economics*, 819–863.

Davis, S., J. Haltiwanger, and S. Schuh, 1996a, *Job Creation and Destruction*, Cambridge, Mass.: The MIT Press.

Davis, S., J. Haltiwanger, and S. Schuh, 1996b, "Small Business and Job Creation: Dissecting the Myth and Reassessing the Facts," *Small Business Economics*, 8(4), 297–315.

De Jong, H. W., 1989, "Free Versus Controlled Competition," in B. Carlsson, ed, *Industrial Dynamics: Technological, Organizational, and Structural Changes in Industries and Firms*. Boston, Dordrecht and London: Kluwer Academic Publishers.

de Meza, D., and D. Webb, 1987, "Too Much Investment: A Problem of Asymmetric Information," *Quarterly Journal of Economics*, 102, 281–292.

Dosi, G., 1988, "Sources, Procedures, and Microeconomic Effects of Innovation," *Journal of Economic Literature*, 26, 1120–1171.

Dunne, T., M. J. Roberts, and L. Samuelson, 1989, "The Growth and Failure of U.S. Manufacturing Plants," *Quarterly Journal of Economics*, CIV, 671–698.

European Network for SME Research (ENSR), 1993, The European Observatory for SMEs, First Annual Report to the European Commission, EIM, Holland.

Evans, D. S., 1987, "Tests of Alternative Theories of Firm Growth," *Journal of Political Economy*, 95(4), 657–674.

Evans, D. S., and B. Jovanovic, 1989, "Estimates of a Model of Entrepreneurial Choice Under Liquidity Constraints," *Journal of Political Economy*, 97, 808–827.

Evans, D. S., and L. Leighton, 1989a, "Some Empirical Aspects of Entrepreneurship," *American Economic Review*, 79, 519–535.

Evans, D. S., and L. Leighton, 1989b, "Why Do Smaller Firms Pay Less?" *Journal of Human Resources*, 24, 299–318.

Fazzari, S. R., G. Hubbard, and B. Peterson, 1986, "Financing Constraints and Corporate Investment," *Brookings Papers on Economic Activity*, March, 19–37.

Feldman, M., 1994, *The Geography of Innovation*, Boston: Kluwer Academic.

Freear, J., J. E. Sohl, and W. E. Wetzel, 1996, "Creating New Capital Markets for Emerging Ventures," Prepared for the U.S. Small Business Administration, Office of Advocacy, under Contract No. SBAHQ-95-m-1062., Washingon, D.C.

Galbraith, J. K., 1956, *American Capitalism: The Concept of Countervailing Power*, revised edition, Boston: Houghton Mifflin.

Garten, Jeffery E., 1992, *A Cold Peace: America, Japan, Germany, and the Struggle for Supremacy*, New York: Times Books.

Gifford, S., 1992, "Innovation, Firm Size and Growth in a Centralized Firm," *Rand Journal of Economics*, 235, 284–298.

Gomes-Casseres, B., 1996, *The Alliance Revolution: The Shape of Business Rivalry*, Cambridge, Mass.: Harvard University Press.

Gort, M., and S. Klepper, 1982, "Time Paths in the Diffusion of Product Innovations," *Economic Journal*, 92, 530–553.

Grossman, G. M., and E. Helpman, 1991, *Innovation and Growth in the Global Economy*, Cambridge, Mass.: The MIT Press.

Hannah, L., 1996, "Marshalls, 'Trees' and the 'Global Forest': Were 'Giant Redwoods' Different?" Presented at a National Bureau of Economc Research Conference, Cambridge, Mass., October.

Harrison, B., 1994, *Lean and Mean*, New York: Basic Books.

Hebert, R. F., and A. N. Link, 1989, "In Search of the Meaning of Entrepreneurship," *Small Business Economics*, 1(1), 39–50.

Hillier, B., and M. V. Ibrahimo, 1993, "Asymmetric Information and Models of Credit Rationing," *Bulletin of Economic Research*, 45(4), 271–304.

Holmes, T. J., and J. A. Schmidts, 1990, "A Theory of Entrepreneurship and Its Application to the Study of Business Transfers," *Journal of Political Economy*, 98, 265–294.

Holtz-Eakin, D., D. Joulfaian, and H. S. Rosen (1994), "Sticking It Out: Entrepreneurial Survival and Liquidity Constraints," *Journal of Political Economy*, 102(1), 53–75.

Jaffe, A., 1989, "Real Effects of Academic Research," *American Economic Review*, 79, 957–970.

Jaffee, D., and T. Russell, 1976, "Imperfect Information, Uncertainty, and Credit Rationing," *Quarterly Journal of Economics*, 90, 651–666.

Joel Popkin and Company, 1997, "Small Business Share of Private, Nonfarm Gross Domestic Product," prepared under contract for the U.S. Small Business Administration, Office of Advocacy, SBAHQ-95-C-0021.

Jovanovic, B., 1982, "Selection and the Evolution of Industry," *Econometrica*, 50(3), 649–670.

Jovanovic, B., and G. M. MacDonald, 1994, "Competitive Diffusion," *Journal of Political Economy*, 102, 24–52.

Kamien, M. I., and N. L. Schwartz, 1975, "Market Structure and Innovation: A Survey," *The Journal of Economic Literature*, 13, 1243–1257.

Kirchhoff, B., 1991, "Employers Large and Small: A Review Article," *Small Business Economics*, 3(3), 233–238.

Kirchhoff, B., 1994, *Entrepreneurship and Dynamic Capitalism*, London: Praeger.

Klepper, S., 1996, "Entry, Exit, Growth, and Innovation over the Product Life Cycle," *American Economic Review*, 86(3), 562–583.

Knight, F., 1921, *Risk, Uncertainty and Profit*, New York: Houghton Mifflin.

Lazerson, M., 1988, "Organizational Growth of Small Firms: An Outcome of Markets and Hierarchies?" *American Sociological Review*, 53(3), 330–342.

Lerner, J., 1994, "Venture Capitalists and the Decision to Go Public," *Journal of Financial Economics*, 35(3), 293–316.

Lerner, J., 1996, "The Government as Venture Capitalist," Harvard Business School, working paper #96-038, Boston, Mass.

Link, A. N., and C. Rees, 1990, "Firm Size, University Research and the Returns to R&D," *Small Business Economics*, 2(1), 25–33.

Loveman G., and W. Sengenberger, 1991, "The Re-Emergence of Small-Scale Production: An International Comparison," *Small Business Economics*, 3(1), 1–39.

Lucas, R. E., 1978, "On the Size Distribution of Business Firms," *Bell Journal of Economics*, 9(2), 7–20.

Lynch, P., and J. Rothchild, 1996, *Learn to Earn*, New York: Simon & Schuster.

Mandel, M., 1997, *The High-Risk Society*, New York: Times Business, Random House.

Marshall, A., 1920, *Principles of Economics*, London: Macmillan.

Marx, K., 1912, *Capital*, Translated by Ernest Untermann, Vol. 1, Chicago: Kerr.

Meyer, B. D., 1990, "Why Are There So Few Black Entrepreneurs?" working paper No. 3537, Cambridge, Mass.: NBER, December.

"Modernization Matters," 1996, The Modernization Forum, Dearborn, Michigan, May, p. 6.

Morales, R., 1994, *Flexible Production*, Cambridge: Polity Press.

Morck, R., B. Yeung, and Y. U. Wayne, 1998, "The Information Content of Stock Markets: Why Do Emerging Markets Have So Little Firm-Specific Risk?" The Davidson Institute Working Paper 44a, August, University of Michigan.

Nelson, R., and S. Winter, 1982, *An Evolutionary Theory of Economic Change*, Cambridge, Mass.: Harvard University Press.

OECD, 1996, *SMEs: Employment, Innovation and Growth*, Paris: The Washington Workshop.

OECD, 1997, "Small Business, Job Creation and Growth: Facts, Obstacles and Best Practices," draft concept paper for the 1997 Denver Summit, Paris.

Oi, W. Y., 1983, "Heterogeneous Firms and the Organization of Production," *Economic Inquiry*, 21(April), 147–171.

Pakes, A., and R. Ericson, 1998, "Empirical Implications of Alternative Models of Firm Dynamics," *Journal of Economic Theory*, 79(1), 1–45.

Piore, M. J., and C. F. Sabel, 1984, "Possibilities for Prosperity: International Keynesianism and Flexible Specialization," *The Second Industrial Divide*, New York: Basic Books.

Pratten, C., 1991, *The Competitiveness of Small Firms*, Cambridge: Cambridge University Press.

Preston, L., and C. Heller, eds., 1997, *Small Business Economics*, Special Issue on Small and Medium Sized Firms in the Global Economy, 9(1), 1–80.

Reid, G. C., 1987, *Theories of Industrial Organization*, Oxford: Basil Blackwell.

Reid, G. C., 1991, "Staying in Business," *International Journal of Industrial Organization*, 9, 545–556.

Saxenian, A., 1991, "The Origins and Dynamics of Production Networks in Silicon Valley," *Research Policy*, 20, 423–437.

Scherer, F. M., 1991, "Changing Perspectives on the Firm Size Problem," in Z. J. Acs and D. B. Audretsch, eds., *Innovation and Technological Change*, Ann Arbor: The University of Michigan Press, 24–38.

Schmookler, J., 1966, *Innovation and Economic Growth*, Cambridge, Mass.: Harvard University Press.

Schumacher, E. F., 1973, *Small Is Beautiful*, New York: Harper & Row.

Schumpeter, J. A., 1934, *The Theory of Economic Development*, Cambridge, Mass.: Harvard University Press.

Schumpeter, J. A., 1942, *Capitalism, Socialism, and Democracy*, New York: Harper & Row.

Servan-Schreiber, J.-J., 1968, *The American Challenge*, London: Hamish Hamilton.

Smith, A., 1776, *The Wealth of Nations*, Oxford: Clarendon Press.

Solow, R., 1956, "Technical Change and the Aggregate Production Function," *Review of Economics and Statistics*, 312–320.

Steindl, J., 1945, *Small and Big Business*, Oxford: Basil Blackwell.

Stiglitz, J. E., and A. Weiss, 1981, "Credit Rationing in Markets with Imperfect Information," *American Economic Review*, 71(3), 393–410.

Stohr, W., 1986, "Regional Innovation Complexes," *Papers of the Regional Science Association*, 59, 29–44.

Storey, D. J., 1994a, "New Firm Growth and Bank Financing," *Small Business Economics* 6(2), 91–102.

Storey, D. J.,1994b, *Understanding the Small Business Sector*, London: Routledge.

Storey, D. J., and S. Johnson, 1987, *Job Generation and Labor Market Changes*, London: Macmillan.

Storper, M., and R. Walker, 1989, *The Capitalist Imperative: Territory, Technology and Industrial Growth*, Oxford: Basil Blackwell.

Suarez-Villa, L., and C. Karlsson, 1996, "The Development of Sweden's R&D-Intensive Electronics Industry: Exports, Outsourcing, and Territorial Distribution," *Environment and Planning*, A, 28, 783–817.

Thurow, L., 1992, *Head to Head: The Coming Battle Among Japan, Europe, and America*, New York: William Morrow.

Trueheart, C., 1997, "French Proudly Hold Fast to Benevolent Central Rule," *The Washington Post*, July 14, A1.

Tyson, Laura D' Andrea, 1992, *Who's Bashing Whom? Trade Conflict in High Technology Industries*, Washington, D.C.: Institute for International Economics.

U.S. Census Bureau, 1998, U.S. Enterprise Statistics 1992. Washington, D.C.

U.S. Small Business Administration, 1984, *The State of Small Business*, A Report of the President, Washington, D.C.

U.S. Small Business Administration, 1992, *The State of Small Business*, A Report of the President, Washington, D.C.

U.S. Small Business Administration, 1994, *The State of Small Business*, A Report of the President, Health Insurance, 65–108, Washington, D.C.

U.S. Small Business Administration, 1995, *The State of Small Business*, A Report of the President, Washington, D.C.

U. S. Small Business Administration, Office of Advocacy, 1996, *White Paper on the Financing of Small Business*, Washington, D.C.

Viner, J., 1932, "Cost Curves and Supply Curves," *Zeitschrift fur Nationalokonomie*, III, 23–46.

von Hippel, E., 1988, *The Sources of Innovation*, New York: Oxford University Press.

The Washington Post, "U.S. Sails on Tranquil Economic Seas," December 2, 1996, p. 1.

Whittaker, D. H., 1997, *Small Firms in the Japanese Economy*, Cambridge: Cambridge University Press.

Williamson, O., 1991, "Comparative Economic Organization: The Analysis of Discrete Structural Alternatives," *Administrative Science Quarterly*, 36(June).

Winter, S. G., 1984, "Schumpeterian Competition in Alternative Technological Regimes," *Journal of Economic Behavior and Organization*, 5, 287–320.

You, J., 1995, "Small Firms in Economic Theory," *Cambridge Journal of Economics*, 19, 441–462.

PART I

Entrepreneurship, Industrial Dynamics and the Macroeconomy

CHAPTER 2

Entrepreneurship and the Theory of
the Firm

Mark Casson

1   Introduction

It is strange that so much economic literature on the firm ignores the
entrepreneur. While several famous economists have touched upon the
subject – Mill and Marshall, for example – what they have had to say
about entrepreneurship has not been fully integrated into their overall
model of the economy. Thus while the later Marshall emphasised entrepreneurship in his more institutional work (Marshall, 1919), he largely
ignored it in his more analytical earlier work (Marshall, 1890). When he
did discuss it analytically, he tended to regard it simply as an additional
factor of production. This exemplifies a general tendency amongst
economists to be excessively reductionist in their handling of the entrepreneur. If they do not dismiss entrepreneurship altogether, then they
normally reduce it to something more familiar to them instead.

The economists who have taken entrepreneurship most seriously have
been those who have viewed the economy as socially embedded
(on embeddedness see Granovetter, 1985). Both Cantillon (1755) and
Schumpeter (1934, 1939) come into this category. Cantillon regarded
entrepreneurs as a distinctive social class formed of people who were
willing to bear the risks shifted onto them by the rest of society. Schumpeter regarded them as a social elite possessing a distinctive psychology
centred on rivalry and domination. In both cases the social psychologies
of different classes play an important role in the analysis.

As the division of intellectual labour amongst the social sciences has
progressed, however, economists have become increasingly reluctant to
venture into fields where a knowledge of other disciplines, such as social
psychology, is required. The recent revival of interest in entrepreneurship owes almost nothing to the intellectual initiative of economists.
It has been driven much more by the perceived political need for the

structure of mature industrial economies to become more flexible, and the consequent promotion of small and medium-size enterprise, which has in turn attracted interest as a purely empirical phenomenon.

Even when intellectual developments directly conducive to the study of entrepreneurship have occurred, the opportunity has largely been wasted. The recent revival of institutional economics has made itself felt in the study of history (North, 1981) and law (Posner, 1973), but not in the study of the entrepreneur. Consider, for example, the influence of institutional economics on recent research in the theory of the firm (Williamson, 1985). Following Coase's (1937) path-breaking work, it has been recognised that the answer to the fundamental question about the nature of the firm lies not, as previously thought, in technology and market structure, but in transaction costs instead. It might have been expected that the new focus on transaction costs would stimulate the reconsideration of other institutional aspects of the firm, such as entre-preneurship. After all, transaction costs explain why markets may be missing and can therefore also explain why initiative is required to set up new markets.

But no such development actually took place. Attention was focused on narrow issues such as the economics of vertical integration and the evolution of the M-form firm. Broader questions concerned with the creation of new markets, the dynamics of firm formation and the growth of the firm were ignored.

What actually happened instead is that rivalry broke out over which particular formulation of transaction cost theory is appropriate for these limited purposes. Coase's original paper was somewhat ambiguous on key points, using phrases such as "the costs of discovering prices", which mean different things to different people. This has allowed writers from agency theory (now a part of contract theory) to challenge the received interpretation of Coase.

Other writers, such as Nelson and Winter (1982) and their followers, have been even more radical, suggesting that it is capabilities based on routines, and not transaction costs, that hold the key to the nature of the firm. What initially seemed to be a highly promising research agenda now appears to be in danger of degenerating into chaos because of these professional rivalries.

It is suggested in this chapter that much of the current confusion about the nature of the firm is directly attributable to the continued omission of the entrepreneur. There are many different aspects of the firm that need explaining, and no one concept – transaction cost, agency cost, capa-bility, or whatever – can explain them all. There are some aspects of the firm which can only be explained satisfactorily using the concept of the entrepreneur. When other theories compete to explain such phenomena, then confusion is natural, for each theorist can legitimately criticise his rivals for not having done a proper job.

The aim of this chapter is not to add to the volume of criticism, but to be constructive instead. It proposes a synthetic model of the firm which incorporates insights from all the strands of theory discussed above. The synthetic model is carefully constructed using a small number of key concepts. One of these concepts – information synthesis – is taken directly from the modern theory of the entrepreneur. Two others – information cost and volatility – are taken, respectively, from the economic theory of teams (a branch of decision theory) and the theory of finance.

These concepts serve to construct a vision of the firm as an information-processing mechanism. The design of the mechanism is discussed in some detail. The personal qualities required to set up the mechanism and to maintain it in working order are considered as well.

The basis for the theory is that the economic environment is continuously disturbed by shocks of both a persistent and a transitory nature. Persistent shocks provide a stimulus to the formation of new firms or the radical restructuring of existing firms. Persistent shocks are intermittent and diverse and are usually dealt with by improvisation. This improvisation is effected by the entrepreneur who founds the firm or restructures it later on. By contrast, transitory shocks are repetitive and conform to a more limited number of types. They are dealt with routinely using procedures devised by the entrepreneur. Applying a division of labour to the implementation of these procedures creates the organisation of the firm.

Information on shocks is costly to collect and communicate (Marschak and Radner, 1972). The initial impact of shocks is localised and dispersed, and that means that some people learn of them before others. Those "in the know" buy up resources which have become more valuable as a result of the shock, in order to make a speculative gain. The gain is realised when the resources are deployed to a more profitable use. The most significant type of shock, so far as firms are concerned, is one which creates a new market opportunity. The shock could be a change in tastes, factor costs, technology, social values, or indeed anything that impinges on the gains from a particular type of trade. A firm is created whenever an entrepreneur speculates that certain resources – including labour time – should be acquired in order to create a new market of some kind.

Market opportunities normally have to be realised through intermediation. Intermediation reduces transaction costs which would otherwise inhibit trade. It is also a profit-extraction mechanism for the entrepreneur. The organisation of intermediation has many different aspects, which are explained below; it is these different aspects that are followed up in different theories of the firm. Embedding all these issues in a common framework clarifies the connections between them. It also reveals a common theme – namely, the importance of synthesising information and of ensuring that the information that is synthesised is true. It is the synthesis of different kinds of persistent information that brings firms into being, and it is their skill in subsequently synthesising transitory information which, together with the quality of the initial synthesis, governs their subsequent success.

2   Defining the Firm

An unnecessary source of confusion in the theory of the firm stems from the lack of consensus on definition. Because of the sheer diversity of legal forms that a firm can take, a purely inductive approach to defining the firm is of little use. It is necessary to identify "firmlike" qualities independently of what any particular real world firm happens to be like. From an economic point of view the most useful way of defining an institution such as the firm is in terms of the function it performs. "The firm is what the firm does", in other words. But what exactly does the firm do?

According to Coase (1937), the firm is a co-ordinator. The market is a co-ordinator, too, but unlike the market, where responsibility is dispersed through negotiations, the firm concentrates this responsibility upon itself. The firm may therefore be defined as an institution which specialises in co-ordination using a single locus of responsibility. Firms exist as "islands of conscious power" in an "ocean of unconscious cooperation" because, for some sets of activities, this approach to coordination is superior to others (Robertson, 1923, p. 85).

This definition needs to be amplified, however. The essence of coordination is decision-making. The firm is therefore a specialised decision-making unit. Specialisation is effected when the firm takes decisions about resources which it does not itself supply and about resources which it does not itself consume. Unlike an individual worker, the firm does not decide how to allocate its own labour time; rather it decides how to allocate labour time purchased from others. In the same way the firm, unlike an individual consumer, does not decide how best to consume certain goods, but how best to allocate the goods it owns among the consumers who would like to purchase them.

But what is the point in an entity that does no work itself acquiring the rights to labour, and an entity that does not consume itself acquiring products whose value ultimately derives from consumption by other

people? The answer lies in the improvement in the quality of the decisions that results when the firm rather than the worker decides how
labour time shall be allocated and the firm rather than the consumer
decides on the ultimate sources from which goods shall be procured.

But how does this improvement in the quality of decisions occur? It
arises because the firm has information at its disposal that other people
lack. Even if it does not have the information immediately at hand, it has
the capacity to acquire this information when needed at lower cost than
other people.

A methodological problem arises here, however, because decisions
are actually taken by people and not by impersonal entities such as firms.
What the firm can do, however, is to structure the activities of the different people who participate in the decision-making process, so that
their individual contributions to the decision-making process are made
in the most effective way. The firm, in other words, is essentially a structure designed to harmonise the decision-making efforts of a group of
people who are focused on a single issue or set of related issues.

Where an individual is confronted with a one-off decision it may
not be worthwhile to transfer the responsibility for the decision to a
firm. The set up cost that is involved may outweigh any benefit to the
individual from the support of the firm. Where recurrent decisions
are required, however, the value of the prospective stream of benefits
may well outweigh the set up cost. It becomes economic to vest decision-
making responsibilities in a firm. Because the set up cost requires time
to pay back, continuity of operation is one of the hallmarks of the
firm.

The firm is more that just a structure, however. From a legal point of
view the firm is a kind of fictional person which can acquire, hold and
dispose of property in its own right (Putterman, 1981). This legal fiction
is a rational institutional response to the function of the firm. When the
firm needs to acquire command of labour services in order to control
their use it can do so by purchasing labour time. Likewise, when the firm
needs to dispose of the product on which labour has done its work it can
do so by selling it. In this way it generates revenue which can be used to
cover the cost of the labour it hires.

But is this fiction really necessary, it may be asked. If the decisions
are taken by a single individual, for example, can this individual not buy
labour services and sell the product on his own account? Why does he
need to operate inside the "legal shell" of the firm? The answer lies in
three legal privileges normally conferred by the corporate form, namely,
limited liability, indefinite life, and the right to set off purchases of inputs
against revenues from output when assessing liability for tax. The

advantages of limited liability to a risk-averse individual are fairly obvious, although there are disadvantages too: shifting risk to creditors could conceivably damage the financial reputation of the firm. Since limited liability is only an option, however, it is available to those who wish to take advantage of it without detriment to those who do not. The unlimited life of the firm allows its contractual rights and obligations to survive the death of its owner and so permits the structure to be perpetuated by his heirs or his trustees. So far as taxation is concerned, most tax systems aim to tax consumption. If an individual employed a worker in a personal capacity, the expenditure could be interpreted as a form of consumption. By employing the worker through a firm the employer makes clear that the expenditure must be set off against revenue so that only the profit is liable for tax.

In the light of this discussion, a firm may be defined as *a specialised decision-making unit, whose function is to improve co-ordination by structuring information flow, and which is normally endowed with legal privileges, including indefinite life.* There are, of course, many other common characteristics of firms, but these are best regarded as following from the implications of this definition rather than being elements of the definition itself.

3   The Firm as a User of Information

A person who takes a decision must be motivated to collect the information that is needed, and this means that he must bear some of the consequences of the decision. Thus the right to take decisions about a resource is normally ascribed to the owner of the resource. Thus people who have the relevant information already, or can collect it more cheaply than others, have an advantage as owners of a resource. They can afford to bid away the resource from others who lack this information or would find it more costly to collect. The advantage conferred on the firm by its structuring of information flow allows it to out-bid ordinary individuals for ownership of certain types of resource, and that is how these resources come to be within the control of the firm.

But why should certain people have better access to information than others? Information has the property of a public good, in the sense that supplying information to someone else does not reduce the supplier's access to it. Information is easy to share, in other words. In this case, why does everyone not have access to the same information?

The sharing of information is restricted in two ways. The first is by the cost of communication. When sources of information are localised and costs of communication are high, those who are closest to these sources can obtain information more cheaply than others (Hayek, 1937). The second is a contractual problem. Sources of information may be costly to discover. In a private enterprise economy people can only specialise in the discovery of information if they can generate an income from this information. Selling information is extremely difficult, however. Transaction costs are very high for the kinds of reasons discussed later on. This obliges those who discover information to exploit it for themselves (Casson, 1982).

But just as information incurs costs of communication, so ordinary resources incur transport costs when they are moved from the custody of one owner to the custody of another. Ordinary resources encounter contractual problems too. So why transfer the ownership of a resource to the person who has the relevant information rather than transfer the relevant information to the person who has the resource? In other words, why is the acquisition of resources explained by the distribution of information amongst prospective owners rather than the acquisition of information explained by the distribution of resource ownership instead?

The answer is that information is more costly to trade than most other resources. Resource ownership therefore moves to the information source, rather than the other way around. This is a special case of the more general proposition that ownership of resources is acquired by people who have a complementary non-tradable resource. This non-tradable resource is normally information-based; if it is not pure information, then it is usually a related resource such as technological know-how.

In the short run this complementary resource may appear as a competitive advantage (Porter, 1980) or absolute advantage (Hymer, 1960; Dunning, 1977) possessed by the owner of the tradable resource. In the long run, however, the advantage possessed by the owner is best construed as a comparative advantage instead. Sustained competitive advantage or absolute advantage is achieved by investments of particular kinds. Anyone can undertake investments of this kind, but in the long run only those with a comparative advantage in making such investments will find that it pays them to do so. In the long run, therefore, the ownership of resources is acquired by people who have a comparative advantage in investing in non-tradable resources. The prime examples of such people are those who have a comparative advantage in collecting and processing information. These people will usually exploit their comparative advantage through the institutional framework of a firm.

Not all information is equally costly to trade, however. Communication costs are greatest for information of a tacit nature (Polanyi, 1964; Winter, 1988). Contractual problems are greatest for information that is difficult to patent and whose quality is difficult to assess (Buckley and Casson, 1976). *Sustainable competitive advantage therefore rests on a comparative advantage in handling tacit information of uncertain quality which is difficult to patent.*

A comparative advantage in scientific research satisfies some of these conditions, but not necessarily all of them. This is because some kinds of technology can be patented, and therefore licensed to those who already possess the resources required for their exploitation. Thus technology can be transferred to the owners of the resources, rather than the other way round.

Information about opportunities for trade, on the other hand, normally satisfies all the conditions for non-tradability. Opportunities for trade hinge on a discrepancy between consumers' valuations and producers' opportunity costs. Information on such subjects is usually impressionistic, and therefore of a tacit nature. Unlike scientific inventions, such information cannot be patented, and because objective evidence to support it is difficult to obtain, its quality is uncertain. There is, therefore, no way in which such information can be adequately conveyed to the people who own the resources required for its exploitation; the costs of communication and the threat to appropriability are just too great. The resources required for exploitation must be purchased by the possessor of the information instead. Instead of selling the information to the producers, therefore, supplies are purchased from the producers and resold to the consumers. It is, therefore, *a capacity for acquiring trade-related information which is pre-eminent as the basis for the long-run comparative advantage of the firm.*

4   Optimism and Competence

Given that information is costly to trade, the exploitation of information is effected by allocating resources in a two stage process. In the first stage the resource is allocated to the appropriate owner and then the owner exercises his power of control to allocate the resource to a particular use. The first stage is based upon trade and the second upon the exercise of control. Trade is a voluntary process which involves the consent of both parties, whereas control is a more autocratic process in which the will of the owner prevails.

Not all ownership confers the same degree of control, though. If the resource can be used in only one way, then the owner really has no choice to make. Only a versatile resource affords the owner control over how it is to be used. It is typical of firms that the resources they own are very versatile indeed. It is the importance of exploiting this versatility effectively that creates the demand for specialised decision-making that the firm is designed to meet. Labour time is the pre-eminent example of a versatile resource. Capital equipment is another example: although capital is less versatile than labour, the manager of a capital-intensive firm still has important decisions to make about the scheduling of equipment use. The third main factor of production, land, is versatile too – but only in the long run.

The information used by firms to control their versatile resources is of two main kinds: long-run information on persistent factors and short-run information on transitory factors. Persistent factors are exemplified by the long-run opportunities for trade alluded to earlier. Transitory factors are exemplified by the impact of fashion on consumer demand (Casson, 1997).

Consider, for example, a unique physical asset that can be used to produce different varieties of a given consumer good. The persistent factor governs whether there is a market for the good. The transitory factor governs which variety is in demand in a given period. No individual can observe the persistent factor directly. Individual judgements about the state of the market are highly subjective, it is assumed. Some individuals – the optimists – believe that general conditions are favourable, but others – the pessimists – believe that they are not. Although the transitory factor can be investigated more objectively, differences in valuation can still exist because investigators differ in their competence.

Now consider the market for this asset. In the course of the negotiations each person signals something of his own valuation of the asset to the other party. This valuation will be high if the individual is an optimist and low if he is a pessimist. It will also tend to be high if the person is competent – i.e., he can observe the transitory factor easily – and low if not. Trade will proceed when the buyer is more optimistic or more competent than the seller. If the seller is more optimistic or more competent than the buyer then no trade will occur. As a result, ownership is conferred on the more optimistic and/or more competent party.

The transitory factor can be investigated either before or after a bid is made. When the transitory factor is fashion, for example, the state of fashion will have a major impact on the style of the product that labour is required to produce. When the transitory factor is highly volatile it pays to investigate after the bid because this ensures that the information governing the use of the resource is up to date. If the value of the resource in its best available use is independent of transitory conditions, then it also pays to wait until afterwards, since investigating beforehand does not significantly improve the quality of the bid. Both these conditions tend to be satisfied in the case of fashion: fashion trends are highly volatile, and the profitability of the most fashionable product may well be the same whatever the fashion happens to be.

A person who is optimistic about the persistent factor also has more incentive to investigate before bidding, since he is more likely than a pessimistic person to finish up acquiring the resource. Thus optimistic people are likely to be better informed than pessimistic people when bidding for the resource. This explains why optimistic people do not make more mistakes on average than pessimistic people do – it pays them to invest more in avoiding them.

It is still possible for optimists to make a mistake, of course. Long run success requires an individual to know when it is right to be optimistic, and when it is appropriate to be pessimistic instead. Because of the highly subjective nature of trade-related information, ownership of resources may be acquired by people who mistakenly think that they have a comparative advantage in handling such information, as well as by people who really do. Those who think that they have a comparative advantage, when they do not, squander resources through over confidence. Conversely, those who have a comparative advantage but do not realise it miss out on the profits they could make because they have too little confidence in themselves. It is only those who have a comparative advantage and have sufficient self-knowledge to be confident of it who benefit themselves (and society) in the long run.

This analysis can be extended in a straightforward way to include other attributes of the owner, such as degree of risk aversion. Given the uncertainty that surrounds the persistent factor, risk-averse individuals will be reluctant to become the owners of resources, just as pessimistic or incompetent people are. Risk aversion may not affect owners so much as pessimism or incompetence does, however. It may simply provide them with a greater incentive to investigate the transitory factor before they make a bid. It is quite possible that a risk-averse individual, provided that he is optimistic and competent, may become the owner of a resource because, as a result of his commitment to investigation, he already knows before the negotiations begin that the transitory factor is favourable.

The implications of these results for the firm are seen by identifying the firm with the legal shell used by the owner of the resource who makes the decision on how it is to be used. *The analysis identifies the owner of the firm as the optimistic and competent individual with low aversion to risk who acquires resources from other people because he believes that in the light of his better information he can put them to better use.* He normally puts them to use by producing goods for sale. If his beliefs about trading opportunities are warranted, then his venture in employing the resources will be a success.

5 The Firm as Employer

The preceding analysis unites three qualities in the owner of the firm. But it may be a tall order for all three qualities to coexist in the same person. Is it possible to organise a division of labour in which different qualities are supplied by different people? It is indeed possible, and the examination of this possibility provides further insight into the nature of the firm. In particular, it elucidates the concept of "employment" introduced above.

The basic idea is that a pessimistic but competent person may undertake to investigate the transitory factor on behalf of an optimistic but incompetent one. The incompetent optimist acquires the ownership of the resource and then hires the competent pessimist to carry out the investigation. The competent pessimist may even have been the person who sold the resource to the owner in the first place. The relevant resource may even be the pessimist's own labour time. The resulting arrangement resembles the employment relation – though not in every respect. The competent pessimist becomes the "employee" of an incompetent but optimistic "employer". He investigates the transitory factor and is then directed to produce the appropriate product – i.e., he is directed to the appropriate use of his own labour time.

In the case of fashion, for example, the incompetent optimist believes that there is a latent demand for a new type of fashion product. He is not sure, however, exactly what style will be in fashion at any given time. He hires a worker, who is willing to sell his labour time because he is not so optimistic, and instructs him to investigate what the current fashion is likely to be. In the light of this the worker is told what style of product to produce.

A further division of labour may be effected which separates the manual and cerebral aspects of this work. Two "employees" may be hired. One is hired to investigate the transitory factor and the other is hired to produce the appropriate output. The former is a pessimist with low information cost while the latter is a pessimist with high information cost. In order to simplify communications, the owner tells the investigator what the implications of each observation are for product choice and leaves the investigator to tell the manual worker what to do. The volatility of the transitory factor favours carrying out the observation at the last possible moment, after negotiations are complete. The manual worker must therefore already be in place at the time the observation is carried out. This creates a simple hierarchy in which the owner prescribes a rule for the "managerial employee" who observes the transitory factor and passes on the appropriate instruction to the "manual employee". This shows that *the employment relation is a natural consequence of a division of labour in information-processing, whereby optimists hire pessimists to stand ready to implement decisions on the basis of information collected by their colleagues or by them.*

6   The Firm as Intermediator

It was suggested that trade-related information is just as important as technological know-how – indeed, more important, perhaps – as a source of competitive advantage to a firm. While technological know-how is typically exploited through production, trade-related information is most naturally exploited through intermediation instead. Rather than sell the information directly, the possessor of it extracts rents from it by intervening in the market process – by buying goods cheap and selling them dear. *Speculation* and *arbitrage* are terms often used to describe such intervention, but these suggest, quite wrongly, that it is usually an intermittent rather than a continuous process. Trade-related information is usually exploited on a systematic basis by organising a market that did not exist before. The intermediator does not intervene in an already existing market so much as set up the market from scratch himself.

Markets need to be specially set up because the conduct of trade is fraught with difficulties. It may be difficult for prospective purchasers to get in touch with existing owners. Discovering the exact specification of what is on offer is another task. Then there is the problem of bluffing in negotiations. The essence of the market process is that each individual keeps his beliefs to himself. People do not share their beliefs and come to a consensus view. Quite the contrary, indeed. Beliefs are encoded in price quotations and these quotations are intended to mislead other people as much as to inform them. The price quotations made at the outset of the negotiation process are likely to give a highly distorted view of the subjective valuations which underpin them. Even when a deal is eventually agreed, default is always a possibility.

Intermediation can reduce transaction costs of this kind. Contact can be made more easily if a middleman provides well-advertised and conveniently situated retail premises. Specification costs are also reduced if buyers can inspect samples of each product. Most importantly, the process of negotiation can be accelerated by having an intermediator intervene. The skill of the intermediator resides, not in knowing exactly how the buyer will use the good he acquires from the seller, but in identifying the appropriate buyer and assessing the maximum he can afford to pay.

Complementing this is a skill in identifying suitable sellers and assessing the minimum payment they are willing to accept. The intermediator, in other words, trades on his special knowledge of valuations to reallocate goods to the people who can put them to the best possible use.

The intermediator exploits his own knowledge in the same way that the buyer and seller do – through negotiations. The essence of his strategy is to out-bluff both the buyer and the seller by claiming to the seller that the buyer can afford no more than the intermediator is offering to pay and persuading the buyer that the seller will not accept less than what the intermediator is asking for it. (The intermediator needs to keep the buyer and seller apart, of course, to do this successfully.) By building a reputation for taking a hard line in negotiations the intermediator can effectively discourage haggling. At the same time, by setting realistic prices he can encourage buyers and sellers regularly to channel transactions through him.

A reputable intermediator can also eliminate default by creating a chain of trust in cases where the direct social link between buyer and seller is very weak. Because the intermediator is a specialist, making his living by trade, he has an incentive to build up a reputation for integrity. Once he has acquired this reputation, he can require the seller to supply goods in advance of payment in a way that the buyer could not. Similarly he can require the buyer to pay in advance of delivery in a way that the seller could not. In this way he can guard himself against default by the parties lacking reputation, whilst passing on the good between them.

Unlike the producer described in the previous section, the intermediator buys resources for resale rather than for use. *His comparative advantage resides not in his knowledge of the use to which the good will be put, but his knowledge of who is the best person to put it to that use.* Although the final users know this too, they do not know the sources of supply as well. The intermediator can obtain both the items of information required for coordination more cheaply than other people. He has the optimism that demand will be buoyant for the goods he has bought, and is not so risk-averse, or devoid of confidence, that he fears the consequences of his judgement's being wrong. That is why he becomes the owner of the goods that he re-sells.

7   The Firm as an Organisation: A Four-Factor Theory of the Firm

A distinction was drawn in Section 4 between the persistent and transitory information used by the market-making firm. It was suggested that the firm typically used just one item of each kind. This is not generally correct: there are at least two items of each type. The long-run profit-

Table 2.1. *A Typology of Information for a Four-Factor Theory of the Firm, with Illustrative Examples of Information in Each Case*

	Type of information	
Source of shock	Transient	Persistent
Demand	Fashion news	Assessment of changes in lifestyles, income distribution, etc.
Supply	Anticipation of temporary shortage of skilled workers	New production technology

ability of the market, and the short-run equilibrium of it, depend upon separate factors governing supply and demand. A separate synthesis of information is required in each case. The relevant typology of information is shown in Table 2.1, together with an example of each type.

Persistent information on demand and supply is synthesised on a once-for-all basis. This is the synthesis that underpins the formation of the firm. Transitory information must be synthesised on a recurrent basis, however. Each period the intermediator faces the same problem of how to synthesise information on the transitory demand factor and the transitory supply factor in order to decide what output to order and what prices to quote. Because the problem is always the same from one period to the next it is advantageous for him to devise a procedure which routinely collects and combines the different items of information. Because information is costly to collect, however, it is not always advantageous to commit in advance to observing both demand and supply factors in every period. It is normally advantageous to adopt a sequential procedure in which the most volatile factor is investigated first.

It can also be advantageous to effect a division of labour in the implementation of the procedure. Two managers may be appointed: a marketing manager who observes demand and a purchasing manager who observes supply, each making observations that are a natural by-product of their other duties. The choice of procedure then governs the distribution of managerial power within the firm.

If demand is more volatile than supply then the procedure will normally begin by investigating demand and proceed to investigate supply only if the observation on demand is indecisive. This makes the manager who monitors demand more powerful than the manager who monitors supply, in the sense that the demand information collected by this manager is used to decide whether to consult the other manager or not. The firm is therefore demand-driven (Casson, 1994; 1996; Carter, 1995). Conversely, if supply is more volatile than demand then the manager who monitors supply becomes the more powerful one, and the firm becomes supply-driven instead.

There are many possible procedures by which information can be synthesised in order to take price and production decisions (Aoki, 1986; Geanakopolous and Milgrom, 1991). These different procedures are analogous to the different techniques that may be used in an ordinary production plant. Different procedures incur different observation costs, communication costs and memory costs. Because they all economise on overall information costs in various ways, they all run some risk of making a mistake. The optimal procedure combines observation, communication and memory in the appropriate proportions and trades off total information cost against the cost of error in an appropriate way. The pattern of volatility in the firm's environment is the principal factor governing the efficient choice. Thus while the efficient choice of technique in a plant is governed by the available technology and by the relative prices of different material inputs, *the efficient choice of procedure in a market-making organisation is governed by the pattern of volatility in the market environment and by the absolute and relative magnitudes of the different components of information cost.* Emphasising the market-making role of the firm therefore gives a quite distinctive perspective on the issue of choice of technique.

8 The Firm as the Producer of the Product It Sells: The Vertical Integration of Marketing and Production

The theory of vertical integration is most commonly applied to successive stages of ordinary production (see, for example, Bernhardt 1977; Carlton, 1979). Introducing market-making into the picture considerably strengthens the theory's relevance. The integration of production and market-making explains a prominent feature of many firms, namely, the coexistence of a strong marketing department and a strong production department within the same firm. Internal conflicts between these two departments are a natural consequence of the internalisation of the market for wholesale supply, which locks the two departments into each other.

Conversely, the possibility of disintegrating such a firm through the subcontracting of production sheds considerable light on recent debates over the "hollow firm". More specifically, it shows that the hollowing out of a firm typically returns it from an integrated form to a pure intermediating role. It is only the mistaken belief that it is ordinary production rather than market-making that is crucial to the firm that leads people to perceive this as a paradoxical development.

What then governs the integration and disintegration decisions of the market-making firm? The structure of the wholesale market is one factor. If the market for supplies is basically competitive then an intermediator who is dissatisfied can always switch to a different producer. If switching is difficult, however, then the producer may realise that he enjoys a monopolistic position, and so the supply price may be set above the marginal cost of production. As a result the intermediator may wish to take steps to reduce the supplier's market power (Waterson, 1982).

Acquiring the seller is one approach, but this has the disadvantage that the monopoly rents accruing to the seller will be capitalised in the purchase price. The alternative is for the intermediator to build his own production plant in competition with his existing supplier. The disadvantage of this is that it may add unnecessarily to capacity in the industry. There are three main reasons why the intermediator may nevertheless wish not only to invest in a plant of his own but also to rely on it exclusively for his supplies. Though logically distinct, they are related because *they all apply with greatest force to the supply of newly innovated products.* This makes the impact of the separate factors difficult to distinguish in practice, since they tend to appear jointly where innovative products are concerned.

The first concerns quality control (Casson, 1987, ch. 4). The intermediator may be unsure whether he can trust the producer to match the specification. He may not believe in the supplier's integrity, as noted above. But even if he trusts the supplier's integrity, he may not trust his competence. With a new product whose manufacture requires a modification of existing processes, the supplier may just not be up to the job.

To assure quality, the intermediator could, of course, insist on supervising the production operation. An independent producer is likely to object to this, however, because the information obtained as a result of supervision is likely to be a package which contains some items of a confidential nature. A by-product of observing the production process may be a fairly accurate assessment of the production costs, for example. Use of this information in subsequent negotiations could improve the intermediator's bargaining power to the detriment of the producer. Again, the producer may have been selected for a special skill he has, which he needs to protect as a trade secret. Allowing supervision would divulge the secret to the intermediator and further encourage him to set up rival production of his own.

The second factor is sunk costs. The intermediator may require the producer to invest in specific equipment or incur other forms of set up cost in order to customise the product to his requirements (Klein et al., 1978). Because of legal shortcomings, the producer cannot sell forward sufficient supplies to cover his costs before they are sunk. His consequent reluctance to customise the product obliges the intermediator to customise it for himself.

The third factor concerns the intermediator's desire to appropriate fully the value of his profit opportunity. In subcontracting the production of a new design the intermediator risks building up a competitor. Unless the design is patented, the intermediator's only method of excluding competitors is through secrecy. Even with a patent, the subcontractor may use his experience of production to improve the design and thereby render the original patent obsolete. For all these reasons, therefore, an intermediator launching an innovative product is likely to integrate backwards into its production.

9   The Foundation of the Firm

Judgements about market prospects are essentially subjective. It was noted in Section 4 that opinions differ about the scope for profitable intermediation. Some people take an optimistic view and others a pessimistic one. This diversity of opinion about the persistent factors may be explained by the fact that the underlying market situation cannot be observed directly, but only through certain symptoms. Some people interpret the situation in terms of one symptom and others in terms of another. Each symptom is correlated with the true situation. Accurate symptoms are highly correlated with the true situation and the most successful owners use these. Others are more weakly correlated. Some symptoms may not be used at all because people realise that they are, on balance, too misleading.

Some symptoms may have a bias to optimism in the sense that while picking out good conditions very accurately they are quite likely to report bad conditions as good as well. Others may have a bias to pessimism in that they pick up bad conditions very accurately but are likely to report good conditions as bad too. Wrongly accepting good conditions as bad is less hazardous than wrongly accepting bad conditions as good, and therefore risk-averse people are likely to avoid using symptoms which are biased to optimism. Although the distinction between pessimism and risk aversion made earlier remains valid, it is also true that when people have a choice between alternative symptoms, risk-aversion is likely to lead to pessimism because of symptom choice.

In principle, of course, people could reduce risks still further by combining information on different symptoms. The principle of synthesis, enunciated earlier in connection with transitory factors, would then apply to different symptoms of the persistent factors too (this is one rationale for the aggregation mechanisms discussed by Sah and Stiglitz, 1986). The subjectivity of opinion about persistent factors is almost certainly explained, however, by the fact that this cannot be easily done. Symptoms may be identified as a highly tacit form of information, each obtained from a quite distinctive source. No-one who has not consulted a particular source directly can fully understand what the symptom shows, and the sources are too diverse for anyone to consult more than one symptom before he has to make a decision.

It is possible, for example, that the identification and interpretation of symptoms operate at a subconscious level. Each individual uses symptoms which accumulated experience has taught him are useful in a particular type of situation. The individual may not know why he uses this symptom or even be aware that he does. The use of symptoms may be a highly pragmatic affair.

People can choose which symptoms to use only in the sense that by choosing a particular occupation and lifestyle they determine what kind of experiences they accumulate. Sophisticated symptoms are likely to be the result of a broad and varied lifetime experience. Because the use of symptoms is subconscious, people cannot share their expertise in any formal way. It is possible, though, to exchange life experiences through conversation, and quite a bit of business wisdom may be transmitted in this way. People may also find it easier to share their expertise when confronted with a specific situation. Each person examines particular symptoms in the situation and gives his opinion on the matter. Because these opinions may be difficult to justify by explicit reasoned argument, however, the weight that other people attach to a given person's opinion may depend more on his reputation and general social standing than on his ability to justify his choice.

The accuracy of the symptoms used is not the ultimate determinant of successful intermediation, however. If two or more people use similar symptoms to arrive at the same conclusions then rents from the exploitation of the general idea will be dissipated through competition between them. The loss is substantial because the costs of discovery are sunk costs and the marginal costs of exploitation are relatively low.

The combination of symptoms used to identify an idea therefore needs to be unique. This in turn suggests that the individual or group that develops the idea needs to be unusual – even eccentric – in some particular way. This makes them alert to opportunities which others simply fail to discover (Kirzner, 1973). Alternatively, it makes them aware that possibilities rejected by others really are opportunities, despite the fact that the others believe that they are foolish to go ahead with exploiting them. They are therefore able to preempt the opportunity and to invest in barriers to entry which will keep competitors out once they realise their mistake. Few barriers succeed in the long run, of course, but they may still be useful in prolonging the otherwise transitory period for which monopoly rents can be earned.

If an individual believes that he has recognised a change that others have not, and realises that this is because of a special symptom that he has used, then he may well ask himself whether he may not be in the wrong and others in the right. He requires self-confidence to back his own judgement. Without self-confidence, moreover, he will probably be unable to get financial backing from others, as discussed later. Whether the individual is successful or not depends upon whether his confidence is well-placed (as noted in Section 4). *People with good self-knowledge, who can assess their own competencies successfully, are more likely to achieve success because their degree of confidence will be matched to their true capability.* People who lack confidence will never found a firm, while those who are over confident are likely to found firms that fail.

10   The Size of the Firm

The synthetic model of the firm presented in this chapter does not suggest that there are intrinsic differences between firms of different sizes. Size is endogenous, being a reflection of the scope of the founder's vision, his organisational capabilities, his leadership qualities and the pattern of volatility in the industry. These factors apply first and foremost to the market-making firm. They affect its size through the size of the organisation it requires. The larger is the organisation needed for routine market-making, the larger is the firm, in other words.

Economies of integration are also important, since these affect the firm's involvement in additional aspects of market-making (wholesaling, retailing, etc.) and in non-market-making activities such as production. Product-specific factors are important in integration – particularly the amount of technological innovation embodied in the product. Finally, if market-making is integrated with production then economies of scale in production influence the size of the firm as well.

The scope of the founder's vision is reflected primarily in the nature of the opportunity for intermediation that he perceives. For example, a retailer who establishes a newsagent's shop to sell magazines in his local town possesses a vision of limited potential. By contrast, an individual who starts a magazine to support a new hobby has a vision with much greater potential. As the market for the magazine develops, the founder will become swamped with detail unless he delegates some decisions. Organisational capability is required to devise a managerial division of labour which structures information flow amongst the delegates efficiently.

Communication between the delegates needs to be truthful. If expensive and intrusive supervision is to be avoided then employees must be inspired to tell the truth through a sense of the moral value of the hobby, and the importance of their collective mission to promote it. The founder must be good at selecting suitable recruits and sharing his enthusiasm with them. Recruits must be competent, in the sense that they have low information-processing costs, and honest, in the sense that they do not impose unnecessary costs on others. If the founder is not an enthusiast himself then he needs to hire a charismatic enthusiast who can recruit and motivate employees on his behalf.

The pattern of volatility is also an important influence on the size of organisation. The more sources of disturbance there are, the more widely they are dispersed, and the more they interact with one another, the larger the organisation, and hence the firm, needs to be. Suppose, for example, that the magazine described has acquired a global market. If the market is homogeneous, because the magazine sells to a cosmopolitan elite in each country, then marketing requires less management attention than if the market is heterogeneous, because it sells to lower income groups and so requires local editions in each country. A homogeneous market has a single dominant source of volatility driving global demand, whilst a heterogeneous market has multiple sources of volatility driven by factors specific to individual countries. A similar distinction can be made on the supply side. If the magazine is exported world-wide from a single printing works then management faces a single major source of supply-side volatility driven by supply conditions at this plant. If the magazine is produced locally in each country, however, then the publisher becomes a multinational and faces multiple supply-side volatility instead.

It is not only the diversity of shocks that affects the size of organisation, however, but the breadth of synthesis that is required to respond effectively to them. In a "multidomestic" multinational, for example, where each national market is self-sufficient in its source of supply, consultation over some decisions can be confined to the national level; it is sufficient for the marketing director and the production director of the national subsidiary to get together. When production is internationally rationalised, though, so that different subsidiaries export to and import from each other, consultation must be global because all subsidiaries need to participate to some extent in planning intra-firm trade. International rationalisation therefore favours large scale organisation, and hence large firms.

This discussion presumes, however, that the extent of integration and the scale of production plants remain unchanged. For example, international rationalisation can encourage counter-movements, leading to the divestment of production, and the sharing of production facilities between different firms, which reduces the size of the market-making firm.

The analysis of volatility can be summarised by saying that small firms with small organisations are best adapted to dealing with just a small number of sources of volatility. If there are just a single source of demand volatility and a single source of supply volatility then a small organisation may cope with decision-making very well, responding rapidly to key information of the relevant type. Indeed, if demand is much more volatile than supply (or vice versa) so that there is just a single dominant source of volatility, then a single autocratic manager who has access to the relevant information source can take all the decisions by himself. At the other extreme, if there are multiple sources of demand and supply volatility then a much more consultative management style is required. There are too many sources of information for any one manager to monitor them all, and no important decisions can be taken on the basis of one source of information alone. It requires a large organisation to collect and synthesise all the relevant information in this case.

The synthetic theory of the firm provides a simple explanation of differences between industries in the average size of firm. To begin with, the theory emphasises the importance of distinguishing between pure market-making firms, pure production firms and firms that integrate market-making with production. Although most industries contain some firms of each type, the way that industries are classified means that many have just one dominant type. In some business service industries, such as employment agencies, the pure market-making firm is a very common type. Pure production firms are common in industries such as construction that make widespread use of subcontracting. In the manufacture of consumer goods the integrated form is common because many manufacturers prefer to make markets for their products themselves, instead of relying on specialist middlemen to do it for them. The optimal size of firm in an industry is not, therefore, a consequence only of scale economies, but of the economics of integration, the pattern of market volatility and the endowments of vision and charisma amongst the entrepreneurs who are attracted to the industry. It is the interaction of these characteristics which determines the average size of firm in an industry.

11   The Growth of the Firm

The size and growth of firms are closely related topics, and it is therefore not surprising that a theory which illuminates one issue should also illuminate the other. Simple comparative static analysis suggests that if there is a change in any of the factors governing the optimal size of firm in an industry, then an increase in optimal size will be associated with the growth of firms and a decrease in optimal size with the contraction of firms in that industry.

However, an increase in the overall size of the industry caused, for example, by a general increase in demand will not have the same effect, because if the optimal size of firm remains unchanged then in the long run adjustment will take place through the entry of new firms of optimal size.

This issue of entry indicates a qualification to the comparative static analysis. For why should the firms of larger size be the original firms grown larger, rather than new firms of large size replacing smaller ones that have left the industry? If people outside the industry are more alert to the relevant changes, will they not preempt the opportunity for the established firms to grow?

Now the synthetic theory indicates that the size of the firm is, in some respects, just an indicator of its structure, which in turn is governed by the nature of the market-making opportunity it exists to exploit. Large firms simply have more complex organisational structures than do small ones. These complex structures exist to process transitory information in an efficient way. The question then becomes whether such organisations are well adapted to collecting persistent information as well. Will they be handicapped in processing persistent information, so that they fail to recognise new opportunities for intermediation when they arise and fail to adjust their organisational structures in an appropriate way?

The answer depends upon whether the persistent change in market-making conditions is incremental or radical. Incremental changes tend to originate inside the industry and radical changes outside it. Incremental changes are often discovered as a by-product of routine activity.

Salesmen report back on lost sales and consumer resistance, for example, and this leads to minor improvements in the product. Large firms are in a good position to respond to such changes since their large scale of operation makes it easier to identify systematic patterns in incidents of this kind.

Radical changes are less likely to originate in this way – they may begin with a successful formula, such as telephone selling, introduced in a quite different industry. Such changes provide an opportunity for firms from the outside industry to enter through diversification. Alternatively, junior managers in the outside industry may leave employment in order to enter the industry by founding their own firms.

Such entry may alert established firms to investigate persistent factors in greater detail. If the established firms realise that they have over-looked a new market-making opportunity, they may still be able to respond in time. For example, even if an entrant has created a valuable brand name, an established firm may be able to license it or, more likely, take over the smaller firm on generous terms. The takeover combines the new branded product with established organisational skills, generating a surplus out of which the takeover can be financed.

This analysis implicitly assumes, however, that the new product requires the old organisational structure to exploit it. How will estab-lished large firms respond if organisational change is required? It may be too costly to change their procedures. Selfish and dishonest managers in the established firm may try to see out their period of employment without the upheaval that reorganisation would incur. It may therefore be cheaper to grow a small firm into a large one than to have the large one change its structure. The advantage of the small firm lies in its freedom to evolve a different kind of organisation without disrupting complex procedures already in place. The price of this flexibility is inex-perience, so small-firm managers of significant organisational ability are needed in order to take advantage of the opportunity that large-firm inertia affords.

To summarise, the synthetic theory highlights four important deter-minants of the growth of new firms. The first is that sources of informa-tion on persistent changes in market-making opportunities are dispersed outside the industry and are not picked up first through the accumulated experience of established firms. The second is that large firms do not diversify into the industry. The third is that the exploitation of new market-making opportunities requires a different organisational struc-ture to that required by the previous market-making opportunity, as embodied in the organisational structures of established firms. The fourth is that the entrants who recognise the new opportunity include people with sufficient ability to grow new organisations more cheaply than the established firms can adapt their own.

It is a feature of this approach that it explains the success of small firms in terms of the weaknesses of large ones, and that it relates the weaknesses of large firms to their inability to adjust their organisational structures to a change in the market environment. Although this approach is clearly anticipated in the work of Penrose (1959) and others, it has not been widely used as an explanation of small firm growth in recent empirical literature. Anecdotal evidence suggests, however, that it works quite well as an explanation of small firm growth in the 1970s and early 1980s, and its subsequent tailing off into the 1990s. Of course, only a small proportion of the small firms founded in the 1970s and 1980s grew very fast at all, and it is also true that corporate growth in general has been depressed by recession in the early 1990s. Nevertheless, it is plausible to associate the growth of small firms in the 1970s and 1980s with the development of new products for niche markets which required more flexible forms of organisation than the large firms of the time were able to provide (Acs and Audretsch, 1990). Many large firms were still wedded to rigidly hierarchical structures adapted to supplying mature products to stable markets. They had slow and complicated procedures inspired by a mass production philosophy. The small firms had simpler decision-making procedures giving faster response to new threats – like the oil crisis – and to new opportunities – especially in the service sector.

The globalisation of markets in the 1980s intensified competition between large firms from different countries. To maintain competitiveness, these firms delayered, "downsized" and dis-integrated, so that their organisations became "leaner" – in terms of employment (though not sales) they became much smaller. As a result, they are now more alert to opportunities both inside and outside their traditional lines of business. The number of opportunities that large firms fail to pick up, it may be surmised, is much smaller than before, and this provides less scope for successful small-firm entry. Small-firm growth has therefore been reduced by increased large-firm flexibility. At the moment this argument is no more than a conjecture, but it would seem to be a promising line of inquiry for case-study research.

12   Reflections on the "Ownership" Theory of the Firm

Having set out the theory and considered its application to small firm growth, it is useful to conclude by comparing the theory with some of the alternative approaches mentioned at the outset. The limitations of these approaches, it is suggested, lie mainly in their partial nature. This partial nature means that the theories become misleading when applied to issues that they are not designed to address.

The comparison begins with the "ownership" theory of the firm (Grossman and Hart, 1986), which argues that a firm is created in order to define a residual claimant – the owner of the firm – who can control team-based activity within it. While the basic idea is quite ingenious, the authors' suggestion that their theory addresses the crucial issue in the theory of the firm seems misplaced.

According to the synthetic theory presented above, ownership of a firm is an essentially speculative activity. The aim of the owner is to appropriate rents from what he believes to be privileged information. The most important case concerns an opportunity for intermediation, as described in Section 6. The opportunity must be kept a secret until it has been preempted, and, since it is difficult to sell a secret, he must preempt the opportunity himself.

Another way of appropriating rent from information is by placing a bet on the subject with other people who are believed to be not so well informed. The rent is extracted when the truth is revealed and the bet is won. This is, in effect, what happens when a successful firm acquires resources from other people. *The owner of the firm bets that his judgement of the situation is better than the judgement of those who sell their resources to the firm.* The profit of the firm is his reward for being right.

Differences in judgement exist because different people use different symptoms to interpret the environment. People with wide-ranging but unusual experiences have the kind of entrepreneurial judgement which is at once both "deviant" in terms of received opinion, and yet often correct. Other people who have confidence in the judgement of a person of this kind may contribute risk capital to the firm he founds. This helps to fund the indivisible sunk cost required to establish a new market. Major investors may also contribute their opinions on how the founder's idea is best exploited. Minor investors may be involved too; they essentially free-ride on the judgement of the principal entrepreneur and the major investors. All these investors count on the entrepreneur to exercise vigilance even though he may own only a modest portion of the equity.

Grossman and Hart offer a very different account of ownership, however. In their account, the emphasis on speculation is missing. According to them the owner seeks control, not in order to specify a decision-making procedure appropriate to the intermediation opportunity he has identified, but simply to gain the upper hand in a game of strategy played out with other people who contribute resources to the firm. Grossman and Hart lay great emphasis on the incompleteness of the employment contract. They argue that this creates an ambiguity which is resolved by allocating residual control – i.e., control over all the decisions not fully specified in the contract – to one particular party, namely, the owner of the firm. *Such an account of ownership is misleading because it overstates the incompleteness of contracts and thereby suggests much more scope for strategic behaviour than is possible in practice.* It ignores the fact that the owner has committed himself to certain procedures and that although he can change these procedures, the probability that he will do this in any given period is actually very small. Moreover, his right to change these procedures in a manner which seriously damages the interests of other parties is constrained by the constitution of the firm. Should the owner breach the constitution he will lose the loyalty of key employees, who can inflict considerable damage on the firm if they quit.

The incompleteness of contracts certainly exists as a rational response to information costs. It does not, however, create a major ambiguity which strategic behaviour by a specialised residual claimant is required to control. Rather it creates a need for employees to acquaint themselves with the constitution and the procedures of the firm and to form rational expectations of how their conduct is likely to be regulated by these procedures on a day-to-day basis.

The only substantial way in which contracts are incomplete is that the owner retains the right to change the procedures in the light of changes he believes he has recognised in the environment of the firm. This is simply the entrepreneurial function. The owner is far too concerned with maintaining procedures that efficiently exploit his intermediation opportunity to be bothered, to any significant extent, with the strategic fine-tuning that Grossman and Hart discuss. Such fine-tuning may well occur, but it is the speculative factor that Grossman and Hart omit that is the principal factor governing the ownership of the firm.

13   Reflections on the New Institutional Economics

Williamson's (1975; 1985) theory of the firm is based on three key assumptions: opportunism, bounded rationality and asset-specificity. None of these assumptions emerges unscathed from the present analysis. The assumption of opportunism is qualified by the fact that many transaction costs are connected with the processing of information and are incurred whether the information concerned is true or false.

The assumption of bounded rationality has been replaced by an assumption that information is costly to collect and to communicate. This new assumption is more precise. It avoids ambiguity over exactly what deviations from substantive rationality are likely to occur. Thus Williamson considers bounded rationality to be a very serious problem when writing contingent contracts, but effectively ignores it when considering how the owner of the firm chooses between alternative boundaries for the firm. Indeed, in Williamson's theory the principal role of bounded rationality is simply to explain why the employment contract is incomplete, along the lines of Coase (1937) and Simon (1957). In addition, by specifying the absolute and relative magnitudes of different components of information cost, the new approach makes it possible to predict in detail the decision-making procedures and the organisational structure of the firm, along the lines described in Section 7. Instead of making ad hoc assumptions about the kind of procedures that are used, predictions are derived using the logic of information costs. The predictions explain why different kinds of organisation are associated with different kinds of market-making opportunity.

Asset-specificity is supplemented in this chapter by other determinants of vertical integration, such as the appropriability of rewards from information, and problems of quality control. Williamson justifies his emphasis on asset-specificity by interpreting the concept so broadly that practically any asset can be made to appear specific when the argument requires it. The problem with asset-specificity is that it is just too successful in accounting for vertical integration. The real challenge is to explain why vertical integration does *not* occur in the many cases where asset-specificity is present, rather than to account for why it *does* occur in a few of the many cases where asset-specificity can be found.

Williamson is undoubtedly correct in his contention that a comprehensive theory of the firm must synthesise the insights of Simon (1947), Commons (1934) and Coase (1937). His own analysis hardly qualifies as comprehensive, though. Williamson has little to say about intermediation and almost nothing to say about the role of entrepreneurship in the formation and the growth of the firm. A sense of the truly global dimension to the exploitation of market opportunities is missing too. The problem seems to be that opportunism is too restricted, bounded rationality is too vague, and asset-specificity too ubiquitous, to build an entire theory on just these foundations. It has been suggested in this chapter that a better approach is to analyse the firm as a specialised intermediator created by an entrepreneur routinely to synthesise information about different sources of volatility. Moral leadership constrains opportunism; information costs take the place of bounded rationality; and asset-specificity is supplemented by a number of other factors to provide a full account of vertical integration. The result is a theory that is entirely consistent with the principle of rational action employed in mainstream economics. *It is the concepts of intermediation, information synthesis and volatility – rather than opportunism, bounded rationality and asset-specificity – which turn out to be most crucial when economic principles are consistently applied to the theory of the firm.*

14   Reflections on Resource-Based Theories of the Firm

Resource-based theories emphasise the competences or capabilities of the firm's management team. This strand of thinking originates with Penrose (1959) and Richardson (1960; 1972); its revival owes much to its synergy with recent evolutionary theorising by Nelson and Winter (1982). When discussing the resource-based approach to the firm it is difficult to be sure whether there is one theory expressed in different ways by different writers or several different theories which are broadly similar to each other.

Some writers, such as Loasby (1976) and Foss, Knudsen and Montgomery (1995), lay great emphasis on the complexity of the real-world processes in which firms are involved. It is suggested that economic agents in general, and managers in particular, cannot behave rationally because they are overwhelmed by the complexity of the decision problems they face. People cope with this situation by relying upon procedures that are institutionalised through political power and social conformity instead (Hodgson, 1988).

This approach, with its emphasis on institutions and their internal organisation, evidently asks the same kinds of question that are raised in this chapter. The nature of the answers given is very different, however. Many resource-based theorists reject formal modelling altogether and adopt the nihilistic stance that in a complex world any model of the firm will distort the analysis more than it illuminates it. This negative attitude runs directly counter to the positive thrust of this chapter, which attempts to rationalise institutions and their procedures in terms of a higher level of rationality – the rationality of choosing between alternative institutions and procedures in order to achieve the best possible trade-off between the quality of decision making and information costs.

Writers who reject rationality are usually opposed to the equilibrium concept too. They argue that economic change is path-dependent (David, 1985; Langlois, 1984); in other words, the final stage that is reached depends upon the path of adjustment that is followed. Path dependence then becomes an endogenous feature of real-world complexity with which individual decision makers have to cope.

A key assumption here is that the path that the adjustment process starts down is essentially a myopic path. Thus in the later stages of the evolution of the system the path that is taken may involve dealing with contradictions thrown up by the inappropriate nature of the initial response. Firms discover too late that they are "locked in" by irreversible decisions made at an earlier stage (Dosi and Metcalfe, 1991).

Because the assumption of myopia is often left implicit, however, these writers rarely consider exactly why the myopic response arises in the first place. They also play down the related issue of whether the costs of myopia are really all that great. The information costs of considering all the possible scenarios that may emerge as a consequence of a given change may well be so high that it is, in fact, efficient to tolerate a certain amount of error, provided that the consequences are not too severe. Analysing the information costs of planning may reveal that an initial decision not to plan is rational in the light of information costs. Any "disequilibria" therefore relate to improbable scenarios whose possible occurrence is fully anticipated by the model. In this modified sense, therefore, the principle of equilibrium still prevails.

Another significant feature of resource-based theories is the emphasis that is placed on the tacit nature of information (Fransman, 1995; Kogut and Zander, 1992). In particular, it is asserted that the ownership and competitive advantages of firms comprise tacit information which could not be transferred to another firm even if contractual arrangements would permit it. A sharp distinction is therefore made between resource-based theories on the one hand and the Coasian internalisation theory on the other, on the grounds that the Coasian theory fails to identify the true obstacle to the diffusion of advantages to other firms. The distinction is, however, overdrawn; for example, Buckley and Casson (1976), in their application of internalisation theory to this issue, clearly identify "psychic distance" as a non-contractual obstacle to information flow.

Indeed, what is required is nothing less than a balanced synthesis of communication costs and contractual costs to provide an integrated account of the nature of the firm. This is what the present chapter provides. The concept of communication cost reduces tacitness to an economically relevant and measurable form, while the concept of monitoring cost addresses the contractual issues. Indeed, the present theory goes beyond this by emphasising that managerial competence resides in handling information in a variety of ways – collecting it, assimilating it, disseminating it and storing it, as well as using it to take

decisions. It avoids the rather restrictive emphasis on technological information characteristic of some of the resource-based literature (Cantwell,
1995) by recognising that an enormous variety of information is involved
in market-making intermediation. In this way the questions raised by
resource-based theories are addressed in a constructive manner. The
theory of the firm, like managerial competence, benefits more from
evolutionary changes of the kind described in this chapter than it does
from a radical reconstruction of the kind that resource-based theories
propose. Radical reconstruction is always expensive, and often unnecessary – as in the present case.

15   Summary and Conclusions

This chapter has provided a definition of the firm as a specialist decision
maker and then employed a small number of key concepts to examine a
number of related facets of it. It has been argued that previous writing
on the firm has been essentially partial, with different writers focusing on
different issues. A synthesis which leads to a theory of the firm centred on
the entrepreneur as the founder and prime mover within it has been
proposed.

The basis of this theory is that an entrepreneur observes the environment in order to detect symptoms of change. This leads him first to
found the firm and subsequently to effect intermittent changes in its procedures. These procedures synthesise information from two main sources
of volatility – namely, the demand factors and the supply factors in the
market that the entrepreneur has set up. Shocks that encourage the
establishment of a market tend to persist for a considerable time, while
shocks to the market that occur once it is set up tend to be of a more
transitory nature. That is why routine procedures are an efficient way of
dealing with them. The managers who are delegated by the entrepreneur
to monitor the transitory factors also have responsibility for implementing decisions. They are supported by administrative staff, who have to be
in post before the decisions are made.

The key to the firm's success lies not in specific business strategies, as
suggested by Porter (1980), nor in specific ownership advantages, such as
technology, as suggested by Dunning (1977). These are both short-run
consequences of long-run decisions about market opportunities and
organisational structure taken previously by the entrepreneur. It is the
quality of entrepreneurial judgement, as reflected in the correctness of
these decisions, which holds the key to long-run success.

Large firms and small firms differ principally in the complexity of the
decision-making procedures and the extent of the managerial division of

labour they employ. Opportunities for small-firm growth are positively related to the dispersion of information about market-making opportunities, the extent to which new opportunities require new organisational forms, the organisational capabilities of small-firm founders and the degree of managerial inertia in established large firms.

From a knowledge of markets, through to a knowledge of technology and a knowledge of people, it is the ability to synthesise information that emerges as the hall-mark of the successful entrepreneur. The only thing to add is that the successful entrepreneur requires self-knowledge as well. When backing his own judgement against that of others, he needs to be sure that his confidence is well-placed. Conversely, he must frankly acknowledge his own shortcomings, because it is these that dictate the nature of the complementary expertise that he must recruit. "Know thyself" is not only a moral injunction, the theory suggests, but a key to entrepreneurial success as well.

Note

I am grateful to Zoltan Acs, Peter Buckley, John Cantwell, Bo Carlsson, Eric Jones, Animesh Shrivastava and two anonymous referees for comments on an earlier draft.

References

Acs, Z. and D.B. Audretsch (1990) *Innovation and Small Firms,* Cambridge, Mass.: MIT Press.

Aoki, M. (1986) Horizontal vs. Vertical Information Structure of the Firm, *American Economic Review*, 76, 971–983.

Bernhardt, I. (1977) Vertical Integration and Demand Variability, *Journal of Industrial Economics*, 25, 213–229.

Buckley, P.J. and M.C. Casson (1976) *The Future of the Multinational Enterprise,* London: Macmillan.

Cantillon, R. (1755) *Essai sur la Nature du Commerce en Générale* (ed. H. Higgs), London: Macmillan, 1931.

Cantwell, J.A. (1995) Multinational Corporations and Innovatory Activities: Towards a New Evolutionary Approach, in J. Molero (ed), *Technological Innovation, Multinational Corporations and New International Competitiveness*, Chur: Harwood Academic, 21–57.

Carlton, D.W. (1979) Vertical Integration in Competitive Markets Under Uncertainty, *Journal of Industrial Economics*, 27, 189–209.

Carter, M.J. (1995) Information and the Division of Labour: Implications for the Firm's Choice of Organisation, *Economic Journal*, 105, 385–397.

Casson, M.C. (1982) *The Entrepreneur: An Economic Theory*, Oxford: Martin Robertson, reprinted Aldershot: Gregg Revivals, 1991.

Casson, M.C. (1987) *The Firm and the Market: Studies in Multinational Enterprise and the Scope of the Firm*, Cambridge, Mass.: MIT Press.

Casson, M.C. (1991) *Economics of Business Culture: Game Theory, Transaction Costs and Economic Performance*, Oxford: Clarendon Press.

Casson, M.C. (1994) Why are Firms Hierarchical? *International Journal of the Economics of Business*, 1, 47–76.

Casson, M.C. (1995) *Entrepreneurship and Business Culture*, Aldershot: Edward Elgar.

Casson, M.C. (1996) Comparative Organisation of Large and Small Firms: An Information Cost Approach, *Small Business Economics*, 8, 1–17.

Casson, M.C. (1997) *Information and Organisation: A New Perspective on the Theory of the Firm*, Oxford: Clarendon Press.

Coase, R.H. (1937) The Nature of the Firm: *Economica* (New series), 4, 386–405.

Commons, J.R. (1934) *The Legal Foundations of Capitalism*, New York: Macmillan.

David, P.A. (1985) Clio and the Economics of QWERTY, *American Economic Review*, 75(2), 332–337.

Dosi, G. and J.S. Metcalfe (1991) On Some Notions of Irreversibility in Economics, in P. Saviotti and J.S. Metcalfe (eds), *Evolutionary Theories of Economic and Technological Change: Present Status and Future Prospects*, Chur: Harwood Academic, 133–159.

Dunning, J.H. (1977) Trade, Location of Economic Activity and the Multinational Enterprise: A Search for an Eclectic Approach, in B. Ohlin, P.O. Hesselbom and P.M. Wijkman (eds), *The International Allocation of Economic Activity*, London: Macmillan, 395–418.

Foss, N.J., C. Knudsen and C.A. Montgomery (1995) An Exploration of Common Ground: Integrating Evolutionary and Resource-Based Views of the Firm, in C.A. Montgomery (ed), *Resources in an Evolutionary Perspective: A Synthesis of Evolutionary and Resource-based Approaches to Strategy*, Dordrecht: Kluwer.

Fransman, M.J. (1995) *Visions of the Firm and Japan*, Oxford: Oxford University Press.

Geanakopolous, J. and P. Milgrom (1991) A Theory of Hierarchies Based upon Limited Managerial Attention, *Journal of Japanese and International Economics*, 5(3), 205–225.

Granovetter, M. (1985) Economic Action and Social Structure: The Problem of Embeddedness, *American Journal of Sociology*, 91(3), 481–510.

Grossman, S.J. and O. Hart (1986) The Costs and Benefits of Ownership: A Theory of Vertical and Lateral Integration, *Journal of Political Economy*, 94, 691–719.

Hayek, F.A. von (1937) Economics and Knowledge, *Economica* (New Series), 4, 33–54, reprinted in F.A. von Hayek, *Individualism and Economic Order*, London: Routledge and Kegan Paul, 1959, 33–56.

Hodgson, G. (1988) *Economics and Institutions*, Oxford: Blackwell.

Hymer, S.H. (1960) *The International Operations of National Firms: A Study of Direct Investment*, PhD thesis, MIT, published 1976, Cambridge, Mass: MIT Press.

Kay, N.M. (1993) Markets, False Hierarchies and the Role of Asset Specificity, in C. Pitelis (ed), *Transaction Costs, Markets and Hierarchies*, Oxford: Blackwell, 242–261.

Kirzner, I.M. (1973) *Competition and Entrepreneurship*, Chicago: University of Chicago Press.

Klein, B., R.G. Crawford and A.A. Alchian (1978) Vertical Integration, Appropriable Rents and the Competitive Contracting Process, *Journal of Law and Economics*, 21, 297–326.

Knight, F.H. (1921) *Risk Uncertainty and Profit*, Boston: Houghton Mifflin.

Kogut, B. and U. Zander (1992) Knowledge of the Firm, Combinative Capabilities and the Replication of Technology, *Organization Science*, 3, 383–397.

Langlois, R.N. (1984) Internal Organisation in a Dynamic Context: Some Theoretical Considerations, in M. Jussawalla and H. Ebenfield (eds), *Communication and Information Economics: New Perspectives*, Amsterdam: North-Holland, 23–49.

Loasby, B.J. (1976) *Choice, Complexity and Ignorance*, Cambridge: Cambridge University Press.

Marschak, J. and R. Radner (1972) *The Economic Theory of Teams*, New Haven, Conn.: Yale University Press.

Marshall, A. (1890) *Principles of Economics*, London: Macmillan.

Marshall, A. (1919) *Industry and Trade*, London: Macmillan.

Milgrom, P.R. and J. Roberts (1992) *Economics of Organisation and Management*, Englewood Cliffs, N.J.: Prentice Hall.

Nelson, R.R. and S.G. Winter (1982) *An Evolutionary Theory of Economic Change*, Cambridge, Mass.: Harvard University Press.

North, D.C. (1981) *Structure and Change in Economic History*, New York: W.W. Norton.

Penrose, E.T. (1959) *The Theory of the Growth of the Firm*, Oxford: Blackwell.

Polanyi, M. (1964) *Science, Faith and Society*, Chicago; University of Chicago Press.

Porter, M.E. (1980) *Competitive Strategy*, New York: Free Press.

Posner, R.A. (1973) An Economic Approach to Legal Procedure and Judicial Administration, *Journal of Legal Studies*, 2, 399–458.

Putterman, L. (1981) *Division of Labour and Economic Welfare*, Oxford: Oxford University Press.

Richardson, G.B. (1960) *Information and Investment*, Oxford: Oxford University Press.

Richardson, G.B. (1972) The Organization of Industry, *Economic Journal*, 82, 883–896.

Robertson, D.H. (1923) *The Control of Industry*, London: Nisbet.

Sah, R.K. and J.E. Stiglitz (1986) The Architecture of Economic Systems: Hierarchies and Polyarchies, *American Economic Review*, 76, 716–727.

Schumpeter, J.A. (1934) *The Theory of Economic Development* (trans. R. Opie), Cambridge, Mass.: Harvard University Press.

Schumpeter, J.A. (1939) *Business Cycles: A Theoretical, Historical and Statistical Analysis of the Capitalist Process*, New York: McGraw-Hill.

Simon, H.A. (1947) *Administrative Behaviour*, New York: Macmillan.

Simon, H.A. (1957) A Formal Theory of the Employment Relation, in H.A. Simon, *Models of Man: Social and Rational*, New York: John Wiley & Sons.

Spence, A.M. (1973) Job Market Signalling, *Quarterly Journal of Economics*, 87, 355–374.

Teece, D.J., R. Rumelt, G. Dosi and S.G. Winter (1994) Understanding Corporate Coherence: Theory and Evidence, *Journal of Economic Behaviour and Organization*, 23, 1–30.

78   **Mark Casson**

Waterson, M. (1982) Vertical Integration, Variable Proportions and Oligopoly, *Economic Journal*, 92, 129–144.
Williamson, O.E. (1975) *Markets and Hierarchies: Analysis and Anti-Trust Implications*, New York: Free Press.
Williamson, O.E. (1985) *The Economic Institutions of Capitalism*, New York: Free Press.
Winter, S.G. (1988) On Coase, Competence and the Corporation, *Journal of Law, Economics and Organisation*, 4, 163–180.

CHAPTER 3

Entrepreneurship and Economic Restructuring: An Evolutionary View

David B. Audretsch

1   Introduction

Two stylized facts that have emerged consistently in the economics literature pose something of a puzzle to scholars of industrial organization.
The first, which has received considerable attention at least since the
seminal study by Herbert Simon and Charles Bonini (1958) some four
decades ago, is the persistence of an asymmetric firm-size distribution
predominated by small enterprises. Ijiri and Simon (1977, p. 2) characterize this as a"regularity in social phenomena that is both striking and
observable in a number of quite diverse situations. It is a regularity in
the size distribution of firms."[1]

In fact, virtually no other economic phenomenon has persisted as consistently as the skewed asymmetric firm-size distribution. Not only is it
almost identical across every manufacturing industry, but it has remained
strikingly constant over time, at least since the Second World War, and
even across developed industrialized nations.

The second puzzling result is that the entry of new firms into an industry is not substantially deterred in industries where scale economies and
innovative activity play an important role. The traditional theory in
industrial organization would have predicted that the presence of daunt-
ing barriers to entry would have deterred the start-up and entry of new
firms in such industries.

These two puzzles in industrial organization are consistent with the
striking conclusion of Acs, Carlsson and Karlsson in the introductory
chapter of this volume that most firms are small. In fact, most of these
firms are so small as to preclude operating at anything approaching an
efficient scale of output, at least for most industries. This observation is
not new and has been the focus of concern in the field of industrial

organization for decades. For example, Leonard Weiss in 1991 (Audretsch and Yamawaki, 1991, p. xiv) concluded, "In most industries the great majority of firms is suboptimal. In a typical industry there are, let's say, one hundred firms. Typically only about five to ten of them will be operating at the MES (minimum efficient scale) level of output, or anything like it. So here is a subject that ought to be measured and critically analyzed and evaluated."[2]

Lucas (1978) attempted to explain the pervasiveness of small enterprises in the firm-size distribution with a static theory. In this chapter, an evolutionary theory is introduced. According to this evolutionary theory, the answer to the question "How are small and suboptimal enterprises able to be viable?" is "They are not – at least not by remaining small and suboptimal." Rather, such new suboptimal scale firms are engaged in the selection process, whereby the successful enterprises grow and ultimately approach or attain the optimal size, whereas the remainder stagnate and may ultimately be forced to exit the market. Thus, the persistence of an asymmetric firm-sized distribution skewed toward small enterprises presumably reflects a continuing process of entry into industries and not necessarily the survival of such small enterprises over a long period of time. That is, although the skewed size distribution of firms persists with remarkable stability over time, it does not appear to be a constant set of small firms that is responsible for this skewness.

In particular, this evolutionary theory analyzes the process by which new firms enter into industrial markets, either grow and survive or exit from the industry, and possibly displace incumbent corporations. At the heart of this evolutionary process is innovation, because the potential for innovative activity serves as the driving force behind much of the evolution of industries. And it is innovative activity that explains why the patterns of industry evolution vary from industry to industry, depending upon the underlying knowledge conditions, or what Nelson and Winter (1982) term *technological regimes*.

The purpose of this chapter is to link this new theory on innovation and industry evolution to the recent empirical evidence. In the following section the theory linking innovation to industry evolution is presented. This theory is evolutionary in that it focuses on the role of new firms in the generation of diversity and the process of selection among diverse alternatives. The evidence supporting this evolutionary theory is provided in the third section. The new evolutionary theory and evidence are combined to present two views of industry evolution in the fourth section. Finally, in the fifth section a summary and conclusion are provided.

2 Innovation and Industry Evolution

Coase (1937) was awarded a Nobel Prize for explaining why a firm should exist. But why should more than one firm exist in an industry?[3] One answer is provided by the traditional economics literature focusing on industrial organization. An excess level of profitability induces entry into the industry. And this is why the entry of new firms is interesting and important – because the new firms provide an equilibrating function in the market, in that the levels of price and profit are restored to the competitive levels.

The model proposed by Audretsch (1995) refocuses the unit of observation away from firms deciding whether to increase their output from a level of zero to some positive amount in a new industry, to individual agents in possession of new knowledge that, because of uncertainty, may or may not have some positive economic value. It is the uncertainty inherent in new economic knowledge, combined with asymmetries between the agent possessing that knowledge and the decision making vertical hierarchy of the incumbent organization with respect to its expected value, that potentially leads to a gap in the valuation of that knowledge.

How the economic agent chooses to appropriate the value of his knowledge, that is, either within an incumbent firm or by starting or joining a new enterprise, will be shaped by the knowledge conditions underlying the industry. Under the routinized technological regime the agent will tend to appropriate the value of his new ideas within the boundaries of incumbent firms. Thus, the propensity for new firms to be started should be relatively low in industries characterized by the routinized technological regime.

By contrast, under the entrepreneurial regime the agent will tend to appropriate the value of his new ideas outside the boundaries of incumbent firms by starting a new enterprise. Thus, the propensity for new firms to enter should be relatively high in industries characterized by the entrepreneurial regime.

Audretsch (1995) suggests that divergences in the expected value regarding new knowledge will, under certain conditions, lead an agent to exercise what Albert O. Hirschman (1970) has termed *exit* rather than *voice* and depart from an incumbent enterprise to launch a new firm. But who is right, the departing agents or those agents remaining in the organizational decision making hierarchy who, by assigning the new idea a relatively low value, have effectively driven the agent with the potential innovation away? Ex post the answer may not be too difficult. But given the uncertainty inherent in new knowledge, the answer is anything but trivial a priori.

Thus, when a new firm is launched, its prospects are shrouded in uncertainty. If the new firm is built around a new idea, i.e., potential innovation, it is uncertain whether there is sufficient demand for the new idea or whether some competitor will have the same or even a superior idea. Even if the new firm is formed to be an exact replica of a successful incumbent enterprise, it is uncertain whether sufficient demand for a new clone, or even for the existing incumbent, will prevail in the future. Tastes can change, and new ideas emerging from other firms will certainly influence those tastes.

Finally, an additional layer of uncertainty pervades a new enterprise. It is not known how competent the new firm really is, in terms of management, organization, and work force. At least incumbent enterprises know something about their underlying competencies from past experience, which is to say that a new enterprise is burdened with uncertainty as to whether it can produce and market the intended product as well as sell it. In both cases the degree of uncertainty will typically exceed that confronting incumbent enterprises.

This initial condition of not just uncertainty, but greater degree of uncertainty vis-à-vis incumbent enterprises in the industry is captured in the theory of firm selection and industry evolution proposed by Boyan Jovanovic (1982). Jovanovic presents a model in which the new firms, which he terms *entrepreneurs*, face costs that not only are random but also differ across firms. A central feature of the model is that a new firm does not know its cost function, that is, its relative efficiency, but rather discovers this through the process of learning from its actual post-entry performance. In particular, Jovanovic (1982) assumes that entrepreneurs are unsure about their ability to manage a new-firm start-up and therefore their prospects for success. Although entrepreneurs may launch a new firm on the basis of a vague sense of expected post-entry performance, they only discover their true ability – in terms of managerial competence and of basing of the firm on an idea that is viable on the market – once their business is established. Those entrepreneurs who discover that their ability exceeds their expectations expand the scale of their business, whereas those discovering that their post-entry performance is less than commensurate with their expectations will contract the scale of output and possibly exit from the industry. Thus, Jovanovic's model is a theory of *noisy selection*, where efficient firms grow and survive and inefficient firms decline and fail.

The role of learning in the selection process has been the subject of considerable debate. On the one hand is what has been referred to as the *Lamarckian* assumption that learning refers to adaptations made by the new enterprise. In this sense, those new firms that are the most flexible and adaptable will be the most successful in adjusting to whatever the demands of the market are. As Nelson and Winter (1982, p. 11) point out, "Many kinds of organizations commit resources to learning; organizations seek to copy the forms of their most successful competitors."

On the other hand is the interpretation that the role of learning is restricted to discovering whether the firm has the *right stuff* in terms of the goods it is producing as well as the way they are being produced. Under this interpretation the new enterprise is not necessarily able to adapt or adjust to market conditions but receives information based on its market performance with respect to its *fitness* in terms of meeting demand most efficiently vis-à-vis rivals. The theory of organizational ecology proposed by Michael T. Hannan and John Freeman (1989) most pointedly adheres to the notion "We assume that individual organizations are characterized by relative inertia in structure." That is, firms learn not in the sense of adjustment of their actions as reflected by their fundamental identity and purpose, but in the sense of their perception. What is then learned is whether or not the firm has the right stuff, but not how to change that stuff.

The theory of firm selection is particularly appealing in view of the rather startling size of most new firms. For example, the mean size of more than 11,000 new-firm start-ups in the manufacturing sector in the United States was found to be fewer than eight workers per firm (Audretsch, 1995).[4] While the minimum efficient scale (MES) varies substantially across industries, and even to some degree across various product classes within any given industry, the observed size of most new firms is sufficiently small to ensure that the bulk of new firms will be operating at a suboptimal scale of output. Why would an entrepreneur start a new firm that would immediately be confronted by scale disadvantages?

An implication of the theory of firm selection is that new firms may begin at a small, even suboptimal, scale of output, and then if merited by subsequent performance expand. Those new firms that are successful will grow, whereas those that are not successful will remain small and may ultimately be forced to exit from the industry if they are operating at a suboptimal scale of output.

Subsequent to entering an industry, a firm must decide whether to maintain its output (Q_{it}), expand, contract, or exit. Two different strands of literature have identified several major influences shaping the decision to exit an industry. The first, and more obvious strand of literature, suggests that the probability of a business's exiting will tend to increase as the gap between its level of output and the MES level of output increases.[5] The second strand of literature points to the role that the technological environment plays in shaping the decision to exit. As Dosi (1988) and Arrow (1962) argue, an environment characterized by more frequent innovation may also be associated with a greater amount of uncertainty regarding not only the technical nature of the product but also the demand for that product. As technological uncertainty increases, particularly under the entrepreneurial regime, the likelihood that the business will be able to produce a viable product and ultimately be able to survive decreases.

These two forces combine to shape the probability of a new firm's remaining in business in period t, or

$$P(Q_{it} > 0) = f(i_{it}, c(Q_{it}) - c(Q^*)), \tag{1}$$

where $c(Q_{it})$ is the average cost of producing at a scale of output Q_i, and $c(Q^*)$ is the average cost of producing at the MES level of output, or the minimum level of production required to attain the minimum average cost, Q^*. One of the main points to be emphasized is that as firm size grows relative to the MES level of output, the more likely the firm is to decide to remain in the industry. This suggests that either an increase in the start-up size of the firm or a decrease in the MES level of output should increase the likelihood of survival. It also implies that, given a level of MES output in an industry, the greater the size of the firm, the less it will need to grow in order to exhaust the potential scale economies. Notice that this theory is strikingly contradictory to the more typical and traditional theory that growth will be positively related to size for new firms, since larger firms are presumed to have access to greater financial resources.

The rather ambiguous role of innovative activity should also be emphasized. On the one hand, a greater perceived likelihood of innovating (i) will lead the firm to remain in an industry, even if other factors, such as the gap between the firm's size and the MES level of output resulting in a cost differential of $c(Q_{it}) - c(Q^*_i)$, would otherwise have led the firm to exit the industry. Seen from this perspective, firms in a highly innovative environment will tend to have a lower propensity to exit, ceteris paribus, as long as the perceived likelihood of innovative activity is relatively high. On the other hand, the likelihood that the firm will actually end up producing a viable product for which there is sufficient demand will clearly be lower in more innovative environments. A paradox could be that new firms may have a greater likelihood of innovating under the entrepreneurial regime than under the routinized regime. Yet, the likelihood that the new firm will emerge with a viable and marketable product is greater in industries where there is less technological and product uncertainty.

That is, the actual innovative activity of the firm, I_{it}, and not the likelihood of that innovative activity, i_{it}, will ultimately determine its actual level of output in period t, Q_{it}, so that

$$Q_{it} = Q_{it} + Q(I_t) \qquad (2)$$

where Q_{it} is a factor of the firm's output in the previous period,

$$Q_{it} = Q_{i0} + aQ_{it-1} \qquad (3)$$

and Q_0 is an autonomous level of output and a is a factor representing the portion of the previous period's output that can be maintained in the market the next period (this could be zero in some cases). Factors such as market growth presumably influence the value of a. That is, if market growth is sufficiently high, a new firm may be able to grow enough so that $Q_{it} = Q^*_i$, even in the absence of innovative activity.

An important implication of the dynamic process of firm selection and industry evolution is that new firms are more likely to be operating at a suboptimal scale of output if the underlying technological conditions are such that there is a greater chance of making an innovation, that is, under the entrepreneurial regime. If new firms successfully learn and adapt, or are just plain lucky, they grow into viably sized enterprises. If not, they stagnate and may ultimately exit the industry. This suggests that entry and start-up of new firms may not be greatly deterred in the presence of scale economies. As long as entrepreneurs perceive that there is some prospect for growth and ultimately survival, such entry will occur. Thus, in industries where the MES is high, it follows from the observed general small size of new-firm start-ups that the growth rate of the surviving firms would presumably be relatively high.

At the same time, those new firms not able to grow and attain the MES level of output would presumably be forced to exit from the industry, resulting in a relatively low likelihood of survival. In industries characterized by a low MES, neither the need for growth nor the consequences of its absence are as severe, so that relatively lower growth rates but higher survival rates would be expected. Similarly, in industries where the probability of innovating is greater, more entrepreneurs may actually take a chance that they will succeed by growing into a viably sized enterprise. In such industries, one would expect that the growth of successful enterprises would be greater, but that the likelihood of survival would be correspondingly lower.

Summarizing these arguments, the theory of firm selection and industry evolution leads to the following predictions, or hypotheses, concerning the likelihood of survival and growth rates of those surviving new firms:

1 The likelihood of new-firm survival should be lower in industries exhibiting greater scale economies. The growth rates observed in surviving firms in high MES industries should be greater.
2 The likelihood of firm survival should be higher for larger firms but growth rates should be lower.
3 The likelihood of firm survival should be lower under the entrepreneurial technological regime but the growth rates of surviving firms should be greater.
4 Both firm growth and the likelihood of survival should be greater in high-growth industries.

3 Empirical Evidence

3.1 Innovation

While the concept of technological regimes does not lend itself to precise measurement, the major conclusion of Acs and Audretsch (1988; 1990) was that the existence of these distinct regimes can be inferred by the extent to which small firms are able to innovate relative to the total amount of innovative activity in an industry. That is, when the small-firm innovation rate is high relative to the total innovation rate, the technological and knowledge conditions are more likely to reflect the entrepreneurial regime. The routinized regime is more likely to exhibit a low small-firm innovation rate relative to the total innovation rate.

3.2 Entry

Empirical evidence in support of the traditional model of entry, which focuses on the role of excess profits as the major incentive to enter, has been ambiguous at best, leading Geroski (1991, p. 282) to conclude, "Right from the start, scholars have had some trouble in reconciling the stories told about entry in standard textbooks with the substance of what they have found in their data. Very few have emerged from their work feeling that they have answered half as many questions as they have raised, much less that they have answered most of the interesting ones."

Perhaps one reason for this trouble is the inherently static model used to capture an inherently dynamic process. Manfred Neumann (1993, pp. 593–594) has criticized this traditional model of entry, as found in the individual country studies contained in Geroski and Schwalbach (1991), because they

are predicated on the adoption of a basically static framework. It is assumed that startups enter a given market where they are facing incumbents which naturally try to fend off entry. Since the impact of entry on the performance of incumbents seems to be only slight, the question arises whether the costs of entry are worthwhile, given the high rate of exit associated with entry. Geroski appears to be rather skeptical about that. I submit that adopting a static framework is misleading ... In fact, generally, an entrant can only hope to succeed if he employs either a new technology or offers a new product, or both. Just imitating incumbents is almost certainly doomed to failure. If the process of entry is looked upon from this perspective the high correlation between gross entry and exit reflects the inherent risks of innovating activities ... Obviously it is rather difficult to break loose from the inherited mode of reasoning within the static framework. It is not without merit, to be sure, but it needs to be enlarged by putting it into a dynamic setting.

Still, one of the most startling results that have emerged in empirical studies is that entry by firms into an industry is apparently not substantially deterred or even deterred at all in capital-intensive industries in which scale economies play an important role (Audretsch, 1995).[6] While studies have generally produced considerable ambiguity concerning the impact of scale economies and other measures traditionally thought to represent a *barrier to entry*, Audretsch (1995) found conclusive evidence linking the technological regime to start-up activity. New-firm start-up activity tends to be substantially more prevalent under the entrepreneurial regime, or where small enterprises account for the bulk of the innovative activity, than under the routinized regime, or where the large incumbent enterprises account for most of the innovative activity. These findings are consistent with the view that differences in beliefs about the expected value of new ideas are not constant across industries but rather depend on the knowledge conditions inherent in the underlying technological regime.

3.3   Survival

Geroski (1995) and Audretsch (1995) point out that one of the major conclusions from studies about entry is that the process of entry does not end with entry itself. Rather, it is what happens to new firms subsequent to entering that sheds considerable light on industry dynamics. The early studies (Mansfield, 1962; Hall, 1987; Dunne et al., 1989; Audretsch, 1991) established not only that the likelihood of a new entrant's surviving is quite low, but that the likelihood of survival is positively related to firm size and age. More recently, a wave of studies has confirmed these findings for diverse countries, including Portugal (Mata et al., 1995; Mata, 1995), Germany (Wagner, 1994), and Canada (Baldwin and Gorecki, 1991; Baldwin, 1995; Baldwin and Rafiquzzaman, 1995).

Audretsch (1991) and Audretsch and Mahmood (1995) shifted the relevant question away from *Why does the likelihood of survival vary systematically across firms?* to *Why does the propensity for firms to survive vary systematically across industries?* The answer to this question suggests that what had previously been considered to pose a barrier to entry may, in fact, constitute not an entry barrier but rather a barrier to survival.

3.4   Growth

What has become known as *Gibrat's law*, or the assumption that growth rates are invariant to firm size, has been subject to numerous empirical tests. Studies linking firm size and age to growth have also produced a number of stylized facts (Wagner, 1992). For small and new firms there is substantial evidence suggesting that growth is negatively related to firm size and age (Hall, 1987; Wagner, 1992; 1994; Mata, 1994; Audretsch, 1995). However, for larger firms, particularly those having attained the MES level of output, the evidence suggests that firm growth is unrelated to size and age.

An important finding of Audretsch (1991; 1995) and Audretsch and Mahmood (1995) is that although entry may still occur in industries characterized by a high degree of scale economies, the likelihood of survival is considerably less. People will start new firms in an attempt to appropriate the expected value of their new ideas, or potential innovations, particularly under the entrepreneurial regime. As entrepreneurs gain experience in the market they learn in at least two ways. First, they discover whether they possess *the right stuff*, in terms of producing goods and offering services for which sufficient demand exists, as well as whether they can produce that good more efficiently than their rivals. Second, they learn whether they can adapt to market conditions as well as to strategies engaged in by rival firms. In terms of the first type of learning, entrepreneurs who discover that they have a viable firm will tend to expand and ultimately survive. But what about those entrepreneurs who discover that they either are not efficient or are not offering a product for which there is a viable demand? The answer is, *It depends*

– *on the extent of scale economies as well as on conditions of demand.* The consequences of not being able to grow will depend, to a large degree, on the extent of scale economies. Thus, in markets with only negligible scale economies, firms have a considerably greater likelihood of survival. However, where scale economies play an important role the consequences of not growing are substantially more severe, as evidenced by a lower likelihood of survival.

3.5   Wages and Compensating Factor Differentials

How are the new firms, many of which operate at a suboptimal scale of output, able to exist? The answer according to the studies on post-entry survival and growth is that they cannot – at least not indefinitely. Rather, they must grow at least to approach the MES level of output. An alternative answer is provided by recent studies focusing on the relationships among firm size, age and employee compensation (Audretsch, 1995). By deploying a strategy of *compensating factor differentials*, where factor inputs are both deployed and remunerated differently than they are by the larger incumbent enterprises, suboptimal scale enterprises are to some extent able to offset their size-related cost disadvantages.

Just as it has been found that the gap between the MES and firm size lowers the likelihood of survival, there is evidence suggesting that factors of production, and in particular labor, tend to be used more intensively (that is, in terms of hours worked) and remunerated at lower levels (in terms of employee compensation). Taken together, the empirical evidence on survival and growth combined with that on wages and firm size suggests how it is that small, suboptimal scale enterprises are able to exist in the short run. In the initial period of learning, during which time the entrepreneur discovers whether he has the *right stuff* and whether he is able to adapt to market conditions, new firms are apparently able to reduce the cost of production in order to compensate for their small scale of production.

In the current debate on the relationship between employment and wages it is typically argued that the existence of small firms which are suboptimal within the organization of an industry represents a loss in economic efficiency. This argument is based on a static analysis, however. When viewed through a dynamic lens a different conclusion emerges. One of the most striking results is the finding of a positive impact of firm age on productivity and employee compensation, even after controlling for the size of the firm. Given the strongly confirmed stylized fact linking both firm size and age to a negative rate of growth (that is, the smaller and younger a firm, the faster it will grow but the lower is its likelihood of survival), this new finding linking firm age to employee compensation and productivity suggests that not only will some of the small and suboptimal firms of today become the large and optimal firms of tomorrow, but there is at least a tendency for the low productivity and wage of today to become the high productivity and wage of tomorrow.

4   Two Models of Industry Evolution

What emerges from the new theories and empirical evidence on innovation and industry evolution is that markets are in motion, with a lot of firms entering the industry and a lot of firms exiting the industry. But is this motion horizontal, in that the bulk of firms exiting are firms that had entered relatively recently, or vertical, in that a significant share of the exiting firms had been established incumbents that were displaced by younger firms? In trying to shed some light on this question, Audretsch (1995) proposes two different models of the evolutionary process of industries over time. Some industries can be best characterized by the model of the conical revolving door, where new businesses enter, but where there is a high propensity subsequently to exit the market. Other industries may be better characterized by the metaphor of the forest, where incumbent establishments are displaced by new entrants. Which view is more applicable apparently depends on three major factors – the underlying technological conditions, scale economies, and demand. Where scale economies play an important role, the model of the revolving door seems to be more applicable. While the rather startling result discussed that the start-up and entry of new businesses are apparently not deterred by the presence of high scale economies, a process of firm selection analogous to a revolving door ensures that only those establishments successful enough to grow will be able to survive more than a few years. Thus the bulk of new entrants that are not so successful ultimately exit within a few years of entry.

There is at least some evidence also suggesting that the underlying technological regime influences the process of firm selection and therefore the type of firm with a higher propensity to exit. Under the entrepreneurial regime new entrants have a greater likelihood of making an innovation. Thus, they are less likely to decide to exit the industry, even in the face of negative profits. By contrast, under the routinized regime the incumbent businesses tend to have the innovative advantage, so that a higher portion of exiting businesses tend to be new entrants. Thus, the model of the revolving door is more applicable under technological conditions consistent with the routinized regime, and the metaphor of the forest, where the new entrants displace the incumbents, is more applicable to the entrepreneurial regime.

Why is the general shape of the firm-size distribution not only strikingly similar across virtually every industry – that is, skewed with only a few large enterprises and numerous small ones – but persistent and tenacious not only across developed countries but even over a long period of time? The evolutionary view of the process of industry evolution is that new firms typically start at a very small scale of output. They are motivated by the desire to appropriate the expected value of new economic knowledge. But, depending upon the extent of scale economies in the industry, the firm may not be able to remain viable indefinitely at its start-up size. Rather, if scale economies are anything other than negligible, the new firm is likely to have to grow to survive. The temporary survival of new firms is presumably supported through the deployment of a strategy of compensating factor differentials that enables the firm to discover whether or not it has a viable product.

The empirical evidence supports such an evolutionary view of the role of new firms in manufacturing, because the post-entry growth of firms that survive tends to be spurred by the extent to which there is a gap between the MES level of output and the size of the firm. However, the likelihood of any particular new firm's surviving tends to decrease as this gap increases. Such new suboptimal scale firms are apparently engaged in the selection process. Only those firms offering a viable product that can be produced efficiently will grow and ultimately approach or attain the MES level of output. The remainder will stagnate, and depending upon the severity of the other selection mechanism – the extent of scale economies – may ultimately be forced to exit out of the industry. Thus, the persistence of an asymmetric firm-size distribution biased towards small-scale enterprise reflects the continuing process of the entry of new firms into industries and not necessarily the permanence of such small and suboptimal enterprises over the long run. Although the skewed size distribution of firms persists with remarkable stability over long periods, a constant set of small and suboptimal scale firms does not appear to be responsible for this skewed distribution.

5　Implications for Public Policy

The vision of the link between the firm and the market typically shapes public policy. The new learning strongly argues for a vision of the firm in the market as one that is dynamic, fluid, and turbulent. Change is more the rule and stability the exception.

The public policies emerging in the post-war period dealing with the firm in the market were essentially constraining in nature. There were three general types of public policies towards business – antitrust (competition policy), regulation, and public ownership. All three of these policy approaches towards the firm in the market restricted the firm's freedom to contract. While specific policy approaches tended to be more associated with one country than with others, such as antitrust in the United States or public ownership in France and Sweden, all developed countries shared a common policy approach of intervening to restrain what otherwise was perceived as too much market power held by firms. Public policies constraining the freedom of the firm to contract were certainly consistent with the Weltanschauung emerging from the theories and empirical evidence regarding the firm in the market during the post-war period. Left unchecked, the large corporation in possession of market power would allocate resources in such a way as to reduce economic welfare. Through state intervention the Williamsonian trade-off between efficiency on the one hand and fairness on the other would be solved in a manner that presumably would be more socially satisfying.

But more recently the relevant policy question has shifted away from *How can the government constrain firms from abusing their market power?* to *How can governments create an environment fostering the success and viability of firms?* The major issues of the day have shifted away from concerns about excess profits and abuses of market dominance to the creation of jobs, growth and international competitiveness. The concern about corporations is now more typically not that they are too successful and powerful but that they are not successful and powerful enough. Thus, the government policies of the 1990s have increasingly shifted away from *constraining* to *enabling*. Governments are increasingly promoting joint R&D programs, fostering efforts to innovate and the creation of new firms. For example, as unemployment in Germany surpassed four million, and stood at 10.8 percent of the labor force, it is not surprising that Chancellor Helmut Kohl would undertake some action to spur the creation of new jobs. Perhaps what is more surprising is the main emphasis announced by the Chancellor in the *Initiatives for Investment and Employment*[7] on January 30, 1996, on new and small firms. The first and main point of this program consists of a commitment to the "creation of new innovative firms."[8] The rationale underlying this commitment is stated by the Chancellor in the program: "New jobs are created mainly in new firms and in small- and medium-sized enterprises."[9]

This Weltanschauung apparent in the Kohl jobs program represents a sharp departure from that found both in Germany as well as throughout

Europe in earlier years. For example, in his widely read *Le Defi Ameri-cain*, Servan-Schreiber (1968, p. 159) advocated "the creation of large industrial units which are able both in size and management to compete with the American giants . . . The first problem of an industrial policy for Europe consists in choosing 50 to 100 firms which, once they are large enough, would be the most likely to become world leaders in their fields." And as is clearly documented in the 1988 Cecchini report, there were significant forces in Europe prepared to implement Servan-Schreiber's policy advice.

How could the Kohl administration draw an inference about the source of jobs, growth and international competitiveness that is seemingly at odds with both scholarship and policy thinking of just a few years prior? In fact, his emphasis on public policies creating an environment where the production and application of new knowledge is encouraged is consistent with public policies towards business throughout Europe and North America. After all, the observation that the structure of firms and markets tends to be remarkably fluid and turbulent is not new. Before the country was even half a century old, Alexis de Tocqueville, in 1835, reported, "What astonishes me in the United States is not so much the marvellous grandeur of some undertakings as the innumerable multitude of small ones."[10]

Notes

An earlier version of this paper was presented at the international conference Entrepreneurship, Small and Medium Sized Enterprises and the Macroeconomy at the Jönköping International Business School, 13–15 June 1996. I am grateful to the participants of the conference, Zoltan J. Acs and the referees for Cambridge University Press for their suggestions and comments. Any omissions or errors remain my responsibility.

[1] Ijiri and Simon (1977, pp. 1–2) observe, "Nature, as it presents itself to the physical scientist, is full of clearly defined patterns . . . The patterns that have been discovered in social phenomena are much less neat. To be sure economics has evolved a highly sophisticated body of mathematical laws, but for the most part, these laws bear a rather distinct relation to empirical phenomena . . . Hence, on those occasions when a social phenomenon appears to exhibit some of the same simplicity and regularity of pattern as is seen so commonly in physics, it is bound to excite interest and attention."

[2] Quotation from "editor's introduction" to Audretsch and Yamawaki (1991, p. xiv).

[3] Coase (1937, p. 23) himself said, "A pertinent question to ask would appear to be (quite apart from the monopoly considerations raised by Professor Knight), why, if by organizing one can eliminate certain costs and in fact reduce the cost of production, are there any market transactions at all? Why is not all production carried on by one big firm?"

[4] A similar start-up size for new manufacturing firms has been found by Dunne, Roberts, and Samuelson (1989) for the United States, Mata (1994) and Mata and Portugal (1994) for Portugal, and Wagner (1994) for Germany.

[5] For example, Weiss (1976, p. 126) argues "In purely competitive long-run equilibrium, no suboptimal capacity should exist at all."

[6] The country studies included in Geroski and Schwalbach (1991) also indicate considerable ambiguities between measures reflecting the extent of scale economies and capital intensity on the one hand and entry rates on the other.

[7] This was announced as the *Aktionsprogramm für Investitionen und Arbeitsplätze* ("Soziale Einschnitte und Steuerreform sollen Wirtschaftswachstum anregen: Bundesregierung beschließt Aktionsprogramm für Investitionen und Arbeitsplätze," *Der Tagesspiegel*, 31 January, p. 1).

[8] The original text of the *Aktionsprogramm* states, "Offensive für unternehmerische Selbständigkeit und Innovationsfähigkeit" ("Ein Kraftakt zu Rettung des Standorts Deutschland," *Frankfurter Allgemeine*, 31 January, 1996, p. 11).

[9] *Ibid.* The original text reads, "New Arbeitsplätze entstehen zumeist in neugegründeten Unternehmen und im Mittelstand."

[10] Quoted from *Business Week*, Bonus Issue, 1993, p. 12.

References

Acs, Zoltan J. and David B. Audretsch (1988), "Innovation in Large and Small Firms: An Empirical Analysis," *American Economic Review*, vol. 78, no. 4, September, 678–690.

Acs, Zoltan J. and David B. Audretsch (1990), *Innovation and Small Firms* (Cambridge: MIT Press).

Arrow, Kenneth J. (1962), "Economic Welfare and the Allocation of Resources for Invention," in R. R. Nelson (ed), *The Rate and Direction of Inventive Activity* (Princeton, N.J.: Princeton University Press).

Audretsch, David B. (1995), *Innovation and Industry Evolution* (Cambridge, Mass.: MIT Press).

Audretsch, David B. (1991), "New Firm Survival and the Technological Regime," *Review of Economics and Statistics*, vol. 73, no. 3, August, 441–450.

Audretsch, David B. and Maryann P. Feldman (1996). "R&D Spillovers and the Geography of Innovation and Production," *American Economic Review*, vol. 86, no. 3, June, 630–640.

Audretsch, David B. and Paula E. Stephan (1996), "Company-Scientist Locational Links: The Case of Biotechnology," *American Economic Review*, vol. 86, no. 3, June, 641–652.

Audretsch, David B. and Talat Mahmood (1995), "New-Firm Survival: New Results Using a Hazard Function," *Review of Economics and Statistics*, vol. 77, no. 1, February, 97–103.

Audretsch, David B. and Hideki Yamawaki (1991), *Structure, Conduct and Performance: Leonard Weiss* (New York: New York University Press).

Baldwin, John R. (1995), *The Dynamics of Industrial Competition* (Cambridge: Cambridge University Press).

Baldwin, John R. and M. Rafiquzzaman (1995), "Selection Versus Evolutionary Adaptation: Learning and Post-Entry Performance," *International Journal of Industrial Organization*, vol. 13, no. 4, December, 501–523.

Baldwin, John R. and Paul K. Gorecki (1991), "Entry, Exit, and Production Growth," in P. Geroski and J. Schwalbach (eds), *Entry and Market Contestability: An International Comparison* (Oxford: Basil Blackwell).

Cecchini, P. (1988), *1992 The European Challenge* (London: Gower).

Coase, R. H. (1937), "The Nature of the Firm," *Economica*, vol. 4, no. 4, 386–405.

Dosi, Giovanni (1988), "Sources, Procedures, and Microeconomic Effects of Innovation," *Journal of Economic Literature*, vol. 26, no. 3, 1120–1171.

Dunne, T., M. J. Roberts, and L. Samuelson (1989), "The Growth and Failure of U.S. Manufacturing Plants" *Quarterly Journal of Economics*, vol. 104, 671–698.

Geroski, Paul A. (1995), "What Do We Know About Entry," *International Journal of Industrial Organization* (Special Issue on *The Post Entry Performance of Firms*, D.B. Audretsch and J. Mata, eds), vol. 13, no. 4, December.

Geroski, Paul A. (1991), "Some Data-Driven Reflections on the Entry Process," in Paul Geroski and Joachin Schwalbach (eds), *Entry and Market Contestability: An International Comparison* (Oxford: Basil Blackwell).

Geroski, Paul A. and Joachim Schwalbach, eds. (1991), *Entry and Market Contestability: An International Comparison* (Oxford: Basil Blackwell).

Hall, Bronwyn H. (1987), "The Relationship Between Firm Size and Firm Growth in the U.S. Manufacturing Sector," *Journal of Industrial Economics*, 35 (June), 583–605.

Hannan, Michael T. and John Freeman (1989), *Organizational Ecology* (Cambridge, Mass.: Harvard University Press).

Hirschman, Albert O. (1970), *Exit, Voice, and Loyalty* (Cambridge, Mass.: Harvard University Press).

Ijiri, Yuji and Herbert A. Simon (1977), *Skew Distributions and Sizes of Business Firms* (Amsterdam: North Holland).

Jovanovic, Boyan (1982), "Selection and Evolution of Industry," *Econometrica*, vol. 50, no. 2, 649–670.

Knight, Frank H. (1921), *Risk, Uncertainty and Profit* (New York: Houghton Mifflin).

Lucas, Robert E., Jr. (1978), "On the Size Distribution of Business Firms," *Bell Journal of Economics*," vol. 9, Autumn, 508–523.

Mansfield, Edwin (1962), "Entry, Gibrat's Law, Innovation, and the Growth of Firms," *American Economic Review*, vol. 52, no. 5, 1023–1051.

Mata, Jose (1994), "Firm Growth During Infancy," *Small Business Economics*, vol. 6, no. 1, 27–40.

Mata, Jose, Pedro Portugal and Paulo Guimaraes (1995), "The Survival of New Plants: Start-Up Conditions and Post-Entry Evolution," *International Journal of Industrial Organization*, vol. 13, no. 4, December, 459–482.

Mata, Jose and Pedro Portugal (1994), "Life Duration of New Firms," *Journal of Industrial Economics*, vol. 27, no. 3, 227–246.

Nelson, Richard R. and Sidney G. Winter (1982), *An Evolutionary Theory of Economic Change* (Cambridge, Mass.: Harvard University Press).

Neumann, Manfred (1993), "Review of Entry and Market Contestability: An International Comparison," *International Journal of Industrial Organization*, vol. 11, no. 4, 593–594.

Scherer, F. M. (1991), "Changing Perspectives on the Firm Size Problem," in Z. J. Acs and D. B. Audretsch (eds), *Innovation and Technological Change: An International Comparison*, Ann Arbor: University of Michigan Press.

Schumpeter, Joseph A. (1942), *Capitalism, Socialism and Democracy* (New York: Harper & Row).

Schumpeter, Joseph A. (1911), *Theorie der wirtschaftlichen Entwicklung. Eine Untersuchung hber Unternehmergewinn, Kapital, Kredit, Zins und den Konjunkturzyklus* (Berlin: Duncker und Humblot.).

Servan-Schreiber, J.-J. (1968), *The American Challenge* (London: Hamish Hamilton).

Simon, Herbert A. and Charles P. Bonini (1958), "The Size Distribution of Business Firms," *American Economic Review*, vol. 48, no. 4, 607–617.

Wagner, Joachim (1994), "Small Firm Entry in Manufacturing Industries: Lower Saxony, 1979–1989," *Small Business Economics*, vol. 6, no. 3, 211–224.

Wagner, Joachim (1992), "Firm Size, Firm Growth, and Persistence of Chance: Testing Gibrat's Law with Establishment Data from Lower Saxony. 1978–1989," *Small Business Economics*, 4 (2), 125–131.

Weiss, Leonard W. (1976), "Optimal Plant Scale and the Extent of Suboptimal Capacity," in R. T. Masson and P. D. Qualls (eds), *Essays on Industrial Organization in Honor of Joe S. Bain* (Cambridge: Ballinger).

Williamson, Oliver E. (1975), *Markets and Hierarchies: Antitrust Analysis and Implications* (New York: The Free Press).

Winter, Sidney G. (1984), "Schumpeterian Competition in Alternative Technological Regimes," *Journal of Economic Behavior and Organization*, vol. 5, September–December, 287–320.

CHAPTER 4

Creative Destruction: Source or Symptom of Economic Growth?

Paul D. Reynolds

1   Introduction

It would be very convenient if large firms and economic stability were the major sources of economic growth. It would simplify the development of accurate theories and predictive models, research would be easier to conduct, and effective public policy would be facilitated. Unfortunately, recent evidence suggests that a dual economy – where growth is created by a small number of large efficient firms and new and small firms have a tangential role – is *not* a useful conceptual framework for contemporary market economies. Assumptions about structural stability do not allow for change and adaptation in an economic system (Barreto, 1989; Baumol, 1968). "Creative destruction," volatility, turbulence, or churning in market economies (Scherer, 1984; Schumpeter, 1942) is frequently cited as a necessary feature of economic growth and change. There has been, however, little empirical evidence on this issue.

Three questions are the focus of this analysis: (1) Is there systematic evidence that creative destruction is associated with economic growth? (2) Is there systematic evidence that creative destruction precedes economic growth? (3) Is there systematic evidence that creative destruction has a significant causal relationship to economic growth?

There have been a few analyses designed to determine the effect of business dynamics on subsequent growth of an economic system. Analyses of labor market areas in Sweden (Davidsson et al., 1994) and the United States (Reynolds, 1994) suggest some distinctive role of business dynamics in subsequent economic growth. Analysis of the relative growth of small versus large firm sectors across the European Union EU-12 and EU-16 countries indicates greater relative small sector growth leads to greater subsequent national economic growth (Thurik,

97

1995). There is some evidence across seven Organization for Economic Cooperation and Development (OECD) countries that manufacturing sectors with a higher proportion of small firms have greater sectoral growth (Schreyer and Chavoix-Mannato, 1995). There is, however, limited systematic evidence regarding the role of volatility and turbulence in economic growth.

The following analysis utilizes unique data on the birth and death of U.S. business establishments and business jobs to consider the relationship to economic growth. The analysis strategy is designed to be simple, although many technical details are complex. They are presented in the Addenda. The unit of analysis is the 382 U.S. labor market areas, presented in Figure 4.1 (discussed in Addenda A). Economic growth is considered from 1976 through 1992, covering periods of both national expansion and contraction. Two different measures of creative destruction or business volatility are developed (discussed in Addenda B and D). Economic growth is measured by considering relative job growth in these 382 labor market areas (discussed in Addenda C). Measures of regional characteristics (discussed in Addenda E and F) are employed to consider concurrent and future changes in job growth in multiple regression models.

The results are robust and powerful. No matter what measures are utilized, higher levels of business volatility, or creative destruction, appear to have a strong association with economic growth. On the other hand, creative destruction does not, by itself, appear to be a source of economic growth. Without creative destruction, there is no growth; creative destruction does not seem to cause growth.

2   Creative Destruction Associated with Economic Growth

Is a higher level of "creative destruction" associated with economic growth? The short answer is yes.

This is illustrated, in Table 4.1, in the correlations between measures of establishment and job volatility with job growth for 382 U.S. labor market areas. Correlations between twelve creative destruction measures and six indices of business volatility are presented in relation to concurrent, subsequent, and economic growth two years in the future. Two-year time periods are used in all cases. Each correlation in Table 4.1 is the average of six correlations over a twelve-year period. The specific analyses, by year, are presented in Appendixes 4.1 and 4.2. There are some year to year variations. The inter-correlations among all measures are provided in Table 4.D1 (see Addenda D). Measures of "creative destruction" and the business volatility indices are discussed below.

The result is an array of positive correlations with two exceptions,

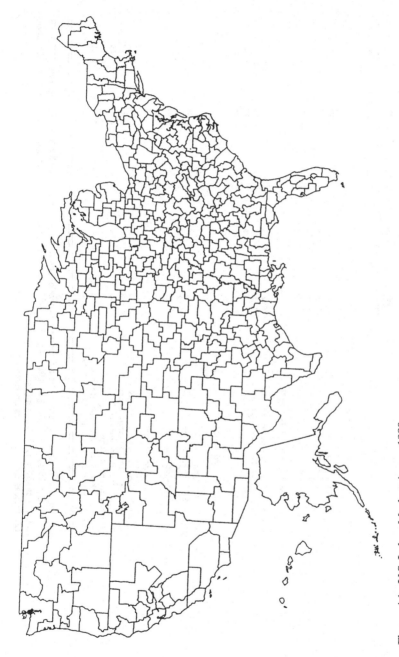

Figure 4.1. U.S. Labor Market Areas: 1980

Table 4.1. *Business Volatility and Job Growth*

	AVERAGE VALUES	STANDARD DEVIATION	CORRELATIONS WITH JOB GROWTH (1)		
			CONCURRENT	SUBSEQUENT	2 YEAR LAG
FIRM DYNAMICS: ESTABLISHMENT BASED					
Births per 100 establishments	10.6	2.41	0.59	0.39	0.19
Deaths per 100 establishments	9.3	1.51	0.03	0.10	0.11
Births/Deaths	1.4	0.29	0.46	0.20	0.07
Births+Deaths	19.9	3.03	0.49	0.36	0.21
FIRM DYNAMICS: POPULATION BASED					
Births per 10,000 human population	20.2	7.02	0.48	0.32	0.16
Deaths per 10,000 human population	17.5	5.05	0.14	0.16	0.13
Births/Deaths	1.2	0.29	0.52	0.27	0.10
Births+Deaths	37.7	11.06	0.36	0.28	0.16
JOB DYNAMICS: WORKING POPULATION BASED					
Job births per 100 jobs	9.9	4.11	0.51	0.30	0.14
Job deaths per 100 jobs	7.8	3.89	-.02	0.05	0.04
Job births/job deaths	1.2	0.50	0.52	0.27	0.10
Job births+job deaths	17.7	7.22	0.34	0.23	0.12
BUSINESS VOLATILITY INDICES					
Distributive Services Sectors	0.0 (2)	0.88	0.43	0.36	0.22
Extractive (Agr, Mining) Sectors	0.0	0.86	-.11	-.15	-.17
Business Services Sectors	0.0	0.73	0.18	0.13	0.05
Manufacturing Sectors	0.0	0.64	0.10	0.05	0.02
Local Market Sectors: Tops, Simples	0.0	0.84	0.42	0.34	0.25
Local Market Sectors: Branches, Subsid	0.0	0.83	0.24	0.17	0.14

(1) Each correlation represents the average of 6 correlations with base periods for the following periods: 1976-78; 1978-80; 1980-82; 1982-84; 1984-86; 1986-88. Any correlation with an absolute value greater than about 0.04 is statistically significant (total n = 2,292).
(2) Indices created to have an average value of zero.

one minor. The minor exception is related to a correlation of -0.02, essentially no relationship, between job deaths and concurrent job growth. The other is related to an index of establishment and job volatility associated with extractive sectors, agriculture, and mining. Regardless of the time frame, more volatility in these sectors is correlated with a reduction in job growth.

Schumpeter's speculations are strongly confirmed: creative destruction accompanies economic growth.

3 Creative Destruction Preceding Economic Growth

The relative impact of creative destruction on subsequent economic growth is assessed in a preliminary way with the correlations presented in Table 4.1. However, this does not provide useful evidence on potential additive effects from measures related to different features of business and job volatility. Neither does it indicate which measures may be redundant in a more sophisticated analysis. Further, the appropriate combination of measures may have a greater association with economic growth.

For this reason, stepwise multiple regression procedures were utilized to determine (1) the relative impact of the different measures on predictions of job growth and (2) the total impact of combinations of different measures of creative destruction and business dynamics.

Table 4.2 presents the results. All measures were entered in a standardized step-wise regression procedure, except that tolerance was adjusted to reduce the inclusion of correlated independent variables. There are three sets of regression models presented – for concurrent, subsequent, and lagged relationships between measures of business dynamics and economic growth. Four time periods are presented for each. The F-test values for all twelve models are presented; all are statistically significant well beyond the 0.0001 level.

The average explained variances are 56 percent for the concurrent predictions; 43 percent for the predictions to the subsequent periods; and 39 percent for predictions to a period with a two-year time lag. The highest individual item correlations in Table 4.1 are about 0.50, which would explain about 25 percent of the variance. Clearly, in combination, these measures of creative destruction or business volatility provide much greater explanatory or predictive power.

But which items are most critical? There is, as can be seen, substantial variation. Some are not included in any of the linear regression models: annual rate of job destruction, establishment based establishment birth/death rate ratios. Several are included in only one of the twelve models: human population based establishment birth/death

Table 4.2. Multiple Regression Analysis on Job Growth: Turbulence, Volatility Measures Only

Standardize Beta values, if included in predictive equation.

		CONCURRENT				SUBSEQUENT				TWO-YEAR LAG			
LABEL	VARIABLE NAME	80-82	82-84	84-86	86-88	82-84	84-86	86-88	88-90	84-86	86-88	88-90	90-92
Creative Destruction Measures													
JBBRA	JOB CREATION: TOTAL PER 100 JOBS	0.75	0.54	0.25								0.29	
JBDTA	JOB DESTRUCT: TOTAL PER 100 JOBS												
JBVOLR	RATIO JOB BIRTHS/DEATHS RATES		0.32					0.16		-.14			
JBCRA	JOB GAIN/LOSS VOLATILITY:TOTAL EFFECT	-.63	-.30					-.18					
ESRPOA	ESTAB CREATION: TOTAL PER 10,000 HUM POP	0.37	0.31					1.16					
ESDTPOA	ESTAB DESTRUCT: TOTAL PER 10,000 HUM POP							-1.08					
ESPVOLR	RATIO EST POP BIRTH/DEATH RATES					0.25		-.66					
ESCHPOA	EST BRTH+DEATH POPUL VOLATILITY								0.21				
ESBRESA	ESTAB CREATION: TOTAL PER 100 ESTAB	0.21	0.29	0.52	0.40	0.58	0.52	0.28	0.64				
ESDTESA	ESTAB DESTRUCT: TOTAL PER 100 ESTAB												
ESEVOLR	RATIO EST EST BIRTH/DEATH RATES										0.17		
ESCHESA	EST BRTH+DEATH ESTAB VOLATILITY										0.28		
Business Volatility Indices													
DISSERV	DIST SERV FIRM,JOB VOLATILITY 4 ITEM INDEX		-.33		-.27		0.22	-.18	-.26			-.15	-.49
EXTRACV	EXTRACTIV FIRM,JOB VOLATILITY 4 ITEM INDEX	0.08	-.43	-.37	-.22	-.59	-.53	-.32			-.47	0.08	0.10
BUSSERV	BUSI SERV FIRM,JOB VOLATILITY 4 ITEM INDEX		-.35		-.35	-.34	-.29	-.37	-.43	0.19			-.26
MANUFGV	MANUFACTU FIRM,JOB VOLATILITY 4 ITEM INDEX		0.16			0.22							
LOCTSV	LOCMKT TS FIRM,JOB VOLATILITY 2 ITEM INDEX							0.12	0.30			0.20	0.40
LOCBSV	LOCMKT BS FIRM,JOB VOLATILITY 2 ITEM INDEX		0.08	-.08		0.21		0.13	0.30			0.28	
Adj R²		0.69	0.69	0.66	0.56	0.50	0.57	0.35	0.32	0.54	0.35	0.20	0.49
	Average for group				0.56				0.43				0.39
F value	(all stat sign at 0.0000 level)	208.49	106.60	126.83	62.39	54.75	127.06	34.79	46.53	89.19	41.22	19.74	74.84

rates ratio; population based establishment birth and death rates total; establishment based establishment death rates; and establishment based birth and death rates total. Among the creative destruction measures, however, those associated with job or firm birth rates tend to have a greater presence in these models, eight times for establishment based establishment birth rate measures; four times for the job birth rate measure; and three times for the population based establishment birth rate measure.

Inspection of Table 4.2 indicates that the six business dynamic indices are much more prevalent in the models, compared to the twelve creative destruction measures. At least one of these measures appears in every model, and four or more in six of the twelve. For this reason, the business dynamics indices are utilized in the following analysis of the relative impact on general models of economic growth.

This preliminary regression analysis indicates that creative destruction and business volatility have a very substantial relationship – on their own – with economic growth. And for most indices it is a positive relationship – more volatility or turbulence is associated with more growth.

4   Creative Destruction Causing Economic Growth

The previous analysis provides strong and consistent evidence that creative destruction measures and business volatility indices have a strong relationship to economic growth. But there is no evidence with regard to potential causal impact. Such evidence would be available if (1) acceptable linear additive models related to regional economic growth could be developed and (2) there was evidence that inclusion of measures related to creative destruction or business volatility provided substantial improvements in these models. If these measures provide no improvements in explanatory power, or the explained variance, then creative destruction is not, presumably, having a significant causal impact. Creative destruction is, then, a reflection of economic growth related to other factors.

The major challenge in implementing this strategy is in the development of a model of regional economic growth, one that might be enhanced with creative destruction measures and business volatility. Five types of measures may be considered as related to labor market area economic growth:

Regional factors or characteristics
Economic sectoral emphasis

Age of establishments by sector
Change in the economic structure
Creative destruction and business volatility

A model of the temporal relationship between these various measures and economic growth adopted for this analysis is presented in Figure 4.2. There are two time lags in this basic model: one is the two years between measures of regional factors or characteristics and the period in which business volatility is measured. The same time lag is developed for all measures of the economic structure (percentage of establishments in each sector, age of establishments by sector, change in establishments by sector). A second time lag is related to measures of creative destruction or business volatility and measures of economic (or job) growth. This time lag varies, as indicated in Figure 4.2, with analysis developed for concurrent predictions, predictions to the next period, and predictions with a two-year time lag. The two-year periods for the data sets available for this analysis are indicated in Figure 4.2.

Assembling the data for such an analysis, however, is neither cheap nor easy. Fortunately, measures of three of the four domains – related to economic sectoral emphasis, age of establishments by sector, and change of establishments by sector – can be developed from the data sets utilized for creative destruction indices and business volatility indices.

REGIONAL
FACTORS

STRUCTURAL
CHARACTERISTICS

       BUSINESS
       VOLATILITY

            JOB GROWTH

		CONCURRENT	SUBSEQUENT	TWO YEAR LAG
1978	1980-82	80-82	82-84	84-86
1980	1982-84	82-84	84-86	86-88
1982	1984-86	84-86	86-88	88-90
1984	1986-88	86-88	88-90	90-92

Figure 4.2. Temporal Periods in Regression Analysis Models. *Note*: Measures of structural change are for four-year periods ending with the first business volatility year.

Measures of regional factors or characteristics are, however, another matter.

Indices of fifteen regional characteristics have been developed for a complementary analysis, to be discussed below, related to analysis of processes related to firm births. These fifteen processes are quite similar to those used in a wide range of other U.S. analyses, summarized by Kusmin (1994). These indices were assembled from information acquired from over a dozen different data sets. These indices, and their relationship to firm births, are reviewed in Addenda E.

4.1   Regional Characteristics

Regional characteristics were chosen as indicators of processes assumed to have a potential for increasing economic growth. The mechanisms, reviewed in Addenda E, are expected to enhance the formation of new business establishments, either independents or branches. The fifteen regional characteristics are listed in Table 4.3. As each characteristic is measured by a multi-item indicator for four different periods, the reliabilities associated with different time periods are also presented in Table 4.3. A summary of the items included in each index and the rationale for their inclusion are presented in Addenda E. A detailed listing of the specific items is found in Reynolds, Miller, and Maki (1995).

4.2   Economic Sectoral Emphasis

The economic sectoral emphasis measures are developed for each labor market area for each time period, by computing the percentage of all establishments in five economic sectors (agricultural and mining; manufacturing; distributive service; business services; and local market sectors). It is assumed that a higher percentage of establishments in export potential economic sectors, particularly extractive and manufacturing, will lead to greater regional economic growth.

4.3   Age of Establishments by Sector

For each economic sector, information is available on the number of establishments that are over five years old. Age, in this case, is based on year of first entry in the Dun and Bradstreet Market Identifier files. The percentage of establishments over five years old in each labor market area is computed for each economic sector. A higher proportion of younger firms may reflect structural change and growth in a given economic sector. If the sector is one with substantial exports, this could lead to general growth in the labor market area. A higher percentage of new

Table 4.3. *Reliability of Regional Growth Process Indices*

		VARIABLE LABEL	Measurement Period			
			1978	1980	1982	1984
1)	Career opportunity	CARERxx(1)	0.87	0.89	0.85	0.82
2)	Industry mix (volatile industries)	ESMIXxxx	0.65	0.65	0.61	0.65
3)	Flexible employment policies (lack of)	LUxx	0.86	0.88	0.88	0.87
4)	Availability of factors of production	PFAVLxxx	0.85	0.90	0.89	0.89
5)	Access to customers,clients	ACCSSxx	0.99	0.99	0.99	0.99
6)	Knowledge, R & D Base	TECHxx	0.91	0.99	0.98	0.98
7)	Unemployment/desperation	DESPxx	0.69	0.67	0.74	0.77
8)	Costs of factors of production	PFCSTxx	0.73	0.69	0.69	0.61
9)	Public infrastructure expenditures	INFEPxx	0.70	0.68	0.70	0.57
10)	Size of economic base	BASExx	1.00	0.99	0.99	0.99
11)	Economic diversity	ECONxxV	0.59	0.59	0.65	0.60
12)	Lack of national transportation access	AIRPxx(2)	--	0.80	--	--
13)	Greater personal wealth	WELTHxx	0.92	0.90	0.89	0.89
14)	Social status diversity	SOCxxV	--	0.72	--	--
15)	Population growth	POPxxD	0.75	0.79	0.77	0.82

(1) In the data set, "xx" varies for the time period represented by the index.
(2) This index was computed only once; it was based on airline hubs identified for 1980.

firms in the local market sectors may be a reaction to growth from other sources.

4.4   Change in the Economic Structure

Changes in five sectors (agricultural and mining; manufacturing; distributive service; business services; and local market sectors) were computed by determining the percentage change in establishments (all types) over the previous four years. A measure of manufacturing change in 1980, for example, would reflect change in the percentage of manufacturing establishments between 1976 and 1980. It is assumed that growth in some sectors, particularly those related to out of region exports, may contribute to overall regional economic growth.

4.5   Linear Additive Models and Multiple Regression

The final step in the process is the development of two multiple regression analyses for each of twelve situations. The models were developed for concurrent, subsequent, and two-year lagged predictions for each of four data sets. On the basic of the results of regression analysis using both creative destruction measures and business volatility indices discussed above, only the six business volatility indices were included in the models along with the fifteen indicators of regional characteristics selected to reflect general growth processes, five measures of economic sector emphasis, six measures of economic sector age, and five measures of economic sector change: a total of thirty-seven independent measures.

The results of the full models for the concurrent analysis are presented in Appendix 3; the patterns for the subsequent year and two-year lag analysis are similar. The average results are presented in Table 4.4. This table indicates that the full models are able to explain, on the average for the four time periods, 66 percent of the variation in concurrent job growth, 64 percent of the variation in subsequent job growth, and 67 percent of the variation in job growth after a lag of two years.

How much do the indices of business volatility contribute to this effort? The same models without these measures are able to explain 61 percent of the variance in concurrent job growth, 62 percent of the variance in subsequent job growth, and 65 percent of the variance in job growth after a two-year lag. The reduction in explained variance, 5 percent, or from 66 percent to 61 percent, in the concurrent case is of

Table 4.4. *Summary of Results of Regression Models*

	CONCURRENT	SUBSEQUENT	TWO-YEAR LAG
TOTAL SET, ALL VARIABLES	0.66	0.64	0.67
TOTAL SET, W/O VOLATILITY MEASURES	0.61	0.62	0.65
DIFFERENCE	0.05	0.02	0.02

Note: Average of the results of four predictions.

some interest. The reduction in the other predictions, 2 percent, is smaller than the range of variation in explained variance for the four different periods.

If the same exercise is repeated using creative destruction measures rather than business volatility indices, there are two differences. The gain in concurrent explained variance, as shown in Appendix 4, is 13 percent for the four periods compared with a total average explained variance of 74 percent. The gain in subsequent and two-year lag explained variance (not shown) is about 1 percent, from 62 percent to 63 percent and 65 percent to 66 percent.

4.6   Final Deduction

On the basis of results of regression analysis utilizing only creative destruction measures and business volatility indices as the estimates of contributions to linear additive models of regional job growth, it is appropriate to conclude that business and job turbulence is an integral component of concurrent job growth but not an independent causal factor in subsequent job growth.

In short, turbulence and growth occur together; turbulence does not cause growth.

5   Sources of Creative Destruction

What, then, causes turbulence *and*, perhaps, growth? On this topic, there is more current and relevant information. There is an earlier analysis in this research program, using the same data sets and variables reported earlier, which has focused explicitly on business volatility (Reynolds et al., 1995). There is also a set of complementary studies completed for a number of countries focusing on the most critical element in any measures of creative destruction or business volatility, new firm birth rates (Reynolds et al., 1994).

5.1   U.S. Business Volatility

An extensive analysis focused on development of linear additive models predicting autonomous firm births, deaths, and an index of business volatility. The index was composed of the average standardized value of four measures: autonomous (tops, simples) firm birth and death rates and branch/subsidiary birth and death rates, computed per 10,000 human population. The independent variables were the fifteen indices of growth described in Table 4.3. A linear structural relations (LISREL) analysis was completed with time lags varied from 0 (subsequent period) to 16 years (no concurrent analysis was completed). It was found that time period did not enter into the analysis so that the program could create a consolidated estimate for up to four different data sets.

The major results are presented in Table 4.5. It is to be noted that the ability to explain variation in the business volatility index varies from 54 percent to 72 percent of the variance explained, with little drop related to longer-term predictions. This is due, in part, to a high level of stability in the relative position of the 382 labor market areas over time. For example, labor market areas (LMAs) with a higher concentration of well educated young adults in 1970 are, relative to the rest of the country, in the same situation in 1980.

Perhaps most remarkably, the very same independent variables are found to have a statistically significant impact in all the models. The four indices with major impact in the short-term predictions of Table 4.5 are greater personal wealth, population growth, the absence of unemployed/economically desperate individuals, and the presence of economic diversity. The gamma coefficients (similar to standardized beta coefficients in linear regression) in these models not only have the same sign, but the same order of magnitude – almost all have the same value to one significant digit.

There is a slight variation when medium-term predictions are based on indices developed for 1970, but the same types of components have a major impact: increased wealth in the region, enhanced growth or turbulence; lack of rigid employment practices; and economic diversity.

Table 4.5. Linear Models Predicting Business Volatility: U.S., 1976–1988

Year date represents: 1970, 1978, 1980, 1982, 1984

Year data represents: (Predicting from)

	SHORT TERM					MEDIUM					
TIME LAG (yrs)	0	2	4	6	8	6	8	10	12	14	16
Predicted	78-80	80-82	82-84	84-86	86-88	76-78	78-80	80-82	82-84	84-86	86-88
Years	78-80	80-82	82-84	84-86							
	80-82	82-84	84-86	86-88							
	82-84	84-86	86-88								
	84-86	86-88									
Variable Name											
FACTOR 1 – Agglomerative/Access											
5) Availability of factors of production — PFAVLxx											
7) Access to customers, clients — ACCSSxx											
8) Knowledge, R & D Base — TECHxx											
12) Size of economic base — BASExx						0.16	0.17	0.25			
FACTOR 2 – Wealth/Costs											
4) Costs of factors of production — PFCSTxx											
6) Public infrastructure expenditures — INFEFxx											
9) Greater personal wealth — WELTHxx	0.22	0.22	0.22	0.20	0.24	0.35	0.37	0.45	0.32	0.27	
FACTOR 3 – Growth/Turbulence											
2) Career opportunity — CARERxx						0.10	0.60	0.31	0.32	0.31	0.54
3) Industry mix (volatile industries) — ESMIxxx						0.36	0.43	0.43	0.48	0.31	0.50
11) Population growth — POPxxD	0.33	0.34	0.34	0.34	0.38	0.36	0.43	0.43	0.48	0.50	0.48

FACTOR 4 - Employment Rigidities

15) Flexible employment policies (lack of)	LUxx										-.15	-.14
1) Unemployment/desperation	DESPxx	-.20	-.24	-.23	-.27	-.19	-.14	-.12	-.15		-.10	-.18

FACTOR 5 - Social Diversity

10) Social status diversity	SOCxxV	

FACTOR 6 - Economic Diversity

13) Economic diversity	ECONxxV	0.51	0.47	0.48	0.49	0.55	0.38	0.33	0.28	0.30	0.33	0.26

FACTOR 7 - National transportation difficulties

14) Lack of national transportation access	AIRPxx	

Average Adjusted Explained Variance (R^2)		0.72	0.72	0.70	0.69	0.64	0.54	0.56	0.60	0.61	0.61	0.63

Source: Reynolds, Miller, and Maki, 1995, Table II, p. 400.
Note: Table values are gamma coefficients from LISREL analysis and may be interpreted similarly to standardized beta weights.

The factors having a major impact on predictors of business volatility were similar to those predicting autonomous firm birth and death rates developed with the same independent variables and using the same analysis procedure. A similar cross-regional analysis, utilizing linear models of regional characteristics to predict firm birth and death rates, was completed for the U.K. (Keeble and Walker, 1994). The researchers also found that the models predicting birth and death rates were very similar, confirming that these may be two aspects of the same underlying feature – creative destruction.

5.2   Cross-National Studies of New Firm Births

A central feature of creative destruction and turbulence are new firm births. There has been, just recently, a considerable effort to explore the regional factors associated with higher levels of firm births in a number of countries, including France (Guesnier, 1994), Germany (Audretsch and Fritsch, 1994), Ireland (Hart and Gudgin, 1994), Italy (Garofoli, 1994), Japan (LaPlant, 1992), Norway (Spilling, 1995), Sweden (Davidsson et al., 1994), the United Kingdom (Keeble and Walker, 1994), and the United States (Reynolds, 1994). All of these studies have found similar results with regard to factors affecting new firm births and, presumably, the level of turbulence or creative destruction (Reynolds et al., 1994).

The results of cross-national comparisons, using forced entry linear regression procedures and single item measures of business start-up processes (including the United States), have been somewhat different from the results summarized above. Separate analyses were completed for all sectors and manufacturing alone.

For all sectors, the average explained variance for firm birth rates using a human population based model was 78 percent and for a firm birth rate using the stock as business as the base was 65 percent. Factors that were statistically significant in most country analyses included regional growth in demand; greater urbanization/agglomeration; higher levels of unemployment; greater personal and household wealth; and more small firms and economic specialization.

Models developed only for the manufacturing sector explained an average of 60 percent (population based) or 32 percent (business stock based) of the variation in firm birth rates. Only three factors were widely prevalent and clearly significant in these models, presence of small firms or specialization, demand growth, and a relative level or urbanization/agglomeration. Similar findings are reported for Norway (Spilling, 1995) as well as Japan (LaPlant, 1992; OECD, 1993).

This would suggest that substantial progress has been made in understanding the regional factors that affect firm births as well as business turbulence. Advanced market economies are similar in that demand growth, greater presence of potential entrepreneurs, economic diversity, and more small businesses contribute to higher rates of firm births, business volatility, and creative destruction. There is little systematic evidence that lower costs, direct government support, or a "positive business climate" has a consistent effect in promoting firm births, firm growth, or business volatility.

6   Observations and Policy Implications

This analysis has provided strong evidence on three points. First, economic growth and creative destruction (or volatility or turbulence or churning) occur together. Second, creative destruction cannot be considered a cause of economic growth. Third, substantial progress has been made in determining, for cross-regional comparisons, those factors that affect firm births, the presence of creative destruction, and – in turn – regional economic growth. This analysis complements that of national economic growth (Thurik, 1995) or relative growth across economic subsectors (Schreyer and Chaviox-Mannato, 1995); it may be that higher levels of turbulence or volatility are associated with national or subsector economic growth.

What is not clear is just what features of the creative destruction or business volatility processes are central to enhancing economic growth. New firm births and small firm expansions presumably lead to job gains, attracting people and resources from other firms. The exact role that firm contraction or death may have in this process is more ambiguous. Some firm contraction may reflect loss of customers to new or expanding firms. Other firm contractions or shut-downs (deaths) may reflect the decisions of the owners to redeploy their resources – money, physical assets, management talent, or entrepreneurial emphasis – to other sectors: sectors with greater profit potential. This is most likely to occur when a regional economic base or structural emphasis is changing.

Creative destruction should, perhaps, be considered in the same way as physiological measures of arousal in biological systems. Biological arousal is associated with an increased heart rate, a greater breathing rate, and a generally enhanced level of alertness. If a biological system is excited, all systems are aroused. Often this arousal is associated with good things – overcoming of a challenge, exhilaration in social contexts, sexual arousal – and occasionally with unpleasant events – the threat of physical danger or unanticipated stress from social confrontations. But the capacity for arousal appears to have many positive attributes. When the potential for arousal is reduced – perhaps with depressants – the ability of the system to adapt to new contexts can be substantially reduced.

It seems clear that most economic systems will not have growth without creative destruction or volatility or churning or turbulence in the business community. Government policy at the local and national levels that accepts and facilitates creative destruction will promote economic adaptation. This may be done by assisting start-ups and expansions and reducing the social cost associated with firm contractions and declines. It is unlikely that utilizing public funds or regulations to subsidize firms that cannot be competitive will be in the public interest. It may only delay the inevitable redeployment of resources from declining to growth sectors. An appropriate role for government would be to reduce the social costs associated with these adaptations.

Addenda A: Labor Market Areas

The 382 labor market areas (LMAs) that provide the unit of analysis are presented in Figure 4.1. They were developed on the basis of journey-to-work patterns reported in the 1980 census of the population (Tolbert and Killian, 1987). They represent combinations of the ±3,142 county or county equivalents in the United States. The number of counties continues to change gradually, as new counties are created with urban expansion and others are consolidated as rural populations decline. One-third of the labor market areas include counties from two or more states, providing strong justification for the use of travel-to-work areas as a basic unit of analysis.

Selected characteristics of these LMAs are presented in Table 4.A1, where the LMAs are classified in five equal groups in terms of population density, which varies from less than 1 person per square mile to 5,400 per square mile. The U.S. population is very concentrated, with 75 percent living on 19 percent of the land area. The lowest density LMAs are clearly the largest, with an average size, with Alaska excluded, of 20,000 square miles. This is slightly larger than New Hampshire and Vermont combined. There is little variation in the average size of the other four categories of LMAs, which average 5,000 square miles, or about the size of Connecticut or twice the size of Delaware.

Despite considerable difference across labor market areas in terms of area, population density, and total population size (which varies from

Table 4.A1. *Selected Characteristics U.S. Labor Market Areas by Density: 1980*

	Labor Market Area Population Density				
	Very Low	Low	Medium	High	Very High
Number of LMAs	76	76	76	76	78
Percent of U.S. Area	58 %	13 %	10 %	9 %	10 %
Average Size (1,000)					
Square miles	27 (20)*	6	4	4	5
Square kilometers	71 (52)*	15	12	10	12
Average Density					
People/square mile	14	42	66	108	426
People/square km	5	16	25	42	164
Percent U.S. Population	7 %	8 %	10 %	15 %	60 %
Population, Avg (1,000)	213	241	294	426	1,751
Workers, Avg (1,000)	87	95	119	181	770
Workers as percent population	41 %	39 %	40 %	42 %	44 %
Industry of Occupation (1980): PerCent of Workers by sector					
Agriculture & Mining	13 %	9 %	7 %	6 %	2 %
Construction	8	7	7	6	6
Manufacturing	12	23	24	25	26
Buss Serv,FIRE **	7	7	7	8	10
Trans,Comm,Whole	11	10	10	10	11
Retail	17	16	16	16	16
Consumer Services	8	7	7	7	8
Health,Educ, Soc Ser	17	17	17	16	16
Government	6	5	5	5	5
Total	99 %	101 %	100 %	99 %	100 %

* Without Alaska (570,833 square miles and 401,851 people in 1980). Removal of Alaska does not substantially affect other figures.
** FIRE: Finance, Insurance, and Real Estate.

100,000 to about 12 million) there are not major differences in the economic structure. The percentage of workers in different economic sectors shows little variation for transportation, communication, and wholesale; retail; consumer services; health, education, and social services, and government employees, which are from 56 to 60 percent of all workers for all LMAs. There is a clear decline in the percentage of agriculture and mining employees in higher density LMAs – dropping from 13 percent to 2 percent – and a less dramatic but clear decline for those in construction, a reduction from 8 percent to 6 percent. There are a dramatic increase of manufacturing employees from very low to low density LMAs – from 12 percent to 23 percent – and a slight increase thereafter to 26 percent in the very high density LMA. There is an increase among business service and financial, insurance, and real estate (FIRE) employees in the high density LMAs, rising from 7 percent to 10 percent.

Addenda B: Measures of Business, Job Dynamics

The basic source of data is developed from the files of a commercial credit rating service, the Dun & Bradstreet Dun's Market Identifier (DMI) files. This information is organized on the basis of individual establishments, a single physical location where economic activity takes place, and a record of sales and employment at each location that is updated continuously. Actual employment is reported by over 90 percent of all establishments. The legal or ownership relationship between establishments is reflected in three basic categories: (1) autonomous, independents, or "simples," which are single site firms; (2) headquarters or tops, which own other establishments; and (3) branches and subsidiaries, which are owned by a headquarters to top establishment. Of the 4 to 5 million establishments in place in the U.S. over the past twenty years, about 8 percent are tops, 24 percent branches or subsidiaries, and the remainder, 68 percent, single site businesses.

The complete U.S. file was leased from Dun & Bradstreet by the U.S. Small Business Administration in December of every even year from 1976 through 1988 (U.S. Small Business Administration, 1988). Substantial editing and revisions were completed to minimize the inability to determine the ownership structure among establishments and resolve inconsistencies in employment counts among branches and total enterprises. Comparisons of two consecutive files are used to identify establishment births (new entry in the second year) or deaths (first year entry not found in second year). This procedure for identifying firm births picks up firms very late in the start-up processes; that procedure leads to somewhat lower birth rates compared to those through other procedures for identifying newly founded firms (Carter et al., 1996; Reynolds, 1997).

A specialized version of these data sets, for six two-year periods, was prepared using the 75 economic sectors (2 digit U.S. SIC code) for each of 3,140 counties as the unit of analysis. Each two-year data set contains about 130,000 records. This is about two-thirds of the potential maximum because there are many economic sectors that are not present across all U.S. counties. For each county/economic sector record, there are 68 variables related to different features of simple and branch birth and death, contraction and expansion, and the subsequent effect on job creation and destruction.

Substantial effort has been devoted to comparing the results of the resultant Small Business Data Base with other national sources of data on establishments and jobs, such as the U.S. Bureau of the Census *Enterprise Statistics* and *County Business Patterns* and the Bureau of Labor Statistics *Employment and Earnings* (U.S. Small Business Administration, 1988, sect. 5). Each of these sources has unique advantages: the Small Business Data Base provides coverage of all business economic sectors (except agricultural production), ability to distinguish between simples and branches, and a potential for comparisons across counties or time. No other data set provides comprehensive coverage across all sectors and the ability to separate single site establishments from multisite enterprises.

Addenda C: Measures of Economic Growth

Annual data on the aggregate income from a variety of sources, as well as jobs provided by all economic sectors, is available for all U.S. counties or county-equivalents in the Regional Economic Indicator System (REIS) data sets (U.S. Department of Commerce, 1994). This allows two choices for measures of economic status and growth, aggregate earned income and jobs. Annual growth in aggregate income, even when transfer payments from retirement or welfare programs are eliminated and figures are corrected for inflation, correlates 0.65 with annual changes in jobs with substantial year to year variation, from 0.3 to 0.8 (Reynolds and Maki, 1990, p. 25).

Job growth was chosen as the primary measure of economic growth. Job based measures of growth do not need to be adjusted for inflation or non wage and salary income. Jobs tabulated in the REIS counts include all workers, owners and proprietors, farm owners and workers, government and military employees, as well as self-employed individuals. As many employed individuals hold several jobs, the number of jobs tends to be somewhat higher than the total number employed in the labor force. Table 4.C1 indicates the total count of jobs and employed individuals for the U.S. for 1980 through 1992. The ratio of jobs to employed persons rose from 113 percent to 117 percent from 1980

118   **Paul D. Reynolds**

Table 4.C1. *Jobs and Employment: U.S., 1980–1992*

Year	Total Job Count	Total Employment	(Jobs/Employment)
1980	113,726,000	100,907,000	1.13
1985	123,693,000	108,856,000	1.14
1990	138,981,000	119,550,000	1.16
1992	139,289,000	119,164,000	1.17

Sources: U.S. Department of Commerce, 1994, Regional Economic Information System (REIS); U.S. Bureau of the Census, 1994, *Statistical Abstract of the United States: 1994*, Table 614, p. 395.
Note: Both counts include all residential jobs or employment, including armed forces, agricultural, government, postal service, and self-employment.

through 1992. This temporal trend would affect any longitudinal analysis using jobs as an indicator of economic growth, but none is involved in the following presentations.

If there were little or no variation in annual job growth across the 382 labor market areas, it would be difficult to determine the relative impact of various factors on economic growth. However, there is substantial variation across these U.S. labor market areas. The annual variation is much greater than the temporal variation for the entire U.S.

The pattern of job growth across the 382 LMAs for the eleven two-year periods covering 1970 to 1992 is presented in Table 4.C2. It indicates substantial variation across the labor market areas in the annual job change in a single time period. The average annual job change for the 382 labor market areas for these 11 two-year periods has varied from a drop of 0.15 percent to an increase of 3.90 percent, a range of 4.05 percent. However, in any two-year period, minimum–maximum range of variation across LMAs is from 8.49 percent to 18.88 percent, two to four times greater than the national variation across time.

There is some indication that the dispersion across LMAs declined in the 1984–92 period, as the measures of the range in changes and standard deviation declined in the latter period. Nevertheless, for the analysis to follow, there is substantial variation in the measure of economic growth (annual job change). To facilitate comparisons of linear, additive models for different years, the annual percentage of job change is normalized to provide a mean of 0 and a standard deviation of 1. The distributions for most years are approximately normal.

Table 4.C2. *Job Growth Distribution Across Labor Market Areas: 1970–1992*

Change in % annual job growth

TIME PERIOD	MEAN	Std. Dev.	PERCENTILE							RANGE 5-95%	RANGE 0-100%
			5%	10%	25%	50%	75%	90%	95%		
70-72	2.42	2.11	-0.38	0.25	1.03	2.18	3.49	4.96	6.32	6.70	18.04
72-74	3.45	1.85	0.82	1.52	2.28	3.28	4.34	5.60	6.83	6.01	15.62
74-76	1.34	2.01	-1.50	-1.06	-0.09	1.02	2.54	3.86	5.04	6.54	14.28
76-78	3.90	2.02	0.88	1.69	2.56	3.69	4.84	6.57	7.35	6.47	14.02
78-80	1.42	2.24	-1.78	-0.98	0.00	1.18	2.40	4.56	5.35	7.10	18.88
80-82	-.15	2.28	-3.30	-2.67	-1.56	-0.54	0.98	2.86	4.20	7.60	17.60
82-84	2.32	2.02	-1.04	-0.11	1.13	2.37	3.45	4.67	5.54	6.58	15.59
84-86	1.46	2.13	-1.82	-1.30	0.02	1.52	2.83	4.07	5.08	6.90	12.97
86-88	2.44	1.70	-0.46	0.24	1.35	2.52	3.52	4.54	5.16	5.62	12.09
88-90	2.05	1.38	-0.19	0.50	1.27	1.96	2.74	3.61	4.67	4.86	11.23
90-92	1.04	1.29	-1.17	-0.57	0.22	1.08	1.85	2.64	3.11	4.28	8.49

MEDIAN
RANGE
1970-
1992 4.05

Source: U.S. Department of Commerce, 1994, Regional Economic Information System (REIS).

Addenda D: Measures of Creative Destruction and Business Dynamics

Two types of measures were developed to represent creative destruction: business turbulence and volatility.

Creative Destruction Indices

There is no one best way to measure "creative destruction." It is generally conceptualized as the level of turbulence or churning in an economic system. Measures based on the birth or death of establishments, standardized by the stock of establishments or the human population, could be developed. But changes in the economic system will affect jobs, so it is possible to measure the job gains (from establishment births and expansions) and job losses (from establishment deaths and contractions). An overall measure of volatility, turbulence, or churning may be developed by adding together the birth and death (creation and destruction) rates. Alternatively, since all geographic regions have some level of births and deaths, the ratio of births to deaths may be computed. Growth (in establishments or jobs) would be associated with a ratio greater than 1, decline by a ratio less than 1, and stability by a ratio equal to 1.

Four versions of all three measures, applied to both the creation and the destruction of establishments and jobs, were developed for utilization in the analysis. As presented in Table 4.D1, the first three sets of rows represent four measures. The first set of rows is based on business job creation and destruction, per 100 jobs present at the beginning of the time period. The second set of rows utilizes the average rates of establishment births and deaths per 10,000 human population present in the LMA at the beginning of the period. The third set of rows is based on establishment birth and death rates per 100 establishments in the labor market area at the beginning of the period.

There tend to be consistent and significant positive correlations among all measures of job and establishment dynamics, as presented in Table 4.D1. The major exception is the relationship between the birth/death ratio and the total rate of births and deaths, which is negative. In labor market areas with higher levels of birth and death rates, death rates tend to be higher than birth rates.

Business Dynamic Indices

Indices were developed to allow incorporation of three different aspects of regional business volatility: business establishments versus jobs; tops and simple versus branch and subsidiary establishments; and five different economic sectors. Jobs versus establishments is a well recognized distinction. A unique advantage of the business data set was the capacity to distinguish between independent or simple establishments, headquarters or top establishments, and those that were branches or subsidiaries. The first two were combined (tops are about 8 percent of all establishments; tops and simples about 76 percent of the total) for comparison with branches and subsidiaries (24 percent of all establishments).

Economic sectors were consolidated to retain out-of-region export potential as a central feature for four categories: extractive (agriculture and mining); manufacturing (durable and non-durable); distributive services (transportation, communication, public utilities and wholesale); and business services (finance, insurance, real estate, consulting and other direct services to business). The fifth category included all sectors (construction, retail, consumer services, and health, education, and social services) where the primary customers would be in the immediate region.

Table 4.D1. *Inter-correlations of Creative Destruction Measures, Business Dynamic Indices*

Variable	Mean	Std Dev	Minimum	Maximum	N	Label
JBBRA	9.91	4.11	3.20	33.48	2292	JOB CREATION: TOTAL PER 100 JOBS
JBDTA	7.77	3.89	1.87	41.52	2292	JOB DESTRUCT: TOTAL PER 100 JOBS
JOBVOLR	1.39	.50	.28	6.61	2292	RATIO JOB BIRTHS/DEATHS RATES
JBCRA	17.68	7.22	6.44	56.59	2292	JOB GAIN/LOSS VOLATILITY:TOTAL EFFECT
ESBRPOA	20.23	7.02	6.77	65.66	2292	ESTAB CREATION: TOTAL PER 10,000 HUM POP
ESDTPOA	17.48	5.05	6.78	49.01	2292	ESTAB DESTRUCT: TOTAL PER 10,000 HUM POP
ESPVOLR	1.17	.29	.39	2.49	2292	RATIO EST POP BIRTH/DEATH RATES
ESCHPOA	37.71	11.06	14.95	102.92	2292	EST BRTH+DEATH POPUL VOLATILITY
ESBRESA	10.63	2.41	5.35	21.34	2292	ESTAB CREATION: TOTAL PER 100 ESTAB
ESDTESA	9.29	1.51	5.41	18.15	2292	ESTAB DESTRUCT: TOTAL PER 100 ESTAB
ESEVOLR	1.17	.29	.39	2.50	2292	RATIO EST EST BIRTH/DEATH RATES
ESCHESA	19.93	3.03	12.37	31.03	2292	EST BRTH+DEATH ESTAB VOLATILITY
DISSERV	.00	.88	-1.37	4.78	1528	DIST SERV FIRM,JOB VOLATILITY 4 ITEM INDEX
EXTRACV	.00	.86	-.78	5.92	1528	EXTRACTIV FIRM,JOB VOLATILITY 4 ITEM INDEX
BUSSERV	.00	.73	-1.78	3.67	1528	BUSI SERV FIRM,JOB VOLATILITY 4 ITEM INDEX
MANUFGV	.00	.64	-1.34	4.75	1528	MANUFACTU FIRM,JOB VOLATILITY 4 ITEM INDEX
LOCTSV	.00	.84	-2.07	5.39	1528	LOCMKT TS FIRM,JOB VOLATILITY 2 ITEM INDEX
LOCBSV	.00	.83	-2.31	4.91	1528	LOCMKT BS FIRM,JOB VOLATILITY 2 ITEM INDEX

Table 4.D1. *(cont.)*

Correlations:

	JBBRA	JBDTA	JOBVOLR	JBCRA	ESBRPO	ESDTPOA	ESPVOLR	ESCHPOA	ESBRESA	ESDTESA	ESEVOLR	ESCHESA
JBBRA	1.0000											
JBDTA	.6285**	1.0000										
JOBVOLR	.2581**	-.4693**	1.0000									
JBCRA	.9080**	.8965**	-.1058**	1.0000								
ESBRPOA	.3572**	.0249	.3182**	-.2168**	1.0000							
ESDTPOA	.0943**	.0367	.0000	-.0735**	.6713**	1.0000						
ESPVOLR	.3244**	-.0460	.4279**	.1600**	.5481**	-.2118**	1.0000					
ESCHPOA	.2697**	-.0326	.2020**	.1712**	.9411**	.8824**	.2513**	1.0000				
ESBRESA	.3452**	-.0505	.4422**	-.1694**	.7394**	.1804**	.7910**	.5516**	1.0000			
ESDTESA	-.0671**	-.0426	-.0347	-.0611**	-.1643**	-.6110**	-.4502**	.3831**	.1545**	1.0000		
ESEVOLR	.3274**	-.0401	.4188**	.1649**	.5372**	-.2194**	.9970**	.2409**	.7910**	-.4525**	1.0000	
ESCHESA	.2409**	-.0613*	.3340**	.1042**	.6689**	.4470**	.4044**	.6286**	.8710**	.6199**	.4032**	1.0000
DISSERV	.4698**	.2459**	.1659**	.4027**	.6174**	.4108**	.2971**	.5649**	.6064**	.3681**	.3062**	.6399**
EXTRACV	.0127	.0529	-.0959**	.0356	.2223**	.3136**	-.0694*	.2815**	.0569	.2201**	-.0675*	.1460**
BUSSERV	.3888**	.2541**	.0748*	.3603**	.5123**	-.4251**	.1598**	.5084**	.4237**	.3306**	.1760**	.4811**
MANUFGV	.2804**	.2686**	.0627	.3054**	-.0172	-.0888**	-.0977***	-.0522	-.1515**	-.0724*	-.1033**	-.1508**
LOCTSV	.3131**	.1538**	.1389**	.2630**	.5309**	.3946**	.2240**	.5053**	.6046**	.5391**	.2108**	.7177**
LOCBSV	.2353**	.1107**	.1212**	.1951**	.2771**	.1149**	.2415**	.2208**	.4890**	.3043**	.2582**	.5194**

Correlations:

	DISSERV	EXTRACV	BUSSERV	MANUFGV	LOCTSV	LOCBSV
DISSERV	1.0000					
EXTRACV	-.1259**	1.0000				
BUSSERV	-.5065*	.1772**	1.0000			
MANUFGV	-.0596	-.1390**	-.1081**	1.0000		
LOCTSV	.4115**	-.0097	.1520**	-.0738*	1.0000	
LOCBSV	.2468**	.0618	.1990**	-.1110**	.3544**	1.0000

Note: Minimum pairwise *N* of cases: 1528. Two-tailed significance: * 0.01; ** 0.001.

This last category would normally include the majority of establishments and jobs in any region.

The indices were developed from summing birth and death rates for establishments and jobs for each of the five economic sectors, a total of twenty separate indicators. A factor analysis was completed on these indicators with all regions pooled across six time periods, a total of 2,292 data points. The results (as shown in Table 4.D2) show a high level of consistency with regard to the four export oriented economic sectors, with one slight aberration related to manufacturing. The results also indicate that a distinction should be retained between autonomous firms and headquarters establishments (tops and simples) and branches for the local market sector.

The result was the construction of six indices. The lowest reliability (presented in Table 4.D2) was associated with manufacturing (0.51), followed by those related to tops and simples in the local market sectors (0.56) and branches and subsidiaries in the local market sectors (0.57). Reliabilities for the other three indices were from 0.70 to 0.90.

The actual indices were developed by taking the average of the standardized values (mean of 0; standard deviation of 1) for the component measures. They have, therefore, no direct interpretation in terms of specific events, but indicate relative levels of volatility among labor market areas.

Addenda E: Regional Characteristics and Firm Start-Up Processes

The rationale and measures included in each regional characteristic index follow. A more detailed presentation of the influence of each dimension on each index can be found in the appendix to Reynolds, Miller, and Maki (1995).

Career Opportunity. Refers to the presence of individuals who may wish to pursue entrepreneurial careers in a labor market area. The presence of such individuals is reflected in an index that combines the proportion of the population thirty-five to forty-four years old, those with college education, and the proportion of managers, professionals, and those in technical occupations in the work force. The reliabilities are from 0.8 to about 0.9.

Industry Mix (Volatile Industries). Refers to a higher proportion of construction, retail, and consumer service businesses in a region. It is measured by a combination of measures of work force and establishment concentrations in these sectors. The reliability is usually above 0.60.

Table 4.D2. *Development of Business Dynamic Indicators: Factor Analysis Loadings and Index Reliability*

	Distributive Services Sectors	Extractive Sectors	Business Service Sectors	Manufacturing Sectors	Local Market: Branches	Local Market: Tops, Simples
DXXTVOLE	.86					
DXXBJVOL	.84					
DXXTJVOL	.84					
DXXBVOLE	.83					
EXXBVOLE		.88				
EXXTJVOL		.87				
EXXTVOLE		.79				
EXXBJVOL		.74				
BXXTVOLE			.74			
BXXTJVOL			.72			
BXXBVOLE			.68			
BXXBJVOL			.56			
MXXBVOLE*		.68		.39		
MXXTVOLE				.77		
MXXTJVOL				.74		
MXXBJVOL				.58		
LXXBVOLE					.87	
LXXBJVOL					.49	
LXXTVOLE						.85
LXXTJVOL						.71
Number of Items	4	4	4	4	2	2
RELIABILITY (Chronback's Alpha)	0.90	0.87	0.70	0.51	0.57	0.56

Notes:

Industry Sectors (first letter):

E = Extractive: Agriculture Services, Mining (US SIC 1, 2, 7, 8, 9, 10–14)
M = Manufacturing: Durables and Non-Durables (US SIC 20–39)
D = Distributive Services: Transportation, Communication, and Public Utilities and Wholesale (US SIC 40–49; 50–51)
B = Business Services: Financial, Insurance, and Real Estate; Other Business Services (US SIC 60–67, 73, 81, 86, 89)
L = Local Market: Construction, Retail; Consumer Services; Health, Education, and Social Services (US SIC 15–17, 52–59, 70, 71, 75, 76, 78, 79, 80, 82, 83, 84, 88) Included in the manufacturing volatility index

Indicators:

?XXTVOLE   Sum of tops, simples birth and death rates; establishment based
?XXBVOLE   Sum of branch, subsidiaries birth and death rates; establishment based
?XXTJVOL   Sum of job birth and death rates from tops, simples births, expansion, contraction, and death
?XXBJVOL   Sum of job birth and death rates from branch, subsidiaries births, expansion, contraction, and deaths

Flexible Employment Policies. Refers to the capacity to adjust employment relations as work demands shift. Its indicator reflects both the percentage of the work force that is unionized as well as the proportion of workers not covered by right to work laws. These laws would allow individuals to work in a unionized establishment without joining the union. Areas without such laws are assumed to have a less flexible employment relationship. The reliability is about 0.90.

Availability of Production Factors. Reflects the importance of access to inputs. It is indicated by up to ten variables, two associated with per capita savings and demand deposits, one related to the proportion of the population in the work years (fifteen to sixty-four), one related to the proportion of the population with high school diplomas, and the remainder the density (per square mile) of various types of workers (sales, clerical, service, skilled craftsmen, machine operatives, transport operatives, and laborers). The reliability is about 0.90 for all time periods.

Access to Customers and Clients. Should refer to the ease with which output could be provided to the user. A two item index reflects the population density and density of establishments (number per square mile). It has a reliability that is almost perfect (0.99).

Knowledge, Research and Development Base. Refers to the capacity for access to specialized technological knowledge. Four items were assembled for inclusion in this measure: population with post college degrees, professional and technical employees, patents granted, and doctorates granted. All were computed as measures of density (per 1,000 square miles). Reliabilities were from 0.90 to 0.99.

Unemployment/Desperation. Refers to a reaction to the absence of traditional work opportunities, which, presumably, leads to personal and household economic despair. A two item index was developed; it included the unemployment rate and transfer payments (much of which are welfare payments) as a proportion of total personal income. Reliabilities were moderate, usually around 0.70.

Costs of Factors of Production. Are assumed to encourage business births when they are lower. The index reflected four measures related to government activity: business taxes per worker, property taxes per worker, per capita local government revenue, and per capita local government debt. A measure of wage rates, earned income per worker, was also included. Reliabilities were generally in the 0.60s.

Public Infrastructure Expenditures. Are assumed to encourage business births if they are low, assuming that greater public value is provided for the taxes collected. It is not possible to estimate the efficiency of government activity, but the per capita expenditures for education, highways, welfare, and police service could be determined. This index has a reliability from about 0.60 to 0.70.

Size of the Economic Base. Should affect the absolute number of business births, but a large economic base may also have a higher birth rate. The total human population, labor force, and establishment population were combined for this index. The reliabilities are almost perfect (0.99 to 1.00).

Economic Diversity. May, by providing a wider range of market opportunities, enhance business births. The index reflects a combination of a measure of the presence of small businesses (establishments/employees) as well as two measures of diversity. One reflects diversity of occupations in the working population and the other the diversity of industries in which they work (Gibbs and Poston, 1975). Reliabilities are about 0.60.

Access to National Transportation. Was determined by identifying the major 29 airport hubs. As both Kennedy and La Guardia airports are in the same labor market area, New York City–Long Island, there are major hubs in 28 different labor market areas. The distance, in miles, from the center of each labor market area to the closest and second closest airline hub was measured. The index was composed of the distance to the closest airline hub and the difference between the closest and second closest airline hubs. As neither Alaska nor Hawaii had a major hub, they were excluded from this analysis. The reliability of this index, which reflects both choice and access to major airports was 0.80. It was computed only for 1980 airline hub designations.

Personal Wealth. Is assumed to increase markets for goods and, in turn, encourage business births. It was measured by an index that combined personal income per capita, income per household, income per family, and property income (dividends, interest, and rent) per capita. Reliability was usually about 0.90 or better.

Social Status Diversity. Is assumed to provide greater diversity of markets and, in turn, encourage business births. As data on the ethnic identification of the population was not available at the county level, this index was restricted to measures of diversity in household income and diversity in educational attainment. Both are widely used to identify social class. As these two measures of diversity correlated 0.57 for 1980, they were combined into a single measure of social status diversity.

Population Growth. Is considered to increase markets and provide opportunities for new businesses. It was measured by an index that included population change over the previous ten years, percent in-migration, and the percent of the residents living in the same county five years earlier. Reliabilities were from 0.7 to 0.8.

In the ideal case, all reliabilities would be perfect, or 1.00. This is achieved for some of these measures, such as access to customers, knowledge and R&D base, or size of the economic system. But reliabilities rarely are perfect and the current "state of the art" determines what is considered acceptable. Most of the reliabilities in Table 4.3 are within the acceptable range. Reliabilities are about the same for the different time periods, suggesting some stability in the potential for measurement.

The major limitation on developing these indices is the availability of data at the right time period and for individual counties. When a critical indicator is not available annually, simple linear extrapolations are made between different periods and the intermediate values estimated. For example, if data is available for 1970 and 1980, an estimate for 1976 is produced by simply determining the ten-year change in the value of the indicator and assuming that 60 percent of the change occurred between 1970 and 1976.

Several important indicators are available annually for each state but not each county, such as the number of patents granted. In this case the absolute count for the state is apportioned among the counties of each state based on some other measure. For example, patents granted were apportioned on the basis of the distribution of those over twenty-five years old, based on the assumption that few patents would be granted to children. Data on the counties is then aggregated for the labor market areas.

From two to eleven specific indicators were used to create indices for each of the start-up processes for each of the periods. To create these indices, the distributions of the specific indicators were transformed to symmetrical distributions (skewness between -1.0 and $+1.0$). The values for each indicator were then standardized (mean of 0.0; standard deviation of 1.0). Each index is the average value of the normalized, standardized values of the indicators.

Appendix 1. Creative Destruction Measures and Economic Growth: By Year

	Establishments: Stock Based (1)			Establishments Human Pop Based (2)				Job Indicators Existing Job Based (3)				
	Births	Deaths	Br/Dth	Br+Dth	Births	Deaths	Br/Dth	Br+Dth	Births	Deaths	Br/Dth	Br+Dth
Average value(4)	10.6	9.3	1.4	19.9	20.2	17.5	1.2	37.7	9.9	7.8	1.2	17.7
Std Deviation	2.4	1.5	0.5	3.0	7.0	5.0	0.3	11.0	4.1	3.8	0.3	7.2
Range: Min	5.4	5.4	0.3	12.4	6.7	6.8	0.4	15.0	3.2	1.8	0.4	6.4
Max	21.3	18.2	6.6	31.0	65.7	49.0	2.4	102.9	33.5	41.5	2.5	56.6
CORRELATIONS WITH LABOR MARKET AREA JOB GROWTH (5,9)												
SAME PERIOD (6)												
From / With												
1976-78 / 1976-78	0.65	-.11	0.30	0.62	0.55	0.13	0.55	0.47	0.53	0.17	0.55	0.48
1978-80 / 1978-80	0.65	0.20	0.38	0.57	0.67	0.51	0.41	0.64	0.49	0.07	0.41	0.41
1980-82 / 1980-82	0.74	0.20	0.66	0.66	0.71	0.40	0.69	0.62	0.61	-.13	0.69	0.32
1982-84 / 1982-84	0.47	0.04	0.51	0.39	0.30	0.01	0.49	0.19	0.49	-.15	0.48	0.21
1984-86 / 1984-86	0.56	-.03	0.51	0.42	0.31	-.09	0.36	0.14	0.53	-.02	0.56	0.36
1986-88 / 1986-88	0.46	-.11	0.39	0.26	0.35	-.10	0.40	0.11	0.43	-.04	0.39	0.26
Average correlation	0.59	0.03	0.46	0.49	0.48	0.14	0.52	0.36	0.51	-.02	0.52	0.34
NEXT PERIOD (7)												
From / To												
1976-78 / 1978-80	0.55	-.13	0.24	0.50	0.60	0.30	0.50	0.56	0.36	0.07	0.50	0.30
1978-80 / 1980-82	0.62	0.19	0.29	0.55	0.60	0.45	0.38	0.57	0.39	0.09	0.38	0.33
1980-82 / 1982-84	0.20	0.29	-.00	0.27	0.09	0.12	0.03	0.11	0.12	0.07	0.03	0.12
1982-84 / 1984-86	0.39	0.12	0.30	0.35	0.18	-.03	0.35	0.10	0.42	0.02	0.34	0.27
1984-86 / 1986-88	0.37	-.06	0.34	0.25	0.19	-.09	-.39	0.07	0.34	-.04	-.38	0.21
1986-88 / 1988-80	0.19	0.19	0.06	0.24	0.29	0.18	-.02	0.25	0.14	0.09	-.02	0.14
Average correlation	0.39	0.10	0.20	0.36	0.32	0.16	0.27	0.28	0.30	0.05	0.27	0.23

TWO YEAR LAG (8)

From	To												
1976-78	1980-82	0.41	-.05	0.22	0.39	0.47	0.32	0.34	0.47	0.34	0.08	0.35	0.29
1978-80	1982-84	0.20	0.06	0.08	0.18	0.09	0.07	0.09	0.09	0.09	-.05	0.10	0.05
1980-82	1984-86	0.20	0.31	-.04	0.28	0.04	0.06	0.02	0.05	0.14	0.14	0.02	0.18
1982-84	1986-88	0.17	0.12	0.18	0.18	0.05	-.01	0.13	0.03	0.29	0.03	0.12	0.20
1984-86	1988-90	0.22	0.10	0.07	0.21	0.24	0.16	0.16	0.22	0.13	0.07	0.15	0.13
1986-88	1990-92	-.06	0.14	-.10	0.04	0.08	0.16	-.17	0.13	-.16	-.01	-.17	-.11
Average correlation		0.19	0.11	0.07	0.21	0.16	0.13	0.10	0.16	0.14	0.04	0.10	0.12

(1) Births: number tops, simples, or branches created per 100 total establishments at beginning of period. Deaths: number tops, simples, or branches deactivated per 100 establishments of all types at beginning of period.
(2) Sum of two measures, for tops or simples and branches or subsidiary establishments. Annual number created or deactivated per 10,000 population.
(3) Annual number of business jobs (excluding self-employment, agricultural production, military, and any other government employment) created or destroyed per 100 jobs (including self-employment, agricultural production, military, and government).
(4) Annual percentage increase in total number of jobs in the labor market area.
(5) Average values for 382 labor market areas over 6 two-year time periods, $n = 2,292$.
(6) Average for six periods ($n = 2,292$) is 3.8%, SD $= 4.82$; min $= -12.4$%; max $= 31.2$%
(7) Average for six periods ($n = 2,292$) is 3.2%, SD $= 4.33$; min $= -12.4$% max $= 43.5$%.
(8) Average for six periods ($n = 2,292$) is 3.1%; SD $= 4.08$; min $= -12.4$%; max $= 36.3$%.
(9) Number of labor market areas for each correlation is 382; any correlation with an absolute value 0.14 or higher is statistically significant.

129

Appendix 2. *Business Dynamic Indices and Economic Growth: By Year*

CORRELATIONS
WITH LABOR
MARKET AREA
JOB GROWTH

		DISSERV	EXTRACV	BUSSERV	MANUFGV	LOCTSV	LOCBSV
SAME PERIOD							
From	With						
1976-78	1976-78	.42**	.08	.24**	.17**	.43**	.37**
1978-80	1978-80	.50**	.24**	.35**	-.04	.53**	.28**
1980-82	1980-82	.44**	.43**	.42**	-.07	.48**	.37**
1982-84	1982-84	.39**	-.46**	.06	.21**	.34**	.14*
1984-86	1984-86	.51**	-.51**	.03	.14*	.46**	.17**
1986-88	1986-88	.32**	-.43**	-.00	.22**	.27**	.11
Average correlation		.43	-.11	.18	.10	.42	.24
NEXT PERIOD							
From	To						
1976-78	1978-80	.48**	.25**	.29**	-.12	.29**	.26**
1978-80	1980-82	.43**	.31**	.34**	-.06	.42**	.34**
1980-82	1982-84	.32**	-.49**	-.03	.22**	.34**	.08
1982-84	1984-86	.48**	-.50**	.07	.11	.35**	.14*
1984-86	1986-88	.33**	-.47**	-.04	.17**	.33**	.03
1986-88	1988-90	.11	.00	.13*	-.04	.34**	.17**
Average correlation		.36	-.15	.13	.05	.34	.17

Appendix 2. (cont.)

CORRELATIONS WITH LABOR MARKET AREA JOB GROWTH		DISSERV	EXTRACV	BUSSERV	MANUFGV	LOCTSV	LOCBSV
TWO YEAR LAG							
From	To						
1976-78	1980-82	.37**	.28**	.26**	-.12	.26**	.34**
1978-80	1982-84	.30**	-.49***	-.13	.21**	.18**	.09
1980-82	1984-86	.41**	-.50**	-.03	.13*	.38**	.13
1982-84	1986-88	.31**	-.47**	.00	.15*	.26**	.00
1984-86	1988-90	.11	-.04	.13*	-.11	.32**	.19**
1986-88	1990-92	-.18**	.20**	.07	-.14*	.12	.10
Average correlation		.22	-.17	.05	.02	.25	.14

Notes:
DISSERV   Tops, simples, & branches in wholesale, transportation, utilities, and communication.
EXTRACV   Tops, simples, & branches in extractive and agriculture.
BUSSERV   Tops, simples, & branches in financial, insurance, real estate, and business services.
MANUFGV   Tops, simples, & branches in manufacturing.
LOCTSV   Tops, simples in construction, retail, health, education, social, and consumer service.
LOCBSV   Branches in construction, retail, health, education, social, and consumer service. Two-tailed statis-
tical sign: * −0.01; ** −0.001.

Appendix 3. *Regression Models: Business Volatility Indices: Concurrent Year by Base Year*

BASE YEAR		1980	1982	1984	1986
VAR NAME		ZJCN200	ZJCN200	ZJCN200	ZJCN200
PREDICTIVE YEARS		80-82	82-84	84-86	86-88
VAR NAME	DESCRIPTION				
EXTRACV	Agr,Min Volat Index	0.32	-.36	-.46	-.21
MANUFGV	Manufac Volat Index				
DISSERV	Dis Ser Volat Index		0.59	0.54	
BUSSERV	Bus Ser Volat Index	0.32			
LOCTSSV	Loc Mkt Aut FrmVol Index	0.28	0.11		0.10
LOCBSV	Loc Mkt Brc,Sub-Vol Index	0.10	0.11		0.12
PFAVL00	Prod Factor Avail Index		-.71		
ACCSS00	Access to Customers Index				.94
TECH00	Access to Tech Index		0.64		-1.02
BASE00	Econ,Mkt Base Size Index		-.31		0.31
PFCST00	Prod Factor Cost Index		-.29		-.31
INFEF00	Public Infra Cost Index				
WELTH00	Personal,HH Wealth Index	-.13	-.45		0.21
CARER00	Career Opportunity Index	0.30			0.26
ESMIX00	Volatile Sector Mix Index	-.31			
POP00D	Pop Growth Index	0.14		0.22	0.62
LU00	Flexible Work Force Index	-.14		0.12	
DESP00	Unemp,Desperation Index				0.22
SOC00V	Social Diversity Index			0.14	
ECON00V	Economic Diversity Index	0.20	0.12		-.20
AIRP00	Airline Hub Access Index	-.17			
E00EPC	PerCent Agr,Min Estab				
M00EPC	PerCent Manufac Estab		0.39		
D00EPC	PerCent Dis Ser Estab				0.23
B00EPC	PerCent Bus Ser Estab			-.26	
L00EPC	PerCent Loc Mkt Estab	0.20			
EPCOLD00	% Old Agr,Min Estab	-.22			-.36
MPCOLD00	% Old Manufac Estab				
DPCOLD00	% Old Dis Ser Estab		-.52		
BPCOLD00	% Old Bus Ser Estab	0.26			
LPCOLD00	% Old Loc Mkt Estab				-.20
TPCOLD00	% Old All Sec Estab		0.62		
EPCEN2C4	% 4 yr Chg Agr,Min Estab	0.09			
MPCEN2C4	% 4 yr Chg Manufac Estab				
DPCEN2C4	% 4 yr Chg Dis Ser Estab				
BPCEN2C4	% 4 yr Chg Bus Ser Estab			0.17	
LPCEN2C4	% 4 yr Chg Loc Mkt Estab				

		1980	1982	1984	1986
Adj R^2		0.70	0.63	0.65	0.66
Average	0.66				
F value		59.03	49.38	100.38	50.80
RESULTS W/O VOL MEASURES					
Adj R^2		0.63	0.57	0.63	0.63
Average	0.61				
F value		59.32	46.44	65.94	60.86
Full Model-Model w/o Volatility					
Change in Adj R^2		0.07	0.06	0.02	0.03
Average	0.04				

Note: Region weighted by number of jobs in base year. Dependent variable normalized with mean of 0 and standard deviation of 1. Entries are standardized beta weights generated by SPSS PC V 5.01, step-wise regression, tolerance increased to 0.01.

Appendix 4. *Regression Models: Creative Destruction Measures: Concurrent Year by Base Year*

BASE YEAR VAR NAME		1980 ZJCN200	1982 ZJCN200	1984 ZJCN200	1986 ZJCN200
PREDICTIVE YEARS		80-82	82-84	84-86	86-88
VAR NAME	DESCRIPTION				
JOBVOLR	Job Births/Job Deaths	0.23	0.22	0.19	0.13
JOBCRA	Job Births+Job Deaths				
ESPVOLR	Est Brth/Est Death/Pop	0.26	0.32		
ESCHPOA	Est Brth+Est Death/Pop	0.58	0.48	0.13	0.31
ESEVOLR	Est Brth/Est Death/Stock			0.32	0.24
ESCHESA	Est Brth+Est Death/Stock				
PFAVL00	Prod Factor Avail Index	-.38			
ACCSS00	Access to Customers Index				
TECH00	Access to Tech Index	0.28			
BASE00	Econ,Mkt Base Size Index			0.20	0.41
PFCST00	Prod Factor Cost Index		-.33		-.35
INFEF00	Public Infra Cost Index	-.15			0.10
WELTH00	Personal,HH Wealth Index	-.11		-.46	
CARER00	Career Opportunity Index	0.25	0.14		0.22
ESMIX00	Volatile Sector Mix Index	-.11			
POP00D	Pop Growth Index	0.10	0.17		0.54
LU00	Flexible Work Force Index			0.23	
DESP00	Unemp,Desperation Index	0.10	0.14		0.17
SOC00V	Social Diversity Index				
ECON00V	Economic Diversity Index				-.16
AIRP00	Airline Hub Access Index	-.22			
E00EPC	PerCent Agr,Min Estab		-.29	-.27	-.19
M00EPC	PerCent Manufac Estab		0.08		-.17
D00EPC	PerCent Dis Ser Estab			0.20	
B00EPC	PerCent Bus Ser Estab		-.22	-.23	
L00EPC	PerCent Loc Mkt Estab		-.21		
EPCOLD00	% Old Agr,Min Estab		-.14		-.30
MPCOLD00	% Old Manufac Estab				
DPCOLD00	% Old Dis Ser Estab		-.27		
BPCOLD00	% Old Bus Ser Estab	0.15			
LPCOLD00	% Old Loc Mkt Estab	-.21		0.14	-.13
TPCOLD00	% Old All Sec Estab				
EPCEN2C4	% 4 yr Chg Agr,Min Estab				0.07
MPCEN2C4	% 4 yr Chg Manufac Estab				
DPCEN2C4	% 4 yr Chg Dis Ser Estab		0.08		0.07
BPCEN2C4	% 4 yr Chg Bus Ser Estab		0.10		
LPCEN2C4	% 4 yr Chg Loc Mkt Estab			-.14	
Adj R^2		0.78	0.73	0.73	0.70
Average 0.74					
F value		95.02	70.06	96.48	57.82
RESULTS W/O VOL MEASURES					
Adj R^2		0.63	0.57	0.63	0.63
Average 0.61					
F value		59.31	46.44	65.94	60.8
Full Model-Model w/o Volatility					
Change in Adj R^2		0.15	0.16	0.10	0.07
Average 0.12					

Note: Region weighted by number of jobs in base year. Dependent variable normalized with mean of 0 and standard deviation of 1. Entries are standardized beta weights generated by SPSS PC V 5.01, step-wise regression, tolerance increased to 0.01.

Note

The analysis is based on data provided by the U.S. Small Business Administration in fulfillment of Contract SBA 3067-0A-88 and financial support provided by the Rural Poverty and Resources Program of the Ford Foundation (Grant 900-13), both to Paul Reynolds and Wilbur Maki, Co-Principal Investigators. Brenda Miller made many contributions in developing the data sets used in this analysis. Neither the sponsors nor other colleagues are responsible for the analysis, interpretations, or implications developed in this chapter.

References

Audretsch, David B. and Michael Fritsch. 1994. The Geography of Firm Births in Germany. *Regional Studies* 28(4):359–366.

Barreto, Humberto. 1989. *The Entrepreneur in Microeconomic Theory: Disappearance and Explanation.* New York: Routledge.

Baumol, William J. 1968. Entrepreneurship in Economic Theory. *American Economic Review* (Papers and proceedings) 58:64–71.

Carter, Nancy, William B. Gartner, & Paul D. Reynolds. 1996. Exploring Start-Up Event Sequences. *Journal of Business Venturing* 11:151–166.

Davidsson, Per, Leif Lindmark, and Christer Olofsson. 1994. New Firm Formation and Regional Development in Sweden. *Regional Studies* 28(4):395–410.

Garofoli, Gioacchino. 1994. New Firm Formation and Regional Development: The Italian Case. *Regional Studies* 28(4):381–394.

Gibbs, Jack P. and Dudley L. Poston. 1975. The Division of Labor: Conceptualization and Related Measures. *Social Forces* 53(3): 568–476.

Guesnier, Bernard. 1994. Regional Variation in New Firm Formation in France. *Regional Studies* 28(4):347–358.

Hart, Mark and Graham Gudgin. 1994. Spatial Variations in New Firm Formation in the Republic of Ireland, 1980–1990. *Regional Studies* 28(4):367–380.

Keeble, David and Sheila Walker. 1994. New Firms, Small Firms, and Dead Firms: Spatial Patterns and Determinants in the United Kingdom. *Regional Studies* 28(4):411–428.

Kusmin, Lorin D. 1994. *Factors Associated with the Growth of Local and Regional Economies: A Review of Selected Empirical Literature.* Washington, DC: U.S. Dept of Agriculture, Agriculture and Rural Economy Division, Economic Research Service, Staff Report No. AGES 9405.

LaPlant, David. 1992. The Effects of Regional Economic Characteristics on New Manufacturing Establishment Formation in Japan. Milwaukee, Wisconsin: Department of Economics, Marquette University, MA essay.

Organization for Economic Cooperation and Development [OECD]. 1993. *Regional Characteristics Affecting Small Business Formation: A Cross-National Comparison.* Co-operative Action Programme on Local Initiatives. ILE Notebooks No. 18.

Reynolds, Paul. 1994. Autonomous Firm Dynamics and Economic Growth in the United States, 1986–1990. *Regional Studies* 28(4):429–442.

Reynolds, Paul D. 1997. Who Starts New Firms? Preliminary Explorations of Firms-in-Gestation. *Small Business Economics* 9:449–462.

Reynolds, Paul D. and Wilbur R. Maki. 1990. *Business Volatility and Economic Growth*. Report Submitted to the U.S. Small Business Administration in fulfillment of Contract SBA 3067-0A-88.

Reynolds, Paul D. and Wilbur R. Maki. 1992. *Regional Characteristics Affecting Business Growth: Assessing Strategies for Promoting Regional Economic Well-Being*. Report Submitted to the Rural Poverty and Resources Program, The Ford Foundation, U.S. Small Business Administration in fulfillment of Grant 900-013.

Reynolds, Paul D., Brenda Miller, and Wilbur R. Maki. 1995. Explaining Regional Variation in Business Births and Deaths: U.S. 1976–88. *Small Business Economics* 7:389–407.

Reynolds, Paul D., Brenda Miller, and Wilbur R. Maki. 1994. Regional Characteristics Affecting Business Volatility in the United States: 1980–84. In Charlie Karlsson, et al. (Eds). *Small Business Dynamics: International, National and Regional Perspectives*. London: Routledge, pp. 78–115.

Reynolds, Paul, David J. Storey, and Paul Westhead. 1994. "Cross-National Comparisons of the Variation in New Firm Formation Rates." *Regional Studies* 28(4):443–456.

Reynolds, Paul and Sammis White. 1993. *Wisconsin's Entrepreneurial Climate Study*. Milwaukee, WI: Marquette University Center for the Study of Entrepreneurship. Final Report to Wisconsin Housing and Economic Development Authority.

Scherer, F. M. 1984. *Innovation and Growth: Schumpeterian Perspectives*. Cambridge, MA: The MIT Press.

Schreyer, Paul and Michelle Chaviox-Mannato. 1995. Quantitative Information on SMEs: OECD Approach, Data Collection and Examples of Analysis. Organization for Economic Co-operation and Development Working Party on SMEs: High-Level Workshop on "SMEs: Employment, Innovation, and Growth." Washington, DC: 16–17 June 1995.

Schumpeter, Joseph. 1942. (1975) *Capitalism, Socialism, and Democracy*. New York: Harper & Row.

Spilling, Olav R. 1995. Regional Variation of New Firm Formation: The Norwegian Case. Piacenza, Italy: Research in Entrepreneurship. 9th Workshop and Doctoral Seminar.

Storey, David J. 1991. "The Birth of New Firms – Does Unemployment Matter?" *Small Business Economics* 3:167–178.

Storey, David J. 1994. *Understanding the Small Business Sector*. London: Routledge.

Thurik, Roy. 1995. Small Firms, Large Firms, and Economic Growth. Presented at SMEs: Employment, Innovation and Growth: The Washington Workshop. Paris, France: Organization for Economic Cooperation and Development.

Tolbert, Charles M. and Molly Sizer Killian. 1987. Labor Market Areas for the United States. Washington, DC: U.S. Department of Agriculture, Agricultural and Rural Economy Division, Economic Research Service, Staff Report AFE870721.

U.S. Bureau of the Census. 1994. *Statistical Abstract of the United States: 1994* (114th Edition). Washington, DC: U.S. Government Printing Office.

136   **Paul D. Reynolds**

U.S. Department of Commerce. 1994. Regional Economic Information System. Washington, DC: Economic and Statistics Administration, Bureau of Economic Analysis, Regional Economic Measurement Division.

U.S. Small Business Administration, Office of Advocacy. 1988. *Handbook of Small Business Data: 1988*. Washington, DC: U.S. Government Printing Office.

U.S. Small Business Administration, Office of Advocacy. 1994. *Handbook of Small Business Data: 1994*. Washington, DC: U.S. Government Printing Office.

CHAPTER 5

Industry Structure, Entrepreneurship and the Macroeconomy: A Comparison of Ohio and Sweden, 1975–1995

Pontus Braunerhjelm and Bo Carlsson

1   Introduction

In the previous two chapters, the focus has been on the role of entrepreneurship in restructuring within industries (Chapter 3) and the contribution of entry and exit of firms ("turbulence") to economic growth (Chapter 4). Audretsch notes the stability of the size distribution of firms over time in various industries and finds that such stability is not necessarily the result of a lack of change in the population of firms but is more likely the result of a continuing process of entry and exit of firms. Reynolds' primary result is that economic growth is strongly associated with a high degree of turbulence. In this chapter we focus on another aspect of restructuring, namely, the interdependence among existing industry structure, entrepreneurship, and the macroeconomy. Clearly, poor macroeconomic conditions can stifle entrepreneurship. But it is also possible, even likely, that lack of entrepreneurship will negatively affect the macroeconomy, particularly economic growth.

The object of this chapter is to compare two economic regions with similar industrial structure and history, facing similar restructuring challenges in recent years, but responding differently to these challenges. This has resulted in different macroeconomic performance, not least in the role played by entrepreneurship.

The two regions we will focus on are the state of Ohio and the country of Sweden. They are similar in terms of population size (10.8 million in Ohio vs. 8.7 million in Sweden in 1993), overall level of development (GDP/capita in 1993 of $23,300 vs. $16,800) and industrial structure (21.5 percent vs. 18.3 percent of the total labor force in manufacturing in 1993). However, there are also distinct differences in terms of economic policy and industrial development in recent years. Economic policies, of course, define the rules of the game and thereby define the framework in which firms operate.

The chapter is organized as follows: We begin in the next section with an overview of the macroeconomic performance of Sweden and Ohio over the last two decades. This is followed by a review of the present industrial structure in both regions, of the overall changes therein since 1975, and of the role of entrepreneurship as reflected in net changes in the number of firms and employment in various industries. We then examine the major industry clusters in each country and their role in encouraging/discouraging new enterprise formation. The findings are discussed in the concluding section.

2   Overview of the Economic Development in Ohio and Sweden, 1975–1995

We have chosen in this study to view Ohio and Sweden as comparable regions, even though one is an independent country and the other is not. For reasons of data availability and convenience we have also chosen to use the United States as an entity to which both regions are compared.

As shown in Figure 5.1, both Ohio and Sweden have performed considerably worse than the United States and the Organization for Economic Cooperation and Development (OECD) area as a whole since 1975 in terms of gross domestic product (GDP) growth. Ohio kept pace with OECD and the rest of the U.S. until 1979 but then went into a steep decline until 1982. After that, there was stable growth until another recession hit in 1990. In Sweden, GDP stagnated in the late 1970s, grew modestly in the 1980s, and then declined sharply in the early 1990s.

As shown in Figure 5.2, manufacturing output in Ohio declined by 20 percent in 1978–83 and then did not exceed its 1978 level again until the early 1990s. In Sweden, manufacturing output was stagnant in 1975–84, then grew steadily until 1989, only to decline again until 1993. The recovery has been strong in both Ohio and Sweden in the last few years (recent strong growth in Ohio is not shown in the figure because of lack of comparable data).

The picture is somewhat different when it comes to employment growth; see Figure 5.3. Ohio has generally expanded employment more quickly than the OECD area as a whole but not as fast as the United States overall. Sweden tracked the OECD average in 1975–85 and then fell below it, disastrously so after 1990. It appears as though Sweden is now experiencing a crisis similar to that which Ohio went through ten years earlier.

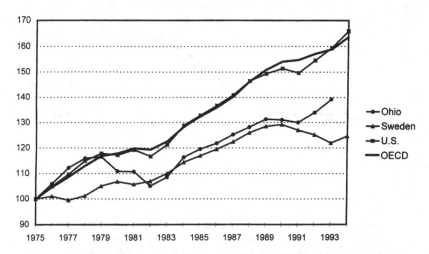

Figure 5.1. GDP in Ohio, Sweden, United States and OECD, 1975–94: Index, 1975 = 100. *Sources*: Sweden and the United States: IMF, 1991 and 1995, *International Financial Statistics, Yearbook* (Washington, D.C.: U.S. Government Printing Office). Ohio, 1963–1977: V. Renshaw, E. A. Trott, Jr., and H. L. Friedenberg, 1988, "Gross State Product by Industry, 1963–1986," *Survey of Current Business*, 68 (5), pp. 30–46. Ohio, 1977–1993: U.S. Department of Commerce, Bureau of Economic Analysis, Regional Economic Analysis Division, diskette file. OECD: OECD, 1993, *National Accounts. Main Aggregates. Volume 1, 1960–1991* (Paris: OECD), OECD data for 1993–1995: OECD, 1996, *Main Economic Indicators* (Paris: OECD).

Employment in manufacturing has declined in most countries over the last two decades, as reflected in the declining OECD average (Figure 5.4). However, the United States maintained its manufacturing employment until the early 1990s and then suffered a decline. (But of course, manufacturing employment declined as a share of total employment in the United States, similarly to developments in other countries.) In Ohio, manufacturing employment increased until 1979, then declined sharply until 1983 as a deep crisis hit, and has remained roughly constant subsequently. In Sweden, manufacturing employment has declined steadily and quite precipitously after 1989.

As shown in Figure 5.5, the unemployment rate increased from about 5.5 percent in the OECD area in the late 1970s to over 8 percent in the early 1980s, where it has basically remained to the present. In the United States, the unemployment rate developed similarly but with greater

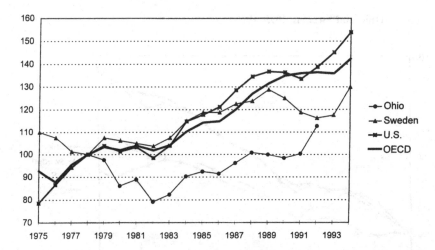

Figure 5.2. Manufacturing Output, 1975–94, in Ohio, Sweden, United States, and OECD: Index, 1978 = 100. *Sources*: Sweden: IMF, 1995, *International Financial Statistics*, *Yearbook* (Washington, D.C.: U.S. Government Printing Office). Ohio: U.S. Department of Commerce, *National Economic, Social, and Environmental Data Bank*, diskette file. OECD: 1978–1992: Real Value Added in Manufacturing, *Historical Statistics* (Paris: OECD), various issues, 1993–1994: Industrial Production, *Main Economic Indicators* (Paris: OECD), 1996. United States: *Economic Report of the President*, 1995 (Washington, D.C.: U.S. Government Printing Office), Table B-49.

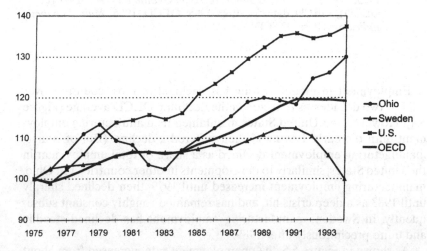

Figure 5.3. Civilian Employment, 1975–94, in Ohio, Sweden, United States, and OECD: Index, 1975 = 100. *Sources*: Sweden, United States, and OECD: OECD, *Historical Statistics* (Paris: OECD), various issues. Ohio: Regional Financial Associates, diskette files.

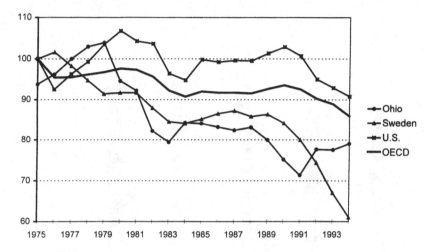

Figure 5.4. Employment in Manufacturing, 1975–94, in Ohio, Sweden,
United States, and OECD: Index, 1975 = 100. *Source*: Sweden, United
States, and OECD: OECD, *Historical Statistics* (Paris: OECD), various
issues. Ohio: Regional Financial Associates, diskette files.

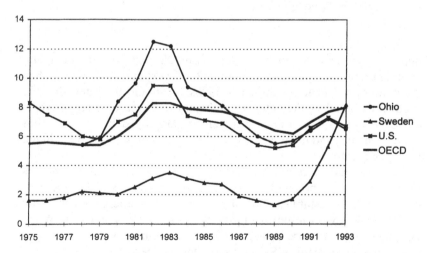

Figure 5.5. Unemployment as percentage of Total Labor Force in Ohio,
Sweden, United States, and OECD, 1975–93. *Source*: Sweden, United
States, and OECD: OECD, *Historical Statistics* (Paris: OECD), various
issues. Ohio: Regional Financial Associates, diskette files.

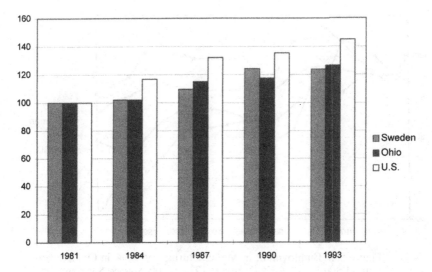

Figure 5.6. Number of Establishments in Ohio, Sweden, and the United States, 1981–93: Index 1981 = 100. *Source*: Ohio: U.S. Bureau of the Census, *Public Employment*, Series GE-No. 1, various years (Washington, D.C.: U.S. Government Printing Office). Regional Financial Associates, diskette files. Sweden: Swedish National Central Bureau of Statistics, diskette files. United States: U.S. Bureau of the Census, *County Business Patterns*, various issues (Washington, D.C.: U.S. Government Printing Office).

amplitude. The same is true, just more so, in Ohio. In Sweden, the unemployment rate stayed around 2–3 percent for most of the period but then increased dramatically in the early 1990s. (It should be noted that the Swedish data reflect the official numbers; the increase in recent years would be even more dramatic if persons employed in various labor market schemes and in involuntary early retirement were included in the unemployment numbers.)

Entrepreneurial activity is difficult to measure. A partial indicator is the net increase in the number of firms in any given activity. The increase in the number of establishments in all sectors in Sweden, Ohio, and the United States over the period 1981–1993 is shown in Figure 5.6. While the number of firms rose by nearly 45 percent in the U.S., it increased by only 24 and 26 percent in Sweden and Ohio, respectively.

Thus, all of these measures of macroeconomic performance indicate lagging performance in both Ohio and Sweden relative to the United States in the last two decades. While there are many factors which have contributed to this, we will focus here on entrepreneurship and structural features in these economies.

3   The Development of Industry Structure

The changes in the distribution of *employment* by industry have been similar in Sweden and Ohio to those in the United States. Mining, construction, and manufacturing have seen their share of total employment decline, while the service sectors have seen theirs increase. At the end of the period considered here (see Table 5.1), the main differences were the following: The employment structure was similar in Ohio to that in the United States, except for a larger manufacturing sector – a feature shared with Sweden. Sweden had a considerably larger share of total employment than both Ohio and the United States in construction; transportation, communications, and public utilities (TCPU); services; and particularly finance, insurance, and real estate (FIRE), while it had a smaller share in public administration[1] and retail trade. The low share for public administration and high shares for TCPU, FIRE, and services reflect the fact that a large portion of the latter three are in the public sector but not reported in the data as public administration.

If we look instead at the distribution of *establishments* by industry in 1993 (also in Table 5.1), differences emerge.[2] Sweden had more establishments than Ohio and the U.S. in manufacturing, TCPU, and particularly FIRE and considerably fewer in services and retail trade, while Ohio again showed a structure similar to that in the United States except for a somewhat larger manufacturing sector.

A comparison of the upper and lower parts of Table 5.1 shows that the shares of establishments in the construction industry are similar across all three countries, while the construction industry's share of employment is considerably higher in Sweden, indicating larger enterprises in this sector in Sweden than in Ohio and the United States. The fact that manufacturing's share of employment is consistently larger than its share of establishments, of course, means that manufacturing firms are considerably larger than firms in other sectors. The large share of employment in TCPU in Sweden corresponds to a similarly large share of establishments. A likely partial explanation is that the Swedish data include public sector employees who are counted as part of public administration in the Ohio and U.S. data. The small shares of both employment and establishments in the retail trade sector in Sweden indicate both that Sweden has relatively few retail establishments and that existing establishments are considerably smaller than those in Ohio and the United States (3.3 employees per establishment in 1993, compared

144   Pontus Braunerhjelm and Bo Carlsson

Table 5.1. *Distribution by Sector of Employment and Establishments in Sweden, Ohio, and the United States, 1993, Percentages*

	Distribution of Employment		
	Sweden	Ohio	U.S.
Mining	0.27	0.34	0.53
Construction	6.42	3.61	4.14
Manufacturing	20.16	20.96	16.33
Transportation, Communications & Public Utilities	8.54	4.15	5.24
Wholesale Trade	5.04	5.65	5.40
Retail Trade	8.00	18.04	17.86
Finance, Insurance & Real Estate	12.28	5.28	6.03
Services	33.96	26.93	27.22
Government	5.33	15.03	17.24
Total	100.00	100.00	100.00

	Distribution of Establishments		
	Sweden	Ohio	U.S.
Mining	0.18	0.39	0.46
Construction	10.30	9.84	9.58
Manufacturing	9.26	7.38	6.20
Transportation, Communications & Public Utilities	8.39	3.78	4.28
Wholesale Trade	8.87	7.92	8.16
Retail Trade	16.92	25.81	24.87
Finance, Insurance & Real Estate	26.21	8.29	9.76
Services	19.87	36.59	36.68
Total	100.00	100.00	100.00

Sources: U.S. Bureau of the Census, *Public Employment*, Series GE-No. 1, various years (Washington, D.C.: U.S. Government Printing Office). Regional Financial Associates, diskette files. U.S. Bureau of the Census, *County Business Patterns*, various issues (Washington D.C.: U.S. Government Printing Office). Swedish National Central Bureau of Statistics, diskette files.

to 13.9 in Ohio and 12.7 in the U.S.). By contrast, the large Swedish shares of both employment and establishments in the finance, insurance, and real estate industry reflect the existence of quite a large number of very small establishments. Finally, the service sector absorbs a larger share of total employment in Sweden than elsewhere (partly because of the inclusion of many public employees in this sector), but a considerably smaller share of the number of establishments. The Swedish service sector firms are comparable in size to those elsewhere, while the average establishment size in the economy as a whole is small: 7.0 employees per establishment vs. 19.9 in Ohio and 17.8 in the U.S. in 1993.

4 Net Growth in Number of Establishments

What can be said about firm formation? Table 5.2 summarizes the development of the number of establishments in each sector over the period 1981–1993. As noted earlier, the number of establishments increased at a higher rate in the United States than in either Sweden or Ohio. In Sweden, the number of establishments declined in mining, construction, and manufacturing, while in the United States only mining contracted and in Ohio manufacturing nearly held its own and the number of mining establishments was cut in half. By contrast, the number of establishments in finance, insurance, and real estate in Sweden doubled while it grew by 46 percent in the U.S. and 26 percent in Ohio.

Why did both Ohio and Sweden lag behind the United States in net creation of new establishments? The rightmost columns in Table 5.2 show that the rate of growth in the number of establishments outpaced that in the United States only in retail trade in Ohio and only in wholesale trade and finance, insurance and real estate in Sweden. In all other sectors, the net growth was lower than in the United States. In Sweden, the shortfall was particularly marked in construction; services; transport, communications, and public utilities; and manufacturing. In Ohio, the shortfall was more evenly spread (with the exception of mining). The relative decline of manufacturing in Sweden and Ohio is not surprising, given the large historical share of that industry in those regions. But their relatively poor performance in the service sector (the largest and fastest growing sector in the United States as a whole) contributed mightily to their lack of dynamism. And, as will be shown, these features are closely interrelated, suggesting a high degree of path dependence.

The hypothesis we want to examine here is that a lot of the lack of entrepreneurship depends on the existing structures; i.e., it depends on history. In order to carry out that analysis, we need to dig a little deeper, i.e., disaggregate more. In the next section, we will compare industry structure in Ohio and Sweden at the two-digit SIC level.

5 Comparison of Industry Structure and Development at the Two-Digit SIC Level

How similar is the composition of employment by industry in Ohio and Sweden at lower levels of aggregation, and how similar has the pattern of development been over time? These are the questions dealt with in this section.

Table 5.2. *Growth in Number of Establishments in Sweden, Ohio, and the United States, 1981–1993, by Industry*

	Number of establishments in 1993 relative to 1981			Growth in number of establishments in 1993/81 relative to the United States		
	Sweden	Ohio	U.S.	Sweden	Ohio	
Mining	0.832	0.497	0.874	0.952	0.569	
Construction	0.929	1.446	1.495	0.621	0.967	
Manufacturing	0.960	0.978	1.205	0.797	0.812	
Transportation, Communications & Public Utilities	1.075	1.314	1.556	0.691	0.845	
Wholesale Trade	1.473	1.083	1.305	1.129	0.830	
Retail Trade	1.054	1.269	1.253	0.841	1.013	
Finance, Insurance & Real Estate	2.002	1.263	1.458	1.373	0.867	
Services	1.175	1.362	1.717	0.684	0.793	
Total	1.237	1.264	1.449	0.854	0.872	

Sources: U.S. Bureau of the Census, *Public Employment*, series GE-No. 1, various years (Washington, D.C.: U.S. Government Printing Office). Regional Financial Associates, diskette files. U.S. Bureau of the Census, *County Business Patterns*, various issues (Washington, D.C.: U.S. Government Printing Office). Swedish National Central Bureau of Statistics, diskette files.

The similarities (and differences) in industry structure are examined by using so-called location quotients (similar to the concept of revealed comparative advantage in the trade literature). The basic idea is that the composition of industry in both Ohio and Sweden is compared to that of the United States. In the case of Ohio, if a given industry has the same share of Ohio's total employment as Ohio does of total U.S. employment (4.6 percent in 1995), its location quotient is 1.0; similarly for a Swedish industry whose share of Swedish employment corresponds to Sweden's "share" of U.S. employment (3.4 percent).

Table 5.3 shows the two-digit SIC industries for which Ohio exhibits the highest location quotients, ranked by the 1995 quotients. The primary metals industries, rubber and miscellaneous plastics products, and fabricated metal products are the largest industries relative to their U.S. counterparts, followed by stone, clay, and glass products; transportation equipment; and industrial machinery and equipment. The ranking of industries according to location quotients was nearly the same in 1975 as in 1995, in spite of the fact that the employment in these industries grew at very different rates. For example, the location quotient of the primary metals industries increased (by 17.1 percent), in spite of the fact that 1995 employment in the industry was only 63 percent of its 1975 level. This indicates that the employment in the primary metals industry was reduced even more in other parts of the United States. In fact, the rubber and miscellaneous plastics products industry is the only one among the top six industries in Ohio whose employment grew over the 20-year period. On the other hand, employment increased in miscellaneous repair services, personal services, and health services, whose location quotients also increased, i.e., whose share of the U.S. total increased.

Table 5.4 shows the corresponding data for Sweden. Metal mining; communications, health, education, and social services; and paper and allied products are the relatively largest industries in Sweden. But except for health, education, and social services and transportation services, all of the relatively largest industries saw their location quotients reduced between 1975 and 1993, contrary to the development in Ohio. But similarly to Ohio, the labor force in these large industries was reduced (again with the exception of the health, education, and social services sector, transportation services, and construction). Also, the number of establishments increased in most of these industries, in spite of declining employment.

Herein lies an important explanation for the relatively poor performance of both Ohio and Sweden relative to the United States in terms of employment growth over the last two decades. They either gained

Table 5.3. *Ohio Location Quotients, 1975 and 1995, Ranked by 1995 Location Quotients*

SIC	Description	Location quotients		Change in location quotients 1995/75	Employment ratio 1995/75	Number of establishments ratio 1995/75
		1975	1995			
33	Primary metal products	2.363	2.768	1.171	0.63	0.83
30	Rubber & misc. plastics products	2.144	2.272	1.060	1.36	1.78
34	Fabricated metal products	2.157	2.233	1.035	0.87	1.04
32	Stone,clay, and glass products	2.046	1.753	0.857	0.67	0.85
37	Transportation equipment	1.749	1.698	0.971	0.85	1.04
35	Industrial machinery and equipment	1.822	1.692	0.929	0.77	0.94
76	Misc. repair services	1.126	1.265	1.123	1.71	1.33
72	Personal services	1.026	1.255	1.223	1.53	1.30
89	Services, nec	2.332	1.242	0.533	1.27	0.48
80	Health services	1.013	1.121	1.107	2.07	2.69

Source: Regional Financial Associates, diskette files.

Table 5.4. *Swedish Location Quotients, 1975 and 1993, Ranked by 1993 Location Quotients*

SIC	Description	Location quotients 1975	Location quotients 1993	Change in location quotients 1993/75	Employment ratio 1993/75	Number of establishments ratio 1993/75
10	Metal mining	3.585	3.276	0.914	0.466	8.500
48	Communications	n.a.	2.241	n.a.	n.a.	n.a.
80,82-84	Health. educ. & social services	0.807	2.090	2.590	4.712	3.455
26	Paper and allied products	2.494	2.003	0.803	0.770	1.000
34	Fabricated metal products	1.685	1.616	0.959	0.825	1.284
37	Transportation equipment	1.743	1.521	0.873	0.786	1.237
24	Lumber and wood products	2.851	1.501	0.526	0.555	0.909
33	Primary metal industries	1.733	1.403	0.809	0.443	0.890
35	Industrial machinery and equipment	1.644	1.320	0.803	0.682	1.364
40-47	Transportation services	1.213	1.304	1.076	1.382	1.333
15-17	Construction	1.514	1.266	0.836	1.058	1.227

Sources: Swedish National Central Bureau of Statistics, diskette files. U.S. Bureau of the Census, *County Business Patterns* various issues (Washington, D.C.: U.S. Government Printing Office).

shares in declining industries (this is true for Ohio) or lost shares in declining industries (as in Sweden). Ohio also gained shares in such rapidly growing industries as holding and other investment offices, social services, business services, and transportation services – but not enough to attain a location quotient exceeding 1.0 in 1995. In Sweden, the most rapidly growing industries (in terms of location quotients) were all service industries: communications, health, education, and social services, and electric, gas, and sanitary services (although, as indicated earlier, a significant share of the increases in these sectors may be due to improved statistical coverage later in the period).

6   Industry Clusters

The industry analysis carried out above is suggestive, but even more insight is gained when the interdependence among industries is also taken into account. Industrial transformation may be the result of broader changes affecting not just individual sectors but whole clusters of industries. Put differently, it is hard enough to change the structure and orientation of an industry in response to new market requirements, but it is even harder when the industry is part of a whole cluster of inter-dependent activities formed over several decades. On the other hand, the existence of strong linkages may also give rise to new market opportunities.

In what follows we will draw upon previous work (see Braunerhjelm and Carlsson, 1996) in which we have identified the most important industry clusters in Sweden and Ohio. The method we used is summa-rized in Appendix 1.

Having surveyed the economic landscape in Ohio and Sweden over the last 20 years by employing conventional industry data, we turn now to a different (and somewhat novel) type of analysis, namely, industry clusters. The main idea is that rather than looking at each industry separately, it makes sense to try to understand industrial transformation as the result of broader changes affecting not just individual sectors but whole clusters of industries. How then can one define such industry clusters?

The methodology chosen for the present analysis is outlined in Appendix 1. We focus on two key ideas: that linkages are important, and that a certain concentration of activity is required to form a cluster.

The results of the various steps used to define clusters are shown in Tables 5.5 and 5.6. The industries which meet the respective criteria (employment exceeding 10,000; location quotient exceeding 1.3; and number of other industries with which the industry interacts at a certain

Table 5.5. Ohio Cluster Summary, 1995

SIC Code	Core industries	Number of establ. 1995	Employment 1995	Crit.: >10,000	Location quotients 1995	Crit.: >1.5	# of contacts excl. itself	Crit.: >4	Total cluster empl.	Total cluster establ.	Three criteria met
35	Industrial machinery and equipment	4,449	158,629	*	1.692	*	15	*	326,995	11,082	•
34	Fabricated metal products	2,942	148,277	*	2.233	*	13	*	254,878	6,111	•
37	Transportation equipment	531	138,179	*	1.698	*	11	*	170,916	794	•
33	Primary metal products	668	91,732	*	2.768	*	10	*	124,384	1,094	•
30	Rubber & misc. plastics products	1,388	101,023	*	2.272	*	5	•	35,773	594	•
32	Stone, clay, and glass products	1,005	44,732	*	1.753	*	5	•	25,265	686	•
50-7,59	Wholesale & retail trade	67,460	898,119	*	0.975		13	*	957,483	86,903	
73,87,89	Bus. serv, engin. & mgmt serv, serv, nec	23,601	391,948	*	0.879		20	*	767,283	55,828	
80,82-3,86	Health, educ. & social services	46,460	743,667	*	1.058		1		485,966	19,496	
40-7	Transportation services	8,595	123,273		0.708		18	*	247,969	20,891	
15,16,17	Construction	29,100	208,282	*	0.878		7	*	197,442	2,115	
60-4	Financial services & insurance	13,276	211,272	*	0.874		5	•	138,667	23,410	
28	Chemicals and allied products	709	45,345		0.927		20	*	112,885	8,571	
48	Communications	1,448	47,185		0.814		15	•	111,675	2,110	
58	Eating and drinking places	21,590	346,132	*	1.023		2		99,076	3,674	
49	Electricity, gas, and sanitary services	540	46,388		0.983		15	•	80,159	6,042	
70,72,76	Hotels, etc., personal & misc services	13,945	126,325	*	0.867		4		56,429	794	
27	Printing and publishing	2,737	77,525		1.073		2		44,757	5,970	
65,67	Real estate, holding & oth invest off	9,004	64,207		0.855		11	•	39,182	1,672	
26	Paper and allied products	419	33,177		1.037		10	•	39,157	6,635	
20	Food and kindred products	721	56,580		0.721		4		26,317	402	
79	Amusement & recreation services	3,830	48,579		0.781		2		22,340	344	
38	Instruments and related products	480	30,040		0.764		2		14,593	1,390	
75	Automotive repair and services	7,633	40,965		0.831		2		13,371	258	
23	Apparel and other textile products	394	14,273		0.327		4		10,752	2,421	
24	Lumber and wood products	1,145	24,211		0.690		2		8,848	295	
39	Miscellaneous manufacturing	711	18,505		1.027		1		7,648	437	
25	Furniture and fixtures	418	16,255		0.692		0		6,652	309	
13	Crude petroleum and natural gas	548	7,822		0.527		5	•	3,045	95	
22	Textile mill products	90	3,537		0.114		6	•	2,979	252	
29	Petroleum refining and related products	182	5,291		0.768		2		2,810	86	
14	Nonmetallic minerals mining	291	4,846		1.059		0		1,835	76	
12	Coal mining	120	4,085		0.842		0		925	67	
31	Leather and leather products	43	1,955		0.371		0		770	27	
10	Metal mining	8	191		0.079		1		446	12	
21	Tobacco products	0	0		0.000		0		40	2	
	TOTAL	278,764	4,474,210	*					4,474,210	278,764	

Table 5.6. Swedish Industry Clusters, 1993

SIC	Description	Employment 1975	Employment 1993	Crit: >10,000	Location quotients 1975	Location quotients 1993	Crit: >1.5	# of contacts excl. itself	Crit: >4	Total cluster employment	Three criteria met
40-47	Transportation services	101,009	139,740	*	1.161	1.698	*	18	*	324,412	*
35	Industrial machinery and equipment	132,532	90,361	*	1.871	2.041	*	15	*	227,267	*
36	Electronic & other electric equipment	76,442	60,133	*	1.554	1.710	*	18	*	188,703	*
34	Fabricated metal products	95,056	78,387	*	1.918	2.498	*	13	*	162,029	*
37	Transportation equipment	115,064	90,452	*	1.984	2.352	*	11	*	137,060	*
28	Chemicals and allied products	36,309	38,170	*	1.058	1.652	*	20	*	111,556	*
33	Primary metal industries	76,703	33,953	*	1.973	2.169	*	10	*	93,984	*
26	Paper and allied products	60,794	46,789	*	2.839	3.097	*	10	*	49,536	*
65,67	Real est., holding & oth. invest. offices	37,404	65,288	*	1.293	1.841	*	11	*	18,156	*
32	Stone, clay, and glass products	36,050	18,376		1.768	1.525	*	5	*	13,355	*
80,82-3,86	Health, educ., social serv., memb. org.	228,075	220,887	*	0.921	0.665		1		453,715	
70,72,76	Hotels, pers.& misc. repair serv.	37,924	41,734	*	0.586	0.607		4		304,784	
48	Communications	43	94,967		0.001	3.466	*	15	*	248,253	
50-57,59	Wholesale & retail trade	396,394	402,282	*	1.082	1.255		13	*	219,552	
60-4	Financial serv. & insurance	61,515	107,779	*	0.542	0.943		5	*	70,722	
58	Eating & drinking places	33,559	42,945	*	0.291	0.269		2		63,691	
49	Electric, gas, and sanitary services	14,814	30,950	*	0.533	1.388	*	15	*	55,105	
27	Printing and publishing	57,510	52,510	*	1.568	1.538	*	2		35,548	
79	Amusement & recreation services	22,937	69,812	*	1.123	2.377	*	2		29,888	
20	Food and kindred products	79,220	66,746	*	1.416	1.801	*	4		25,719	
30	Rubber and misc. plastics products	26,164	19,450		1.203	0.926		5	*	16,412	
24	Lumber and wood products	69,273	38,461	*	3.245	2.321	*	2		13,395	
73,87,89	Business, engineering serv., services nec	73,195	171,220	*	0.757	0.813		20	*	12,212	
22	Textile mill products	28,330	10,248		0.965	0.697		6	*	9,381	
38	Instruments and related products	113,115	14,257	*	4.124	0.767	*	2		7,792	
29	Petroleum and coal products	2,472	3,134		0.379	0.963		2		5,959	
23	Apparel and other textile products	25,729	6,074		0.612	0.294		4		4,623	
13	Oil & gas extraction	2	14		0.000	0.002		5	*	4,551	
75	Auto repair, services, and parking	27,160	17,997	*	1.792	0.773		2		4,260	
25	Furniture and fixtures	16,093	12,928	*	1.130	1.166		0		2,974	
39	Miscellaneous manufacturing industries	7,538	5,678		0.544	0.667		1		2,506	
10	Metal mining	12,344	5,752		4.081	5.066	• •	1		2,263	
14	Nonmetallic minerals, except fuels	6,734	3,315		1.708	1.534	*	0		1,797	
31	Leather and leather products	3,324	943		0.388	0.379		1		264	
21	Tobacco products	1,353	1,050	*	0.531	1.265		0		226	
	TOTAL	2,112,180	2,102,782		1.000	1.000					

level in terms of input/output coefficients) are marked with an asterisk (*) in the appropriate column. The industries which meet all three criteria are listed in descending order of total cluster employment, followed by nonqualifying industries (i.e., those meeting fewer than the three criteria) in descending order of cluster employment.[3]

As shown in the tables, six clusters are identified in Ohio and seven in Sweden, representing 21.0 and 32.3 percent of total employment, respectively. According to the selected criteria, the largest clusters in Ohio are industrial machinery and equipment, followed by fabricated metal products and transportation equipment; see Table 5.5. All of the identified clusters consist of traditional, "hard-core" manufacturing activities, reflecting Ohio's long-standing traditions. It turns out that the location quotient criterion is the dominant one in Ohio (as well as in Sweden). However, the selection criterion would have to be reduced from 1.3 to 1.0 in order for more industries to qualify, but only one of these (electronic and other electric equipment) also meets the "contacts" criterion. The employment criterion would have to be raised above 50,000 and the "contacts" criterion above 5 to be constraining.

The corresponding results for Sweden are shown in Table 5.6. The seven clusters identified in Sweden contain a mixture of service and manufacturing industries. The largest is transportation services and the second largest, communications (i.e., postal and telecommunications services). This result is somewhat surprising. It is due in large measure to high location quotients, which, in turn, reflect the inclusion of government workers in these sectors in the Swedish data but not in the Ohio data. Further exploration of this finding is certainly warranted. The other identified clusters are traditional manufacturing industries for which Sweden has long been known: industrial machinery and equipment; fabricated metal products; transportation equipment; primary metal industries; and paper and allied products. This list contains no surprises. If the location quotient criterion were lowered to 1.2, one more industry (construction) would qualify. If the criterion were reduced to 1.1, another four industries would qualify: electronics and other electric equipment; real estate, holding and other investment offices; food and kindred products; and amusement and recreation services. On the other hand, if the criterion were raised to 1.4, transportation services would no longer qualify, and primary metal industries would not qualify if the limit were set at 1.5. Further inspection of Table 5.6 reveals that the employment criterion would have to be raised above 30,000 and the number of "contacts" above 10 in order to be constraining.

Thus, the list of selected clusters appears not only sensible but also fairly robust to alternate assumptions in both regions. That all of the

selected clusters in Ohio and most of those in Sweden are in manufacturing is not really surprising, in spite of the rapid growth in many service
industries in recent years. They still do not qualify as "clusters" under the
criteria chosen here, in most cases because their location quotients rarely
exceed 1.0 (i.e., neither Sweden nor Ohio has a comparative advantage
in service industries) but also because their linkages to other industries
are relatively weak. Only rarely do they constitute a core which generates other economic activity; more often they provide support for other
industries. Perhaps this is inherent in "service" industries. The most
notable non-qualifier here is business services, which has numerous linkages to other industries and therefore has a cluster employment twice as
large as the core industry employment. But its location quotient was
0.879 in Ohio in 1995 and only 0.521 in Sweden in 1993; both had
increased by about 8 percent since 1975.

It turns out that the four largest manufacturing clusters are exactly
the same in Ohio and Sweden. The industrial machinery and equipment
industry constitutes the core of the largest cluster (in terms of total
employment) in Ohio and the largest manufacturing cluster in Sweden.
Fabricated metal products, transportation equipment, and primary metal
products are the next largest manufacturing clusters in both regions. The
combined employment in these four clusters is 877,200 (19.6 percent of
total employment) in Ohio vs. 479,400 (14.7 percent) in Sweden. The
number of establishments in these clusters is 19,081 (6.8 percent of the
total) in Ohio vs. 31,658 (6.3 percent) in Sweden.

7   Discussion and Concluding Remarks

In spite of all our efforts to avoid a priori notions of what constitute
major agglomerations of economic activity, the industry clusters we have
come up with contain no surprises and are all basically in mature industries. This suggests that the path dependence is extremely strong. At least
at the surface, i.e., at the relatively high level of aggregation in this study,
there is not much indication of industrial transformation taking place in
either Ohio or Sweden. This seems partially to support Audretsch and
Feldman's result (1996, partly drawing on Klepper, 1996) that the
beneficial effects of clusters diminish or even turn negative in the mature
phase of the product cycle.

An analysis of the development over the period 1975–1995 of the clusters identified for Ohio shows that all of them declined in terms of
employment. The electronic and other electrical equipment and primary
metal products clusters also suffered declines in the number of establishments. This is hardly indicative of dynamism. Wholesale and retail

trade and business services, etc., grew rapidly but did not qualify as the core of an industry cluster according to the criteria used here. They also saw substantial increases in the number of establishments.

Looked at from another angle, none of the fastest growing two-digit industries (except business services) in Ohio is among the clusters we have identified. Quite the contrary, all of the industries which constitute the core of a cluster are at the bottom of the list of growing industries.

Thus, if Ohio seems to be lacking in entrepreneurship, this is at least in part due to the legacy of the past. The industries which once led Ohio to a leading position in industrial development among the states may now be retarding the transition to a more modern structure. At the same time, it may also be true that lack of vigorous entrepreneurship has contributed to the relatively slow transformation of the economy.

Unfortunately, we are unable because of lack of data to make a similar comparison over time for Sweden. But because the clusters we have identified are largely the same in both countries, the same conclusion is likely to hold for Sweden as well.

And yet, this may be too rash and too pessimistic a conclusion. Studies in both Ohio and Sweden indicate that new firms tend to continue to cluster in industries in which the region exhibits traditional strength. For example, recent studies of the aerospace cluster in northeast Ohio (Berry et al., 1996) and the biotechnology sector in Ohio (Berry, 1996) show that both of these clusters draw heavily upon traditional strength in the machinery industry in Ohio. The aerospace cluster focuses on jet engines and parts, relying on strength in the supporting machinery industries. Similarly, the biotech activity is closely tied to instruments, measurement equipment, and industrial machinery – also areas of traditional strength in Ohio. Studies by Rickne (1996) on new technology-based firms and industrial renewal in Sweden and by Holmén and Jacobsson (1996) on industry clusters in western Sweden also suggest strong path dependence. Clustering is also revealed in the direct foreign investment by knowledge-intensive Swedish firms, which tend to locate their foreign operations in regions in which their respective industries are already well represented (Braunerhjelm and Svensson, 1996).

Thus, there is reason to suspect that there is much more of a dynamic nature going on than meets the eye at the aggregate level. Therefore, one of the objects of our continued research will be to examine whether or not the old "flagship" industries are stagnating or continuing to evolve. What is the role of entrepreneurship in their recent development? What shifts have there been in the size distribution of firms in these clusters? What do the gross and net exit and entry numbers show? Is there renewal taking place, and are those renewal processes similar or different in different settings? These are some of the questions for further analysis.

Having come up with a methodology for identifying industry clusters, we have reached the first station on a much longer journey. The next stage will be to select a subset of clusters in each country and do a more in-depth analysis and comparison of the specific linkages (in terms of both interaction and spatial concentration) among various entities within each country or region.

Appendix 1

The methodology chosen for the definition of industry clusters is the following: The focus is on two key ideas: that linkages are important, and that a certain concentration of activity is required to form a cluster. We use four steps to identify clusters:

1 It is desirable that the clusters we identify be fairly broadly defined. Therefore, we started with two-digit SIC industries. Broad industry definitions facilitate identification of important linkages via input–output tables which may be difficult to obtain at lower levels of aggregation. We imposed the condition that to be considered the core in a cluster, the industry should have total employment exceeding 10,000.

2 Each core industry should constitute a significant share of economic activity in the relevant fields. Therefore, for each industry we calculated the "location quotient," i.e., Ohio's and Sweden's share of total U.S. employment in the industry. This means that an industry which is large relative to other industries in the same region may not qualify, unless it is also large relative to the same industry elsewhere. We imposed the condition that the location quotient at the end of the period studied should be at least 1.3 (i.e., the region should have at least 30 percent more than its "fair share" of U.S. employment in the industry).

3 Industries which have significant linkages to other industries should be included and others excluded. Thus, we obtained the commodity by commodity total requirement coefficients from the U.S. input–output table for 1987 (two-digit level).[4] We counted the number of both horizontal and vertical coefficients for each industry exceeding certain levels (0.1, 0.15, and 0.2, respectively); each coefficient meeting the requirement was

referred to as a "contact." The sum of the number of contacts (excluding the industry's deliveries to and purchases from itself) was computed. The distribution of the number of contacts across industries was found to be similar at all three levels. We chose the 0.15 level and imposed the criterion that the number of contacts should exceed four in order for an industry to be considered the core of a cluster. An industry may fail to meet this criterion either by having fewer "intense" contacts with other industries or by not having sufficiently close links to at least five other industries.

4 We calculated the total employment in each cluster by adding to each core industry its share of "contact" industry employment as represented by the input–output coefficients. This means that a core industry with few contacts has larger employment in the core than in the cluster, whereas the industries with the most significant contacts have considerably larger cluster employment than core industry employment.

Notes

[1] It should be noted, however, that "public administration" is defined rather narrowly in Sweden, consisting of state and local government, defense, police, and fire-fighting services. The "public sector" is much more broadly defined, but in the data reported here, public employees are not shown separately but are distributed to the various industries in which they are employed (mainly services). For Ohio and the United States, by contrast, all government workers are reported as a separate "industry" (Gov). Thus, the distribution of employment by industry is not strictly comparable between the regions for this reason, particularly with respect to government and public administration. Also, the statistical coverage of public employment in Sweden was poor in the 1970s but improved dramatically in the 1980s. Thus, the increase in employment in services and public administration prior to 1984 is exaggerated in Table 5.1.

[2] Public administration/government is omitted from the lower portion of Table 5.1 because of lack of comparable data.

[3] Because of the fact that the total employment in each cluster is obtained by adding to each core industry its share of "contact" industry employment as represented by the input–output coefficients, a core industry with few contacts has larger employment in the core than in the cluster, whereas the industries with the most significant contacts have considerably larger cluster employment than core industry employment.

[4] The U.S. input/output table for 1987 is the latest one available. Input/output tables for both Ohio and Sweden are currently not available for later years. The U.S. input/output table for 1975 has been used for certain calculations for 1975.

References

Audretsch, D., 1995. *Innovation and Industry Evolution*, Cambridge, MA, and London: MIT Press.

Audretsch, D., and Feldman, M., 1996. "Innovative Clusters and the Industry Life Cycle," *Review of Industrial Organization*, 11 (2), pp. 253–273.

Berry, D.E., 1996. "Technological Innovation and Diffusion in Cleveland's Biomedical/Biotechnology Industries," mimeo, Case Western Reserve University, May.

Berry, D.E., Johnson, S., and Stavros, J., 1996. "Technological Innovation and Diffusion in Cleveland's Aerospace Industry," mimeo, Case Western Reserve University, May.

Braunerhjelm, P., and Carlsson, B., 1996. "Industry Clusters in Ohio and Sweden, 1975-1995," mimeo, The Industrial Institute for Economic and Social Research and Case Western Reserve University.

Braunerhjelm, P., and Svensson, R., 1996. "Host Country Characteristics and Agglomeration in Foreign Direct Investment," *Applied Economics*, 28, pp. 833–840.

Economic Report of the President, 1995. Washington, D.C.: U.S. Government Printing Office.

Holmén, M., and Jacobsson, S., 1996. "Characterising the Competence Base of a Region: The Case of Western Sweden." Paper presented at the conference on Regional Production Systems in the Nordic Countries, Copenhagen, May 31–June 2.

IMF, 1991 and 1995. *International Financial Statistics Yearbook*. Washington, D.C.: International Monetary Fund.

Klepper, S., 1996. "Entry, Exit, Growth, and Innovation over the Product Life Cycle," *American Economic Review*, 86 (3), pp. 562–583.

OECD, various years. *Historical Statistics*. Paris: OECD.

OECD, 1996. *Main Economic Indicators*. Paris: OECD.

OECD, 1993. *National Accounts. Main Aggregates. Volume 1, 1960–1991*. Paris: OECD.

Regional Financial Associates, diskette files.

Renshaw, V., Trott, Jr., E.A., and Friedenberg, H.L., 1988. "Gross State Product by Industry, 1963–1986," *Survey of Current Business*, 68 (5), pp. 30–46.

Rickne, A., 1996. "New Technology Based Firms: An Exploratory Study of Technology Exploitation and Industrial Renewal," mimeo, Department of Industrial Management and Economics, Chalmers University of Technology, Gothenburg.

Swedish National Central Bureau of Statistics, diskette files.

U.S. Bureau of the Census, *County Business Patterns*, various issues. Washington, D.C.: U.S. Government Printing Office.

U.S. Bureau of the Census, *Public Employment*, Series GE-No. 1, various issues. Washington, D.C.: U.S. Government Printing Office.

U.S. Department of Commerce, Bureau of Economic Analysis, Regional Economic Analysis Division, diskette files.

U.S. Department of Commerce, *National Economic, Social, and Environmental Data Bank*, diskette file.

PART II

Financing Entrepreneurship and SMEs

CHAPTER 6

Small Business Failure: Failure to Fund or Failure to Learn?

Robert Cressy

1   Introduction

The distribution of business failure by time trading has two salient characteristics demanding explanation. Firstly, the distribution is inverse U-shaped, with a positive skew. Most business failures occur in the first two years of existence. Thereafter, riskiness declines monotonically with time trading, being very low for the mature business.[1] Secondly, this distribution is surprisingly stable over time. Virtually the same mean failure rate (11 percent of the stock of value added tax [VAT]-registered businesses) occurs throughout the whole decade of the 1980s (Ganguly, 1985; Storey, 1994). This fact must be viewed as quite astonishing in the light of the vast economic changes wrought in that period, which witnessed the massive privatisation and deregulation programs of the Thatcher government and large changes in the structure of industry.

The Literature

These facts seem to have escaped the notice of economists. Despite the publication of the Ganguly book some ten years ago, to the present author's knowledge, no explanation has been offered.

What might explain these facts about failure? On an intuitive level, it is tempting to argue that if failure is largely independent of macro-economic conditions and seems to respond little to changes in industry structure, it must be determined by more fundamental underlying factors such as the levels of human capital embodied in the business's employees (including, critically, the owners). These factors may be less changeable than the macroeconomy and therefore provide some basis as an underlying stability of the failure distribution. This, in fact, is the thesis put forward in Cressy (1996b), where it is shown that human capital significantly explains the failure rate of UK startups over a three-and-

161

half-year period. Financial capital is shown to be relatively unimportant, or determined by human capital. Other empirically oriented work in a similar vein (henceforth referred to as the "static" literature) also indicates a significant role for human capital – though often in conjunction with business assets (see, e.g., Evans and Jovanovic, 1989; Bates, 1989; Holtz-Eakin et al., 1994a,b).

Mata (1994), in one of the few panel data studies in this area (henceforth referred to as the "dynamic" literature), shows that current, rather than initial, employment size is a predictor of imminent failure of small Portuguese businesses. He is also able to identify the importance of firm-specific heterogeneity in the determination of firm growth rates. However, his data does not permit the full analysis of the impact of human and financial capital on survival over time. Audretsch and Mahmood (1995) on US panel data show that current financial conditions measured by the interest rate (etc.) are also significant predictors of imminent failure.

Audretsch (1994), moreover, finds on similar data that among the factors determining survival, time trading of the business is significant. This finding is consistent with another important strand of theory in the literature, which emphasises the role of *learning* in the process of business evolution. Jovanovic (1982), in an influential theoretical contribution, argues that we should expect early failure to predominate because business is an *experiment*. Learning about one's costs as an entrepreneur is something that can only be done by *entering* business. Early exit is likely, in that priors are dispersed and "bad news" plays a "disproportionate" role in the entrepreneur's estimate of her costs. Importantly, the empirical literature seems largely to confirm the Jovanovic model's predictions. However, the model is not specific enough consistently to generate the inverse U-shaped curve of failure that we have identified.

The Jovanovic model also assumes that all firms start with the same initial cost estimates and hence sizes. By contrast Frank (1986) argues that there are important differences in the priors of individuals starting in business that result in differing initial firm sizes and subsequent performance. One interpretation of this thesis might be that some general learning has already taken place, for example, via work experience in the sector. This is consistent with the human capital approach of Cressy discussed earlier and provides us with an important element in the dynamic modelling process.

The Current Study

This study explores empirically the timing of early business failure. The theoretical basis of the study differs from that of other work on the same phenomenon – using the standard entry–exit model of industrial economics – by drawing on the Jovanovic idea of business as a learning experiment and combining this with the human capital approach of Cressy (1996b). The learning process that takes place in our model, in contrast to that of Jovanovic, is embodied in the stock of human capital that accumulates through the individual's lifetime and includes the business experience implicit in time trading. Variations in this human capital, measured at startup, are treated as proxy for variations in business cost prior distributions, ignored in the Jovanovic model. By the nature of the Bayesian updating process, individuals with more dispersed priors will react more to temporary changes in the environment. Therefore, their sales will display greater temporal variation than those of their older colleagues.[2]

The database is a panel of some 2,000 UK startups commencing in business during 1988 and tracked on a quarterly basis thereafter.[3] A large range of human and financial capital variables, together with survival data, is recorded. This makes it ideally suited to testing a model in which these variables play a central role. The econometric estimation techniques employed in the study are those of duration analysis using the logistic and hazard function approaches.

Human Capital and Business Dynamics

Human capital, in the static literature, is identified with the endowments of individual proprietors at the startup stage. However, the important contribution of Jovanovic (1982), as we have seen, is to view business as a learning experiment. This adds a *temporal* dimension to the analysis. Imminent failure may thus be related not merely to *initial* values of human and financial capital but to *current* ones also. Human and financial capital are both properly regarded as *stocks* that can accumulate through time and whose current values may influence the likelihood of business survival.[4] Initial values of the stocks (e.g., proxying the parameters of the ability-prior of the entrepreneurs, in the case of the human capital) then play a role in shifting (and pivoting) the survival curve rather than in moving along it.

The empirical failure density for one of the cohorts of our sample of startups (88q2) is shown in Figure 6.1.[5] The density is bell-shaped and positively skewed. Peak failure occurs at about six quarters or eighteen months, mirroring the UK VAT deregistrations data (Ganguly, 1985). However, our density has higher failure rates in the early periods, reflecting the higher proportion of the smallest businesses in the sample. The reasons for this shape are to be explained in the following model.[6]

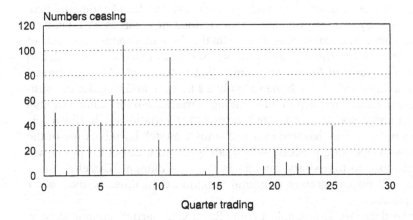

Figure 6.1. Survival Rates for Business Startups: 1988q2 Cohort Cessation Rate by Quarters

2   The Theory

The capital stocks of entrepreneurs influence survival via individual and aggregate hazard functions. Statistically, the hazard function shows the probability of failure in the next instant given that failure has not occurred to date. The general form of the hazard function for the economy is defined as

$$h(t) = \Pr\{\tau\varepsilon(t, t + dt)|\tau > t\}$$
$$= f(t)dt/[1 - F(t)] \tag{1}$$

where τ is the (random) time to failure of the business, $f(t)$ and $F(t)$ are the density and cdf of failure at t, respectively, and $h(t)$ is the conditional failure rate or hazard function. This yields an expression for the failure density, $f(t)$:

$$f(t) = h(t) \exp\left\{-\int_0^t h(\tau)dt\right\} \tag{2}$$

which has slope

$$f'(t) = \left[-h(t)^2 + h'(t)\right] \exp\left\{-\int_0^t h(\tau)dt\right\} \tag{3}$$

Now, the expression in brackets needs to be of variable sign with t if inverted U-shaped distribution is to arise. Pursuing this, we can show that the aggregate density, $f(t)$, can be written as the weighted sum of the component densities, $f_i(t)$, $i = 1, 2$ for the High and Low human capital groups, respectively. Assuming the hazard rate is constant for the High group the sign of $f'(t)$ is determined by the slope of the hazard for the Low human capital group. This slope, h'_2, can be written

$$dt_2(t)/dt = H_c \cdot c'(t) + H_e e'(t) \tag{4}$$

where $H = H\{c(t), e(t)\}$ is the hazard rate as a function of human and financial capital stocks $c(t)$ and $e(t)$, respectively. If we assume that $H_c, H_e < 0$ (larger stocks at t will reduce imminent failure) and that $c' > 0$, $e' < 0$ (human capital increases, and financial capital decreases, with time trading), then we can find functions $H(t)$ for which f' is positive for $t < t^*$ and negative for $t > t^*$.

The form of the human capital and financial stocks is plausibly linear:

$$c(t) = c(0) + ct; c(0), c > 0 \tag{5}$$

$$e(t) = e(0) + pt - et; e(0), c, p > 0 \tag{6}$$

where $c(0)$ and $e(0)$ are the initial stocks of human and financial capital of group 2, pt the level of retained profits at time t, and c, e the rates of appreciation and depreciation of the stocks through time trading, respectively. This formulation then implies that the initial stocks and reserves for group 2 will be positively related to survival, and that in the case of the financial stocks, the faster the rate of run-down the greater the failure rate.[7]

This line of reasoning is thus consistent with the idea of the aggregate failure distribution resulting from an initial division of the population of entrepreneurs into Low and High human capital individuals, and with a process of *selection* occurring through time. More specifically, older proprietors will be expected to start off with higher human, and hence financial, capital stocks than younger proprietors (Cressy, 1996b). However, stocks of both younger and older individuals may grow over time. In particular, financial stocks will respond positively to retained profits from operations ($p(t)$), and negatively to drawdown to fund adverse changes in costs of operations ($-et$). Accumulated profits may be withdrawn as owner earnings, invested in fixed capital, or retained as reserves. Accumulated reserves create more viable businesses, since the chances of profits falling below the opportunity cost threshold[8] are lower the greater the accumulated financial capital stocks, ceteris paribus.

Older proprietors will have either no growth or gradual growth since their need to learn in business is smaller and their decisions will respond less to short run news (estimates of costs being close to true values). Thus the overdraft facilities of mature proprietors will not need to take up the slack as a result of judgement errors. Young proprietors by contrast will grow erratically, as they respond sharply to short run news. Their mistakes in turn will cause them to rely on initial and subsequent overdrafts to cope with poor investment decisions that have raised their costs. Thus younger proprietors will be likely to deplete their financial capital stocks as time passes and may be making increasing demands on the bank for overdraft funds which simply stave off their demise.[9] If the immature entrepreneurs' profits grow at all, they will do so at an unsteady rate, making failure more likely. The resulting scenario is that businesses run by the youthful will tend to drop out of the cohort early on, leaving an increasingly viable set of firms, run largely by mature owners, continuing into the future.

3   The Data

The data used in this chapter comes from a panel of some 2,000 startups who commenced business by opening a business account with a major UK bank in 1988. Some eighty variables are recorded. The variables are in four subsets:

- a *Background information* on the businesses and their proprietors – including legal type, industry, employees, proprietor age, qualifications, etc., available only at the startup stage;
- b *Bank account information* – borrowing parameters, charges, account turnover, etc., available on a quarterly/six-monthly basis;
- c *Survival information* – when the account terminated, available on a quarterly/six-monthly basis;
- d *Macro environment information* – industry, gross domestic product (GDP), base rates, etc., available on a quarterly basis.

Appendix A to this chapter contains detailed definitions and descriptions of the main variables. The main variable groups are listed below for ease of reference.

Key Variable Groups

Time Trading (T).   The number of quarters from the opening of the business account.

Failure (D).   Failure event and time to failure – whether the business account, opened in 1988, was still open in quarter *t*; how long the account survived, etc.

Human Capital
HC1 General human capital – the number and average age of proprietors.
HC2 Specific human capital – work and business experience in the area of the start; time the business (if acquiring new management) has traded; and startup model.
HC3 Specific human capital: education – the fraction of the business's proprietors with O and A levels and degrees, respectively.
HC4 Specific human capital: vocational qualifications – trade apprenticeship, Higher National Certificate (HNC), Higher National Diploma (HND), and professional qualifications of the proprietors.

Financial Capital
F1 Borrowing limit – the overdraft limit set by the bank on the business account (the *maximum* authorised borrowing allowed for working capital purposes).
F1 Overdraft drawdown – the amount of the overdraft *actually used* by the business in the current quarter.
F2 Reserves of the business – the balance of the current account, if positive.
F2 Expected cash reserves – arithmetic mean reserves of the business from startup to time t.

Sales
S1 Debit turnover (DTO) – a measure of the money flowing through the business account at time t.
S1 Expected sales – mean DTO from startup to the present.
S2 Variance of debit turnover – the time-variance of DTO from startup to current period; treated as a proxy for the dispersion of the entrepreneur's production cost estimate.

Opportunity Cost of Entrepreneurship (O). The pre-entrepreneurial wage, and alternative expected wage at time t (simulated).[10]

Industry (I). SIC codes are used to define appropriate industry sectors.

Macro
M Base rate – rate at which the bank borrows on the money market at time t.
M GDP – index of real gross domestic product at time t.

M   Growth of GDP – mean growth rate of real GDP from business startup to time t.

Table 6.1 summarises the predictions of the empirical model given the proxies for the theoretical variables available.

4   Empirical Modelling

Table 6.2 presents the descriptive statistics for main variables in the sample. The sample size of 10,343 reflects the fact that each of the 2,000 firms is counted several times as a result of the individual time series on each. This sample size represents only complete observations, i.e., those for which there are non-missing values for each of the variables in the model.[11] The businesses were small, having on average about two employees – often part time (figures not presented) – and between one and two proprietors (N) with an average age of thirty-five years. Some two thirds of the proprietors had work experience in the area of the start (FWKFLD). One in eight businesses was purchased (PURCH) rather than a de novo startup. Most businesses were in retailing (17 percent), property/finance/professional services (12 percent), construction (12 percent) and other (mainly personal services) (25 percent) (not shown in the table). The average income of proprietors prior to start (AVINCOME) was quite low, some £10,000 per annum. From the table, the average overdraft limit (LIMIT) over the period was £3,000 per quarter, and overdraft borrowing (DRAWDOWN) was around £2,000 per business. However, this is matched by the £800 reserves (POSBAL) of the businesses. The measure of sales employed here (DEBTO) indicates that cash flowed in from this source at around £8,000 per quarter.[12] As regards survival (CESS) the average lifespan of the businesses in this sample was some sixteen quarters or four years; however, the distribution is skewed, so that this overstates quite considerably the true or median figure. The sample is right censored at twenty-seven quarters (maximum CESS = 27).

Bivariate Analysis

Figure 6.2 shows the plot of average lifespan of the business (CESS) against the average age of its proprietors (AVAGE). The relationship is concave, increasing with an apparent maximum at around the proprietor age of 50 years, where the business lifespan reaches about eighteen quarters or 4.5 years.[13] However, the chart also shows that a business run by a sixteen year old will be expected to last only about half this time, or

Table 6.1. *Predictions of the Model*

CONCEPT		VARIABLE	PREDICTED EFFECT ON FAILURE
TIME TRADING	TIME TRADING	TIMQ	+
	DITTO, SQUARED	TIMQ2	-
	DITTO, CUBED	TIMQ3	+[a]
HUMAN CAPITAL	HC1: AGE OF PROPRIETORS	AVAGE	-
	DITTO, SQUARED	AVAGE2	+
	HC1: TEAM SIZE	N	-
	DITTO, SQUARED	N2	?
	HC2: WORK EXPERIENCE	FWKFLD	-
	HC4: VOCATIONAL QUALIFICATIONS	FTRAD	-
	HC2: STARTUP MODE[d]	PURCH	-
SALES	S1:TURNOVER	DEBTO	?[b]
	S1: EXPECTED TURNOVER	MEANDTO	-
	S2: DISPERSION OF ENTREPRENEUR'S COST ESTIMATE	VARDTO	+
FINANCIAL CAPITAL	F1: CURRENT OVERDRAFT LIMIT	LIMIT	+/0
	F1: CURRENT USE OF OVERDRAFT	DRAWDOWN	?
	F1: MEAN USE OF OVERDRAFT	MEANDRAW	-
	F1: GROWTH OF BORROWING[c]	VARDRAW	+
	F2: CURRENT CASH RESERVES	POSBAL	-
	F2: MEAN CASH RESERVES	MEANPOS	-
MACRO	M: GROWTH OF GDP	GROWGDP	-
	M: BASE RATE	MEANBRAT	+

[a] We have adopted a cubic specification for the time dimension of the logistic function.
[b] A positive sign of DEBTO is consistent with overtrading (sales above average). However, it is also consistent with growing profitability. Hence the ambiguous sign.
[c] Growth of borrowing is the target variable, but because of the large number of missing values that this created (many initial values of borrowing are zero) we substituted variance of borrowing.
[d] The idea is that purchase of a business embodies human capital of the past owner that is transferred to the present owner. See Appendix B for details.

Table 6.2. *Descriptive Statistics for the Sample*

Variable	Mean	Std Dev	Minimum	Maximum
T: TIMQ	6.6549	6.8155	1.0000	27.0000
HC1: AVAGE	35.2842	10.0630	16.0000	71.3333
HC1: N	1.3776	0.6113	1.0000	5.0000
HC2: FWKFLD	0.7140	0.4121	0	1.0000
HC4: FTRAD	0.1901	0.3791	0	1.0000
HC2: PURCH	0.1341	0.3408	0	1.0000
I:AGRI	0.0303	0.1715	0	1.0000
I:TRANS	0.0512	0.2205	0	1.0000
O:AVINCOME	9505.19	16230.33	0	586000.00
F1:LIMIT	2855.45	11164.57	0	500000.00
F1:MEANLIM	2535.22	8555.73	0	183750.00
F1:VARLIM	37479353.75	519711589	0	27067187500
F1:DRAWDOWN	2293.73	9038.99	0	188317.67
F1:MEANDRAW	1980.72	7347.27	0	141223.85
F1:VARDRAW	22356044.57	238028381	0	10312243085
M:BRATE	11.7588	2.7861	5.3500	14.9500
M:MEANBRAT	11.8203	1.2377	7.6400	13.7450
M:GDP	99.2188	1.2876	96.2000	104.1000
M:MEANGDP	98.7407	0.6696	96.2000	100.3888
M: GROWGDP	0.113125	0.00173	-0.00710	0.00787
F2:POSBAL	800.5266	2271.70	0	55418.43
F2:MEANPOS	799.3979	1677.92	0	47281.71
F2:VARPOS	2617384.58	19467198.75	0	978880146
S1:DEBTO	8897.09	31471.38	0	2268790.00
S1: MEANDTO	8031.35	22455.2	0	1361274.00
S2: VARDTO	327221605	1625443192	0	1.6472E12
D:FAIL	0.7007	0.4579	0	1.0000
D:NOWFAIL	0.0963	0.2951	0	1.0000
D:CESS	15.563	8.2049	1.0000	27.0000

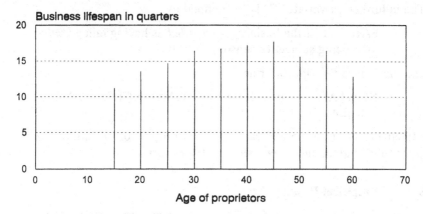

Figure 6.2. Business Lifespan: By Age of Proprietors

eleven quarters. Thus the figure is consistent with the hypothesis of the model, namely, that businesses run by proprietors with low human capital die early. A similar relationship to lifespan holds for several of the human capital measures, including work experience in the area of the startup.

The Logistic Model

The logistic model is a useful starting point for the multivariate analysis of failure time. The logistic procedure allows one to define a failure variable (NOWFAIL) as a function of time trading of the business (TIMQ) and a set of covariates which can be either constant (e.g., the qualifications of the proprietors at startup) or time-varying (e.g., the mean turnover of the business by quarter).

The coding for the logistic regression is as follows:

Define[14]

> FIRSTFIN = first calendar quarter of trading of the business (88q1, 88q2, . . .)
> LASTFINQ = last calendar quarter of trading of the business (88q1, 88q2, . . .)

> TIMQ = index of current quarter of trading (1, 2, . . .)

Define

> CESS = index of last period of data for the firm (1, 2, . . .)

by

> CESS = TIMQ if FINDATQ = LASTFINQ.

The failure *event* variate (FAIL) is defined by

> FAIL = 1 iff the business is *recorded* as having failed (*rather* than being subject to censoring); = 0 else;

and the failure *time* indicator as

> NOWFAIL = 1 if FAIL = 1 and TIMQ = CESS; NOWFAIL = 0 else.

Effectively, then, the model calculates the proportion of failures for a *given* time trading and *given* values of the covariates.

5   Empirical Results

We argued that the variance of sales and the growth of borrowing will be smaller for High human capital individuals and that these factors influence the subsequent survival of the business. Their influence on survival may not be completely "explained away" by the human capital itself, and insofar as this is the case the residual effect will show up in the estimated survival equation (Table 6.3).

Model 1: The Dynamic Human Capital Model

Table 6.3 shows that the logistic regression with human capital measures as regressors is highly significant (Pr > χ^2 = 0.0001). The most significant individual variable in the model is the time trading (TIMQ), which enters, as expected, in cubic form. It is thus consistent with the theoretical model. However, the sign of the third term (TIMQ3) is "wrong" and only just significant (p = 0.09). The signs of the covariates are precisely as expected, with the human capital measures all acting to reduce failure in every trading period. The most significant human capital variables are the fraction of proprietors that have work experience in the area (FWKFLD) followed by average age (AVAGE) and the trade apprenticeship qualification (FTRAD). Overall the results are very similar to the static model of Cressy (1996b) that predicts failure over a three and a half year period from inception, but here we control for time trading.

Model 2: Human Capital + Sales

Model 2 adds current sales measures to model 1. The model now becomes quadratic rather than cubic (unless, e.g., we reject variables

Table 6.3. *Logistic Estimates of the Hazard Function*

	Model 1: Human Capital	Model 2: Human Capital+SALES	Model 3: Human Capital+SALES +BORROWING	Model 4: Human Capital+SALES +BORROWING +MACRO
Variable	PARAM EST PR > χ^2	PARAM EST PR > χ^2	PARAM EST PR > χ^2	PARAM EST PR > χ^2
MODEL χ^2(df)	609.692(12)	611.710(13)	727.617(22)	1008.136(23)
PR > χ^2	0.0001	0.0001	0.0001	0.0001
INTERCPT	-1.5737	-2.1736	-2.1855	-5.5536
	0.0003	0.0001	0.0001	0.0001
TIMQ	0.4235	0.4415	0.4444	0.4560
	0.0001	0.0001	0.0001	0.0001
TIMQ2	-0.0104	-0.0114	-0.0117	-0.0261
	0.0353	0.0215	0.0188	0.0034
TIMQ3	-0.00023	-0.00021	-0.0002	0.000431
	0.0898	0.1264	0.1455	0.0612
AVAGE	-0.0763	-0.0509	-0.0511	-0.0488
	0.0004	0.0192	0.0183	0.0263
AVAGE2	0.000766	0.000471	0.000492	0.000479
	0.0065	0.0992	0.0840	0.0980
N	-0.2360	-0.0855	-0.0378	-0.0633
	0.2876	0.7022	0.8670	0.7866
N2	0.00374	-0.0152	-0.234	-0.0169
	0.9462	0.7845	0.6764	0.7737
FWKFLD	-0.4408	-0.3440	-0.3112	-0.2864
	0.0001	0.0001	0.0003	0.0008
FTRAD	-0.3123	-0.3199	-0.3218	-0.3036
	0.0014	0.0011	0.0011	0.0022
PURCH	-0.1751	-0.0410	-0.0168	0.0115
	0.1041	0.7109	0.8801	0.9185

Table 6.3. *(cont.)*

AGRI	-0.7844	-0.8204	-0.8102	-0.7408
	0.0019	0.0012	0.0014	0.0036
TRANS	-0.3623	-0.2914	-0.2802	-0.2722
	0.0331	0.0877	0.1019	0.1152
DEBTO		-0.0002	-0.00001	-0.00001
		0.0003	0.0145	0.0278
MEANDTO			-0.00002	-0.00002
			0.0104	0.0030
MEANDTO2			7.35E11	7.15E-11
			0.0146	0.0183
VARDTO			2.41E-10	2.56E-10
			0.0049	0.0026
LIMIT			6.382E-6	7.518E-6
			0.1654	0.1709
DRAWDOWN			-2.24E-6	-2.24E-6
			0.8110	0.8176
MEANDRAW			-0.00003	-0.00003
			0.0360	0.0184
VARDRAW			5.37E-10	6.43E-10
			0.0206	0.0058
POSBAL			-0.00021	-0.00022
			0.0001	0.0001
VARPOS			-327E-12	
			0.9013	
GROWGDP				-205.5
				0.0001
MEANBRAT				0.3289
				0.0001

Note: Number of observations = 10,343.

at below the 15 percent level). The time-varying covariate measuring business turnover (DEBTO) is highly significant in this equation, as is its mean (MEANDTO). The sign of both is negative, indicating the role of sales in profitability. On the other hand, the variance of sales (VARDTO), also measured at time t (TIMQ), is positively related to failure, as predicted. The effect of a higher variance of sales is thus to *increase* the business's failure probability at any point in time. Thus a more "noisy" firm is a more failure-prone firm, as we would expect from the analysis. Finally, note that the team size variables (N, $N2$), though individually insignificant, are in fact collinear and turn out to be jointly significant at the 5 percent level; and the addition of sales variables renders the startup mode variable (PURCH) insignificant.

Model 3: Human Capital + Sales + Borrowing

Model 3 adds measures of borrowing to model 2, namely, the over-draft limit (LIMIT), current overdraft borrowing (DRAWDOWN), and current reserves (POSBAL). The result is once again a quadratic model in time trading, with highly significant effects of borrowing levels and reserves on failure: *Mean* borrowing (MEANDRAW) and (current) reserves (POSBAL) both stave off failure[15]. The variance of borrowing (VARDRAW), as predicted, increases the chances of imminent failure. Regarding the existence of capital constraints, however, the current overdraft limit is insignificant, perhaps because of its correlation with firm sales levels.[16] This suggests the absence of borrowing constraints over time, since under such restrictions we should expect a relaxation of any constraint to impact survival chances positively.[17]

Model 4: Human Capital + Sales + Borrowing + Macro

The addition of the macro variables is expected from the theory to have a significant impact on survival only if the deviations from the average of the last decade were substantial. The recession of 1990–92 was indeed one of the most severe in the last half century, suggesting that a repetition of the stability of the last ten years is unlikely. This conclusion is in fact borne out in the estimation. Both the GDP growth variable (GROWGDP) and the base rate variable (MEANBRAT) are highly significant and quantitatively important, with the former having a negative, and the latter a positive, sign as expected.[18] As one might expect, major variations in the macro environment will impact significantly on the small firm given the quality of human capital they possess.

Model 5 (Not Reported): Human Capital + Sales + Macro + Opportunity Cost: Discussion

An obvious criticism of the methodology above is that it ignores the influence of labour market variables, in particular the opportunity cost of staying in business. It is to be expected that older entrepreneurs will have a declining chance of re-employment, thus creating a lock-in effect that may explain some of the longevity associated here with human capital. In Cressy (1996b) I addressed this issue by including a weighted average of the previous wage of the entrepreneur and unemployment benefit, with the weights being the probability of being unemployed given age, industry, etc. The estimation indicated that the alternative wage was positively, rather than (as predicted) negatively, related to survival, but on controlling for human capital the effect on survival became insignificant. Thus the alternative wage seemed to be proxying human capital rather than opportunity cost of entrepreneurship. However, the results were found to be invariant to substantial variations in the unemployment probability.

In the absence of the appropriate data it is difficult to deal with the issue adequately. Simulation is one approach to the problem, but then we need to choose between alternative rates of decline if the results turn on them. To address the latter issue, we ran logistic regressions with simulated exponential declines in the wage over time, where initial values were the pre-entrepreneurial (i.e., pre-startup) wage, AVINCOME. The formula applied was

$$NINC = AVINCOME * EXP(R * (1 - TIMQ))$$

where the variable R is the rate of depreciation of the initial income AVINCOME. This was tried for values of 10 percent up to 50 percent. The results were that the NINC coefficient was uniformly positive (contradicting the theory) and highly insignificant (usually at or above the 30 percent significance level). Thus the results in the dynamic case mirror those for the static case.

6   Summary and Conclusions

We started with the objective of explaining the positive skew of the failure distribution and its apparent stability over calendar time. The basic hypothesis was that the shape of the distribution would be determined by a division of the population of entrepreneurs into High human capital and Low human capital types. We argued that firms with higher initial human capital (indicating higher mean and lower variance priors of ability) and higher current variance of borrowing and sales (indicating higher variance posteriors of ability) would fail more often. The failure-prone (low human capital) young would therefore die out early, leaving the failure-resistant mature entrepreneurs to continue into the longer run. This hypothesis was borne out by the estimation. The predicted effects of growth in borrowing were also established empirically, with Low human capital types seemingly compensating for mistakes in investment by increasing their overdraft requirements. Financial capital was insignificant given human capital, sales, and reserves, suggesting the absence of borrowing constraints. Finally the theory predicted that demand factors represented by the mean sales of the business and the growth rate of GDP would reduce the hazard rate. However, these were found to do so in a quite unexpectedly dramatic way, reflecting the particular characteristics of the UK macro economy over the period studied.

Appendix A: Definitions of Terms and Variables in the Database

Basic Information

FINDATQ = date (quarter) of the financial data (931 = 1993q1)
LASTFINQ = quarter of last financial data of the business
FIRSTFIN = first quarter of financial data of the business
TIMQ = quarter of business trading (1, 2, . . .)

Lifespan Data

CESS = last quarter of trading (i.e., last quarter of financial data) (= last TIMQ)

Background Data

General Human Capital (HC1)

AVAGE, AVAGE2 = average age of the proprietors at startup, and its square
N, N2 = number of proprietors in the business at startup, and its square

Specific Human Capital: Experience **(HC2)**

FWKFLD = fraction of the proprietors with work experience in the same area as the start
FEXSB = fraction of the proprietors who had small business experience
PURCH = 1 if the business start is a purchase; = 0 else
TRADTIME = time since the business first started trading

Specific Human Capital: Education **(HC3)**

FNOAC* = fraction of proprietors with no academic qualifications
FNOLEV = fraction of proprietors with a maximum of O level academic qualifications
FNALEV = ditto A levels
FNDEG = ditto a degree

Specific Human Capital: Vocational Qualifications **(HC4)**

FTRAD = fraction of proprietors with trade apprenticeships
FPROF = ditto professional qualifications
FHND = ditto Higher National Diploma or Certificate
FOTHQUAL = ditto other vocational qualifications
FNOVOC* = ditto no vocational qualifications

Opportunity Cost of Entrepreneurship Variables **(O)**

AVINCOME = income of proprietors prior to startup

Financial Assets: Collateral Availability **(F2)**

TOTHEQ, TOTHEQ2 = total housing equity of the business's proprietors,[19] and its square

Industry Dummies **(I)**

AGRI = 1 if the business was in agriculture[20]
RETAIL = 1 if in retail
CATER = 1 if in catering
PROP = 1 if in property/finance/professional services
CONST = 1 if in construction
MOTOR = 1 if in motor trades
PROD = 1 if in production/manufacturing
TRANS = 1 if in transport/distribution

WHOLE = 1 if in wholesale
OTHER* = 1 if the business was not located in any of the
industrial categories listed

Financial Data

The terms below mainly refer to the overdraft (OD) facility operated by
UK and other European and US banks. This facility enables the firm to
borrow at a pre-determined interest rate over a fixed period up to a
maximum amount. Interest is then only paid on the amount drawn down.
Security is often posted on the OD limit. This amounts to a fixed or
floating charge on the firm's assets – usually house equity of the owners.
The security may be forfeited if the firm fails to pay its interest or principal as per the OD schedule.

Sales Turnover and Debit Turnover

A measure of the cash flowing out of the account is provided by the variable DEBTO, or *debit turnover* on the last day of quarter t. In the case
of a "stationary" account, for which the balance of the account, B_t, is constant ($B_t = B_{t1}$), we can get a very simple relation between DEBTO and
sales of the business, namely,

$$Sales_t = \gamma \, DEBTO_t, \quad \gamma > 0 \tag{A1}$$

However, this assumes that the business does not accumulate profits, but
instead draws out any surplus for the directors/shareholders.

Averages and Standard Deviations of Turnover

Averages and standard deviations of debit turnover are used as measures
of the mean return and riskiness of the business. The latter variables were
defined as follows: Let x_{it} denote the debit turnover (DEBTO) of the
business I in period t of trading (TIMQ). Then, we define

$$\bar{x}_{ni} = \sum_{t=1}^{\tau=ni} x_{it} \Big/ ni$$

$$s_{ni}^2 = \sum_{t=1}^{\tau=ni} (x_{it} - \bar{x}_{ni})^2 \Big/ ni \tag{A2}$$

respectively, as firm i's mean and variance of debit turnover, at quarter
n_i, the number of periods trading for the ith firm.

Macro Data

BRATE = base rate, set by the government's open market

operations as the rate at which the bank has to borrow short term from the money market.

Appendix B: Elements of a Theory of General Human Capital and Business Survival

The model described below incorporates measures of both general and specific human capital and is based on a set of hypotheses relating human capital to survival; further details can be found in Cressy (1994,1996b).

H1. *There is a positive, concave relationship between general human capital of the business's proprietors, measured by age, and the survival of the business.*

Expected utility of self-employment is assumed to be a function of the accumulated general stock of human capital, given age. Owner maturity brings experience, a form of investment in general "human capital." This enhances business skills, the utility of which represents the return to being in business. However, as part of the human ageing process, the capital stock depreciates over time and requires investment to maintain its value. If investment decreases (say) exponentially with age (broadly, "it is more difficult to teach an old dog new tricks"), the relationship between human capital stock and age will be concave with a turning point where depreciation exceeds investment. Recent evidence indicates that the utility of human capital in entrepreneurship is expected to be greater than the utility of the same stock in wage employment: the self-employed are, other things equal, *happier* than those in wage employment (Blanchflower and Oswald, 1995). We assume, specifically, that the utility of self-employment is proportional to the capital stock. Then the *expected difference* in utility of self-employment over wage employment will increase with age. Because of uncertainty about the return to self-employment, even for the self-employed person (Jovanovic, 1982), the probability of a self-employed individual's utility exceeding that from wage employment, i.e., the probability of survival in self-employment, will then be increasing in proprietor age and the human capital stock.[21] The resulting survival function will be concave in age with survival prospects increasing at a decreasing rate, eventually declining.[22]

H2. *The number of proprietors in the business is positively associated with "group" human capital and so with survival.*

Team size embodies both individual human capital of the proprietors and a synergistic human capital effect associated with their grouping. Two effects in team size that enhance survival can be identified: *homeostasis* and *balance*. The homeostasis effect refers to the fact that the resilience of the management team to chance depletion and/or damage increases with team size. For example, if one owner is ill, or leaves, or is inactive (e.g., the proverbial "free rider"), a business run by a larger management team will be less affected than one run by a smaller team. The balanced team effect, on the other hand, arises from the fact that a larger number of proprietors allows specialisation of function. Different individuals in a larger team can engage in general management, finance, marketing, production, etc., rather than (say) one owner-manager's attempting to perform all functions.[23]

H3. The specific human capital of the proprietors measured by work experience in the same area as the startup enhances business survival.
This hypothesis asserts that human capital is *not* entirely *activity-specific*, in the sense that skills acquired in one context may be useful in another context. Work experience, in particular, may allow the proprietor to use skills previously acquired in the service of an employer in his/her own business to his/her advantage. Established business contacts that have been built up over time may also be utilised as clients for the new business. This latter is the familiar spinoff effect of an enhanced client base via proprietor work experience in the same area as the start.

H4. The specific human capital embodied in vocational qualifications of the proprietors enhances survival.
The human capital embodied in vocational qualifications is intuitively more appropriate for the success of the typical small business than academic qualifications.[24] The three-year trade apprenticeship is particularly valuable in starting a small business by providing training of direct relevance to the skills needed in the initial stages of self-employment. It also provides a benchmark for evaluating the skills of potential future employees. Value-for-money is more likely to be forthcoming from individuals who are genuinely skilled at their job. Finally, the investment of three years' time is also indicative of a *commitment* to the trade in question.

H5. Business purchases embody "frozen" human capital and survive longer than wholly new starts.
Purchases are more viable than de novo starts for two reasons: Firstly, there is likely to be *already* an established *clientele* for the product/service ("goodwill"). This itself means a guaranteed initial demand for the product or service and obviates the problem of identifying/establishing one. Secondly, there is *already* an established network of *suppliers* for the business. This again helps to prevent the problem of

availability and reliability of inputs to the business. These facts jointly imply less "spade work" by the new proprietor. To some extent the new proprietor has, simply by the fact of purchase, "bought in" the business experience of his predecessor(s).[25] The choice of purchase mode may also itself be evidence of a more sophisticated entrepreneurial attitude of the proprietors.

H6. *Some industry sectors in which the business is located will be associated with higher survival chances.*
Whilst there may be macro-economic effects influencing survival, structural effects also play a role. In general we expect that growing sectors will enhance survival as a result of increasing general demand. However, theories of turbulence suggest that competitive sectors will have both high birth *and* high death rates (Beesley and Hamilton, 1984). The precise sectoral effects applicable to a given time period, however, cannot be hypothesised with any certainty.

Notes

[1] For example, whilst a business one and one half years old has a failure rate of some 16 percent and so is highly risky, one of five years' standing has a failure rate of a mere 3 percent and is a relatively safe bet (Ganguly, 1985, p. 145).
[2] A feature of business reality known in the UK as *overtrading* is also implicitly incorporated into the model. This is the distinction between individuals that *misinterpret* market signals and those that don't. In particular it distinguishes those that interpret temporary changes as permanent ones. Older people starting in business, for example, will have acquired life experience that enables them better to distinguish temporary from permanent changes in the environment. They will therefore make their output decisions "more slowly", taking into account information in a more balanced way. The *same* information (price or cost change, say) will affect their decisions less than those of their younger colleagues. The effect of this behaviour on their decisions is, however, analytically indistinguishable from the effect of dispersed priors. The prior estimate of the mean for an older person is divided by n_o, whereas that for a younger person is divided by $n_y \ll n_o$.
[3] The composition of the sample differs from that of the VAT statistics mainly because it has a higher proportion of sole traders and small partnerships not registering for VAT. The general shape of the failure curve is, however, the same (Figures 6.1–6.2), though because of the sample composition mentioned it has a larger mass of failure in the early quarters.
[4] In the recent literature, for example, Mata (1994) showed that current measures of business size were significantly better predictors of imminent failure than was initial size.

[5] There are in fact five cohorts in the analysis rather than the four expected from the dates of interviews. Although the businesses were all interviewed in 1988, some did not record bank data until 1988q1.

[6] The data is subject to some degree of interval truncation (some observations are at six-monthly rather than quarterly intervals) and a smaller amount of right truncation due to continuing firms. Experiments with alternative specifications that take these features into account suggest that this is not a major source of bias in the results.

[7] A pure human capital model would have a function of t only through c, so that human capital "explains" financial capital entirely.

[8] This refers to the opporunity cost of staying in the present business.

[9] The spurts of growth experienced by the Low human capital types are commonly described as *overtrading* and constitute an excessive response to temporary changes in the environment. This is why they will be followed by equally precipitate reverses. This growth may be associated, as we have noted, with interpreting short run changes in demand as *permanent* changes justifying fixed investment. When demand returns to its long run (lower) value, the firm finds it has excess capacity, resulting in lower profitability, and greater chances of failure. If (at the extreme) capital costs incurred are entirely sunk, then the firm has little option but to incur the higher costs through time. However, if there is only some degree of sunkenness, the younger proprietor will then make a large reduction in capacity to accommodate a "permanent" fall in demand.

[10] See below for details of simulation.

[11] As far as we are able to tell this selection produced no bias to the results.

[12] Strictly, to obtain the value of sales the inflow to reserves should be added to this figure. See Appendices.

[13] The relationship parallels that of three and a half year survival to age in Cressy (1996b).

[14] These definitions are repeated for completeness in Appendix A.

[15] The reason mean borrowing is significant relates to the liquidity providing role of the overdraft. In general, higher sales levels require larger overdraft requirements to finance the larger working capital deficit from such sales.

[16] A separate ordinary least squares (OLS) regression of limit against sales produced the following equation:

$$\text{LIMIT} = 1532.43 - 0.2163 \text{ DEBTO} + 417823 \text{ MEANDTO},$$
$$\bar{R}^2 = 0.09, \quad \Pr > F = 0.0001,$$

with both coefficients significant at 0.0001.

[17] This is consistent with the static results of Cressy (1996b), who found no effects of initial borrowing constraints on survival over a three and a half year period from startup.

[18] Both the odds ratio and the standardised coefficient (not presented) provide measures of the quantitative importance of a variable. The odds ratio measures the effect on the odds of failure of a unit change in the variable in question. The standardised estimate of the effect does something similar but on the probability of failure, with the independent variable being standardised (divided by its standard deviation) and the change in the variable being measured relative to its mean value.

[19] Housing equity is defined as the difference between the aggregate market value of their houses and the aggregate outstanding mortgages.

[20] The sector definitions used here do not exactly match the SIC but were used by the bank because of conformity to marketing definitions.

[21] Uncertainty is likely to be at most constant and is more likely to be *decreasing* with age, since self-knowledge increases with age. This is part of the Bayesian learning process.

[22] The theory produces a dynamic capital stock equation exactly analogous to physical capital stock of production theory.

[23] This concept of course is not new and can be traced back to Adam Smith. It is also argued by some modern authors to be relevant to the growth potential of the business.

[24] This argument does not apply to the typical high-tech start, where academic qualifications are paramount. The typical startup is in fact very low-tech in nature, as evidenced in the present database.

[25] There is empirical support for the superior longevity of business purchases in the work of Bates (1989).

References

Audretsch, D. 1991. "New Firm Survival and the Technological Regime." *Review of Economics and Statistics 68(3):* 520–526

Audretsch, David B. 1994. "Business Survival and the Decision to Exit." *Journal of the Economics of Business 1(1):* 125–138

Audretsch, David B. and Talat Mahmood. 1995. "New Firm Survival: New Results Using a Hazard Function." *Review of Economics and Statistics 77(1),* February: 97–103

Bates, Timothy. 1989. "Entrepreneur Human Capital Inputs and Small Business Longevity." *Review of Economics and Statistics LXXII (4):* 551–559

Beesley, M. and R. Hamilton. 1984. "Small Firms Seedbed Role and the Concept of Turbulence." *Journal of Industrial Economics,* December: 217–232

Blanchflower, D. and Andrew Oswald. 1995. "What Makes an Entrepreneur?" *NBER Working Paper # 3252,* NBER, Dartmouth College, Hanover, New Hampshire

Cressy, Robert. 1996a, "Pre-Entrepreneurial Income, Cash-Flow Growth and Survival of Startup Businesses: Model and Tests on UK Data," *Small Business Economics 8(1),* February: 49–58

Cressy, Robert. 1996b, "Are Business Startups Debt-rationed?" *The Economic Journal 106(438),* September: 1253–1270

Cressy, Robert C. 1994. "Are Startups Debt-Rationed?" *SME Centre Working Paper #20, Warwick Business School*

Cressy, Robert C. 1993. *The Startup Tracking Exercise: Third Year Report.* National Westminster Bank of Great Britain, November

Cressy, Robert C. and M. Cowling. 1994. "Credit Rationing or Monetary Illusion? Evidence from Defaults Under the Loan Guarantee Scheme." *SME Centre Working Paper #26,* Warwick Business School

Evans, David and Boyan Jovanovic. 1989. "An Estimated Model of Entrepreneurial Choice Under Liquidity Constraints." *Journal of Political Economy 97(4):* 808–827

Frank, Murray Z. 1986. "An Intertemporal Model of Industrial Exit," *Quarterly Journal of Economics 103*, May: 333–344

Ganguly, P. 1985. *UK Small Business Statistics and International Comparisons.* Small Business Research Trust, London, Harper Row

Holtz-Eakin, D., D. Joulfaian, and H.S. Rosen. 1994a. "Sticking It Out: Entrepreneurial Survival and Liquidity Constraints." *Journal of Political Economy 102(11):* 53–75

Holtz-Eakin, D., D. Joulfaian, and H.S. Rosen. 1994b. "Entrepreneurial Decisions and Liquidity Constraints." *Rand Journal of Economics, 25(2)*, Summer: 34–347

Jovanovic, Boyan. 1982. "Selection and the Evolution of Industry." *Econometrica 50(3)*, May: 649–670

Mata, Jose. 1994. "Firm Growth During Infancy." *Small Business Economics 6:* 27–39

Storey, David J. 1994, *Understanding the Small Business Sector.* London, Routledge

CHAPTER 7

Capital Structure at Inception and the Short-Run Performance of Micro-Firms

Gavin C. Reid

1   Introduction

This chapter examines the financial structure and performance of young micro-firms. As regards age, their average time from financial inception is one and a half years; as regards size, their average number of employees is just three full-time, and two part-time workers. Short-run performance is measured over one year, in terms of continuing to trade.

The key issue explored is the extent to which financial structure close to inception has a bearing on early performance of the micro-firm. In a neoclassical theory of the small firm, generalised to incorporate money capital (Vickers, 1987), the conditions for maximising profit will determine an optimal asset structure for the small firm, along with the familiar marginal conditions for production optimality. It requires that the full marginal cost of debt should equal the full marginal cost of equity, which in turn should equal the discount factor on the marginal income stream. Thus optimal amounts of debt and equity (and hence gearing) are determined, along with optimal hiring of factors of production. Previous evidence (Reid, 1991) has suggested that this optimality requirement has been reflected in a strong measured association between gearing and survival of the small firm. In particular, lower gearing significantly raised survival prospects for the small firm over a three-year time horizon. It is likely that this arises because of both the lower risk exposure and the lower debt servicing associated with lower gearing. In this chapter, a principal goal is to look at asset structures much closer to inception, to see which types best promote survival.

An additional goal is to ask whether an unequal distribution of entrepreneurial ability has implications for even the youngest of small firms. Specifically, in the small firms model of Oi (1983), the size distribution of small firms is generated by entrepreneurial ability. Higher ability entrepreneurs raise the marginal productivities of their workers by more

186

successfully coordinating all factor inputs, and more effectively monitoring labour inputs. Thus they enjoy better performance and create larger firms than do lower ability entrepreneurs. Oi (1983) also shows that this implies that if there is *also* a distribution of efficiency of workers, more productive workers will be paired with more productive entrepreneurs. This conclusion is reinforced by other notable small firm theories, including the influential theory of Jovanovic (1982), which predicts a positive association between firm size and entrepreneurial ability.

Whilst the approach taken is deliberately empirical, and heavily "grounded" in business practice, it is informed by the relevant economic theory as cited above. Direct interviews with one hundred and fifty entrepreneurs in the early stage of their firms' life-cycles were used to provide a particularly detailed picture of financial structure: an area in which (given reporting conventions) the state of our current knowledge is extremely poor.[1] The information obtained was on sales, profits, debt, equity, gearing, credit, assets and financial history (e.g., on personal financial injections, loans and grants).

The general finding is that financial structure is not a major determinant of performance in this, the very earliest, phase of the life-cycle of the micro-firm. Whilst it is possible to identify specific financial features which may favour survival (e.g., the availability of trade credit) or may threaten survival (e.g., the use of extended purchase commitments), conventional features of financial structure (e.g., assets, gearing) do not play a significant role. However, other (non-financial) explanations of early-stage survival are available, including the use of advertising and business planning and the avoidance of precipitate product innovation. This suggests that market features and internal organisation of the micro-firm may dominate financial structure as determinants of survival in the very earliest phase of the life-cycle. A subsidiary finding favours the view that high efficiency entrepreneurs tend to form larger firms which attract higher efficiency and higher paid labour. This can be seen to support an "efficiency wage" view of micro-firm labour hiring policy.

2   The Data

Data were gathered in 1994 by face-to-face interviews with owner–managers of new micro-firms. The sampling frame was established on a regional basis, with nineteen geographical areas within lowlands Scotland providing sub-samples. Ports of entry to the field were through enterprise stimulating institutions (sometimes called "incubators"), known as Enterprise Trusts,[2] in the relevant areas. The Directors of these Enterprise Trusts were willing to act as "gatekeepers" and provided random samples of an average size of around nine firms from their case loads of new business starts. The only two restrictions imposed were that the Enterprise Trust could positively identify the firm's starting date and that no firm should be more than three years from inception at the time of sampling.

In this way, very detailed evidence on a stratified sample of one hundred and fifty new business start-ups in Scotland was obtained. These data were obtained by using an administered questionnaire with sections on markets, finance, costs, business strategy, human capital, organisation and technical change. Of main concern in this chapter is the Finance section, which posed twenty-one questions to entrepreneurs, several of which had filters to further questions (e.g., a question on outside equity which, if answered, inquired further about the size of equity stake and the dividend paid to equity holders). The Finance section inquired into net and gross profits; sales; debt; form and function of equity; extent and cost of bank loans; grants and subsidies; past and present gearing; trade creditors and debtors; extended, hire and lease purchase; net (and gross) assets and their ratio to stocks; forms of share capital; and issuing of debt.

For the sample as a whole, average gross and net profits were £49,000 and £15,000, respectively,[3] with gross sales being £227,000. Just over half of the firms (51 percent) had debt (including business overdrafts). Only a small proportion (5 percent) had any outside equity (including investment by "business angels", who had sunk money into the business), and the percentage share of equity held in this way was just a majority holding (54 percent). This figure had slightly fallen since financial inception. No dividend had been paid to equity holders. The average personal cash injection by entrepreneurs at business start-up had been £13,000.

About one third (32 percent) of entrepreneurs had used a bank loan to launch the business, taking out an average loan of £30,000 at an interest rate of approximately 11 percent. Most entrepreneurs (78 percent) had received a grant or subsidy[4] in starting their businesses, and the average value of this was £4,000. The great majority of recipients had found this assistance of help, and evaluated its contribution as crucial (34 percent), important (17 percent) and helpful (43 percent). Gearing (typically bank loan divided by personal financial injections) stood at an average value of 158 percent at launch and 169 percent at time of interview. Being well above 100 percent, this put the average firm into the highly geared category. The target level of gearing over the next three years was much lower, on average being 73 percent, putting it into the lower geared category. A common explanation given for this desire to lower gearing was to reduce dependence on banks.

Three quarters of the firms had trade credit arrangements. Suppliers, on average, allowed one and a half months' time to pay, and the average creditor balance was £24,000. Customers, on average, were allowed a rather shorter time to pay, one month, and the average debtor balance was £29,000. Thus, an average net debtor status prevailed, as regards trade credit, for the sample as a whole. Of the various tied methods of purchasing plant and equipment, only hire purchase was moderately widely used (26 percent), followed by extended purchase (5 percent) and lease purchase (4 percent). The gross value of fixed assets was £23,000 and the net value was £18,000, with entrepreneurs tending to depreciate fixed assets on a straight line basis over a period of three or four years. The ratio of the value of stocks to net assets averaged 160 percent for the sample as a whole, but displayed considerable variation across firms. Less than a third (31 percent) of firms had issued share capital in their businesses.[5] The issuing of debt was very uncommon (3 percent) and, when it was used, it was proportionally much higher than equity finance (230 percent on average). The interest paid to holders of debt was low (2 percent).

Concerning data on non-financial features of these micro-firms, the evidence is too extensive to report upon here in any detail, as over five hundred quantitative measures are available, as well as dozens of coded qualitative comments. However, a brief overview of general features may be helpful. Further detail will be given, as appropriate, in the next section.

By the design of the sample, firms were typically less than three years old, and the average age was twenty-one months. No firms employed more than fifty full-time employees, and the average number was three, implying that these enterprises are at the very bottom end of the micro-firm size distribution. For part-time employees, the average number was two. No firm had a greater number of product groups than thirty, and the average number was four. Just over a third of firms had the local market as their main customer base. The average number of major rivals each firm had was eleven. Goods were perceived to be only mildly differentiated; nearly 80 percent of firms competed independently (rather than conjecturally or collusively); and 70 percent of firms advertised.

Over a half (56 percent) of the entrepreneurs had previous experience of running a business. By business type, proportions were: sole trader (from home) (26 percent); sole trader (from business premises) (29 percent); partnership (19 percent); private company (27 percent). In terms of internal organisation within the average micro-firm, superiors typically had moderate discretion over subordinates, and it was usually the case that subordinates understood and acted on the orders of superiors. Of the entrepreneurs interviewed, 83 percent said that their personnel were knowledgeable about each others' skills. Typically, the micro-firm had engaged in minor process innovation, but rivals were perceived to have engaged in even less. Between one and five product innovations had been undertaken, on average, and 62 percent of entrepreneurs perceived that there had been a lot of technical change in their industry.

3   Continuing or Ceasing to Trade

Econometric analysis of the data will be dealt with in the next section. Here the emphasis will be on detailing statistical differences, such as they are, between two types of micro-firms, those which went out of business within a year of the interview and those which remained in business. The general finding will be that over a surprisingly wide range of characteristics (about three dozen), each type of micro-firm differs very little. For that reason, when differences in attributes are observed, given the dichotomous outcome (viz., to continue or to cease trading), such attributes are especially worthy of further attention.

One such set of differences relates to size and the wage rate. Relevant to these differences is the small firm model of Walter Oi (1983). According to this theory, entrepreneurs allocate efforts optimally over coordinating and monitoring activities. A small firm will be the larger, the greater is the ability of the entrepreneur to use time efficiently to coordinate production, and hence to increase the size of the business. The better the development of entrepreneurial skill, the higher the marginal productivities of factors used in the more efficient small firms. Thus it is the distribution of entrepreneurial ability which generates the size distribution of small firms, with the larger ones being associated with higher ability. Further, the larger, more efficient small firms reward factors of production, including labour, relatively highly because their superior efficiency at coordination shifts marginal productivity schedules upwards.[6]

Considering first Table 7.1, which deals with general characteristics of the micro-firms, it is apparent that firms that continue to trade are larger than those that do not, especially in terms of gross profits (*Grprof*) and sales (*Grsales*), and in some measure in terms of employment (*Ftime*, *Ptime*). Furthermore, firms which continue to trade pay premium wages (*Wagerate*) (i.e., the wages of their best skilled workers), which are higher (indeed 16 percent higher, on average) than those that cease to trade. A 95 percent confidence interval for the difference between these mean (μ) wage rates is given by $\Pr(15.688 < \mu_1 - \mu_2 < 242.632) = 0.95$, which does

Table 7.1. *General Characteristics*

Variable	n_1	Continued Trading $N_1 = 122$		n_2	Ceased Trading $N_2 = 28$	
		Mean	St. Dev.		Mean	St. Dev.
Grprof	100	56,442	(88,044)	24	31,082	(53,242)
Netprof	106	13,329	(29,890)	25	14,514	(24,651)
Grsales	119	0.26047×10^6	(0.9351×10^6)	27	0.11468×10^6	(0.2418×10^6)
Ftime	122	2.9754	(6.8544)	28	2.0357	(4.1498)
Ptime	122	2.0082	(12.781)	28	0.71429	(1.3569)
Wagerate	61	919.16	(462.01)	12	790.00	(312.24)
Hrswk	122	58.123	(19.332)	28	56.679	(13.676)
Secschl	122	4.7623	(1.1787)	28	4.6786	(0.9833)
Impact	121	16.442	(20.427)	27	11.093	(9.1673)

Notes: Definitions of variables are given in the Appendix to this chapter. There were 122 (N_1) firms which continued trading, and 28 (N_2) firms which ceased trading, in the sample as a whole. However, data are incomplete for some variables, for some firms. Hence n_1 and n_2 indicate the relevant sample sizes for each category of firm, for which means and standard deviations were computed.

not contain the origin, rejecting the hypothesis of equal mean wage rates. This finding is consistent with the small firms model of Oi (1983), which suggests that more productive workers (with higher efficiency and hence higher wages) will tend to be matched to more able entrepreneurs (with better performance).[7] It is also consistent with an "efficiency wage" view of employment, of the sort discussed by Yellen (1984). According to this view, firms which operate in the non-union sector, which is typical of micro-firms, have a tendency to pay an "efficiency wage" which is at a slight premium on the going wage rate for similar work. This may increase efficiency by reducing labour turnover, making workers feel more committed, etc. Surprisingly, given its emphasis in the informal literature,[8] there is very little difference in terms of hours worked between firms which cease and firms which continue to trade. Further, years of secondary schooling (*Secschl*) differ little between the two groups, though, as human capital arguments suggest, schooling may be important for some aspects of performance.[9]

The last variable listed in Table 7.1 measures how many months the entrepreneur looks ahead in decision-making within the firm (*Impact*). It suggests that, on average, entrepreneurs who continue trading have a 48 percent longer time horizon than those who do not. A 95 percent confidence interval for the difference between mean time horizons is provided by $\Pr(0.3320 < \mu_1 - \mu_2 < 10.3659) = 0.95$, which does not contain the origin, so we reject the hypothesis that the means are the same. This is an interesting result and certainly works against a widespread myth of extreme short-termism in micro-business decision-making. The exact question asked was, "How far ahead do you look when evaluating the impact that planned decisions may have?" The mean response was 15.466 months; and this response was itself set in the context of other questions on business strategy. Despite contrary evidence by the likes of Storey (1995), the evidence reported here makes sense in a business strategy context.[10] For example, 89 percent of respondents had a business plan, and it was a formal written plan for the great majority (79 percent). This plan was reviewed on average every five months. Thus the average impact planning time horizon would involve about three business plan revisions, which is a convincingly coherent picture, and one which accords well with field work perception of small business planning.

The next body of evidence to be considered is presented in Table 7.2 and concerns key financial variables, like net profit (*Netprof*) and net assets (*Netfixas*), as well as various financial ratios, like the debt/equity ratio at financial inception (*Gearst*) and the ratio of stocks to net assets (*Stkass*). The evidence on size, as measured by the net and gross fixed assets variables, and the amount of cash (*Owncash*) entrepreneurs put into their businesses at launch, is that firms which continued trading were on average much larger than (about twice the size of) those that did not. This is consistent with the evidence on gross profits and sales in Table 7.1. To be noted again is the lower net profit of those continuing (explained earlier by a higher wage bill), which is now reinforced by evidence of their lower net profitability (measured by *Nprass = Netprof ÷ Netfixas*). Indeed, for the firms which continued to trade, average net profitability was negative (−4.0 percent), compared to the positive net profitability of those which ceased to trade (+3.5 percent). It must be borne in mind that many well specified business plans do operate on the assumption of unprofitable trading for a considerable part of the early life-cycle of the small firm, so these results should not be assumed to be surprising, but rather as likely to be in accordance with entrepreneurs'

Table 7.2. *Financial Variables and Ratios*

Variable	Continued Trading N₁ = 122			Ceased Trading N₂ = 28		
	n_1	Mean	St. Dev.	n_2	Mean	St. Dev.
Netprof	106	13,329	(29,890)	25	14,514	(24,651)
Netfixas	120	20,957	(45,957)	27	9,072	(23,467)
Grfixass	120	27,227	(47,915)	27	12,264	(31,185)
Nprass	122	-3.984	(27.718)	25	3.4628	(71.246)
Gearst	119	158.69	(341.46)	24	136.88	(294.99)
Gearnow	118	165.68	(377.96)	24	172.38	(444.33)
Stkass	120	97.963	(278.82)	25	421.88	(1486.0)
Owncash	117	14,331	(32,768)	24	7,008	(6,187)

Notes: Definitions of variables are given in the Appendix to this chapter. There were 122 (N₁) firms which continued trading, and 28 (N₂) firms which ceased trading, in the sample as a whole. However, data are incomplete for some variables, for some firms. Hence n_1 and n_2 indicate the relevant sample sizes for each category of firm, for which means and standard deviations were computed.

plans. It may be that the types of markets the firms which have ceased to trade have are characterized by rather different features from those of firms which continue to trade, like a shorter product life-cycle and a shorter time to harvest. Indeed, this is suggested by the significantly shorter impact planning horizon of those firms which ceased trading, noted in Table 7.1.

The gearing (i.e., debt/equity) ratios at financial inception (*Gearst*) and at the time of interview (*Gearnow*), typically measured by the ratio of bank indebtedness to owner–manager's personal financial injections, appear to be unrevealing. There is a slight tendency for gearing to rise after inception, and a slight indication that firms which continued trading redeemed debt more quickly (starting higher geared, and ending lower geared), but this difference is certainly not statistically significant. Whilst apparently unremarkable, this bland feature of the gearing evidence contravenes earlier evidence that gearing is a major predictor of staying in business, and that highly geared small firms, being both relatively risk-exposed and prone to debt servicing crises, have survival prospects significantly inferior to those of lower geared firms. However, the earlier evidence related to firms which were on average three years old at the time of initial interview and were investigated three years later to see whether they were still in business (Reid, 1991). By contrast, the micro-firms in the present sample were never more than three years old at the time of the first interview (and indeed had an average age of just one and a half years) and the time frame for examining whether they were still in business was just one further year. Thus the evidence appears to indicate that gearing, as a crucial feature of financial structure, has an effect on survival which is highly sensitive to the stage of the life-cycle of the micro-firm. At, or close to, inception, it appears unimportant; six or more years from inception, it appears to be crucial.

The final feature to be remarked upon in Table 7.2 is the financial ratio *Stkass*, which measures the ratio of the value of stocks to the net value of fixed assets (i.e., after depreciation, which was typically set at something like 25–33$\frac{1}{3}$ percent per annum). For the sample as a whole, this ratio was 160 percent, but as Table 7.2 indicates the micro-firms which continued to trade had a much lower ratio (98 percent) of stocks to net assets compared to those which ceased to trade (422 percent). This might be caused by a difference in sectoral composition of the micro-firms, and this seems perhaps to be the case. If the samples are dichotomised by SIC code, according to whether the micro-firm is, broadly speaking, in manufacturing ($01 \leq SIC \leq 49$) or in services ($50 \leq SIC \leq 99$), the results are as follows: 67 percent of firms which continued trading were in services; whereas just 61 percent of firms which ceased to trade were in services. Thus micro-firms which ceased to trade were more predominantly in manufactures, where circulating capital requirements are typically much higher than in services. Arguably, micro-firms which have to tie up far greater capital in circulating form are at a survival disadvantage compared to firms which can more immediately put their capital to work.

To conclude this section, Table 7.3 reports on further variables which may impinge on whether a micro-firm continues, or ceases, to trade. They are all qualitative variables, being based on binary responses (Yes/No) to questions. From a macro-economic perspective, grants and terms of credit may be directly influenced by policy makers, and it is of interest to observe whether variables which capture such influence had a different effect on micro-firms which continued to trade, as opposed to those which ceased trading. The *Grant* dummy variable measures whether a firm had received a grant or subsidy when it was launched. This was evidently very common, with firms that stayed in business being less likely (78 percent) to have received much support than those that did not (84 percent). There is evidence that micro-firms can be heavily driven by grant/subsidy regimes and tax breaks, to the extent that a variety of

Table 7.3. *Qualitative Financial Variables*

Variable	Continued Trading N₁ = 122			Ceased Trading N₂ = 28		
	n_1	Mean	St. Dev.	n_2	Mean	St. Dev.
Trcredit	122	0.8032	(0.3991)	25	0.6000	(0.5000)
Debt	122	0.5082	(0.3992)	25	0.4400	(0.5066)
Outeq	121	0.0578	(0.2344)	25	0.0400	(0.2000)
Bankloan	121	0.3141	(0.4661)	25	0.3200	(0.4761)
Grant	121	0.7769	(0.4181)	25	0.8400	(0.3742)
Extpur	122	0.0410	(0.1991)	25	0.1200	(0.3317)
Hirpur	122	0.2869	(0.4542)	25	0.1600	(0.3742)
Leaspur	122	0.0492	(0.2171)	25	0.0000	(0.0000)
Finown	122	0.9098	(0.2876)	25	0.9200	(0.2769)
Finbank	122	0.5082	(0.5020)	25	0.3200	(0.4761)

Notes: Definitions of variables are given in the Appendix to this chapter. There were 122 (N₁) firms which continued trading, and 28 (N₂) firms which ceased trading, in the sample as a whole. However, data are incomplete for some variables, for some firms. Hence n₁ and n₂ indicate the relevant sample sizes for each category of firm, for which means and standard deviations were computed.

so-called paper entrepreneurship has been identified, which depends more on bureaucratic than market opportunity.[11] This view is consistent with these figures, though they do not provide strong supporting evidence.

Table 7.3 indicates that the use of outside equity (*Outeq*), extended purchase (*Extpur*) and lease purchase (*Leasepur*) was slight for both classes of firm. In the pecking-order theory of finance (Myers, 1984), these – being amongst the most expensive – are amongst the least desired forms. Hire purchase (*Hirpur*) was more common, especially amongst the firms that remained trading (29 percent compared to 16 percent). Both types of firm had been equally likely to use a bank loan to launch the business (just under 50 percent in each case), and both had been equally likely to have been financed by the owner–manager (about 90 percent in each case). The proportions in which these forms of finance were used are consistent with a pecking-order of finance,[12] which would put inside equity first (e.g., *Finown*), debt finance next (e.g., *Debt*), and outside equity last (e.g., *Outeq*). Whether micro-firms continue or cease to trade, they appear, on average, to conform to the predictions of this theory.

These observations having been made, emphasising the neutrality of financial structure across the continued/ceased trading divide, two salient features which differ are worthy of further examination. First, whilst 80 percent of firms which continued trading have trade credit arrangements, just 60 percent of the firms which ceased trading had such facilities. A 95 percent confidence interval for the difference between these proportions is given by 0.2 ± 0.02, which does not contain the origin, so the difference between these proportions is statistically significant. At, and close to, inception, the use of trade credit arrangements is of great importance to the relatively fragile, nascent micro-firm. It often cannot implement more formal devices for cash flow management so "time to pay" (usually thirty days, but occasionally up to ninety) can be important for survival. Second, whilst just over one half (51 percent) of the micro-firms which had continued to trade had previously been financed by bank loans (*Finbank*), just less than one third (32 percent) of those who had ceased to trade had enjoyed this form of outside finance. A 90 percent confidence interval for the difference between these proportions is 0.19 ± 0.17, suggesting a statistically discernible difference between them.

In financial markets where information asymmetries arise (e.g., between lender and borrower) an inability to raise loan finance may be signalling a business which is perceived to be unworthy of support (e.g., because of inadequate collateral or excessive risk). The pattern of bank loan support suggested by the variable *Finbank* is consistent with the evidence of Table 7.2, which indicated that firms which continued trading had on average over twice the assets of firms which ceased trading, and their owner–managers had put in over twice the equity at launch.[13]

Before proceeding to the formal inferential methods of the next section, it is useful to summarise what the evidence has indicated so far.

a   The firms which continued trading were on average about twice the size of those which ceased trading, as measured by sales, cash invested in the business and assets.

b   In terms of many other attributes, these firms looked similar: employment, hours worked, years of high school education of owner–manager, gearing (past and present), use of financial instruments (e.g., bank loans, debt, hire purchase, lease purchase, outside equity), and access to grants or subsidies.

c   Financial structures were similar whether firms continued trading or not and indicated a preference for finance capital which conformed with that predicted by the pecking order theory of finance: inside equity, debt, outside equity, in decreasing order of importance.

d There is little difference in net profit between the firms which continued trading and those that did not, but net profitability was negative, on average, for the former, and positive, on average, for the latter, possibly because of the significantly higher (by 16 percent) wages paid in the former firms.

e The finding of greater size and greater wages within surviving, compared to non-surviving, firms supports theories of entrepreneurship, which suggest that abilities of economic agents are unequally distributed, and that the better ability agents receive greater rewards.

f Important distinct features of micro-firms which continued trading, compared to those which did not, were significantly longer (by 48 percent) impact planning time horizons and significantly greater (by 33 percent) access to trade credit arrangements.

4   Probit Estimates

In earlier work, such as that of Reid (1991), it was possible to think of the decision to stay in business as being based on a notional calculation which hinged on positive net economic profitability. In the current context, where, as we have seen in the previous section, the average net profitability of micro-firms which remained trading was negative, this line of reasoning is probably inappropriate, even if one would want to put aside the possibility that accounting and economic profitability may differ. With micro-firms being so close to financial inception, the use of what is in reality a *long-run* net profitability criterion is not relevant. Indeed, given start-up costs, the need to build up a customer base, and the progression up learning curves by both entrepreneur and workers, one would naturally expect an early phase of negative profitability. However, it is still of great interest to know how micro-firms survive this early stage of the life-cycle. The purpose of this section is to provide a statistical model of survival over a one-year period.

If a micro-firm were still trading one year after the entrepreneur was interviewed, then a dependent variable y (which in this study was called *Inbusin*) was coded as unity. If the micro-firm had ceased trading, y was coded as zero. Then the statistical model adopted was that of binary probit analysis, with $y = x'\beta$ where x is a vector of independent control variables (like current gearing, *Gearnow*; and net fixed assets, *Netfixas*) and β is a corresponding vector of coefficients. Assuming that an error term can be added to this model, which is independent normal, the value of β may be estimated by the method of maximum likelihood. Further, a variety of statistical tests may be applied to the estimated model and its coefficients.

Table 7.4 reports on a large set of control variables which may provide a statistical explanation of the probability that a micro-firm will continue trading an additional year. As well as using all the financial variables already discussed in Section 3, it introduces more variables (like whether the firm advertises, *Advert*; how important rapid occupation of a market niche is, *Rapidocc*; and the extent of product innovation, *Prodinn*). Variables, estimated coefficients, asymptotic *t*-ratios, and Hencher–Johnson weighted elasticities are given in the four columns of this, and the following, table. On a likelihood ratio test the model has a 1 percent probability level, and the Cragg–Uhler R^2 of 0.516 is very high for this sort of cross-sectional model. There is also a high percentage (86 percent) of correct predictions, but reference specifically to the statistical significance of the coefficients of over twenty financial structure variables, of the sort discussed in Section 3, does not present a strong picture of their predictive importance. For example, outside equity (*Outeq*) and gearing at inception (*Gearst*) have coefficients which are not significant. However, the coefficient on *Trcredit* is statistically significant ($\alpha = 0.025$). Access to trade credit (*Trcredit*) is obviously important to continued trading as it keeps cash-flow healthy – probably a more important consideration, shortly after launch, than is profitability. The holding of business debt (*Debt*) is also significant ($\alpha = 0.025$) and affects adversely the probability of the micro-firm's continuing to trade. The weighted elasticity for this variable is also relatively high. Although debt is shown to be important, this is not true of the two ratios of debt to equity (i.e., gearing ratios), *Gearst* and *Gearnow*, gearing at inception and gearing at the time of the interview. This finding is an important qualification to earlier evidence (Reid, 1991), based on considerably older small firms, suggesting gearing was a significant determinant of performance. The use of an extended purchase facility (*Extpur*) to buy plant and equipment has a highly statistically significant ($\alpha = 0.010$) negative coefficient, although the elasticity is not high (-0.023). The use of hire purchase (*Hirpur*) has a marginally significant positive coefficient ($\alpha = 0.10$), but again a low elasticity (-0.025).

The *Stkass* variable which measures the ratio of stocks to net assets, which has been analysed in detail, has the expected negative effect. A higher value of *Stkass* lowers the probability of continuing to trade. Its coefficient is statistically significant at the usual level ($\alpha = 0.05$), but

Table 7.4. *Binary Probit with Large Set of Control Variables*

Variable	Coefficient	t-Ratio	Weighted Elasticity
Advert	1.311	3.120***	0.125
Trcredit	0.902	2.070**	0.089
Debt	-1.365	-2.065**	-0.103
Outeq	3.974	0.063	$0.185.10^{-5}$
Bankloan	-0.467	-0.500	-0.028
Grant	0.489	0.461	0.073
Gearst	$-0.458.10^{-4}$	-0.059	-0.001
Gearnow	$-0.855.10^{-4}$	-0.142	-0.003
Extpur	-1.826	-2.493***	-0.023
Hirpur	0.757	1.352^{+}	-0.025
Leasepur	5.304	0.089	$0.104.10^{-5}$
Grfixass	$-0.110.10^{-4}$	-0.851	-0.031
Netfixas	$0.707.10^{-5}$	0.526	-0.015
Impact	$0.787.10^{-4}$	0.518	0.002
Sicdum	-0.184	-0.439	-0.017
Owncash	$0.248.10^{-4}$	0.943	0.030
Rapidocc	0.291	-1.037	-0.077
Stkass	-0.017	-1.831*	-0.027
Othbus	1.517	1.754*	0.016
Procinn	-0.249	-1.348^{+}	-0.062
Prodinn	-0.456	-2.332**	-0.095
Prodgrp	0.023	0.361	0.015
Timplan	0.076	1.850*	0.088
Timdeal	-0.023	-0.710	-0.021
Hrswk	$0.748.10^{-3}$	0.066	0.007
Secschl	-0.026	-0.131	-0.021
Runbef	0.148	0.373	0.014
Finown	-0.610	-0.721	-0.101
Finbank	2.009	1.959*	0.142
Fingrnt	-0.169	-0.181	-0.023
Nprass	0.006	1.210	-0.008
Constant	0.491	0.323	0.087

Likelihood Ratio test:

$$\chi^2 = 51.7 > \chi^2_{01}(31) = 50.9$$

Cragg-Uhler R^2 = 0.516; Binomial Estimate = 0.815
Sample Size (n) = 135; Percent Correct Predictions = 86%
Critical t-values: $t_{0.10} = 1.289^{+}$, $t_{0.05} = 1.658^*$, $t_{0.025} = 1.980^{**}$, $t_{0.010} = 2.358^{***}$

again the elasticity is low (-0.027). The *Finbank* variable, which measures whether a firm has been financed by a bank loan, has also received earlier discussion and appears here with a significant coefficient ($\alpha = 0.05$) and, most importantly, a relatively high elasticity (0.142). Indeed this is the highest estimated elasticity for this probit, suggesting that being in receipt of a bank loan is a major determinant of whether a micro-firm will continue to trade. This in turn suggests that banks are now rather effective monitors of small firm performance and potential. All other financial variables perform badly in this probit equation, including net profitability (*Nprass*), assets (*Grfixass, Netfixas*), gearing (*Gearst, Gearnow*), use of a bank loan at launch (*Bankloan*), outside equity (*Outeq*), and raising of finance from personal financial injections (*Finown*).

Thus it is clear from this probit that non-financial, rather than financial factors appear to play a large part in determining whether a micro-firm will continue to trade one year down the line. The shape and form of these variables are too diverse to be explored fully here, so what has been attempted is to indicate what non-financial factors may be important. Heading the list is whether or not the micro-firm advertises (*Advert*). The coefficient of this variable is highly statistically significant ($\alpha = 0.010$) and the elasticity is the second largest (0.125), next to that of *Finbank* (0.142). This evidence is contrary to earlier evidence (Reid, 1993) suggesting the relative unimportance of advertising for older micro-firms. For the younger firms being examined here, clearly advertising is important in establishing the initial market, after which it may become less important as firms depend more on repeat purchases, and the spreading of information by "word of mouth". Running another business, *Othbus*, arguably a sign of superior business acumen, has a significant positive coefficient ($\alpha = 0.05$), but a small elasticity. It seems that firms can attempt to innovate too early: process and product innovation (*Procinn, Prodinn*) are both negatively associated with continuing to trade. It seems likely that early innovation imposes too high resource and adjustment costs and may be indicative of an ill-judged initial target market niche. In view of what was said earlier about time horizons for judging the impact of plans, it is of note that the proportion of time in a week spent planning (*Timplan*) has a significant ($\alpha = 0.05$) positive coefficient. To summarise the picture of the significant coefficients in Table 7.4, just five are attached to financial variables.

However, it is also clear that some non-financial variables do not have the expected effect in the very early stages of the life-cycle of micro-firms. For example, Ungern-Sternberg (1990) has argued that diversification into several products is a tactic used by small firms to

Table 7.5. *Parsimonious Binary Probit*

Variable	Coefficient	t-Ratio	Weighted Elasticity
Advert	0.853	2.774***	0.111
Trcredit	0.848	2.609***	0.118
Debt	-0.580	-1.483⁺	-0.060
Extpur	-1.238	-2.165**	-0.024
Hirpur	0.492	1.302⁺	0.019
Stkass	$-0.805.10^{-3}$	-1.719*	-0.023
Othbus	0.983	1.520⁺	0.012
Prodinn	-0.254	-2.039**	-0.069
Timplan	-0.048	2.033**	0.080
Finbank	0.845	2.051**	0.073
Constant	-0.347	-0.920	-0.080

Likelihood Ratio test:

$\chi^2 = 36.4 > \chi^2_{.001}(10) = 29.6$

Cragg-Uhler $R^2 = 0.357$; Binomial Estimate = 0.816
Sample Size (n) = 147; Percent Correct Predictions = 83%
Critical t-values: $t_{0.10} = 1.289^+$, $t_{0.05} = 1.658^*$, $t_{0.025} = 1.980^{**}$, $t_{0.010} = 2.358^{***}$

attempt to cope with fluctuations in the demand for individual products. This implies that the number of product groups (*Prodgrp*) should be positively associated with continued trading. However, here this variable's coefficient is statistically insignificant. This does not rule out the validity of this argument at a later stage in the life-cycle, but it does not seem to apply at this earlier stage. Given the many insignificant coefficients in the probit of Table 7.4, it is of importance to seek a more parsimonious model in a statistical sense. This is presented in Table 7.5.

In going to the parsimonious model of Table 7.5, the process innovation variable (*Procinn*) has been dropped. The sample size has increased for this estimated probit, because fewer missing observations have to be dealt with when fewer variables are present. All the variables in this probit have coefficients which are statistically significant, and as a matter of robustness it is reassuring to note that the signs of coefficients are stable. Naturally, the Cragg–Uhler R^2 has fallen, but it still remains high. Using a likelihood ratio test, the model has a very small probability level of 0.1 percent. The percentage of correct predictions is high at 83 percent. Comparing the models of Table 7.4 and Table 7.5 using a likelihood ratio test, one gets a χ^2 value of 26.16 which is less than the $\chi^2_{0.05}(21)$ critical value of 32.7. Thus the data do not accept the extra restrictions of the probit in Table 7.4, compared to the probit in Table 7.5. The parsimonious model of Table 7.5 is therefore the preferred one on statistical grounds.

5   Conclusion

This chapter has examined empirically the potential financial determinants of a young micro-firm's decision to continue trading one further year. It is found that many financial features do not change across firms which continue to trade and firms which cease to trade. For example, both classes of firms follow a pecking-order financial format. Traditionally important financial features, like gearing and assets, appear to be unimportant in the early life-cycle. At this stage, other financial features appear to be important to continued trading, notably the existence of trade credit arrangements and the avoidance of extended purchase commitments. To obtain a satisfactory parsimonious probit model which predicts well whether micro-firms will continue to trade, non-financial variables need to be introduced. It is found that the use of advertising and business planning is important to a micro-firm's continued market activity in the early stage of its life-cycle, and that the more able entrepreneurs tend to run larger firms and to hire more able employees. The overall view reached is that purely micro-economic factors provide an incomplete account of the propensity of micro-firms to continue trading. In some measure one must look to macro-economic effects for further illumination, particularly to the consequences of business cycle fluctuations for pricing, production, employment, and innovation. A panel database that the author is currently constructing for this same set of micro-firms should enable a longitudinal analysis to be undertaken of how micro-firms modify their behaviour as the business cycle evolves.

Appendix: Definitions of Variables Used in Text and Tables

Advert   = 1 if firm advertised, otherwise 0
Bankloan   = 1 if a bank loan was used to launch the business, otherwise 0
Debt   = 1 if business had debt, otherwise 0
Extpur   = 1 if firm had extended purchase commitment, otherwise 0
Finbank   = 1 if firm had previously been financed by a bank loan, otherwise 0
Fingrnt   = 1 if firm had previously been financed by grant/subsidy, otherwise 0

Finown	= 1 if firm had previously been financed by the owner–manager, otherwise 0
Ftime	= number of full-time employees
Gearnow	= gearing (i.e., debt/equity) ratio at time of interview
Gearst	= gearing ratio at launch of business
Grant	= 1 if grant or subsidy was received at launch, otherwise 0
Grfixass	= gross value (£) of fixed assets
Grprof	= gross profits (£) for last financial year
Grsales	= gross sales (£) for last financial year
Hirpur	= 1 if firm had hire purchase commitments, otherwise 0
Hrswk	= number of hours per week devoted to the business
Impact	= number of months entrepreneur looked ahead in evaluating impact of decisions
Inbus	= number of months firm had been in business
Leasepur	= 1 if business had any lease purchase commitments, otherwise 0
Loan	= size of bank loan (£) at launch of business
Netfixas	= net value (£) (after depreciation) of fixed assets
Netprof	= net profits (£) for last financial year
Nprass	= *Netprof* ÷ *Netfixas*
Othbus	= 1 if respondent runs any other business, otherwise 0
Outeq	= 1 if business had any outside equity, otherwise 0
Owncash	= cash (£) put in by inside equity holder(s) at launch
Procinn	= 0 (no change), = 1 (slight change), = 2 (significant change), = 3 (important change) in process innovation since starting business
Prodgrp	= number of product groups produced
Prodinn	= 0 (none), = 1 (1–5), = 2 (6–10), = 3 (11–20), = 4 (>20) new products since starting business
Ptime	= number of part-time employees
Rapidocc	= 0 (not at all), = 1 (moderately), = 2 (very) important to occupy a market niche rapidly
Runbef	= 1 if entrepreneur had run a business before, otherwise 0
Secschl	= number of years spent at high school
Sicdum	= 1 if firm was in manufacturing (01 ≤ SIC ≤ 59), 0 if it was in services
Stkass	= ratio of value of stocks to net fixed assets
Timdeal	= proportion of time spent doing deals in a week
Timplan	= proportion of time spent planning in a week
Trcredit	= 1 if business has trade credit arrangements, otherwise 0

204   Gavin C. Reid

Wagerate   = wage-rate (£) for best skilled full-time workers per month

Notes

The research on which this chapter is based is funded by the Leverhulme Trust, to which grateful acknowledgement is made. Research assistance was provided by Julia A Smith of the Centre for Research into Industry, Enterprise, Finance and the Firm (CRIEFF), University of St Andrews, Scotland, to whom the author expresses thanks. Thanks are also given to delegates of the Jönköping conference, including Zoltan Acs, David Audretsch, Mark Casson, Paul Gompers, Paul Reynolds and David Storey, and three anonymous referees, for useful comments. The author remains responsible for any errors of omission or commission that this chapter may yet contain.

[1] See the comments made by van der Wijst and Thurik (1993, pp. 55–56) in introducing their study of small firm debt ratios.

[2] See Reid and Jacobsen (1988, ch. 5) for a detailed explanation of the role of this type of institution.

[3] Requested deductions from gross profits to get net profits were taxes, directors' remunerations, and all costs.

[4] Often in the form of Enterprise Allowance. Others included Enterprise Trust grants or interest free loans, and Regional Enterprise grants.

[5] Typically in quite simple forms. Representative cases included 100 × £1 shares, often split in simple ways like 50/50, 30/70, 10/90, with partners, who were often the spouse or offspring.

[6] Though this is partially offset by monitoring costs.

[7] Empirically, it is also consistent with a widely confirmed size-wage effect, which is more generally associated with wider size dispersion than is present in this study. See Brown and Medoff (1989) for six alternative explanations.

[8] See Barrow's (1986, p. 16) analysis of "total commitment" in his *Routes to Success*, where he writes, "You will need single-mindedness, energy and a lot of hard work ... working 18-hour days is not uncommon". By contrast, Dunkelberg and Cooper (1990) (see next note) find that the more able the entrepreneur, the fewer the hours worked.

[9] See Dunkelberg and Cooper (1990), who argue, using US National Federation of Independent Business data, that human capital (more widely measured than here) is of greater significance than finance capital early in the life-cycle of the small firm.

[10] Cf. presentation by Smith (1996), University of Abertay Dundee, "Small Business Strategy in new Scottish Firms".

[11] "Paper entrepreneurship" has been defined by Kent (1984, p. 117) as "meeting standards of political conduct associated with taxation and regulation that may be of dubious value. Such activities may neither increase national income, produce any new products, nor generate additional jobs".

[12] See Chittenden et al. (1996) for recent support for this theory in a small firms context.

[13] Cf. the evidence presented by Storey (1994), using his Cleveland (England) data, which suggests that bank lending is unrelated to those characteristics of founders which are thought to be conducive to small firm performance, but is

clearly positively related to the use of personal savings in financing the firm at start-up.

References

Barrow, C. 1986. *Routes to Success: Case Studies of 40 UK Small Business Ventures*. London: Kogan Page.

Brown, C. and J. Medoff. 1989. "The employer size-wage effect," *Journal of Political Economy* 97, 1027–1059.

Chittenden, F., G. Hall and P. Hutchinson. 1996. "Small firm growth, access to capital markets and financial structure: review of issues and an empirical investigation," *Small Business Economics* 8, 59–67.

Dunkelberg, W. C. and A. C. Cooper. 1990. "Investment and capital diversity in the small enterprise," in Z. Acs and D. B. Audretsch (eds), *The Economics of Small Firms: A European Challenge*. Dordrecht: Kluwer, 119–134.

Jovanovic, B. 1982. "Selection and the evolution of industry." *Econometrica* 50, 649–670.

Kent, C. A. (ed). 1984. *The Environment for Entrepreneurship*. Lexington, Mass.: D. C. Heath.

Myers, S. C. 1984. "The capital structure puzzle," *Journal of Finance* 39, 575–592.

Oi, W. Y. 1983. "Heterogeneous firms and the organization of production," *Economic Inquiry* 21, 147–171.

Reid, G. C. 1991. "Staying in business," *International Journal of Industrial Organization* 9, 545–556.

Reid, G. C. 1993. *Small Business Enterprise: An Economic Analysis*. London: Routledge.

Reid, G. C. and L. R. Jacobsen. 1988. *The Small Entrepreneurial Firm*. Aberdeen: Aberdeen University Press.

Smith, J. A. 1996. "Small business strategy in new Scottish firms." Paper presented to Postgraduate Conference, University of Abertay Dundee, 23 February 1996.

Storey, D. 1994. "New firm growth and bank financing," *Small Business Economics* 6, 139–150.

Storey, D. 1995. "Small firms: the risky organization." Paper presented to the ESRC sponsored conference on Risk in Organisational Settings, White House, London, 17 May 1995.

Ungern-Sternberg, T. von. 1990. "The flexibility to switch between different products," *Economica* 57, 355–369.

Vickers, D. 1987. *Money Capital in the Theory of the Firm*. Cambridge: Cambridge University Press.

Wijst, N. van der and R. Thurik. 1993. "Determinants of small firm debt ratios: an analysis of retail panel data," *Small Business Economics* 5, 55–65.

Yellen, J. 1984. "Efficiency wage models of unemployment," *American Economic Review* 74, 200–205.

CHAPTER 8

Resource Allocation, Incentives and Control: The Importance of Venture Capital in Financing Entrepreneurial Firms

Paul A. Gompers

1   Introduction

Small firms and new business creation have become potent forces for economic development in the United States. The growing importance of small firms in job generation, innovation, and industry development has been increasingly studied. For example, during the past decade, the rate of new firm incorporation rose dramatically. In 1981, there were only 581,661 new businesses incorporated in the U.S. That number expanded to 741,657 in 1994. Scherer (1991) demonstrates that during the 1980s, small firms were more innovative than large firms. He finds that during the 1980s, firms with fewer than 500 employees created 322 innovations annually for each million employees while large companies contributed only 225 innovations per million employees.

The dramatic shift towards small firms makes it imperative that capital sources for funding startup companies are efficient and well understood. Venture capital is one source of financing for a small number of very promising young firms. Each year 1,000 to 2,000 of the nearly one million startup firms receive venture capital financing. The firms that receive venture capital are primarily high growth, high potential companies that have the opportunity to become dominant players in their industries. Many successful firms received venture capital financing in their early stages and created tremendous growth in both technological development and jobs. This group includes industry leaders such as Microsoft, Netscape, Sun Microsystems, Apple, Genentech, Starbucks, and Staples.

The dramatic success of the U.S. venture model has not been transferred internationally. Outside the U.S., substantially smaller amounts of venture funding flow into the hands of young entrepreneurs. Black and

Gilson (1997) compare the international venture capital markets and argue that the U.S. market is substantially more efficient than the venture market in other countries. The private equity capital that is invested abroad tends to finance later stage, buy-out firms rather than technology-based startups. The sources of the U.S. venture capital competitiveness need to be explored fully. Only then can recommendations be made.

This chapter examines the control mechanisms and resource allocation in venture capital investments. Venture capitalists employ many unique control mechanisms. The asymmetric information associated with startup companies makes project governance extremely important. During the screening process, venture capitalists review business plans of young companies and design contracts with entrepreneurs that minimize potential agency costs. Sahlman's extensive field research (1990) describes venture capital in terms of the control mechanisms employed to manage these agency costs. Three control mechanisms are common to nearly all venture capital financing: (1) use of convertible securities; (2) syndication of investment; and (3) staging of capital infusions. This chapter will examine the usefulness of each of these mechanisms in alleviating various agency costs that may result from the information asymmetries and uncertainty associated with early stage firms.

The rest of the chapter is organized as follows: Section 2 provides a brief introduction to the venture capital industry. The growth and importance of the venture industry are highlighted. The role of staged capital commitments in controlling potential conflicts is examined in Section 3. Section 4 analyzes the syndication of venture capital investments. Incentive and control features of convertible securities used in venture investments are explored in Section 5. Section 6 develops a control theory of venture capital and concludes the chapter.

2   Startup Financing and Venture Capital

Entrepreneurs often develop products and ideas that require substantial capital during the formative stages of their companies' life cycles. Many entrepreneurs do not have sufficient funds to finance projects themselves and must therefore seek outside financing. Several alternative capital sources exist. The informal risk capital market consists of individuals known as "angels." These are wealthy businesspeople, doctors, lawyers, and others, who are willing to take an equity stake in a fledgling company in return for money to "start up." Wetzel (1987) estimates that 250,000 individuals are active in the informal risk capital market and invest between $20 billion and $30 billion annually. Firms that require substantial amounts of money, however, may not be able to receive sufficient capital from the "angel" network because the market is dispersed with little information sharing and the amount of invested capital tends to be small (usually less than $100,000). Banks are an important source of startup financing for a subset of new businesses. Companies that lack substantial tangible assets and have a large degree of uncertainty about their future are unlikely to receive significant bank loans, however. These firms face many years of negative earnings and are unable to make interest payments or meet principal repayments. These are the firms that Fazzari, Hubbard, and Petersen (1988) show are severely capital constrained. It is difficult for these firms to get the necessary outside financing to fund their projects. It is this inability which hampers growth of new business in many countries.

Venture capital firms in the U.S. will finance these high-risk, potentially high-reward projects. Venture capitalists are professional investors who raise money from third parties to invest in promising startup companies. The investment is also not passive. Venture capitalists take an equity-linked stake in the firms they finance, sharing in both upside and downside risks. Most firms that receive venture capital financing are unlikely candidates for alternative sources of funding. They have few tangible assets to pledge as collateral and they produce operating losses for many years.

A common misperception is that venture capital funds only high-technology companies. A substantial portion of high-tech startups have received venture capital, including such present-day industry giants as Apple Computer, Microsoft, Netscape, and Genentech. Yet low-tech companies such as Staples, Starbucks, and Federal Express also received significant amounts of venture capital money. Each of these firms had a unique idea or product, and venture capital was able to help the entrepreneur exploit that opportunity.

Between 1972 and 1992 venture capitalists brought 962 firms to the public market (Brav and Gompers, 1997). These firms have been a source of innovation and job creation. The companies represent various industries and firms at various stages of development. Within certain high-technology industries, e.g., biotechnology, semiconductor manufacturing, and computer hardware, almost every major firm in existence today received venture financing in its early stages.

Whether the project is in a high- or low-technology industry, venture capitalists are active investors. They monitor the progress of firms, sit on boards of directors, structure compensation packages, mete out financing based on attainment of milestones, and help in hiring management talent. Venture capitalists retain important control rights including the ability to appoint key managers and remove members of the entrepreneurial team. Venture capitalists also provide entrepreneurs with access to consultants, investment bankers, lawyers, and accountants.

Venture capital has grown substantially over the past fifteen years and has had a dramatic impact on the economic landscape of this country. The size of annual contributions to the venture capital industry is closely tied to the initial public offering (IPO) market. As Figure 8.1 shows, when the IPO market is active, more money flows into the industry. This relationship is largely due to the link between returns on venture capital funds and the IPO market. When the IPO market is hot, many more venture capital–backed firms can go public, increasing returns in the industry. This increases investors' interest in the industry and ultimately leads to a greater capital infusion.

Table 8.1 presents a variety of statistics related to the size, activity, and success of the venture capital industry during the period 1980–1994. In nominal terms, capital under management increased more than seven times. The number of firms rose from 254 to 674 while the number of professionals increased by a factor of 2.5. These data point to the dramatic growth in the industry.

In panel B of Table 8.1, the contributions to venture capital are analyzed in greater detail. The independent private funds are now the dominant form of financing, controlling roughly 80 percent of the total capital pool. This growth has been fueled largely by the growth in venture capital limited partnerships. These organizations are the subject of two recent academic papers (Gompers and Lerner, 1996a; 1996b). Notice that while the size of corporate and Small Business Investment Company (SBIC) venture funds has not changed substantially, the size of the average independent private fund has more than doubled.

An interesting trend in venture capital fund raising is the flight to quality or reputation. Follow-on funds (i.e., second or later funds of venture capital firms) have garnered an increasing share of the capital raised over the course of the decade. It is increasingly difficult for new entrants to raise capital. Without a reputation as a good venture capitalist, it is nearly impossible to raise money. A new fund that has not shown any success with its investment portfolio will also have a difficult time raising capital. For old, established firms, however, a new fund can usually be raised with a dozen phone calls. Everyone wants in on the next Greylock or Kleiner Perkins fund.

The source of commitments to the industry has also shown substantial evolution. During the 1970s, individuals were the largest source of commitments to new venture capital funds. In 1978 individuals accounted for 32 percent of the commitments to new funds, which totaled

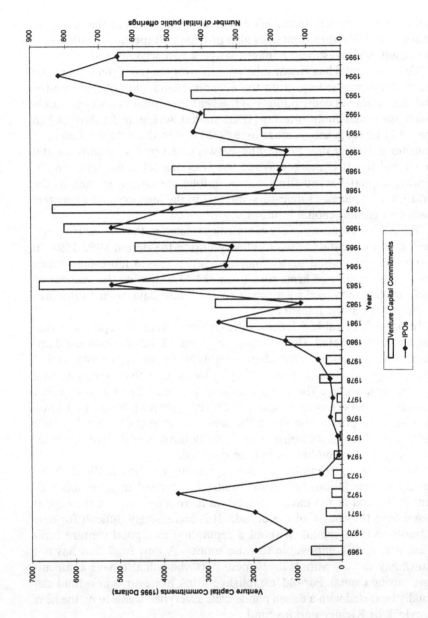

Figure 8.1. Annual Amount of Venture Capital Commitments in Constant 1995 Dollars and the Aggregate Number of Initial Public Offerings

only $216 million. Pension funds accounted for only 15 percent of the total. By 1994 pension funds supplied nearly half the capital (47 percent) and individuals contributed only 12 percent.

The investment activity of venture funds is shown in panel C. The number of companies receiving venture financing is not large. In the most active year, only 1,729 firms received financing. While this is significantly greater than the number that received funding in the 1970s, it is only a small fraction of the 800,000 or so businesses that are started each year.

Investment focus has also changed over the decade. As the venture portfolio of firms has grown, the number of new company investments has declined as a percentage of total capital invested. Likewise, venture funds have moved towards later stage investments. In 1980 25 percent of all investments made by venture capitalists were in seed or startup firms. The percentage invested in seed and early stage investments reached a low of 10 percent in 1989 and 1990 but has increased since then. Late stage investments and leveraged buyouts have grown in importance over the decade.

The importance of venture capital in the initial public offering market is presented in panel D. During the decade, venture capital–backed firms have accounted for about 30 percent of the number, total amount raised, and total market value of all initial public offering companies. In certain industries (e.g., biotechnology, computers, software), venture capital–backed firms account for a significantly larger fraction of the IPO firms.

3   Staged Capital Infusions

Gompers (1995) examines the role that staged capital infusions play in controlling potential agency costs in young entrepreneurial firms. The evidence indicates that the staging of capital infusions allows venture capitalists to gather information and monitor the progress of firms, maintaining the option to abandon projects periodically.

Sahlman (1990) notes that staged capital infusion is the most potent control mechanism a venture capitalist can employ. Prospects for the firm are periodically reevaluated. The shorter the duration of an individual round of financing, the more frequently the venture capitalist monitors the entrepreneur's progress and the greater the need to gather information. The role of staged capital infusion is analogous to that of debt in highly leveraged transactions, keeping the owner/manager on a "tight leash" and reducing potential losses from bad decisions.

Predictions from agency theory (e.g., Jensen and Meckling, 1976) shed light on factors affecting the duration and size of venture capital investments. Venture capitalists weigh potential agency and monitoring costs when determining how frequently they should reevaluate projects and supply capital. Venture capitalists are concerned that entrepreneurs' private benefits from certain investments or strategies may not be perfectly correlated with shareholders' monetary return. Because monitoring is costly and cannot be performed continuously, the venture capitalist will periodically check the project's status and preserve the option to abandon. The duration of funding and hence the intensity of monitoring should be negatively related to expected agency costs.

Agency theory predicts that the information generated by venture capitalists is valuable. Models of venture capital have emphasized the role of information production.[1] Chan (1983) develops a model in which venture capitalists improve allocational efficiency by overcoming

Table 8.1. *Selected Data on the United States Venture Capital Industry, 1980–1994*

	1980	1981	1982	1983
Panel A: Aggregate Venture Capital Industry Statistics				
1 Total Venture Capital Pool ($ millions)	$4,500	$5,800	$7,600	$12,100
2 Number of Venture Capital Firms	254	282	331	448
3 Number of Industry Professionals	NA	NA	1,031	1,494
4 Net New Commitments to the Venture Capital Industry ($ millions)	$700	$1,300	$1,800	$4,500
Panel B: Data on the Independent Private Sector (noncorporate and non-SBIC venture capital organizations)				
1 Net New Commitments to the Independent Private Sector	$661	$867	$1,400	$3,400
Sectoral Analysis (% of Total Capital)				
2 Independent Private	40.0%	44.0%	58.0%	68.7%
3 Corporate	31.1%	28.0%	25.0%	21.0%
4 SBIC	28.9%	28.0%	17.0%	10.3%
Sectoral Analysis - Average Capital per Firm ($ millions)				
5 Independent Private	NA	NA	$27	$36
6 Corporate	NA	NA	$30	$37
7 SBIC	NA	NA	$6	$5
8 Median Size of Independent Private Firm	NA	NA	$22	$18
Independent Private Sector Partnership Formation				
9 Total Number of Funds Raising Capital	22	37	54	89
10 Total Capital Raised ($ millions)	$661	$866	$1,423	$3,460
11 Number of Follow-on Funds	12	13	18	47
12 Capital Raised by Follow-on Funds	$418	$477	$628	$2,383
13 Number of New Funds	10	24	36	42
14 Capital Raised by New Funds	$243	$389	$795	$1,077
Sources of Capital to the Independent Private Sector				
15 Corporations	19.0%	17.0%	12.0%	12.0%
16 Individuals	16.0%	23.0%	21.0%	21.0%
17 Pension Funds	30.0%	23.0%	33.0%	31.0%
18 Foreign	8.0%	10.0%	13.0%	16.0%
19 Endowments	14.0%	12.0%	7.0%	8.0%
20 Insurance Companies	13.0%	15.0%	14.0%	12.0%

asymmetric information. Admati and Pfleiderer (1994) derive robust financial contracts when lead venture capitalists are better informed than other investors. They demonstrate that a contract in which the lead venture capitalist maintains a constant fraction of the firm's equity is the only form of financing that is robust to small changes in possible outcomes.

Venture capitalists claim that the information they generate and the services they provide for portfolio companies are as important as the capital infused. Many entrepreneurs believe that venture capitalists provide little more than money. If the monitoring provided by venture capitalists is valuable, predictions can be made about the structure of staged capital infusions.

If monitoring and information gathering are important, venture capitalists should invest in firms in which asymmetric information is likely

1984	1985	1986	1987	1988	1989	1990	1991	1992	1993	1994
$16,300	$19,600	$24,100	$29,000	$31,100	$34,400	$35,900	$32,870	$31,070	$34,760	$34,130
509	532	587	627	658	674	664	640	617	637	591
1,760	1,899	2,187	2,378	2,474	2,558	2,602	2,072	NA	NA	NA
$4,200	$3,300	$4,200	$4,900	$2,900	$3,107	$2,309	$1,589	$2,740	$3,142	$4,766
$3,200	$2,300	$3,300	$4,200	$2,100	$2,400	$1,847	$1,271	$2,548	$2,545	$3,765
72.0%	73.0%	75.0%	78.0%	80.0%	79.0%	80.0%	80.0%	93.0%	81.0%	79.0%
18.0%	17.0%	16.0%	14.0%	13.0%	16.0%	15.0%	14.0%	3.0%	11.0%	16.0%
10.0%	10.0%	9.0%	8.0%	7.0%	5.0%	5.0%	6.0%	4.0%	8.0%	5.0%
$45	$52	$57	$65	$65	$62	$56	$53	$56	$57	$59
$36	$37	$34	$32	$29	$35	$31	$31	$21	$54	$34
$5	$5	$5	$6	$5	$4	NA	NA	NA	NA	NA
$21	$25	$30	$30	$30	$30	$21	$21	$22	$22	$25
101	77	77	110	84	76					
$3,300	$2,327	$3,320	$4,184	$2,710	$2,400	$1,847	$1,271	$2,548	$2,545	$3,765
58	40	44	66	59	57	41	27	32	36	56
$2,300	$1,396	$2,800	$3,347	$2,422	$2,260	$1,708	$1,209	$2,380	$2,241	$3,016
43	37	33	44	25	19	16	3	9	10	24
$1,000	$931	$520	$837	$388	$280	$139	$62	$168	$304	$748
14.0%	12.0%	11.0%	10.0%	12.0%	20.0%	7.0%	5.0%	3.0%	8.0%	9.0%
15.0%	13.0%	12.0%	12.0%	8.0%	6.0%	11.0%	12.0%	11.0%	7.0%	12.0%
34.0%	33.0%	50.0%	39.0%	47.0%	36.0%	53.0%	42.0%	42.0%	59.0%	47.0%
18.0%	23.0%	11.0%	14.0%	13.0%	13.0%	7.0%	12.0%	11.0%	4.0%	2.0%
6.0%	8.0%	6.0%	10.0%	11.0%	12.0%	13.0%	24.0%	18.0%	11.0%	21.0%
13.0%	11.0%	10.0%	15.0%	9.0%	13.0%	9.0%	5.0%	15.0%	11.0%	9.0%

Table 8.1. *(cont.)*

Panel C: Investment Activity of Venture Capitalists				
Disbursements				
1 Estimated Value of Disbursements ($ millions)	$610	$1,160	$1,450	$2,580
2 Number of Companies Financed	504	797	918	1,320
3 Average Investment per Company	$1.21	$1.46	$1.58	$1.95
Allocation of Investments				
4 New Company Commitments as % of Total	58.0%	55.0%	39.0%	34.0%
5 Follow-on Financings as % of Total	42.0%	45.0%	61.0%	66.0%
Stages of Financing				
6 Seed and Startup as % of Total	75.0%	22.6%	20.0%	17.2%
7 Expansion and Later-Stage as % of Total	25.0%	77.4%	68.0%	70.8%
8 Leveraged Buyouts as % of Total	NA	NA	12.0%	12.0%

Panel D: Exiting Venture Capital Investments				
1 Number of Venture Capital-backed Companies That Are Acquired	28	32	40	49
Venture Capital-Backed Initial Public Offerings				
2 Number of Companies	27	68	27	121
3 Total Amount Raised	$420	$770	$549	$3,031
4 Total Market Value of Companies	$2,626	$3,610	$2,374	$14,035
All IPOs				
5 Number of Companies	95	227	100	504
6 Total Amount Raised	$1,089	$2,723	$1,213	$9,580
7 Total Market Value of Companies	$5,717	$10,922	$5,466	$40,473
Venture capital-Backed IPOs as % of Total IPOs				
8 Number of Companies	28.4%	30.0%	27.0%	24.0%
9 Total Amount Raised	38.6%	28.3%	45.3%	31.6%
10 Total Market Value of Companies	45.9%	33.1%	43.4%	34.7%

Sources: Various publications of Venture Economics (Needham, MA). Data on inital public offerings in panel D, rows 5–7, come from Securities Data Corporation.
Note: NA: Not available.

to be a problem. The value of oversight will be greater for these firms. The capital constraints faced by these companies will be very large and the information gathered will help alleviate the constraint. Early stage companies have short or nonexistent histories to examine and are difficult to evaluate. Similarly, firms in industries with significant growth opportunities and high R&D intensities are likely to require close monitoring. A significant fraction of venture investment should therefore be directed towards early stage and high-technology companies.

Total venture financing and the number of financing rounds should also be higher for successful projects than for failures if venture capitalists utilize information in investment decisions. Venture capitalists monitor a firm's progress and discontinue funding the project if they learn negative information that indicates the project is not valuable. In Venture Economics' (1988) review of returns on venture capital investments, venture capital–backed companies that went public in an initial

$2,760	$2,670	$3,230	$3,940	$3,653	$3,261	$2,301	$1,358	$2,543	$3,071	$2,740
1,469	1,377	1,504	1,729	1,472	1,355	1,219	792	1,087	969	1,011
$1.88	$1.94	$2.15	$2.28	$2.48	$2.41	$1.89	$1.71	$2.34	$3.17	$2.71
31.0%	23.0%	37.0%	39.0%	33.0%	35.9%	29.8%	20.4%	26.4%	35.7%	30.6%
69.0%	77.0%	63.0%	61.0%	67.0%	64.1%	70.2%	79.6%	73.6%	64.3%	69.4%
21.0%	15.0%	19.0%	13.0%	12.5%	13.2%	10.0%	10.0%	11.0%	14.0%	19.0%
67.0%	69.0%	58.0%	69.0%	67.5%	65.8%	72.0%	87.0%	82.0%	80.0%	75.0%
12.0%	16.0%	23.0%	18.0%	20.0%	21.0%	18.0%	3.0%	7.0%	6.0%	6.0%
86	101	120	140	135	136	76	65	69	57	97
53	46	97	81	35	39	42.00	122	157	165	136
$743	$838	$2,118	$1,840	$756	$996	$1,148	$3,899	$4,575	$4,861	$3,351
$3,495	$3,258	$8,434	$6,893	$3,122	$3,900	$5,344	$18,637	$21,869	$23,236	$16,018
213	195	417	259	96	254	213	403	605	819	646
$2,545	$3,166	$8,490	$5,220	$2,392	$13,706	$10,117	$25,148	$39,947	$57,517	$33,841
$10,792	$11,618	$31,616	$23,813	$11,759	NA	NA	NA	NA	NA	NA
24.9%	23.6%	23.3%	31.3%	36.5%	15.4%	19.7%	30.3%	26.0%	20.1%	21.1%
29.2%	26.5%	24.9%	35.2%	31.6%	7.3%	11.1%	15.5%	11.5%	8.5%	9.9%
32.4%	28.0%	26.7%	28.9%	26.5%	NA	NA	NA	NA	NA	NA

public offering yielded the highest return for venture investors, an average 59.5 percent per year (7.1 times invested capital returned over 4.2 years). Acquisitions provided mean returns of only 15.4 percent per year (1.7 times invested capital returned over 3.7 years) while liquidations lost 80 percent of their value over 4.1 years. Firms going public should, therefore, receive greater total funding and more rounds of financing than firms that are acquired or liquidated.

The positive relationship between going public and level of investment is not obvious unless venture capitalists utilize information in the continuation decision. If venture capitalists only provide cash, firms that go public might quickly turn profitable and would need *less* venture capital financing and fewer rounds than companies that are acquired or liquidated.

If asymmetric information and agency costs do not exist, the structure of financing is irrelevant. Hart (1991) points out that if entrepreneurs pursue shareholder value maximizing strategies, financing is simple. Venture capitalists should give entrepreneurs all the money they need and entrepreneurs would decide whether to continue the project on the basis of their information. In the case of startups, entrepreneurs would derive stopping rules that maximized shareholder value. These methods are developed in Roberts and Weitzman (1981) and Weitzman, Newey, and Rabin (1981). On the basis of their private information, they would decide whether to continue the project or not.

The private benefits from managing the firms they create, however, may not always be perfectly correlated with shareholders' monetary returns. Entrepreneurs may have incentives to continue running projects they know have negative net present values (NPVs). Similarly, entrepreneurs may invest in projects that have high personal benefits but low monetary returns for investors. If venture capitalists could costlessly monitor the firm, they would monitor and infuse cash continuously. If the firm's expected NPV fell below the stopping point, the venture capitalist would halt funding of the project.

In practice, venture capitalists incur costs when they monitor and infuse capital. Monitoring costs include the opportunity cost of generating reports for both the venture capitalist and entrepreneur. If venture capitalists need to "kick the tires" of the plant, read reports, and take time away from other activities, these costs can be substantial. Contracting costs and the lost time and resources of the entrepreneur must be imputed as well. Each time capital is infused, contracts are written and negotiated, lawyers are paid, and other associated costs are incurred. These costs mean that funding will occur in discrete stages.

Even though venture capitalists periodically "check up" on entrepreneurs between capital infusions, entrepreneurs still have private information about the projects they manage. Gorman and Sahlman (1989) indicate that between financing rounds, the lead venture capitalist visits the entrepreneur once a month on average and spends four to five hours at the facility during each visit. Non-lead venture capitalists typically visit the firm once a quarter for an average of two to three hours. Venture capitalists also receive monthly financial reports. Gorman and Sahlman show, however, that venture capitalists do not usually become involved in the day-to-day management of the firm. Major review of progress, due diligence, and the decision to continue funding are generally done at the time of refinancing. Venture capitalists are concerned that between evaluations, entrepreneurs might behave opportunistically.

Two well-known companies illustrate how venture capitalists use staged investment to evaluate a firm's progress periodically. Apple Computer received three rounds of venture capital financing. In the first round, venture capitalists invested $518,000 in January 1978 at a price of $0.09 per share. The company was doing well by the second round of venture financing in September 1978. Venture investors committed an additional $704,000 at a price of $0.28 per share, reflecting the progress the firm had made. A final venture capital infusion of $2,331,000 was made in December 1980 at $0.97 per share. At each stage, the increasing price per share and the growing investment reflected resolution of uncertainty concerning Apple's prospects.

Federal Express represents a second example of how venture capitalists utilize staged capital infusions to monitor the firm. Federal Express also received three rounds of venture capital financing, but the firm's prospects developed in a much different manner. The first venture financing round occurred in September 1973, when $12.25 million was invested at a price of $204.17 per share. The firm's performance was well below expectations and a second venture financing round was necessary in March 1974, when $6.4 million was invested at $7.34 per share and reflected the poor performance of the company. Performance continued to deteriorate and a third round of financing was needed in September 1974. At this stage, the venture capital investors intervened extensively in the strategy of the company. The $3.88 million investment was priced at $0.63 per share. Ultimately, performance improved and Federal Express went public in 1978 at $6 per share, but the staged investment of the venture capitalist allowed the venture investors to intervene and price subsequent rounds so they could earn a fair rate of return.

Two related types of agency costs exist in entrepreneurial firms. Both agency costs result from the large asymmetric information that affects young, growth companies in need of financing. First, entrepreneurs might invest in strategies, research, or projects that have high personal returns but low expected monetary payoffs to shareholders. For example, a biotechnology company founder may choose to invest in a certain type of research that brings him/her great recognition in the scientific community but provides less return for the venture capitalist than other projects. Similarly, because entrepreneurs' equity stakes are essentially call options,[2] they have incentives to pursue high variance strategies like rushing a product to market when further testing may be warranted.

Second, if the entrepreneur possesses private information about the firm and chooses to continue investing in a negative NPV project, the entrepreneur is undertaking inefficient continuation. For example, managers may receive initial results from market trials indicating little demand for a new product, but entrepreneurs may want to keep the company going because they receive significant private benefits from managing their own firm.

The nature of the firm's assets may have important implications for expected agency costs and the structure of staged venture capital investments as well. The capital structure literature motivates a search for those factors. Much of this literature (Harris and Raviv, 1991) has emphasized the role of agency costs in determining leverage. Asset characteristics that increase expected agency costs of debt reduce leverage and make monitoring more valuable. Therefore, factors reducing leverage should shorten funding duration in venture capital transactions.

Williamson (1988) argues that leverage should be positively related to the liquidation value of assets. Higher liquidation values mean that default is less costly. Liquidation value is positively related to the tangibility of assets. Tangible assets (e.g., machines and plants) are, on average, easier to sell and receive a higher fraction of their book value than do intangible assets like patents or copyrights. In empirical research on capital structure, many researchers, including Titman and Wessels (1988), Friend and Lang (1988), and Rajan and Zingales (1995), use the ratio of tangible assets to total assets as a measure of liquidation value. All find that use of debt increases with asset tangibility.

In the context of staged venture capital investments, intangible assets would be associated with greater agency costs. As assets become more tangible, venture capitalists can recover more of their investment in liquidation, and expected losses due to inefficient continuation are reduced. This reduces the need to monitor tightly and should increase funding duration.

Shleifer and Vishny (1992) build upon Williamson's model by exploring how asset specificity might affect liquidation value and debt levels. They show that firms with highly industry- and firm-specific assets should use less debt because asset specificity significantly reduces liquidation value. Firms with high R&D intensities likely generate assets that are very firm- and industry-specific. Bradley, Jarrell, and Kim (1984) and Titman and Wessels (1988) use the ratio of R&D to sales to measure uniqueness of assets in investigating the use of debt. Both find a negative relationship between leverage and R&D intensity. Similarly, Barclay and Smith (1995) utilize the ratio of R&D to firm value to explore debt maturity.

Asset specificity would also influence the structure of staged venture capital investments. Industries with high levels of R&D intensity would be subject to greater discretionary investment by the entrepreneur and increase risks associated with firm- and industry-specific assets. These factors increase expected agency costs and shorten funding durations.

Finally, Myers (1977) argues that firms whose value is largely dependent upon investment in future growth options would make less use of debt because the owner/manager can undertake investment strategies that are particularly detrimental to bondholders. Myers suggests that a firm's market-to-book ratio may be related to the fraction of firm value accounted for by future growth opportunities. Empirical results support this prediction. Rajan and Zingales (1995) discover a negative relationship between firm market-to-book ratios and leverage. Similarly, Barclay and Smith (1995) show that debt maturity declines with a firm's market-to-book ratio.

Entrepreneurs have more discretion to invest in personally beneficial strategies at shareholders' expense in industries where firm value is largely dependent upon future growth opportunities. Firms with high market-to-book ratios are more susceptible to these agency costs, thus increasing the value of monitoring and reducing funding duration.

Why can other financial intermediaries (e.g., banks) not do the same sort of monitoring? First, because regulations limit banks' ability to hold shares, they cannot use equity to fund projects.[3] Asset substitution becomes a problem if banks provide debt financing for very high-risk projects. Though several papers focus on monitoring by banks (James, 1987; Petersen and Rajan, 1994; 1995; Hoshi et al., 1991), banks may not have the necessary skills to evaluate projects with few collateralizable assets and significant ex ante uncertainty. In addition, Petersen and Rajan (1995) argue that banks in competitive markets will be unable to finance high-risk projects because they are unable to extract rents in subsequent transactions with the company. Taking an equity position in the firm allows ex post settling up, guaranteeing that the venture capitalist benefits if the firm does well.

In addition, because the probability of failure is so high, venture capitalists need a substantial fraction of the firm's equity in order to make a fair return on their portfolio of investments. Even if banks were to make loans to high-risk firms, required interest payments would be extraordinarily high, creating severe liquidity problems that would limit a firm's growth and exacerbate risk-shifting problems. Finally, venture capital funds' high-powered compensation schemes examined by Gompers and Lerner (1996a) give venture capitalists incentives to monitor firms more closely because their individual compensation is closely linked to the funds' returns.

Gompers (1995) utilizes a unique data set to test the agency and monitoring cost predictions. A random sample of 794 venture capital–financed companies provides a detailed picture of the structure of venture capital investments and the distribution of outcomes for venture-backed projects (e.g., IPO, merger, bankruptcy). The results confirm the predictions of agency theory. Venture capitalists concentrate investments in early stage companies and high-technology industries where informational asymmetries are significant and monitoring is valuable. Venture capitalists monitor the firm's progress and if they learn negative information about future returns, the project is cut off from new financing. Firms that go public (these firms yield the highest return for venture capitalists on average) receive more total financing and a greater number of rounds than other firms (those that go bankrupt or are acquired). Gompers also finds that early stage firms receive significantly less money per round. Increases in asset tangibility increase financing duration and reduce monitoring intensity. As the role of future investment opportunities in firm value increases (higher market-to-book ratios), duration declines. Similarly, higher R&D intensities lead to shorter funding durations. These results provide evidence of the important monitoring and information generating role played by venture capitalists.

4   Syndication of Venture Capital Investments

Most venture capital investments are made in syndicates. One venture firm will originate the deal and look to bring in other venture capital firms. This syndication of investment serves multiple purposes. It allows the venture capital firm to diversify into more investments. If the venture capitalist had to invest the entire amount into all its companies, then she could make many fewer investments. Because the total risk of any particular investment is so high compared to the systematic risk, diversification is very beneficial. By investing in more projects (the typical venture capital fund invests in fifteen to twenty companies), the venture capitalist can largely diversify away idiosyncratic risk.

For example, a typical venture capital firm may raise fifty to one hundred million dollars. In any one particular round, the company receives between two and five million dollars. If the typical venture-backed company receives three rounds of venture financing, any one firm might require ten to twenty million dollars of financing. If the venture capital firm originating the deal were to make the entire investment, the lack of diversification would be very large; i.e., they could only make five to ten investments. Hence the value of bringing in syndicate partners from purely diversification benefits is large.

Another potential explanation for syndication patterns is that bringing in other venture firms to provide their own due diligence acts as a second option on the investment opportunity. There is usually no clearcut answer with any of the investments the venture firm undertakes.

Having other investors okay the deal makes it much less likely that bad deals get funded. This is particularly true when the company is early stage and/or technology-based.

Lerner (1994a) tests this "second opinion" hypothesis in a sample of biotechnology venture capital investments. In a sample of 271 firms, Lerner finds that in the early rounds of investing, experienced venture capitalists tend to syndicate only with venture capital firms that have similar experience. Lerner argues that if a venture capitalist is looking for a second opinion, then he will want to get a second opinion from someone of similar or better ability, certainly not from someone of lesser ability.

After several rounds of investment, venture capital firms tend to add new syndicate partners. These syndicate partners are generally less experienced and less well known. Admati and Pfleiderer (1994) present a model that potentially explains this pattern; they argue that the venture capitalist originating the investment has superior information relative to its syndicate partners. Because the venture capitalist does not have enough capital to bring all projects to fruition without resources from other venture firms, he must syndicate. The lead venture capitalist might have an incentive to increase his percentage investment in firms he thinks have particularly good prospects and let the syndicate partners take a larger fraction of the investments that he feels are not so good. This potential adverse selection problem reduces the types of feasible contracts. The only type of contract that is robust to small changes in agency costs and information structures is a fixed fraction of equity contract. This implies that the originating venture capitalist keeps his percentage of the company constant in each round. This implies bringing on new venture capitalists in each new investment round.

Finally, syndication of investment may increase the bargaining power of the venture capitalists (Gompers, 1993). If the relationship were one venture capitalist and one entrepreneur, a bilateral monopoly would result. The entrepreneur could always threaten to walk away from the project if the venture capitalist did not renegotiate the terms of the contract. Few projects would get funded because the venture capitalist would realize that the possibility of this opportunistic behavior existed. An extensive literature in the bargaining area has shown that bilateral monopolies often lead to situations that are difficult to resolve.

By syndicating the investment, the venture capitalist creates a holdout problem that credibly commits the venture capital syndicate not to renegotiate should the entrepreneur attempt to gain any advantage ex post. This may be particularly true if one of the venture firms has a reputation as a tough bargainer. This commitment device may be particularly useful in industries without significant tangible assets where the bargaining power of the entrepreneur may otherwise be significant.

5   Contracting and Incentive Design

5.1   Theory

Venture capital provides a unique perspective in which to examine the nature of financial contracting and corporate control. Venture capitalists raise money from individuals and institutions to invest in early stage entrepreneurial projects. These projects are characterized by their extreme riskiness, asymmetric information, and potentially high rewards. Venture Economics (1988), however, noted that 6.8 percent of all venture-backed projects accounted for almost 50 percent of the return for venture capital funds; 34.5 percent of all projects experienced either a partial or total loss of invested capital. The variance in potential outcomes is quite high.

Security design and corporate control mechanisms are central concerns for venture capitalists given the uncertainty and asymmetric information associated with start-up firms. This asymmetric information and uncertainty may make firms impossible to finance and exacerbate capital rationing. Amit, Glosten, and Muller (1990a; 1996b) develop one model of venture capital in which adverse selection drives out all but the least able entrepreneurs. They claim that the average quality of venture capital–financed firms will be less than that of comparable non-venture-capital–financed companies.

The contractual relationships between venture capitalists and entrepreneurs need to align entrepreneurs' incentives with venture capitalists' goals. The venture capital industry has developed control mechanisms to deal with incentive problems in an uncertain environment that try to minimize capital rationing. In this section, I focus on the ubiquitous use of convertible securities in the financing arrangement between venture capitalists and entrepreneurs and show how convertible debt is an incentive compatible financial instrument that alleviates Amit, Glosten, and Muller's adverse selection problem and leads to better allocation of control rights.

While many theories of financial instruments have been developed around optimal control allocation, the use of cash flow to determine control right allocation may not be optimal in an entrepreneurial setting. Other contractual measures within venture capital financings can address the issue of state contingent control. Venture financing agreements give the venture capitalist the right to control the board of directors, fire the entrepreneur, and dilute the entrepreneur's equity stake if performance is below expectations. Periodic review and staged capital infusions allow venture capitalists to determine control allocation on a recurring basis (Gompers, 1995). Sahlman (1990) hypothesizes that the most important roles of convertible securities are to align the incentives of entrepreneurs and venture capitalists properly and to provide information about the entrepreneur.

Returns on venture capital investments declined substantially during the mid-1980s. These declining returns motivate Amit, Glosten, and Muller (1990a; 1990b) to develop an adverse selection model of venture capital financing. In their model, risk aversion motivates entrepreneurs to seek insurance by utilizing outside funding. Amit et al. assume that the venture capital market is competitive and that competition ensures that venture capitalists make zero risk-adjusted profits. If entrepreneurial ability is common knowledge, then the financing market will be efficient and all positive NPV projects will be funded by venture capitalists. Each contract correctly prices ability and risk sharing benefits are realized.

Amit, Glosten, and Muller extend the model by assuming entrepreneurial ability is private information. Venture capitalists cannot distinguish between good and bad entrepreneurs. Consequently, venture capitalists price their bid at the average ability of those entrepreneurs who are willing to accept it in equilibrium. Because the authors assume entrepreneurs can self-finance or seek other financing (albeit at a higher cost) and because they assume venture capital contracts are pure equity, high-ability entrepreneurs choose to opt out of the venture capital market. Only low-ability entrepreneurs accept venture capital financing. The Akerlof "lemons" (1970) problem implies that failure rates will be higher for venture capital–backed firms than they are for comparable non-venture-backed firms. Amit, Glosten, and Muller claim their model suggests that new methods of startup financing need to be developed.

The adverse selection problem described by Amit, Glosten, and Muller (1990a; 1990b) is recognized in the venture capital market and control mechanisms attempt to deal with it. By using industry expertise and close monitoring, venture capitalists reduce the asymmetric information inherent in startup ventures. The adverse selection problem can also be alleviated with various contractual features included in venture capital. Convertible debt can act as both a screening and an incentive compatible financing mechanism. The adverse selection result holds only because the venture capital market is unable to sort bad entrepreneurs from good ones with equity.

The screening/incentive model developed in Gompers (1996b) focuses on the incentive effects of cash flow allocation created by financing choice. Gompers assumes that control rights are not necessarily allocated proportionally to cash flows. The model has two periods. In period 1, risk neutral venture capitalists make bids to wealth constrained entrepreneurs. A bid is either (1) a fraction of equity demanded, (2) a fixed debt repayment, or (3) a fixed debt repayment that is convertible into a fraction of equity if convertible debt is used. Debt and equity have the common payoff structures assumed in practice. Debt has a fixed claim on the terminal cash flows of the project. Equity receives a proportional payout of the profits. Two types of entrepreneurs exist. High-ability entrepreneurs are present in proportion ϱ with $0 < \varrho < 1$. Low-ability entrepreneurs are a fraction $1 - \varrho$ of the population. Ability is private information. Each type of entrepreneur has access to a project that can utilize one of two types of assets: risky and safe assets. Each asset requires the same level of investment and both are mutually exclusive. Investment choices are impossible to monitor or verify but returns are verifiable. The probability of the larger payoff is higher if the safe asset is developed. In addition, the high-ability entrepreneur always has a higher probability of generating the bigger payoff. Both high- and low-ability entrepreneurs can enter an alternative labor market and earn their marginal product in that market.

Under mild assumptions, some very strong results can be derived. The only assumptions that are necessary for deriving the optimality of convertible debt or convertible preferred equity are the following: (1) If high-ability entrepreneurs employ the safe asset, the expected return is greater than the investment cost plus the entrepreneurs' opportunity cost. This implies that it is efficient for high-ability entrepreneurs to enter the entrepreneurial sector. (2) Low-ability entrepreneurs, however, generate expected returns that are less than the investment and opportunity costs. Therefore, it is inefficient for low-ability entrepreneurs to invest in a project. (3) The risky asset always expects to return less than the safe asset. While all start-up companies are risky, the entrepreneur usually has the opportunity to change strategy or investment and potentially increase the project's riskiness. For example, an entrepreneur may rush a product to market before complete testing has shown whether the product is reliable. Similarly, a firm's founder may choose to devote all resources to a single development path when parallel paths might be better. (4) A lower bound for the opportunity cost exists and the opportunity cost is high enough to ensure that low-ability entrepreneurs can be punished relative to what they would earn by not developing a project. If the outside opportunity cost were insignificant, entrepreneurs would always want to develop projects and only pooling equilibria would be possible.

Amit, Glosten, and Muller (1990a; 1990b) implicitly assume that venture capitalists use equity to finance projects. The choice of financing instrument is critical for the adverse selection results. Gompers shows that an equity contract that separates low-ability entrepreneurs and yields zero profits for the venture capitalist does not exist. Because low-ability and high-ability entrepreneurs pool in the pure equity case, high-ability entrepreneurs are making less profit than they could if they had other financing options. If high-ability entrepreneurs can self-finance their projects or finance them with non-venture-capital sources, they might opt out of the venture capital market. This is what Amit, Glosten, and Muller demonstrate.

The intuition behind this result is straightforward. Equity is a "soft" security because it shares equally in the upside and downside. Because low-ability entrepreneurs do not bear the entire cost of poor outcomes if they develop projects when straight equity is used, they would choose to invest more often than is socially optimal.

Debt contracts might offer hope of separating high- and low-ability entrepreneurs. Other agency costs, however, may increase if debt is used to finance the entrepreneur. Gompers (1996b) shows that given the assumption in his model, if entrepreneurs did not have access to risky assets, a competitive debt contract would separate the two types of entrepreneurs. When entrepreneurs have access to risky assets, however, they always have incentives to increase risk.

This is clearly evident if we view levered equity as a call option on the assets of the firm as Merton (1973) suggests. In this case, the value of levered equity increases with the volatility of the potential returns. The entrepreneur would therefore always have an incentive to increase the riskiness of the project.

The potential problems of straight debt and straight equity financing can be reduced using convertible debt. The hybrid nature of convertible debt means that it can both screen out bad entrepreneurs and reduce incentives to take risk. Because the convertible maintains its debt like features when returns are low, low-ability entrepreneurs would not receive any return. Venture capitalists maintain priority. But because the debt converts into equity, the entrepreneur does not gain by increasing risk. Some of the upside potential from increasing risk is captured by the convertible portion of the contract. The contract can therefore reduce both types of agency costs.

The use of convertible debt is consistent with Sahlman's (1990) description of venture capital financing structure. In the incentive/

screening model, Gompers (1996b) shows that convertible debt is a competitive, incentive compatible financing instrument. The venture capitalist earns a fair return, high-ability entrepreneurs develop safe projects, and low-ability entrepreneurs choose not to invest and become entrepreneurs.

Unknown ability is likely to be an important concern for venture capitalists. Because the project's success is so dependent upon the entrepreneur's human capital, the venture capitalist spends significant time and resources determining the management team's ability. The single most important factor determining whether a project is funded or not is the entrepreneur's perceived ability. Many business plans look similar, but establishing the ability of the entrepreneur becomes pivotal. Lack of management skills is the reason cited most often for failure of venture capital–backed projects (Gorman and Sahlman, 1989). In designing contracts, venture capitalists must always be wary of the desire of incompetent entrepreneurs to see their projects funded.

Venture capitalists do need to be concerned about actions that the entrepreneur might take to increase the riskiness of a project. Although venture capitalists take an active role in advising and monitoring entrepreneurs, they are usually not involved in the day-to-day activities of the firm unless things go drastically wrong. Entrepreneurs are free to cut corners in the desire to get to market quickly even if this substantially increases risk. Venture capitalists usually cannot observe or verify these "cut corners" or changes in strategy. One mechanism to reduce the desire to take such risks is to use convertible debt.

5.2   Conversion and Call Provisions

The incentive/screening model emphasizes the asymmetric information about the entrepreneur's ability and the riskiness of the project. If convertible debt is used to sort out low-ability entrepreneurs and reduce risk taking, then the venture capitalist would want to delay conversion either until an exit is achieved or until information arrives that signals the project is a success and the entrepreneur has high ability.[4] If the entrepreneur could call the debt before new information about the project outcome arrived, the equilibria of the model would unravel. Low-ability entrepreneurs would have a greater incentive to mimic high-ability entrepreneurs.

An analysis of the common features of venture capital contracts in Gompers (1996b) shows that they are quite different from public convertible contracts and their features are consistent with the incentive/screening model developed. None of the issues was callable within a five year period and only 8 percent (four contracts) allowed the entrepreneur voluntarily to redeem the convertible after that time. Because most firms achieve some exit within five years (Gompers [1996a] shows that the median holding period is approximately three years from first investment to IPO), the call protection is effectively 100 percent; 92 percent of the contracts had mandatory conversion at the time of IPO. The conversion at IPO was contingent upon the price per share and the amount of money raised by the firm. A substantial minority (38 percent) were automatically converted if certain profit, sales, and/or performance milestones were attained.

Benton and Gunderson (1983) describe the conversion features in their legal textbook on venture capital contracts:

> Venture capitalists are often reluctant to invest in a Preferred Stock that is callable. . . . Accordingly, most venture capitalists will opt for automatic conversion events instead of agreeing to voluntary redemption provisions. . . . The venture capitalist will prefer automatic conversion provisions to voluntary redemption provisions, however, because the venture capitalist can, at the investment's outset, agree upon automatic conversion events that, if achieved, will mean that the venture capitalist's investment has been a successful one (by the venture capitalist's own standards).[5]

Clearly, venture capitalists only want conversion when they have some information about projects' outcomes. This motivation is consistent with the incentive/screening model presented in this chapter.

The conversion provisions are clearly consistent with the incentive compatible financing model developed in Gompers (1996b). Conversion occurs only at the time of IPO or when sales and profits reach certain defined levels. These two events are likely to be very strong signals that the project is a success and are able to limit low-ability entrepreneurs' gain from accepting venture capitalists' offers. Gompers finds that the only variable that is related to the inclusion of automatic conversion provisions is whether the company was an early stage investment. The probability of including such an automatic conversion covenant increases if the investment is early stage. Conversion of early stage investments would be tied closely to indicators of success.

5.3   Separation of Cash Flow Allocation and Control Rights

Marx (1994) and Berglöf (1994) both emphasize the control and intervention aspects of convertible debt or convertible preferred equity in venture capital financing. The actual contracts between venture capitalists and entrepreneurs separate control and cash flow allocation, however. First, the contracts usually contain explicit control rights that are allocated to the venture capitalist independently of the allocation of cash flows. These include rights to appoint and remove key managers, voting control of the board of directors, and explicit approval of large expenditures. In addition, Gompers (1995) demonstrates that the staged investment structure of venture capital can effectively control the entrepreneur. The threat of withholding additional financing is, as Sahlman (1990) points out, the most important control mechanism that the venture capitalist can employ.

Separation of control and cash flow allocation may be important in an entrepreneurial setting. The use of financing choice as an incentive and screening device is effective because the entrepreneur's ability and effort are critical to the success of the new company. Rewarding the entrepreneur when the firm is sold or goes public ensures that the entrepreneur's incentives are closely aligned with those of the venture capitalist. Large private benefits may make it difficult to control opportunistic behavior and provide proper incentives to exert effort. Grossman and Hart (1986) argue that ownership, which they define as the ability to control an asset and exclude people from it, should be allocated to the contracting party that is least likely to engage in opportunistic renegotiation. Under mild assumptions, venture capitalists should be given control over certain aspects of the firm. This control might be independent of cash flow allocation. Explicitly assigning certain control rights to the venture capitalist (independently of cash flow allocation) may improve efficiency. Venture capitalists often remove entrepreneurs from the firm or bring in a new CEO when the entrepreneur is no longer the best manager. These changes in control are the result of explicit control rights or the power of staged investment.

Gompers (1996b) finds that every contract had covenants that restricted various decisions of the entrepreneur. For example, most of the documents had restrictions on major acquisition or disposal of assets that required approval of the venture investors. Similarly, all contracts restricted the ability of the entrepreneur to issue new securities that were senior to the current issue. Using these types of restrictions gave the venture investors considerable control over the firm's activities.

Several other control mechanisms showed more variation. An important mechanism of control is representation on the board of directors. The average venture capital–backed company in the sample had just over five board members. Venture capitalists controlled 2.68 seats on average, essentially giving them control of the board of directors.

Two other control mechanisms that were often included in the convertible preferred agreement were superpriority and redemption rights. In each contract, acquisitions were treated the same as liquidations.

Convertible preferred shareholders would receive highest priority and receive the return of their total investment before the common shareholders receive anything. Over half (66 percent) combined the claims of the convertible preferred and common in any claim after the initial amount given back to the convertible shareholder, essentially superpriority.[6] Of the contracts 54 percent gave the common some specified payoff before the residual claims of the preferred and common were lumped together. Finally, over half of the contracts (68 percent) gave the venture investors optional redemption rights, which gave the venture investors the ability to put the stock to the company, forcing them to repay the face value of the convertible plus any accrued but unpaid dividends.

6   A Control Theory of Venture Capital

The preceding analysis highlights the importance of nonmonetary aspects of venture capital. The capital is clearly important. In order to overcome capital rationing, however, the other aspects of venture capitalists' investment process are clearly paramount. Without cash, these firms could not invest. Many of these firms are subject to severe credit rationing. It is the very nature of asymmetric information and uncertainty that leads to the inability to finance many startup firms. In order to understand the role of venture capital, capital theory must be put into a proper framework.

The work of Modigliani and Miller (1958) demonstrates that under certain conditions, the instrument and source of financing are irrelevant to the value of a firm and hence to its investment decisions. There should be no difference between internal and external sources of capital. If cash flow is insufficient to meet investment needs, the firm can issue securities (it does not matter if they are debt or equity) and invest at the optimal level. In a world with taxes and costly financial distress, the firm has an optimal capital structure, but the investment decision of the firm is still independent of the source of capital if markets are efficient.

The assumption that the source of capital does not matter has been challenged in recent work. Jensen and Meckling (1976) demonstrate that agency costs between managers and outside claimants to the firm result if the managers raise outside capital. If the firm is financed by outside equity, the manager has an incentive to consume perquisites because she does not bear the entire cost. Similarly, if the firm is financed by outside debt, the manager may increase risk. Because providers of capital recognize the incentives of the manager, the pricing of outside financing reflects the agency problems and therefore has a higher cost of capital than internally generated funds.

Even if the manager is motivated to maximize shareholder value, informational asymmetries may make external capital more expensive. Myers and Majluf (1984) and Stiglitz and Weiss (1983) demonstrate that equity offerings of firms may be associated with an Akerlof's (1970) lemons problem. If the manager is better informed about the investment opportunities of the firm and acts in the interest of current shareholders, then managers only issue new shares when the company's stock is overvalued. Stock prices decline at the announcement of equity issues because of the negative signal it sends to the market. This reasoning leads Myers (1984) to propose a pecking order theory of financing. Firms tap the cheapest sources of capital first. Internally generated capital is cheaper than debt issues, which are cheaper than equity issues.

Models of the debt market have also focused on the effects of informational asymmetries. Stiglitz and Weiss (1981) show that because banks cannot discriminate among companies, raising interest rates to reflect the risk associated with the projects financed can lead to adverse selection problems. In this case, the bank restricts credit rather than increasing interest rates. Borrowers who are willing to borrow at prevailing interest rates do not receive credit. The key factor leading to higher cost of external capital in models of debt and equity financing is asymmetric information. Eliminate the asymmetric information and the financing constraint disappears.

The inability to verify outcomes leads to noncontractabilities that make external financing costly. Many of the models of ownership (Grossman and Hart, 1986; Hart and Moore, 1990) and financing choice (Hart and Moore, 1989) rely on the inability of investors to verify that certain actions have been taken or certain outcomes have occurred. While actions or outcomes might be observable, meaning that investors know what the entrepreneur did, they would not be verifiable; i.e., investors could not convince a court of the action or outcome. Startup firms that have tremendous uncertainty associated with the future evolution of events are subject to exactly these types of situations. Such conditions lead to external financing's being costly or difficult to obtain.

Fazzari, Hubbard, and Petersen (1988) and Hoshi, Kashyap, and Scharfstein (1991) examine the effects of capital constraints on investment behavior of firms. Both papers classify firms into groups that are ex ante expected to be more or less affected by capital constraints. Fazzari et al. divide firms into high dividend payout firms and low dividend payout firms. Low payout firms are assumed to be more capital constrained. Fazzari et al. find that cash flows are more highly correlated with investment in the low payout group and conclude that capital constraints are more severe for this group.

Hoshi, Kashyap, and Scharfstein (1991) present similar results for keiretsu and non-keiretsu companies in Japan. Keiretsu members have closer ties to a large bank than non-keiretsu companies. Member firms are likely to be less capital constrained than nonmember firms because the informational asymmetries between the bank and the firm are reduced. When they estimate various investment equations, Hoshi et al. find that cash flow helps to explain investment levels in non-keiretsu firms better than in keiretsu firms. The evidence supports the role of informational asymmetries and their effect on generating capital constraints.

Venture capital firms specialize in collecting and evaluating information on startup and growth companies. These types of companies are the most prone to asymmetric information and potential capital constraints. Because the venture capitalist alleviates some of the asymmetric information, we would expect that the investment behavior of venture capital–backed firms would be less dependent upon internally generated cash flows. Whether the project is in a high- or low-technology industry, venture capitalists are active investors. As the results reviewed in this chapter indicate, venture capitalists employ numerous control mechanisms to overcome agency costs and efficiently allocate resources. They monitor the progress of firms, sit on boards of directors, and mete out financing based on attainment of milestones. Venture capitalists retain the right to appoint key managers and remove members of the entrepreneurial team.

The control mechanisms that are implemented by venture investors often change the ability of the entrepreneur to exploit his information advantages or the noncontractabilities. They make the entrepreneur financeable. This is the competitive advantage of the U.S. venture capital model. It is the nonmonetary aspects of venture capital that are critical to its success. The evolution in contractual terms and operating strategy should be implemented if the U.S. experience is to be replicated. While the elements mentioned in this chapter may not be sufficient for promoting an effective venture capital sector, they are clearly necessary.

Notes

I would like to thank Josh Lerner, Andrew Mertrick, Randall Morck, Richard Ruback, Bill Sahlman, Andrei Shleifer, and Jeremy Stein for comments on various sections of this chapter as well as participants at the conference Entrepreneurship, SMEs, and the Macroeconomy in Jönköping, Sweden. This research

232   **Paul A. Gompers**

was funded by the Division of Research at the Harvard Business School. Any errors are my own.

[1] Amit, Glosten, and Muller (1990a) present an alternative model in which venture capitalists cannot generate information and separate high-ability entrepreneurs from low-ability entrepreneurs. In this case, adverse selection leads only low-ability entrepreneurs to accept venture capital financing.

[2] The entrepreneurs' equity stakes are almost always junior to the preferred equity position of venture capital investors. The seniority of the venture capitalists' stake makes the entrepreneur's payoff analogous to levered equity; hence it is also equivalent to a call option. Similarly, if the firm is doing poorly and the option is "out of the money," entrepreneurs may have incentives to increase risk substantially.

[3] Banks and their affiliates in other countries do venture capital–like financing (Sahlman, 1992), but their ability to hold equity is critical.

[4] If the project is a success, the optimal strategy is for the venture capitalist to take compensation as equity. Low-ability entrepreneurs still have no incentive to accept the financing if conversion occurs only after information of success arrives.

[5] Parentheses are in original.

[6] The convertible preferred shares were treated as the maximum number of common shares into which they convert for determining their share in this residual claim at liquidation.

References

Admati, A., and P. Pfleiderer, 1994, Robust financial contracting and the role for venture capitalists, *Journal of Finance* 49, 371–402.

Akerlof, G., 1970, The market for "lemons": Qualitative uncertainty and the market mechanism, *Quarterly Journal of Economics* 84, 488–500.

Amit, R., L. Glosten, and E. Muller, 1990a, Entrepreneurial ability, venture investments, and risk sharing, *Management Science* 36, 1232–1245.

Amit, R., L. Glosten, and E. Muller, 1990b, Does venture capital foster the most promising entrepreneurial firms? *California Management Review*, 102–111.

Asquith, P., 1991, Convertible debt: A dynamic test of call policy, MIT working paper.

Barclay, M., and C. Smith, 1995, The priority of corporate liabilities, *Journal of Finance* 50, 899–917.

Barry, C., C. Muscarella, J. Peavy, and M. Vetsuypens, 1990, The role of venture capital in the creation of public companies: Evidence from the going public process, *Journal of Financial Economics* 27, 447–472.

Benton, L., and R. Gunderson, 1983, in M. Halloran, L. Benton, and J. Lovejoy (eds), *Venture Capital and Public Offering Negotiation*, New York, Harcourt Brace Jovanovich.

Berglöf, E., 1994, A control theory of venture capital finance, *Journal of Law, Economics, and Organizations* 10, 247–267.

Black, Bernard, and Ronald Gilson, 1997, Venture capital and the structure of capital markets: Banks versus stock markets, Columbia University Law School working paper.

Blanchard, O., F. Lopez de Silanes, and A. Shleifer, 1994, What do firms do with cash windfalls? *Journal of Financial Economics* 36, 337–360.

Bradley, M., G. Jarrell, and E. H. Kim, 1984, On the existence of an optimal capital structure: Theory and evidence, *Journal of Finance* 39, 857–878.

Brav, A., and P. Gompers, 1997, Myth or reality? The long-run underperformance of initial public offerings: Evidence from venture and nonventure-backed companies, *Journal of Finance* 52, 1791–1822.

Brennan, M., and A. Kraus, 1987, Efficient financing under asymmetric information, *Journal of Finance* 42, 1225–1243.

Brennan, M., and E. Schwartz, 1988, The case for convertibles, *Journal of Applied Corporate Finance* 1, 55–64.

Chan, Y., 1983, On the positive role of financial intermediation in allocation of venture capital in a market with imperfect information, *Journal of Finance* 38, 1543–1568.

Essig, S., 1991, Convertible securities and capital structure determinant, unpublished Ph.D., University of Chicago.

Fazzari, S., R. G. Hubbard, and B. Petersen, 1988, Investment and finance reconsidered, *Brookings Papers on Economic Activity*, 141–195.

Friend, I., and L. Lang, 1988, An empirical test of the impact of managerial self-interest on corporate capital structure, *Journal of Finance* 43, 271–281.

Gompers, P., 1993, Syndication, hold-out problems, and venture capital, University of Chicago working paper.

Gompers, P., 1995, Optimal investment, monitoring, and the staging of venture capital, *Journal of Finance* 50, 1461–1490.

Gompers, P., 1996a, Grandstanding in the venture capital industry, *Journal of Financial Economics* 42, 133–156.

Gompers, P., 1996b, An examination of convertible securities in venture capital investments, Harvard University working paper.

Gompers, P., and J. Lerner, 1996a, An analysis of compensation in the US venture partnership, University of Chicago and Harvard University working paper.

Gompers, P., and J. Lerner, 1996b, The use of covenants: An analysis of venture partnership agreements, *Journal of Law and Economics* 39, 463–498.

Gorman, M., and W. Sahlman, 1989, What do venture capitalists do? *Journal of Business Venturing* 4, 231–248.

Grassmuck, Karen, 1990, The much-praised and often-criticized 'architect' of Harvard's endowment growth steps down, *Chronicle of Higher Education*. 36 (June 6), A25–A27.

Green, R., 1984, Investment incentives, debt, and warrants, *Journal of Financial Economics* 13, 115–136.

Grossman, S., and O. Hart, 1983, An analysis of the principal-agent problem, *Econometrica* 51, 7–45.

Grossman, S., and O. Hart, 1986, The costs and benefits of ownership: a theory of vertical and lateral integration, *Journal of Political Economy* 94, 691–719.

Harris, M., and A. Raviv, 1991, The theory of capital structure, *Journal of Finance* 46, 297–356.

Hart, O., 1991, Theories of optimal capital structure: A principal agent perspective, Harvard University working paper.

Hart, O., and B. Holmstrom, 1987, The Theory of Contracts, in T. Bewly (ed),

234   Paul A. Gompers

Advances in Economic Theory, Fifth World Congress, Cambridge, Cambridge University Press.
Hart, O., and J. Moore, 1989, Default and renegotiation: A dynamic model of debt, Harvard University working paper.
Hart, O., and J. Moore, 1990, Property rights and the nature of the firm, *Journal of Political Economy* 98, 1119–1158.
Hellman, T., 1994, Financial structure and control in venture capital, Stanford University working paper.
Holmstrom, B., 1982, Moral hazard in teams, *Bell Journal of Economics* 13, 324–340.
Holmstrom, B., and P. Milgrom, 1987, Aggregation and linearity in the provision of intertemporal incentives, *Econometrica* 55, 303–328.
Holmstrom, B., and P. Milgrom, 1990, Multi-task principal-agent analysis, MIT working paper.
Hoshi, T., A. Kashyap, and D. Scharfstein, 1991, Corporate structure, liquidity, and investment, *Quarterly Journal of Economics* 106, 33–60.
James, C., 1987, Some evidence on the uniqueness of bank loans: A comparison of bank borrowing, private placements, and public offerings, *Journal of Financial Economics* 19, 217–235.
Jensen, M., 1986, Agency cost of free cash flow, corporate finance and takeovers, *AER Papers and Proceedings* 76, 323–329.
Jensen, M., and W. Meckling, 1976, Theory of the firm: Managerial behavior, agency costs, and capital structure, *Journal of Financial Economics* 3, 305–360.
Lerner, J., 1994a, The syndication of venture capital investments, *Financial Management* 23, 16–27.
Lerner, J., 1994b, Venture capital and the oversight of privately-held firms, *Journal of Financial Economics* 35, 293–316.
Marx, L., 1994, Negotiation and renegotiation of venture capital contracts, University of Rochester working paper.
Merton, R., 1973, A theory of rational option pricing, *Bell Journal of Economics and Management Science* 4, 141–183.
Modigliani, F., and M. Miller, 1958, The cost of capital, corporation finance, and the theory of investment, *American Economic Review* 48, 261–297.
Myers, S., 1977, Determinants of corporate borrowing, *Journal of Financial Economics* 5, 147–175.
Myers, S., 1984, The capital structure puzzle, *Journal of Finance* 39, 575–592.
Myers, S., and N. M. Majluf, 1984, Corporate financing and investment decisions when firms have information that investors do not have, *Journal of Financial Economics* 13, 187–221.
Petersen, M., and R. Rajan, 1994, The benefits of firm-creditor relationships: A study of small business financings, *Journal of Finance* 49, 3–35.
Petersen, M., and R. Rajan, 1995, The effect of credit market competition on lending relationships, *Quarterly Journal of Economics* 110, 407–444.
Pindyck, R., 1991, Irreversibility, uncertainty, and investment, *Journal of Economic Literature* 29, 1110–1148.
Rajan, R., and L. Zingales, 1995, What do we know about capital structure? Some evidence from international data, *Journal of Finance* 50, 1421–1460.
Roberts, K., and M. Weitzman, 1981, Funding criteria for research, development, and exploration projects, *Econometrica* 49, 1261–1288.

Sahlman, W., 1990, The structure and governance of venture capital organizations, *Journal of Financial Economics* 27, 473–524.

Sahlman, W., 1992, Insights from the venture capital industry, Harvard University working paper.

Sahlman, W., and H. Stevenson, 1987, Capital market myopia, Harvard Business School Case.

Scherer, F., 1991, Changing perspectives on the firm size problem, in Z. Acs and D. Audretsch (eds), *Innovation and Technological Change: An International Comparison*, Ann Arbor, MI, University of Michigan Press, 24–28.

Shleifer, A., and R. Vishny, 1992, Liquidation value and debt capacity: A market equilibrium approach, *Journal of Finance* 47, 1343–1366.

Stiglitz, Joseph, and Andrew Weiss, 1981, Credit rationing in markets with incomplete information, *American Economic Review* 71, 393–409.

Stiglitz, Joseph, and Andrew Weiss, 1983, Incentive effects of terminations: Applications to the credit and labor markets, *American Economic Review* 73, 919–927.

Titman, S., and R. Wessels, 1988, The determinants of capital structure, *Journal of Finance* 43, 1–19.

Venture Economics, 1988, *Exiting Venture Capital Investments*, Needham. Venture Economics.

Weitzman, M., W. Newey, and M. Rabin, 1981, Sequential R&D strategy for synfuels, *Bell Journal of Economics* 12, 574–590.

Wetzel, W., 1987, The informal venture capital market, *Journal of Business Venturing* 2, 299–314.

Williamson, O., 1988, Corporate finance and corporate governance, *Journal of Finance* 43, 567–591.

PART III

Job Creation and Destruction

CHAPTER 9

Job Creation and Destruction by Employer Size and Age: Cyclical Dynamics

John Haltiwanger

1   Introduction

The decomposition of net employment fluctuations into job creation and destruction has yielded considerable new insights regarding the driving forces for business cycle fluctuations (Blanchard and Diamond, 1989; 1990; Caballero and Hammour, 1994; Davis and Haltiwanger, 1990; 1992; 1996; 1997; Mortensen and Pissarides, 1994). The novel feature of the current chapter is its exploration of the cyclical dynamics of job creation and destruction classified by employer size and age. Analysis of the cyclical dynamics by employer size and age permits a richer characterization of the channels through which disturbances affect employment. Several questions arise in this context: Do small and young establishments exhibit different cyclical job creation and destruction dynamics than large and mature establishments? Do small and young establishments respond to shocks in the same manner as large and mature establishments? Is employer size or employer age more important for characterizing differences across establishments in terms of cyclical employment dynamics? This analysis seeks to address these questions by exploiting high frequency job creation and destruction series by employer size and age over the 1970s and 1980s for the United States.

The empirical approach taken in this chapter is based on the insight that the decomposition of net employment fluctuations into job creation and destruction yields a natural two-way decomposition of the forces influencing employment. First, some events may have an important common component causing a general tendency for all establishments to respond in the same direction. In terms of job creation and destruction, such common shocks cause opposite movements in job creation and destruction. For example, an adverse monetary policy shock may induce a recession, causing job destruction to rise and job creation to fall. As

239

emphasized in the recent literature, the more interesting question is whether an adverse aggregate shock has symmetric effects on creation and destruction. Simple theories of business cycles that stress no connection between the process of reallocation and aggregate fluctuations predict symmetric movements of creation and destruction over the cycle. This prediction is at odds with the empirical evidence for total manufacturing in the United States in that the cyclical volatility of job destruction is much greater than the volatility of job creation. The current chapter looks more deeply at this question by examining the nature of this asymmetry when the evidence is evaluated separately across groups of plants classified by employer size and age.

Second, some events may change the intensity of the forces generating reallocation across individual producers. The latter forces alter the closeness of the match between the desired and the actual distributions of labor across production sites. The observed high rates of job creation and destruction in every period suggest that there is a continuous stream of allocative shocks inducing job reallocation. However, even though there is a continuous stream of allocative shocks, the intensity of the arrival rate of such shocks may vary over time. Defining a *reallocation shock* as a change in the intensity of the stream of allocative disturbances, a positive reallocation shock will cause both job creation and destruction to rise. A key question is whether the rise in job creation and destruction is symmetric: That is, does the event leading to an increase in the intensity of reallocation also affect net employment? Recent theories that stress the time and resource consuming nature of reallocation suggest that net employment will be adversely affected in the short run since job destruction will respond more quickly than job creation. In such environments, the contemporaneous effect on creation and destruction will not be symmetric. This chapter directly investigates the dynamic response of creation and destruction by employer size and age groups to events that change the intensity of reallocation within the group.

In addition to allowing a generic two-way decomposition of the forces influencing employment, the decomposition of net employment into job creation and destruction provides a novel way of investigating the impact of observable disturbances (like monetary or oil shocks) on employment. Following from the above discussion, one question is whether observable disturbances yield movements in creation and destruction in the same or opposite directions; another is whether the changes are symmetric. More generally, for current purposes, the decomposition permits investigating the differential impact of monetary/credit market conditions and oil price shocks across establishments classified by employer size and age.

The chapter proceeds as follows: In Section 2, some basic facts regarding the cyclicality of job creation and destruction by employer size and age are presented. Section 3 outlines the structural vector autoregression (VAR) empirical methodology used in this analysis and characterizes some results based upon simple two variable VAR systems. Section 4 presents the results from a richer VAR structure with both observable (e.g., monetary/credit and oil price shocks) and unobservable disturbances. Concluding remarks are provided in Section 5.

2   Measurement Methodology and Basic Facts

Job creation and destruction measures are constructed from establishment-level employment changes over three-month intervals.[1] Job creation equals the sum of employment gains at new and expanding establishments; job destruction equals the sum of employment losses at dying and shrinking establishments. To express these gross job flow measures as rates, these flows are divided by the average of current and previous period's employment. This methodology is based upon that described in detail in Davis, Haltiwanger, and Schuh (1996).

There has been considerable debate regarding the appropriate classification methodology for employer size in evaluating the contribution of small vs. large employers to employment growth. Davis, Haltiwanger, and Schuh (1996) emphasize that the results on the contribution of small businesses to employer growth are sensitive to the manner in which this classification is undertaken. In particular, classifying establishments by the base period size over which the period of growth is measured can result in interpretation problems given regression to the mean problems from measurement error or transitory shocks.[2] While there is no ideal solution to this problem, in this chapter an intermediate approach is taken in that establishments are classified into size classes in a particular quarter in a given year based upon the average of total employment (including nonproduction workers) at the establishment in March of the current year and the prior year. By permitting establishments to switch size classes only if the change exhibits some persistence, this method has the advantage of mitigating the regression to the mean problems from transitory shocks or measurement error without locking establishments into specific size classes for the entire sample period. Given the detailed analysis of the cyclical components of the flows, only two size classes are considered: establishments with the average of current and prior year March employment less than 500 and establishments with the relevant average greater than or equal to 500.[3]

The analysis also considers the role of employer age. Age for a plant is measured from the time of the birth of the plant (the year of first positive employment). Again, given the detailed cyclical analysis and the nature of the data,[4] plants are divided into two age groups: young plants that have been in existence less than 10 years and mature plants that have been in existence for 10 years or more. Putting the size and age classifications together, the analysis is based upon a four-way classification: small, young plants; small, mature plants; large, young plants; and large, mature plants.

Figure 9.1 displays time series of job creation and destruction along with implied net employment growth rates and gross job reallocation (the sum of creation and destruction) for each of the groups.[5] The series depicted are based upon the U.S. manufacturing sector from the second quarter of 1972 to the fourth quarter of 1988. Table 9.1 summarizes important features of the data and includes summary statistics for all plants for purposes of comparison. One key feature emphasized in the recent literature is the large magnitude of gross job flows. In an average quarter, the number of newly destroyed (newly created) manufacturing jobs equals 5.5 percent (5.2 percent) of manufacturing employment. These large magnitudes imply that the economy continually adjusts to a stream of allocative disturbances that cause large scale reshuffling of employment opportunities across production sites. The average rates of job creation and destruction differ sharply across employer size and age. Small, young plants have the highest average creation and destruction rates. Large, mature plants have the lowest average creation and destruction rates. However, even among large, mature plants, the quarterly rates of job creation and destruction imply substantial variation in the fortunes of these individual plants.

Employment is concentrated in mature (10 years or older) plants, which account for more than 75 percent of total manufacturing employment. Most young plants are also small plants. There is only a modest fraction of employment at large, young plants. For this sample period, net employment growth for mature plants is negative, with small, mature plants exhibiting the largest (in absolute value) negative average growth. Net employment growth for young plants (whether small or large) is, on average, positive, with particularly robust average growth for large, young plants.

Sharp differences in the cyclical patterns of job creation and destruction are evident across employer size and age groups. Table 9.1 indicates that the standard deviation of the job destruction rate for all plants is much larger than that for job creation. This general pattern of asymmetry is driven entirely by large, mature plants and small, mature plants. Young plants (whether large or small) exhibit about the same volatility of creation and destruction. As seen in Figure 9.1, among mature plants (whether large or small), recessions are times of sharp increases in job destruction with relatively mild decreases in job creation. Thus, recessions among mature plants have a greater impact on contracting than expanding plants. For young plants (whether large or small), recessions are times of substantial increases in job destruction accompanied by substantial decreases in job creation. Thus, recessions have roughly symmetric effects on contracting and expanding young plants.

The sharp differences in the basic cyclical patterns across age and size groups suggest that these groups may be subject to different shocks at business cycle frequencies and/or that they respond differently to common shocks. The subsequent empirical analysis seeks to characterize the response of job creation and destruction by employer size and age to alternative types of shocks.

Before proceeding to the analysis of the patterns over the business cycle, it is worth noting the systematic patterns over the seasons. Table 9.2 reports quarterly averages for all plants and the four groups classified by employer size and age. Overall, job creation tends to be highest in the second and third quarters while job destruction is the highest in the first and fourth quarters. Interestingly, the seasonal patterns are dominated by small plants. The large rates of job destruction in the first and fourth quarters are driven primarily by small plants and the high job creation rates in the second and third quarters are also dominated by seasonal increases in the rates of job creation among small plants. Even in the presence of nontrivial seasonal volatility, the subsequent analysis does not use seasonally adjusted data in the decompositions of employment fluctuations into alternative driving forces. The motivation for this treatment of the data is that seasonal variation may interact with cyclical variation in complex ways.[6] Accordingly, it is arguably more appropriate to retain the seasonal variation in the data but to evaluate the results in light of the fact that some of the variation (particularly for small plants) is being driven by seasonal factors.[7]

3   Two-Variable System

3.1   The VAR Specification

In this section, the cyclical variations in job creation and destruction for a particular group are decomposed into shocks that move job creation and destruction in opposite directions (referred to as common shocks) and shocks that move job creation and destruction in the same direction (referred to as reallocation shocks).[8] It is important to emphasize that

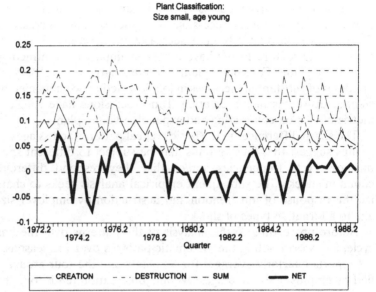

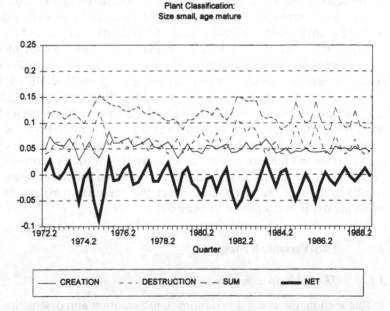

Figure 9.1. Net and Gross Job Flows by Employer Size and Age. *Note*: See Table 9.1, footnote 1, for explanation of size and age classifications.

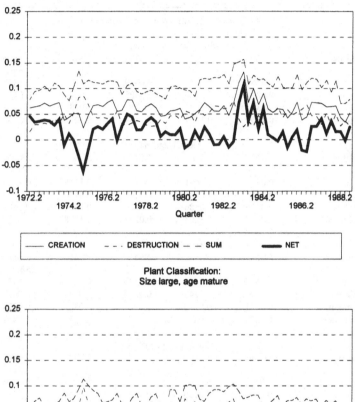

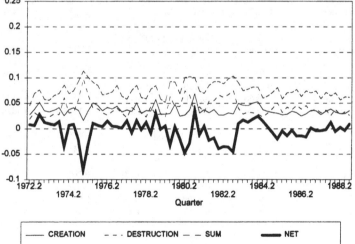

Figure 9.1 *(cont.)*

Table 9.1. *Net and Gross Job Flow Rates in the U.S. Manufacturing Sector, 1972: Q2–1988:Q4*

	A. Summary Statistics (Share of Employment)				

		Size small, age young[1]			
Statistic	POS[2]	NEG	NET	SUM	Employment Share
Mean	0.0762	0.0703	0.0059	0.1465	0.1875
St. Dev.	0.0214	0.0229	0.0305	0.0323	0.0417
Minimum	0.0381	0.0382	-0.0761	0.0932	0.1157
Maximum	0.1357	0.1337	0.0764	0.2227	0.2463

		Size small, age mature			
Statistic	POS	NEG	NET	SUM	Employment Share
Mean	0.0524	0.0631	-0.0107	0.1155	0.4238
St. Dev.	0.0104	0.0184	0.0243	0.0174	0.0537
Minimum	0.0276	0.0386	-0.0870	0.0864	0.3480
Maximum	0.0837	0.1203	0.0297	0.1528	0.5195

		Size large, age young			
Statistic	POS	NEG	NET	SUM	Employment Share
Mean	0.0618	0.0443	0.0176	0.1061	0.0378
St. Dev.	0.0170	0.0148	0.0267	0.0174	0.0077
Minimum	0.0231	0.0160	-0.0625	0.0705	0.0238
Maximum	0.1320	0.0855	0.1070	0.1570	0.0491

		Size large, age mature			
Statistic	POS	NEG	NET	SUM	Employment Share
Mean	0.0361	0.0396	-0.0035	0.0758	0.3508
St. Dev.	0.0091	0.0156	0.0209	0.0146	0.0178
Minimum	0.0160	-0.0817	-0.0817	0.0456	0.3212
Maximum	0.0684	0.0365	0.0365	0.1138	0.3870

		Overall			
Statistic	POS	NEG	NET	SUM	
Mean	0.0520	0.0555	-0.0036	0.1075	
Std.Dev.	0.0082	0.0141	0.0186	0.0136	
Minimum	0.0383	0.0360	-0.0586	0.0791	
Maximum	0.0749	0.0969	0.0285	0.1455	

Table 9.1. *(cont.)*

B.Selected Contemporaneous Correlations

Size small, age young

ρ(POS, NET)	ρ(NEG,NET)	ρ(SUM,NET)	ρ(POS,NEG)	ρ(NET,mfgNET)[3]
0.6604	-0.7117	-0.0666	0.0576	0.7245

Size small, age mature

ρ(POS, NET)	ρ(NEG,NET)	ρ(SUM,NET)	ρ(POS,NEG)	ρ(NET,mfgNET)
0.7115	-0.9182	-0.5464	-0.3749	0.6986

Size large, age young

ρ(POS, NET)	ρ(NEG,NET)	ρ(SUM,NET)	ρ(POS,NEG)	ρ(NET,mfgNET)
0.8625	-0.8137	0.1506	-0.4076	0.7564

Size large, age mature

ρ(POS, NET)	ρ(NEG,NET)	ρ(SUM,NET)	ρ(POS,NEG)	ρ(NET,mfgNET)
0.7275	-0.9166	-0.5246	-0.3925	0.8835

Overall

ρ(POS, NET)	ρ(NEG,NET)	ρ(SUM,NET)	ρ(POS,NEG)	ρ(mfgNET,mfgNET)
0.7038	-0.9107	-0.5189	-0.3475	1

[1] Establishments with employment less than 500 are "small" and establishments with employment greater than or equal to 500 are "large." Establishments that have been in existence for less than 10 years are "young" and establishments that have been in existence for 10 years or more are "mature."
[2] POS = job creation; NEG = job destruction; NET = net employment growth; SUM = job reallocation.
[3] mfgNET is NET for all manufacturing.

"common" shocks are shocks that are common to plants in a specific size and age group. It may be that the "common" shocks are common to all plants, but in this part of the analysis no such restriction is imposed. Thus, in what follows, the terminology often used is "group-common shocks" and "within group reallocation" shocks.[9] In the succeeding section, specific observable shocks (e.g., oil and monetary policy) are considered. Thus, the analysis in the next section permits direct investigation of the hypothesis that plants of different sizes and ages respond differently to specific observable shocks.

Table 9.2. *Quarterly Means of Job Creation and Destruction Rates by Size and Age Class*

A. Quarterly Means of Job Creation

Class	First Quarter	Second Quarter	Third Quarter	Fourth Quarter
Small, young	0.0770	0.0857	0.0769	0.0652
Large, young	0.0613	0.0644	0.0590	0.0626
Small, mature	0.0470	0.0512	0.0619	0.0492
Large, mature	0.0324	0.0329	0.0356	0.0435
Overall:	0.0544	0.0585	0.0584	0.0551

B. Quarterly Means of Job Destruction

Class	First Quarter	Second Quarter	Third Quarter	Fourth Quarter
Small, young	0.0951	0.0687	0.0536	0.0651
Large, young	0.0487	0.0383	0.0458	0.0445
Small, mature	0.0803	0.0597	0.0458	0.0648
Large, mature	0.0437	0.0342	0.0425	0.0383
Overall:	0.0670	0.0503	0.0476	0.0532

Note: See Table 9.1, footnote 1, for explanation of size and age classifications.

For a given employer size and age group, consider the following specification (group-specific subscripts are omitted for expositional clarity; the VAR system is estimated separately for each employer size and age group). Let Z_t be a vector containing structural disturbances and let $Y_t = [POS_t, NEG_t]'$ be a vector containing observed values of job creation and destruction. By assumption, the relationship between the structural disturbances, Z_t, and the observed outcomes, Y_t, has the linear moving average representation

$$Y_t = A(L)\varepsilon_t \tag{1}$$

where $\varepsilon_t = [\varepsilon_{at}, \varepsilon_{st}]'$ is a vector of white noise innovations to the structural disturbances and $A(L)$ is an infinite-order matrix lag polynomial. Elements of ε_t are innovations in the common (subscript a) and reallocation (subscript s) disturbances, respectively.[10] The coefficients in $A(L)$ reflect both the responses to the structural disturbances and the serial correlation of the disturbances.

Estimating a VAR on Y_t does not immediately produce either the matrix lag polynomial, $A(L)$, or ε_t. Instead, the estimated VAR yields

$$Y_t = D(L)\eta_t, \qquad D(0) = I \tag{2}$$

where $D(L)$ is an infinite-order matrix lag polynomial implied by the estimated VAR coefficients and $\eta_t = [p_t, n_t]'$ is the vector of reduced-form innovations. Comparing equations (1) and (2) implies that $\eta_t = B_0 \varepsilon_t$ and $A(L) = D(L)B_0$, so knowledge of B_0 permits recovery of estimates of both $A(L)$ and ε_t. Given these, it is possible to evaluate the roles played by the respective types of disturbances as driving forces behind employment fluctuations.

3.2 Identifying Assumptions

The time-series data on Y_t do not identify B_0. Thus, identifying the role played by the various disturbances requires additional, a priori information. To illustrate the assumptions, it is useful to write the system for B_0 as:

$$\begin{bmatrix} p_t \\ n_t \end{bmatrix} = \begin{bmatrix} 1 & b_{ps} \\ b_{na} & 1 \end{bmatrix} \begin{bmatrix} \varepsilon_{at} \\ \varepsilon_{st} \end{bmatrix} \tag{3}$$

The assumption that $b_{pa} = b_{ns} = 1$ is simply a normalization. The group-common and reallocation innovations are assumed to be contemporaneously uncorrelated, i.e., $p(\varepsilon_{at}, \varepsilon_{st}) = 0$. This assumption imposes a zero covariance between the structural disturbances, a standard assumption in the structural VAR literature.[11]

The system (3) implies three moment conditions that relate elements of the variance–covariance matrix of reduced-form innovations to the parameters of B_0 and to elements of the variance–covariance matrix of structural innovations. There are four unknowns: the contemporaneous response coefficients, b_{na} and b_{ps}; and the standard deviations of the structural innovations, σ_a and σ_s. Hence, the system is underidentified on the basis of assumptions made thus far. However, the moment condition implied by the zero covariance restriction yields a one-to-one mapping between b_{ps} and b_{na}: namely,

$$b_{ps} = \frac{\sigma_{pn} - b_{na}\sigma_p^2}{\sigma_n^2 - b_{na}\sigma_{pn}} \tag{4}$$

where σ^2_p, σ^2_n, and σ_{pn} are the variances and covariance of the reduced-form innovations. Given (4), the other two moment conditions generate a unique mapping of each value of b_{na} into values for σ_a and σ_s. Hence, although the system is underidentified it permits characterization of the trade-offs between the estimated short-run responses to common and reallocation shocks as well as the trade-off in the relative magnitudes of the shocks.

In the next subsection, results characterizing these identification trade-offs are presented to allow the reader to assess the implications of alternative identifying assumptions and draw conclusions. However, there are a number of alternative identifying assumptions to impose that pertain to various theories in the literature that serve as a guide to these trade-offs. Of these, two types are considered: (1) qualitative restrictions on the sign of the short-run contemporaneous response of Y_t to structural disturbances; and (2) exact identifying assumptions on the short-run responses to structural disturbances.[12]

Consider first the qualitative assumptions that $b_{na} < 0$ and $b_{ps} > 0$. These assumptions reflect the assumed qualitative effects that common and reallocation disturbances have on the joint movement of job creation and destruction. That is, common disturbances to a particular group cause creation and destruction for that group to move in opposite directions, while reallocation disturbances cause creation and destruction to move in the same direction for that group.[13]

Exact identifying and/or tighter qualitative restrictions can be generated by considering implications of alternative models. For example, the assumption that $b_{na} = -1$ implies that common shocks to a group have symmetric (but opposite) effects on job creation and destruction for that group. This assumption fits well with models that treat the net employment fluctuations for a group as being generated by common shocks with symmetric effects on all plants in the group. Standard, representative agent models are consistent with this assumption. More generally, this assumption is consistent with models in which group-common shocks amount to a simple mean translation of the distribution of growth rates without any effects on the higher moments of the distribution. This assumption is not consistent with models that stress that common shocks may have an effect on the pace of job reallocation (and thus on the higher moments of the growth rate distribution).

Next consider the assumption that $b_{ps} = 1$. This assumption implies that reallocation shocks have a symmetric positive effect on job creation and destruction. In contrast to the assumption that $b_{na} = -1$, this assumption restricts the impact that reallocation shocks have on the dynamics of job creation and destruction. Even though it is a very different type of restriction, this assumption also fits well with models that imply that net employment fluctuations for a group are primarily driven by common shocks to the group. However, in this case, this idea takes the form of restricting the potential role of reallocation shocks in affecting net employment growth contemporaneously.

As should be clear from this discussion, models that emphasize a connection between net employment fluctuations for a group and the timing and intensity of reallocation within the group are inconsistent with either $b_{na} = -1$ or $b_{ps} = 1$ (e.g., models considered by Davis and Haltiwanger, 1990; Caballero and Hammour, 1994; Mortensen and Pissarides, 1994). While the latter literature provides limited guidance about the precise magnitude of the effects of common shocks on within group reallocation and reallocation shocks on net employment growth for a group, the literature does provide some further guidance about the range of relevant parameters relative to these benchmark identifying assumptions.

For example, the model of Davis and Haltiwanger (1990) generates the following reallocation timing relationship: Since worker reallocation and job reallocation entail forgone production due to costs associated with search and moving, retraining, changes in the scale of operations, plant retooling and other factors, unfavorable (and temporary) common disturbances increase the pace of within group reallocation, implying that $b_{na} < -1$. In addition, the time consuming nature of job and worker reallocation creates an asymmetry between the matching and separation processes in the labor market. Separations can occur instantaneously in response to new information that drives the surplus value of a job–worker match below zero, but the creation of new matches with positive surplus requires time.[14] These considerations suggest that an increased intensity of reallocation within a group will initially impact job destruction more than job creation within the group so that $b_{ps} < 1$.[15]

The empirical strategy in the remainder of this section is summarized as follows: First, the results implied by the simple qualitative sign restrictions and the trade-off characterized in (4) are examined. Second, the implications of the benchmarks $b_{na} = -1$ and $b_{ps} = 1$ (and the accompanying tighter qualitative restrictions) are investigated.

3.3   Results for the Simple Two-Variable System

Figure 9.2 depicts the contribution of group-common shocks to the forecast error variances of job creation and destruction across the range of parameters that satisfy the minimal sign restrictions. The contributions for 4 and 16 step horizons for each of the employer size and age groups are depicted. Table 9.3 provides similar information for the specific

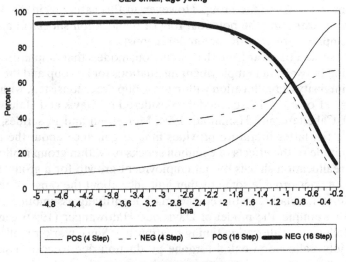

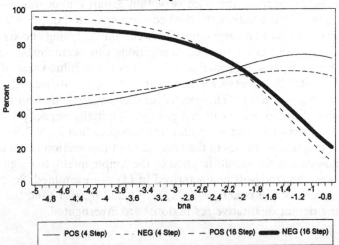

Figure 9.2. Forecast Error Variance Decomposition 1972:2–1988:4, 2-Equation System. *Note:* See Table 9.1, footnote 1, for explanation of size and age classifications.

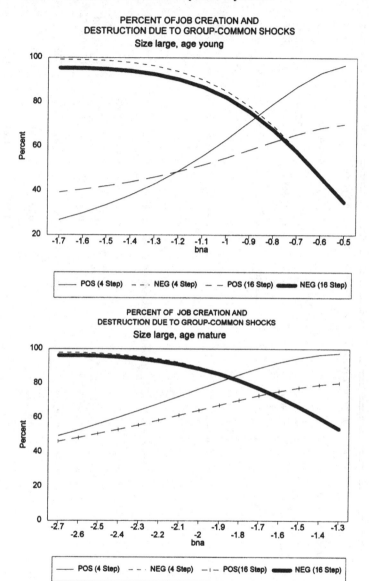

Figure 9.2 *(cont.)*

Table 9.3. *Forecast-Error Variance Decompositions for Job Flows, Two-Variable System, 1972: Q2–1988:Q4*

A. *Fraction of Variance of Job Creation due to Group-Common Shocks*

	Size small, age young			*Size small, age mature*		
Forecast Horizon	$b_{na}=-1$ $b_{ps}=0.8224$	$b_{na}=-1.145$ $b_{ps}=1$	$b_{na}=-1.073$ $b_{ps}=0.9065$	$b_{na}=-1$ $b_{ps}=0.1068$	$b_{na}=-2.720$ $b_{ps}=1$	$b_{na}=-1.860$ $b_{ps}=0.4572$
1 quarter	0.63	0.56	0.60	0.97	0.45	0.70
4	0.56	0.49	0.52	0.74	0.57	0.69
8	0.52	0.47	0.49	0.64	0.58	0.63
16	0.54	0.52	0.53	0.64	0.58	0.63

B. *Fraction of Variance of Job Destruction due to Group-Common Shocks*

	Size small, age young			*Size small, age mature*		
Forecast Horizon	$b_{na}=-1$ $b_{ps}=0.8224$	$b_{na}=-1.145$ $b_{ps}=1$	$b_{na}=-1.073$ $b_{ps}=0.9065$	$b_{na}=-1$ $b_{ps}=0.1068$	$b_{na}=-2.720$ $b_{ps}=1$	$b_{na}=-1.860$ $b_{ps}=0.4572$
1 quarter	0.54	0.62	0.58	0.25	0.86	0.63
4	0.58	0.66	0.62	0.23	0.81	0.59
8	0.64	0.71	0.67	0.29	0.81	0.62
16	0.65	0.71	0.68	0.31	0.79	0.62

C. Fraction of Variance of Job Creation due to Group-Common Shocks

Size large, age young

Forecast Horizon	$b_{na}=-1$ $b_{ps}=1.734$	$b_{na}=-0.8389$ $b_{ps}=1$	$b_{na}=-0.9194$ $b_{ps}=1.329$
1 quarter	0.65	0.79	0.72
4	0.63	0.76	0.70
8	0.54	0.61	0.57
16	0.55	0.61	0.58

Size large, age mature

Forecast Horizon	$b_{na}=-1$ $b_{ps}=-0.0996$	$b_{na}=-2.081$ $b_{ps}=1$	$b_{na}=-1.541$ $b_{ps}=0.1961$
1 quarter	0.98	0.72	0.95
4	0.94	0.73	0.94
8	0.84	0.65	0.81
16	0.80	0.62	0.77

D. Fraction of Variance of Job Destruction due to Group-Common Shocks

Size large, age young

Forecast Horizon	$b_{na}=-1$ $b_{ps}=1.734$	$b_{na}=-0.8389$ $b_{ps}=1$	$b_{na}=-0.9194$ $b_{ps}=1.329$
1 quarter	0.85	0.72	0.79
4	0.85	0.73	0.80
8	0.84	0.72	0.79
16	0.82	0.71	0.77

Size large, age mature

Forecast Horizon	$b_{na}=-1$ $b_{ps}=-0.0996$	$b_{na}=-2.081$ $b_{ps}=1$	$b_{na}=-1.541$ $b_{ps}=0.1961$
1 quarter	0.29	0.92	0.65
4	0.33	0.92	0.68
8	0.29	0.91	0.68
16	0.31	0.91	0.67

Note: See Table 9.1, footnote 1, for explanation of size and age classifications.

256   John Haltiwanger

benchmark identification assumptions. For each employer size and age group, results are also presented for a set of "midpoint" results that reflect the average of the b_{na} values between the benchmark at -1 and the value of b_{na} that emerges under the assumption that $b_{ps} = 1$.[16]

Several results stand out from Figure 9.2. First, the range of b_{na} that jointly satisfies the restriction that $b_{na} < 0$ and $b_{ps} > 0$ varies substantially across size and age groups. Second, the minimal qualitative restrictions on the sign of the effects do not yield very precise implications regarding the contributions of the alternative driving forces. Third, while the implications of the sign restrictions are not precise, some interesting trade-offs are observed. For all groups, large (in absolute value) negative values of b_{na} imply a larger role for group-common shocks for job destruction and a lesser role of group-common shocks for job creation.

The nature of the trade-offs and the differences across the size and age groups are more easily summarized by considering the results in Table 9.3 for the alternative benchmark identifying assumptions. The results exhibit sharply different patterns across employer size and age groups. The benchmark assumptions of either $b_{na} = -1$ or $b_{ps} = 1$ yield quite similar results for small, young plants. Thus, the data for small, young plants are mutually consistent with the hypotheses that group-common shocks yield symmetric (opposite) effects on creation and destruction, while within group reallocation shocks yield roughly symmetric effects on creation and destruction. Under these maintained hypotheses, more than half of the time series forecast error variances (at different horizons) of job creation and destruction for young, small plants are accounted for by group-common shocks.

For all other age and size groups, the results are *not* mutually consistent with symmetric effects of both group-common and within group reallocation shocks. For mature plants (whether large or small), the assumption of symmetric (opposite) effects from group-common shocks (i.e., $b_{na} = -1$) yields reallocation shocks having a much larger absolute effect on destruction relative to creation (i.e., b_{ps} is much less than 1). Further, the assumption of symmetric effects of group-common shocks for these groups yields that a relatively large fraction of job creation is accounted for by group-common shocks but a relatively small fraction of job destruction is accounted for by group-common shocks. Considering the alternative hypothesis that reallocation shocks have symmetric effects (i.e., $b_{ps} = 1$) yields substantially different results. In the latter case, group-common shocks have a much larger absolute effect on job destruction as opposed to job creation (i.e., $b_{na} < -1$). Further, group-common shocks in this latter case account for a very large fraction of the variation in job destruction.

For large, young plants yet another pattern emerges. The assumption of symmetric effects of group-common shocks yields that reallocation shocks have a disproportionate effect on job creation (i.e., $b_{ps} > 1$). Further, in this case, group-common shocks account for a much larger fraction of job destruction relative to job creation. The alternative hypothesis that reallocation shocks have symmetric effects yields a disproportionate effect of group-common shocks on creation (i.e., $b_{na} > -1$). In this latter case, aggregate shocks account for a very large share of the fluctuations in job creation and destruction.

In terms of the alternative theories, the results for small, young plants are consistent with the view that the process of job reallocation and the business cycle are not closely linked. That is, it is possible to maintain jointly the hypotheses that shocks common to a group yield roughly symmetric (opposite) effects on job creation and destruction and that within group reallocation shocks yield roughly symmetric effects. Under these maintained hypotheses, net employment growth for small, young plants is driven primarily by group-common shocks while time variation in the pace of observed job reallocation is driven primarily by time variation in the intensity of reallocation disturbances.

For mature plants (whether large or small) and to a lesser extent large, young plants, the results are consistent with the view that the process of job reallocation and net employment growth are closely linked. That is, one cannot maintain the joint hypotheses of symmetric effects of aggregate shocks and reallocation shocks for these groups. Further, for mature plants, the hypothesis that common shocks have a symmetric effect on creation and destruction implies that much of the fluctuation in destruction is accounted for by reallocation shocks. Since net employment for mature plants is primarily driven by job destruction, this would in turn imply that reallocation shocks play a major role in accounting for net employment fluctuations for mature plants. Thus, for mature plants, the results indicate either that there is a large role for reallocation shocks in accounting for destruction and net employment growth or that common shocks have a disproportionate effect on job destruction.

4   Five-Variable System

4.1   An Expanded VAR Specification

A five-variable VAR specification is now considered that includes the job creation rate, the job destruction rate, a monetary policy or credit variable, an index of the change in real growth rate of oil prices, and the absolute value of the change in this index. These systems are again estimated separately for each size and age group. However, in this case, there are specific observable shocks that are the same in each subsystem.[17]

The real price of oil is measured as the nominal price of crude petroleum deflated by the producer price index. To focus attention on changes in oil prices that are not quickly reversed, an index of oil price series is constructed as the ratio of the current real price of oil to a weighted average of the real price of oil over the prior 20 quarters with weights that sum to 1 and decline linearly to 0.[18] The index of monetary policy innovations and credit intermediation shocks used is the spread (*SPREAD*) between the six-month commercial paper rate and the 6-month Treasury bill rate. This variable has been used extensively in the recent literature (e.g., Stock and Watson, 1989) as an index of monetary/credit conditions.[19]

Figure 9.3 depicts the real oil price index (scaled on left axis) and the index of monetary policy/credit market conditions. The oil price index series is dominated by four events: the sharp increase in oil prices in late 1973, the subsequent sharp increases in 1979 and 1981, and the somewhat transitory decrease in oil prices in 1986. Large increases in the monetary/credit indicator precede each of the major recessions over this period.

4.2   Identification

Let $Y_t = [OIL_t, MAGOIL_t, POS_t, NEG_t, CREDIT_t]'$ be a vector containing observed values of the oil price index, the absolute value of the change in the oil price index, the job creation rate, the job destruction rate, and the monetary policy/credit conditions indicator. Let $\varepsilon_t = [\varepsilon_{ot}, \varepsilon_{mt}, \varepsilon_{pt}, \varepsilon_{nt}, \varepsilon_{ct}]'$ where the elements of ε_t correspond to the time-t values of innovations to the oil price index, the magnitude of the change in the index, the group-common, the reallocation and the monetary/credit disturbances, respectively. Also, let $\eta_t = [o_t, m_t, p_t, n_t, c_t]'$ be the vector of reduced-form innovations.

To identify the five-variable system, it is assumed to be block recursive. The two oil price series are assumed to be exogenous relative to the other innovations. It is not necessary to impose any causal ordering in the subsystem involving the two oil price series since only their joint effect is considered. The unobservable group-common and reallocation shocks reflect the decomposition of the reduced form innovations to job creation and destruction after exogenous oil innovations are taken into account. This implies that there is a two-variable subsystem in job creation and destruction similar to that given in (3) for the components of the reduced form innovations to creation and destruction that are

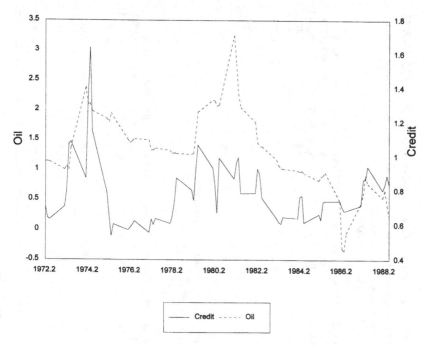

Figure 9.3. Oil Price Index and Monetary/Credit Index

orthogonal to the oil price innovations. Thus, for this subsystem the same type of qualitative and exact identifying assumptions can be used to identify the contributions of group-common and reallocation shocks. The credit/monetary innovation is assumed to be last in the causal ordering of this block recursive system. This reflects the view that movements in monetary policy and credit variables often respond in a passive, systematic manner to developments in the real side of the economy. Thus, in what follows, the contribution of the monetary/credit shocks is based on that component of the reduced form monetary/credit innovation that is orthogonal to the oil price innovations, the group-common shocks and the reallocation shocks.[20]

4.3   Results for the Five-Equation System

The results from the estimation of the five-equation system are summarized in Tables 9.4–9.7 and Figures 9.4–9.11. Tables 9.4–9.7 are the analogue to Table 9.3 for the two-equation system. That is, Tables 9.4–9.7

Table 9.4. *Forecast-Error Variance Decompositions for Job Flows, Five-Variable System, 1972: Q2–1988:Q4*

A. Variance Decompositions of Job Creation
Size small, age young

Forecast Horizon	Fraction due to: Oil Shock	Credit Shock	Common Shock ($b_{na} = -1$) ($b_{ps} = 1.041$)	Common Shock ($b_{na} = -0.9637$) ($b_{ps} = 1$)	Reallocation Shock ($b_{na} = -1$) ($b_{ps} = 1.041$)	Reallocation Shock ($b_{na} = -0.9637$) ($b_{ps} = 1$)
1 quarter	0.025	0	0.50	0.51	0.48	0.46
4	0.09	0.01	0.40	0.41	0.51	0.49
8	0.11	0.04	0.35	0.36	0.50	0.50
16	0.19	0.08	0.36	0.36	0.38	0.37

B. Variance Decompositions of Job Destruction
Size small, age young

Forecast Horizon	Fraction due to: Oil Shock	Credit Shock	Common Shock ($b_{na} = -1$) ($b_{ps} = 1.041$)	Common Shock ($b_{na} = -0.9637$) ($b_{ps} = 1$)	Reallocation Shock ($b_{na} = -1$) ($b_{ps} = 1.041$)	Reallocation Shock ($b_{na} = -0.9637$) ($b_{ps} = 1$)
1 quarter	0.01	0	0.52	0.50	0.47	0.48
4	0.12	0.14	0.39	0.38	0.35	0.36
8	0.25	0.14	0.37	0.36	0.24	0.25
16	0.27	0.13	0.39	0.38	0.22	0.38

Note: See Table 9.1, footnote 1, for explanation of size and age classifications.

Table 9.5. *Forecast-Error Variance Decompositions for Job Flows*

A. Variance Decompositions of Job Creation
Size large, age young

Forecast Horizon	Fraction due to: Oil Shock	Credit Shock	Common Shock ($b_{na} = -1$) ($b_{ps} = 8.417$)	Common Shock ($b_{na} = -0.6316$) ($b_{ps} =1$)	Reallocation Shock ($b_{ps} = 8.417$) ($b_{na} = -1$)	Reallocation Shock ($b_{ps} = 1$) ($b_{na} = -0.6316$)
1 quarter	0.02	0	0.47	0.86	0.52	0.13
4	0.05	0.01	0.42	0.76	0.53	0.19
8	0.10	0.07	0.38	0.57	0.46	0.27
16	0.21	0.11	0.31	0.45	0.36	0.22

B. Variance Decompositions of Job Destruction
Size large, age young

Forecast Horizon	Fraction due to: Oil Shock	Credit Shock	Common Shock ($b_{na} = -1$) ($b_{ps} = 8.417$)	Common Shock ($b_{na} = -0.6316$) ($b_{ps} =1$)	Reallocation Shock ($b_{ps} = 8.417$) ($b_{na} = -1$)	Reallocation Shock ($b_{ps} = 1$) ($b_{na} = -0.6316$)
1 quarter	0.02	0	0.98	0.72	0.02	0.28
4	0.15	0.26	0.57	0.43	0.03	0.16
8	0.23	0.25	0.49	0.37	0.04	0.16
16	0.22	0.24	0.50	0.37	0.04	0.17

Note: See Table 9.1, footnote 1, for explanation of size and age classifications.

Table 9.6. *Forecast-Error Variance Decompositions for Job Flows*

A. Variance Decompositions of Job Creation
Size small, age mature

Forecast Horizon	Fraction due to: Oil Shock	Credit Shock	Common Shock ($b_{na} = -1$) ($b_{ps} = 0.2578$)	Common Shock ($b_{na} = -2.355$) ($b_{ps} = 1$)	Reallocation Shock ($b_{na} = -1$) ($b_{ps} = 0.2578$)	Reallocation Shock ($b_{na} = -2.355$) ($b_{ps} = 1$)
1 quarter	0.03	0	0.84	0.39	0.13	0.58
4	0.22	0.07	0.53	0.31	0.18	0.40
8	0.32	0.07	0.47	0.23	0.20	0.38
16	0.34	0.13	0.36	0.21	0.17	0.32

B. Variance Decompositions of Job Destruction
Size small, age mature

Forecast Horizon	Fraction due to: Oil Shock	Credit Shock	Common Shock ($b_{na} = -1$) ($b_{ps} = 0.2578$)	Common Shock ($b_{na} = -2.355$) ($b_{ps} = 1$)	Reallocation Shock ($b_{na} = -1$) ($b_{ps} = 0.2578$)	Reallocation Shock ($b_{na} = -2.355$) ($b_{ps} = 1$)
1 quarter	0.02	0	0.30	0.78	0.68	0.21
4	0.20	0.08	0.20	0.50	0.53	0.22
8	0.36	0.10	0.18	0.37	0.37	0.17
16	0.37	0.09	0.23	0.37	0.32	0.18

Note: See Table 9.1, footnote 1, for explanation of size and age classifications.

Table 9.7. *Forecast-Error Variance Decompositions for Job Flows*

A. Variance Decompositions of Job Creation
Size large, age mature

Forecast Horizon	Fraction due to: Oil Shock	Credit Shock	Common Shock ($b_{na}=-1$) ($b_{ps}=0.1122$)	Common Shock ($b_{na}=-1.568$) ($b_{ps}=1$)	Reallocation Shock ($b_{na}=-1$) ($b_{ps}=0.1122$)	Reallocation Shock ($b_{na}=-1.568$) ($b_{ps}=1$)
1 quarter	0.05	0	0.94	0.69	0.01	0.26
4	0.13	006	0.79	0.59	0.02	0.22
8	0.20	0.08	0.60	0.42	0.13	0.31
16	0.20	0.09	0.55	0.38	0.15	0.33

B. Variance Decompositions of Job Destruction
Size large, age mature

Forecast Horizon	Fraction due to: Oil Shock	Credit Shock	Common Shock ($b_{na}=-1$) ($b_{ps}=0.1122$)	Common Shock ($b_{na}=-1.568$) ($b_{ps}=1$)	Reallocation Shock ($b_{na}=-1$) ($b_{ps}=0.1122$)	Reallocation Shock ($b_{na}=-1.568$) ($b_{ps}=1$)
1 quarter	0.11	0	0.42	0.76	0.46	0.12
4	0.13	0.28	0.31	0.50	0.29	0.10
8	0.38	0.18	0.22	0.36	0.21	0.08
16	0.40	0.17	0.22	0.35	0.21	0.08

Note: See Table 9.1, footnote 1, for explanation of size and age classifications.

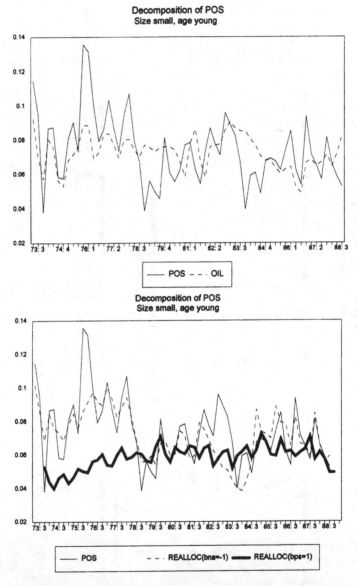

Figure 9.4. Decomposition of Job Creation 1973:2–1988:4, 5-Equation
System. *Note*: See Table 9.1, footnote 1, for explanation of size and age
classifications.

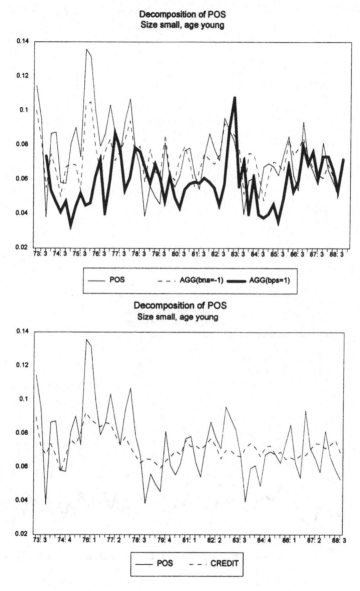

Figure 9.4 *(cont.)*

266   John Haltiwanger

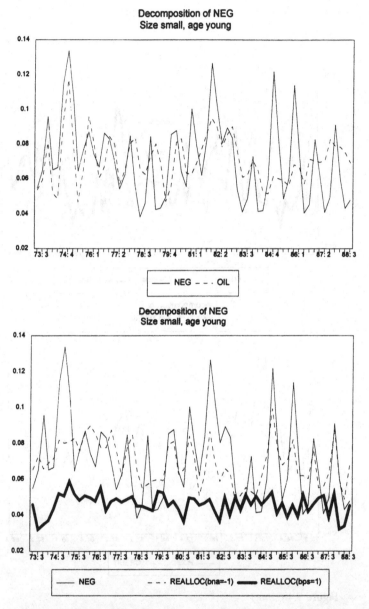

Figure 9.5. Decomposition of Job Destruction 1973:2–1988:4, 5-Equation System. *Note*: See Table 9.1, footnote 1, for explanation of size and age classifications.

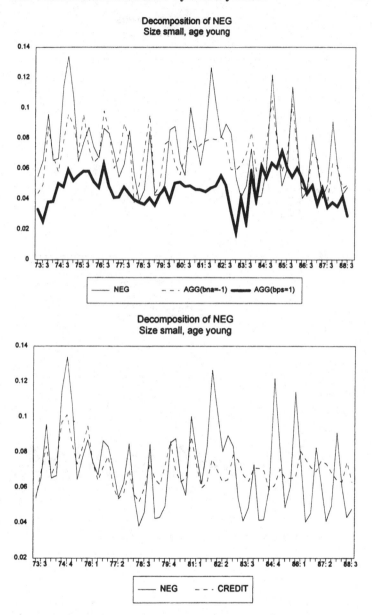

Figure 9.5 *(cont.)*

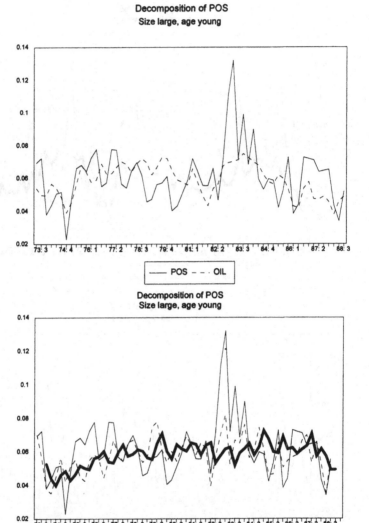

Figure 9.6. Decomposition of Job Creation 1973:2–1988:4, 5-Equation System. *Note*: See Table 9.1, footnote 1, for explanation of size and age classifications.

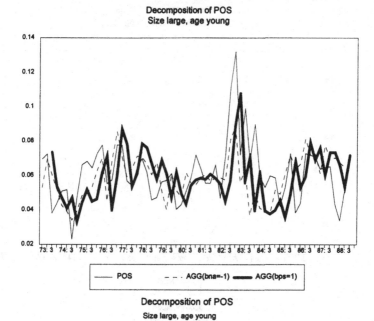

Decomposition of POS
Size large, age young

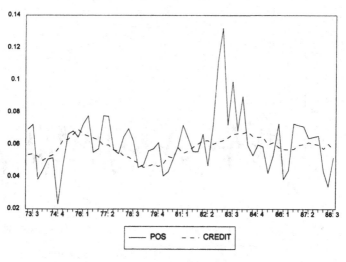

Decomposition of POS
Size large, age young

Figure 9.6 *(cont.)*

Decomposition of NEG
Size large, age young

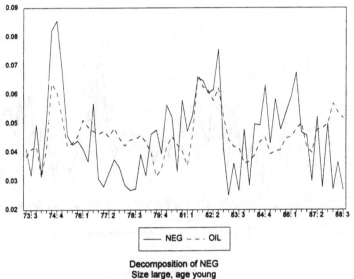

Decomposition of NEG
Size large, age young

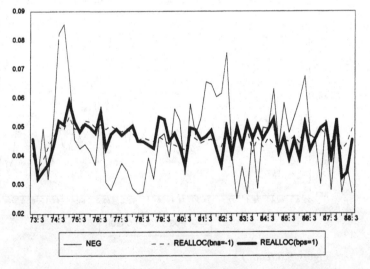

Figure 9.7. Decomposition of Job Destruction 1973:2–1988:4, 5-Equation System. *Note*: See Table 9.1, footnote 1, for explanation of size and age classifications.

**Decomposition of NEG
Size large, age young**

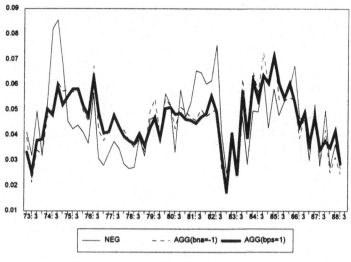

**Decomposition of NEG
Size large, age young**

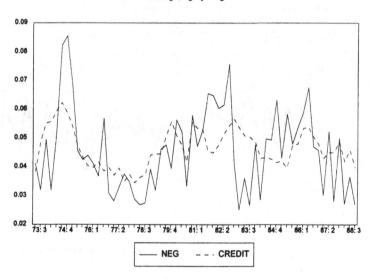

Figure 9.7 *(cont.)*

272   John Haltiwanger

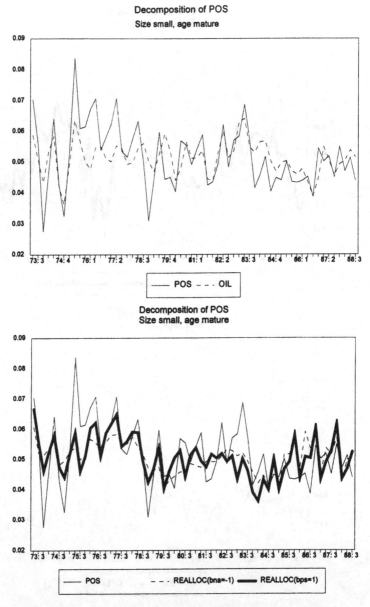

Figure 9.8. Decomposition of Job Creation 1973:2–1988:4, 5-Equation System. *Note*: See Table 9.1, footnote 1, for explanation of size and age classifications.

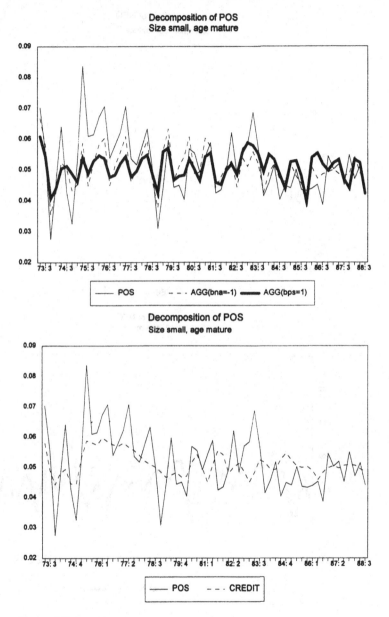

Figure 9.8 *(cont.)*

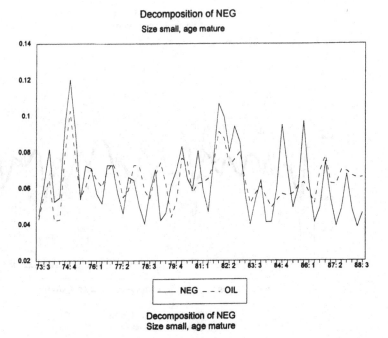

Decomposition of NEG
Size small, age mature

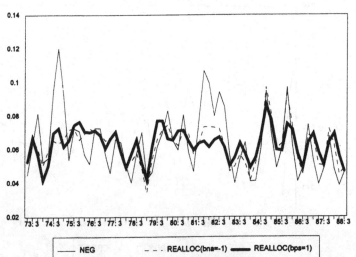

Decomposition of NEG
Size small, age mature

Figure 9.9. Decomposition of Job Destruction 1973:2–1988:4, 5-Equation System. *Note*: See Table 9.1, footnote 1, for explanation of size and age classifications.

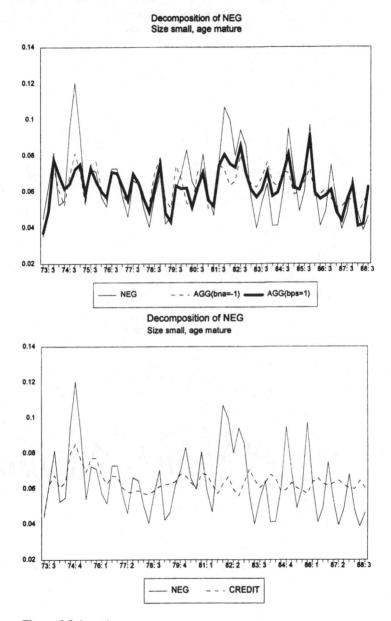

Figure 9.9 *(cont.)*

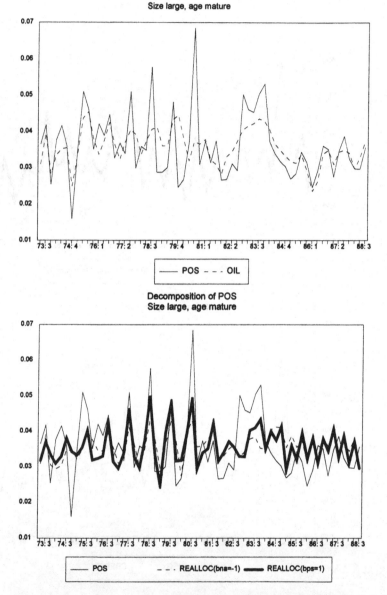

Figure 9.10. Decomposition of Job Creation 1973:2–1988:4, 5-Equation System. *Note*: See Table 9.1, footnote 1, for explanation of size and age classifications.

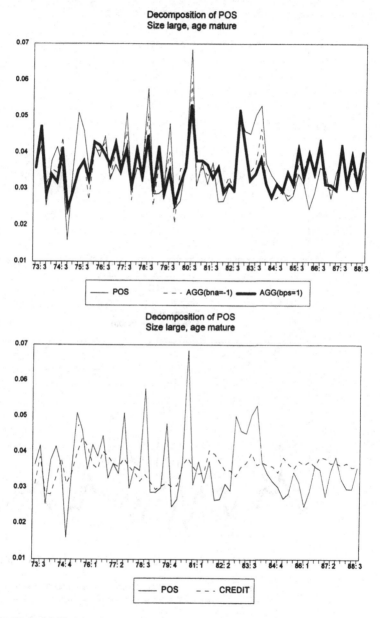

Figure 9.10 *(cont.)*

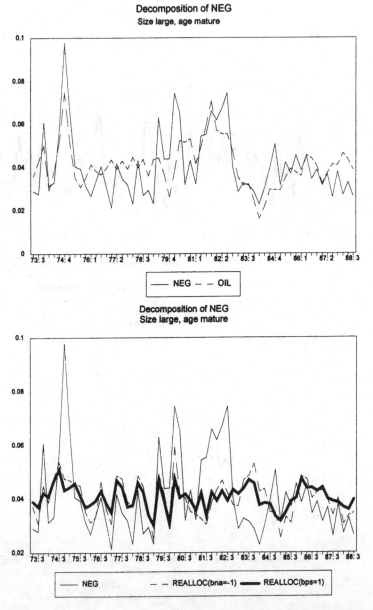

Figure 9.11. Decomposition of Job Destruction 1973:2–1988:4, 5-Equation System. *Note*: See Table 9.1, footnote 1, for explanation of size and age classifications.

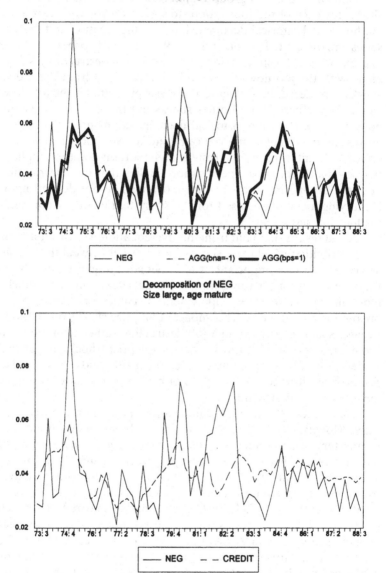

Figure 9.11 *(cont.)*

summarize the respective contributions of the oil price shocks, group-common shocks, within group reallocation shocks and monetary/credit shocks for each of the four groups to forecast error variances at different horizons. Historical decompositions of the creation and destruction series are presented in Figures 9.4–9.11. In each panel of the latter figures, the actual respective job flow (creation or destruction) is depicted along with the job flow that would have emerged from the individual shocks considered. In each case, the series presented is the job flow that would have emerged if all other shocks but the shock in question had been set to 0. Thus, the historical decompositions provide a metric for evaluating the relative importance of alternative shocks across different episodes. In interpreting the results, an important point to emphasize is that the block recursive specification implies that the contributions of both the oil and monetary/credit innovations do not depend upon the identifying assumptions used for the subsystem involving common and reallocation shocks.

Several results stand out from this five-equation system. First, consider the contribution of oil price shocks. Tables 9.4–9.7 reveal that oil shocks are typically more important at intermediate (8 quarter forecast error variances) and longer run horizons (16 quarters). Oil price shocks are more important for the employment dynamics of mature plants as opposed to young plants. The impact of oil price shocks on employment dynamics is primarily through job destruction rather than job creation. From Figures 9.4–9.11, the impact of oil price shocks is particularly evident for job destruction in the mid-1970s and early 1980s. The decrease in oil prices in 1986 did not have much of an effect on either job creation or destruction.

Now consider the impact of innovations in the monetary/credit indicator. Monetary/credit innovations tend to be more important at short (4 quarter) and intermediate run (8 quarter) horizons. The impact of monetary/credit innovations on employment dynamics is primarily via job destruction rather than job creation. Somewhat surprisingly, the contribution of the monetary/credit innovations is more important for large plants rather than small plants. This latter finding may reflect the fact that key credit sensitive sectors (e.g., transportation equipment) have a greater fraction of employment in large establishments.[21] From Figures 9.4–9.11, monetary/credit innovations are especially important in the increases in job destruction in the mid-1970s and the late 1970s. Monetary/credit innovations did not play much of a role in the prolonged increase in job destruction in the early 1980s.

Even taking into account specific observable shocks like oil and monetary/credit innovations, much of the variation in job creation and destruction is accounted for by unobserved group-common and reallocation shocks. In terms of the hypotheses regarding symmetry, the joint hypotheses that both common shocks and reallocation shocks have symmetric effects on job creation and destruction are supported only for small, young plants. Also, if one assumes that common shocks have a symmetric contemporaneous effect on job creation and destruction, then this implies for most groups that reallocation shocks play a major role in job destruction. These results are quite similar in spirit to those found in the two-equation system. Thus, a robust finding of this analysis is that, for mature plants, one of the following two conclusions must be accepted: either reallocation shocks play a major role in the cyclical fluctuations in net employment via job destruction *or* common shocks have a disproportionate effect on job destruction.

5 Concluding Remarks

The main results of this analysis are summarized as follows:

- For U.S. manufacturing, small and young plants exhibit much higher average rates of job creation and destruction than larger and more mature plants.
- The cyclical patterns of job creation and destruction across employer size and age groups differ substantially. On the basis of rates tabulated from all plants, the cyclical volatility of job destruction is much greater than that for job creation. This finding is driven entirely by the behavior of mature plants (both large and small). Young plants (whether large or small) exhibit about the same cyclical volatility in job creation and destruction.
- Observable shocks such as real oil shocks and monetary/credit policy indicators affect job destruction more than job creation. Real oil shocks are relatively more important for mature plants (whether large or small) than for young plants. Somewhat surprisingly, shocks to monetary policy/credit market conditions are also relatively more important for mature plants (whether large or small) than for young plants.
- Even after accounting for observable shocks like oil and monetary policy shocks, much of the cyclical variation in job creation and destruction is accounted for by other (unobservable) factors. In the analysis, these latter factors are decomposed into the respective contributions of common and reallocation

shocks. The results indicate that, for mature plants, either real-location shocks are quite important for net employment fluctuations via job destruction or common shocks affect job destruction disproportionately relative to job creation.

Overall, these results point towards the conclusion that employer age is more important than employer size for understanding the cyclical dynamics of job creation and destruction. This conclusion holds in terms of the basic cyclical properties of the raw data as well as in the estimated dynamic responses. Young plants do not exhibit the cyclical asymmetry in job creation and destruction that is exhibited by more mature plants. This difference in the basic cyclical properties carries over to distinct differences between young and mature establishments in the dynamic response to observable and unobservable shocks.

Notes

The results and conclusions presented in this chapter are those of the author and do not necessarily reflect the concurrence of the Bureau of the Census. I am grateful to David Audretch, Zoltan Acs, and Participants at the conference for their comments. Catharine Buffington and Andrew Figura provided excellent research assistance. I also want to acknowledge and thank the NSF for financial support.
1 The quarterly job flows are based on production worker employment.
2 That is, consider the growth rate for establishments between period $t - 1$ and t. The base period methodology would assign establishments to size classes based upon the level of employment in period $t - 1$. Establishments with adverse transitory shocks (actual or measurement error driven) in period $t - 1$ are more likely to be classified as small, while establishments with positive transitory shocks are more likely to be classified as large establishments. Since transitory shocks reverse themselves, establishments that are classified as small in the base year are likely to expand and establishments that are classified as large in the base year are likely to contract.
3 As discussed in Davis, Haltiwanger, and Schuh (1996), the basic cyclical properties of job creation and destruction by employer size are robust to a variety of different methods for classifying establishments into size classes.
4 See Davis, Haltiwanger, and Schuh (1996) for discussion of issues involving defining employer age.
5 In many of the tables and figures, the following abbreviations are used: POS = job creation, NEG = job destruction, NET = net employment growth (equal to POS − NEG), and SUM = job reallocation (equal to POS + NEG).
6 See, for example, Cooper and Haltiwanger (1993) for theoretical and empirical evidence indicating the nature of the connection between seasonal variation and cyclical variation in employment.
7 To determine the sensitivity to seasonal adjustment, the subsequent analysis has been conducted after controlling for seasonal dummies. The results for the latter analysis (not reported) are quite similar to those reported in the text.

The primary difference is that common shocks play a somewhat more important role using the seasonally *unadjusted* data. This latter finding makes sense given that seasonal shocks are likely to act as a common shock.

[8] The specification of the VAR system (for both the two-variable and five-variable systems) follows that in Davis and Haltiwanger (1996). In the latter paper, the VAR systems are estimated and analyzed for total manufacturing job flows over the period 1948:1–88:4. Further, as mentioned later, the Davis and Haltiwanger (1996) paper considers a wide variety of alternative identifying assumptions (e.g., long run neutrality restrictions) and focuses more on the implications of the results for net employment growth and job reallocation. As noted in the introduction, the novel emphasis of the current chapter is a consideration of these issues in the context of an analysis of job flows by employer size and age. Note that job flows by employer size and age are not available for the longer sample period considered in Davis and Haltiwanger (1996).

[9] In principle, the different groups could be pooled and a panel VAR across employer size and age groups could be estimated. In this case, one could potentially distinguish between shocks common to all groups and group-specific shocks. However, this would require stipulating identifying restrictions about which there is relatively little guidance. It would be interesting in future work to develop appropriate identifying restrictions in a fully specified model with unobserved aggregate, sectoral, and idiosyncratic shocks. The latter is beyond the scope of this exploratory chapter. For analysis that makes some progress along these lines, see Davis and Haltiwanger (1997).

[10] Again, it should be emphasized that "common" refers to disturbances that are common to all plants in the group while "reallocation" disturbances alter the intensity of the allocative disturbances within the group.

[11] As discussed in Davis and Haltiwanger (1996), the standard arguments for the zero covariance restriction are less compelling in this environment because the reallocation and common innovations may represent different aspects of the same unobserved events. However, as noted by Davis and Haltiwanger (1996), an alternative justification for this assumption is available. The key idea is that some events with reallocation consequences generate positive common effects while others generate negative common effects. In a large sample, the correlation between the common and reallocation shocks associated with these primitive events will be approximately zero, so that the zero covariance restriction holds.

[12] An alternative approach is to consider relevant long run neutrality restrictions. See Davis and Haltiwanger (1996) for consideration of the latter in a related setting.

[13] While these assumptions are almost definitional, Davis and Haltiwanger (1996) discuss reasons that reallocation disturbances may not have a positive *contemporaneous* impact on job creation.

[14] Mortensen and Pissarides (1994) also look at the implications of this separation/matching asymmetry.

[15] While it is possible to consider alternative sign restrictions, observe that allowing for $b_{ps} > 1$ amounts to saying that the impact effect of a reallocation shock is to *increase* net employment. This favorable short-run effect of a reallocation innovation is at odds with the literature – from Lilien (1982) through Blanchard and Diamond (1990) – on the net consequences of reallocation

disturbances. Indeed, the chief question in this literature has been whether reallocation disturbances cause recessions, not whether they cause booms.

[16] Bootstrapped standard errors have been calculated for the variance decompositions reported in Tables 9.3–9.7. For ease of exposition, they are not reported. The standard errors range between 0.06 to 0.11.

[17] This does not imply that plants across different groups face identical credit market conditions. Rather, a common index of monetary policy and credit market conditions is used to evaluate the cyclical dynamics of job creation and destruction across groups.

[18] See Davis and Haltiwanger (1996) for further motivation of this measure.

[19] Relevant alternative indices (e.g., the federal funds rate) have been considered with very similar results in a related setting (Davis and Haltiwanger, 1996).

[20] Note that this implies that we do not restrict the orthogonal component of credit market innovations to be the same across groups. Rather, the orthogonal component of credit market innovations for a particular group reflects the innovation to credit market conditions after controlling for oil price disturbances, group-common shocks, and within group reallocation shocks.

[21] For example, the employment-weighted average establishment size (what Davis and Haltiwanger [1990] denote the coworker mean) varies considerably across industries. In 1988, the coworker mean in the transportation industry was 7829 (implying that the typical worker in the transportation industry is employed at a plant with 7829 workers) while the coworker mean in the food industry was 537 workers. Note that Gertler and Gilchrist (1994) argue that there are not substantial differences in the fraction of output accounted for by large firms across durable and nondurable industries. However, their industry breakdown was very broad (just two categories), missing some important components of the variation across industries. Given the results reported here, investigating the within industry variation across size and age categories would be of substantial interest.

References

Blanchard, Olivier and Peter Diamond, 1989, "The Beveridge Curve," *Brookings Papers on Economic Activity 1*, 1–60.

Blanchard, Olivier and Peter Diamond, 1990, "The Cyclical Behavior of Gross Flows of Workers in the United States," *Brookings Papers on Economic Activity 2*, 85–155.

Caballero, Ricardo and Mohamad Hammour, 1994, "The Cleansing Effects of Recessions," *American Economic Review*, *84*, no. 5 (December), 1350–1368.

Cooper, Russell and John Haltiwanger, 1993, "The Aggregate Implications of Machine Replacement: Theory and Evidence," *American Economic Review*, *83*, no. 3 (June), 360–382.

Davis, Steven J. and John Haltiwanger, 1990, "Gross Job Creation and Destruction: Microeconomic Evidence and Macroeconomic Implications," *NBER Macroeconomics Annual*, *V*, 123–168.

Davis, Steven J. and John Haltiwanger, 1992, "Gross Job Creation, Gross Job

Destruction, and Employment Reallocation," *Quarterly Journal of Economics, 107*, no. 3 (August), 819–863.

Davis, Steven J. and John Haltiwanger, 1996, "Driving Forces and Employment Fluctuations: New Evidence and Alternative Interpretations," NBER Working Paper No. 5775, September.

Davis, Steven J. and John Haltiwanger, 1997, "Sectoral Job Creation and Destruction Responses to Oil Price Changes and Other Shocks," mimeo.

Davis, Steven J., John Haltiwanger, and Scott Schuh, 1996, *Job Creation and Destruction in U.S. Manufacturing Industries*, Cambridge: The MIT Press.

Gertler, Mark and Simon Gilchrist, 1994, "Monetary Policy, Business Cycles and the Behavior of Small Manufacturing Firms," *Quarterly Journal of Economics, 109*, no. 2 (May), 309–340.

Lilien, David, 1982, "Sectoral Shifts and Cyclical Unemployment," *Journal of Political Economy, 90*, 777–793.

Mortensen, Dale T. and Christopher Pissarides, 1994, "Job Creation and Destruction and the Theory of Unemployment," *Review of Economic Studies, 61*, no. 3 (July), 397–415.

Stock, James H. and Mark W. Watson, 1989, "New Indexes of Coincident and Leading Economic Indicators," *NBER Macroeconomics Annual, IV*, 351–394.

CHAPTER 10

SMEs and Job Creation During a Recession and Recovery

Per Davidsson, Leif Lindmark and Christer Olofsson

1   Introduction

During the last two decades studies in many countries have found small firms to be overrepresented as generators of new jobs (Birch, 1979; Baldwin and Picot, 1995; Fumagelli and Mussati, 1993; Kirchhoff and Phillips, 1988; Spilling, 1995; for further reference to studies carried out in a large number of countries see also Aiginger and Tichy, 1991; ENSR, 1994; Loveman and Sengenberger, 1991; OECD, 1987; Storey and Johnson, 1987). According to our own previous study of the 1986–89 period the same holds true for the Swedish economy (Davidsson, 1995a; Davidsson et al., 1993; 1994a; 1995a).

That period, however, was characterized by relatively favorable economic conditions. Internationally most of the research on small and medium enterprises' (SMEs') role in job creation has been carried out under such conditions. There are indications that job creation by firm class might vary over the business cycle (Davis et al., 1996a; Haltiwanger, this volume; Kirchhoff and Phillips, 1988; Kirchhoff and Greene, 1995). In the early 1990s Sweden was struck by the deepest recession since the Great Depression (Braunerhjelm and Carlsson, this volume). If it can be shown that SMEs' role in job creation in Sweden is radically different during recession conditions compared with boom conditions, the same is likely to hold true also for other economies.

2   Purpose

There is thus a need for further empirical insight into the cyclical pattern of job creation among SMEs. Another shortcoming of previous studies is that they are often not able to distinguish between firms and establishments, to capture the heterogeneity among small firms in terms of

286

differences between industries and types of small firms, or to partial out the constituent parts of net job creation (births, deaths, expansions, and contractions). Our purpose is therefore to provide empirical insights into the following issues:

1   What is the role of SMEs in job creation under different business cycle conditions?
2   What is the role of SMEs in job creation in different industry sectors?
3   What is the relative importance of different types of SMEs and different forms of business dynamics for net job creation?

While we focus on job creation in this chapter the study forms part of a project which has a broader scope. The broader project is a continuation and refinement of our earlier work on business dynamics in Sweden during the 1980s (Davidsson, et al., 1993; 1994a; 1994b; 1995a; 1995b; 1995c).

3   The Data Set

Four features of the data set used are especially noteworthy in comparison with related studies: (1) it covers all sectors, whereas many other studies have had to rely on data for single sectors, often manufacturing, or have only analyzed the economy as a whole; (2) while it is based on establishment level data, the size of the larger structure (firm or company group) of which the establishment may form a part is known; (3) the researchers have been extensively involved in the design of the data set and in checking of data quality; and (4) it covers varying business cycle conditions, including a very deep recession period. The period studied is November 1988 to November 1994, which allows for seven static descriptions and six year-by-year comparisons. For convenience, we refer to changes occurring between November 1988 and November 1989 as "1989," and so on. The first year marks the end of a boom period. During 1990–93 the country experienced the deepest recession since the 1930s, while a dramatic recovery occurred in 1994 although unemployment levels remain high. All our analyses build on annual changes.

The data set was designed to make it possible to:

*   monitor individual establishments and their employment figures over time in order to identify births, deaths, expansions, and contractions and the associated job changes with accuracy;
*   identify different types of establishments, i.e., autonomous single-site firms, corporate headquarters, and branch plants;

- separate establishments in SMEs from establishments in larger firms or corporations;
- group the establishments according to sectorial affiliation;
- group the establishments according to size of employment;
- relate the establishments to labor market areas;
- locate geographically the ownership of branch plants, including foreign ownership.

Extensive effort was put into data compilation and screening. In close cooperation with register experts and programmers at Statistics Sweden (Swedish Bureau of Census [SCB]), data from various data bases and different (annual) versions thereof were combined and checked in order to achieve the highest possible quality of the input data. Altogether, data from four data bases have been matched for the compilation of business dynamics data. These are:

- the Central Establishment Register (CFAR)
- the Regional Employment Register (ÅRSYS)
- the Register over Groups of Companies (KCR)
- the Register over Establishments and Firms with Foreign Ownership

Our primary unit of analysis is the *establishment*. The establishments were grouped into five size classes based on their number of employees: 0–4, 5–19, 20–49, 50–199, and >200. By comparing different annual versions of CFAR, births, deaths, expansions, and contractions among these establishments can be tracked. As our interest concerns job creation in small *firms*, the data should ideally be firm level data. However, while unique codes exist for legal firms, these are often changed even if no real birth or death has occurred. The same seems to be true for business statistics in other countries. Researchers therefore tend to favor establishment size class analysis, as establishment identification codes are more stable in the registers. This is not satisfactory, as large corporations may have many small establishments and fairly large firms may have no large establishments.

Hence, by choosing establishments rather than legal firms as the basic unit of analysis, monitoring changes over time becomes truer in terms of reflecting real changes, but less adequate as regards assigning those changes to the right (size) category of firm. In order to circumvent this problem, we first identified three *types* of establishments, following the example of Reynolds and Maki (1990):

- *Simples*, which are autonomous, single-establishment firms
- *Branches*, which are either units other than headquarters in

company groups or units other than headquarters in independent multi-establishment firms
* *Tops*, which are headquarters either in company groups or in
independent, multi-establishment firms.

The identification of establishment types involves extensive search
and matching of data in CFAR, KCR, and the Register over establishments and firms with foreign ownership. This identification allows for
using Simples as a conservative proxy for "small firms." This is what we
did in our previous study. A major improvement in the present study is
that we have been able to identify the size of the larger structure (firm
or company group) of which the Tops and Branches form part. This
involved a very extensive data processing procedure in which the
employment figures for each Branch that was associated with a particular Top were added to the size of the Top itself. In that way, it could be
determined for each of the approximately 600,000 establishments in the
data base whether it should be regarded as a small and medium-sized
enterprise (SME) establishment or a large enterprise (LE) establishment. The firm or company group employment size chosen for this
dichotomization was set at 200 employees. In this study we thus deal with
six establishment types:

1 SME Simples
2 SME Tops
3 SME Branches
4 LE Simples
5 LE Tops
6 LE Branches

For Simples, the firm size figure is the same as the establishment size
figure. It should be noted that LE Simples are a very insignificant category. Only some 50 such units exist; i.e., only about one out of ten thousand Simples has more than 200 employees. LE Branches can be further
subdivided into those with domestic versus foreign ownership. Although
the size of foreign firms is not known, we regard all foreign-owned establishments as LE Branches.

In the analyses to follow, changes occurring in different establishment
categories are aggregated in various ways. Categories 1–3 may be combined to the "SME sector"; categories 2 and 3 to "Multi-establishment
SMEs." While our methodology has taken us far in combining the merits
of better data quality of establishment data with the conceptual
adequacy of firm level analysis, it is very important to note that the
different forms of business dynamics – birth, death, expansion, and

contraction – refer to changes on the *establishment* level. "Multi-establishment SME birth job gains" thus includes not only the event that new multi-establishment SMEs (firms that already have more than one establishment in their first year in operation) are created. When what was previously a Simple or a Multi-establishment SME opens up a new branch, the jobs created in this new branch are regarded as "Multi-establishment SME birth job gains." On the firm level, this event is likely to constitute growth, but we do not really know; employment may have been reduced elsewhere in the firm. Therefore, in our principles for aggregation we stick to what we do know: that *establishments* affiliated with a certain size category of firm went through a change of a certain kind.

As data quality of the CFAR was judged less satisfactory as regards employment figures, the original size measure has in most cases been exchanged for more accurate figures from the ÅRSYS register, which tracks specific individuals. The CFAR figure was retained if the registers did not match, and for the entire construction industry. A correction has been made so that the owner–manager is counted as an employee irrespective of the legal form of the firm. This correction increases static figures for SME employment in the private sector by 100,000 or 10 percent as compared to the original registers. As some of this employment is likely part-time, the correction leads to an exaggerated static figure. What is important about this correction, however, is that artificial *job changes* due to change of legal form are avoided.

As to industries, the data base covers the entire economy. That is, all commercially active establishments are included, whether they are for-profit or non-profit. This amounts to about 600,000 establishments and 4 million jobs. In this chapter, however, we have excluded the public sector (which also includes foundations and some other small categories judged to be mainly non-profit) and the primary industries. The remaining *private sector* (400,000 establishments; 2 million jobs), which the analyses in this chapter concern, is subdivided into 15 industry sectors. However, in the present study we apply a less disaggregated delineation into four major sub-sectors: manufacturing, professional services, retailing/hospitality, and miscellaneous. The latter includes construction, various service industries, and unclassified establishments. For establishments that lacked industry classification forward searches were conducted in subsequent annual versions of the CFAR, and if a code was found, that code was used also for previous years.

Problems occur when establishments change categorical affiliation (labor market area [LMA], type, size, etc.) from the beginning to the end of an analysis year. For establishments that change industry or region, we have assigned negative changes to the category of origin and positive changes to the new category. In the analyses presented in this chapter, this rule of thumb affects how changes in units that flow in from or out to the excluded sectors are treated, but should be of little significance for our present purposes.

As regards establishment type and size class, all changes are attributed to the original category. Importantly, this makes the results sensitive to what Davis, Haltiwanger, and Schuh (1993; 1996a; 1996b) call the "regression fallacy," which is a systematic bias in favor of SME job creation. In order to check the extent of this problem, we ordered special runs from SCB that list all establishment category changes and their associated employment changes that took place during each analysis year. These data have been analyzed in a separate paper (Davidsson et al., 1996b) but the main results will be reiterated in the present chapter.

Two one-shot changes in the original registers occurred for tax reasons during the period studied. These changes led to the exclusion of a substantial number of surviving, very small firms in 1991, and their re-entry into the register in 1994. If not corrected for, this would lead to gross over-estimation of deaths (and death job losses) for SME Simples in 1991 and, similarly, gross overestimation of births and birth job gains for the same category in 1994. Through various checks we have been able to obtain reliable information on the extent of overestimation caused by these one-shot changes. In the analyses presented below, SME Simples death job losses in 1991 – and aggregates including this measure – have been reduced by 22,000 compared with the original register data. Likewise, SME Simples birth job gains in 1994 have been reduced by 25,000. The sectorial division of these corrections was made proportionate to the sectors' shares of total job gains or losses in these respective years.

4   Results Concerning Job Creation in SMEs and Large Firms over Time

Figures 10.1 through 10.3 display our results regarding annual job changes in SMEs and in large firms. Figure 10.1 displays the absolute figures for gross job gains and losses in the respective categories. In Figure 10.2 these numbers are transformed to shares, i.e., percentages of total job gains or losses in a given year. Finally, Figure 10.3 repeats the same information in terms of an index where the figures for subsequent years are compared with the corresponding figure for the first year, 1989. Combining the figures for 1989 in Figure 10.1 reveals that in that year total net employment creation was positive by approximately 14,000. This figure is lower, however, than in the years immediately before, when the net surplus exceeded 50,000 annually (Davidsson et al., 1993; 1994a; 1995a). It may also be noted that among large firms the net job creation

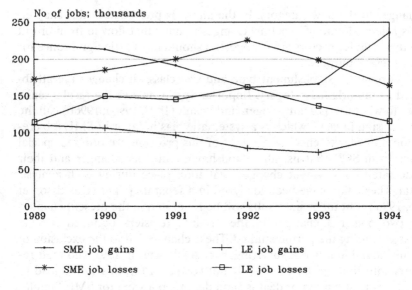

Figure 10.1. Job Volatility Count

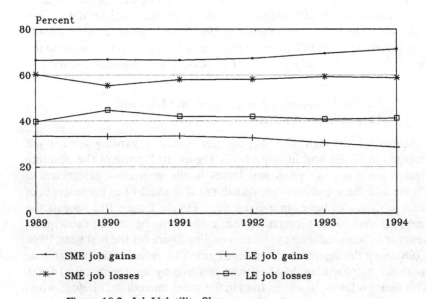

Figure 10.2. Job Volatility Shares

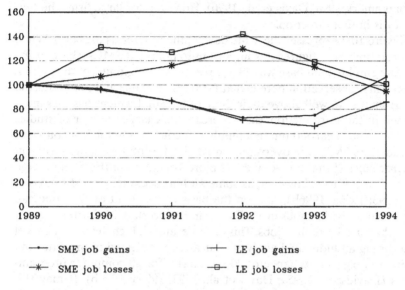

SME job gains   LE job gains
SME job losses   LE job losses

Figure 10.3. Job Volatility Index; 1989 = 100

was already negative. After 4 years of consecutive negative net job creation in 1990–93, the economy returned in the last year, 1994, to net job creation in excess of 50,000 in the private sector. For both SMEs and large firms annual job losses increased until they peaked in 1992. Through 1993 and 1994 job losses declined in a similar fashion for SMEs and large firms. Job gains fell for both categories during 1990–92. In 1993 job gain figures started to rise again for SMEs, and this turned into a dramatic upswing in 1994, contributing to positive net job creation for SMEs that year. For large firms the job gain figure continued to drop in 1993, albeit at a lower rate. In 1994 large firm job gains turned upwards again, but not as dramatically as among SMEs, and large firms therefore remained net losers of jobs in 1994.

There are in this exhibit two cyclical differences between SMEs and large firms that are particularly noteworthy. Firstly, SMEs seem to lag in the downturn. While large firms as a group already had slightly negative net job creation in 1989, the job losses among SMEs did not exceed their job gains until 1991. Secondly, as just mentioned, SMEs actually seem to have led the upswing (employment-wise), with earlier and more dramatic increase in gross job gains. The pattern is not in clear agreement with US findings that over time, net employment fluctuations are associated more with fluctuations in losses than in gains (Eberts and

Per Davidsson, Leif Lindmark and Christer Olofsson

294   **Per Davidsson, Leif Lindmark and Christer Olofsson**

Montgomery, 1994; Davis et al., 1996). However, for large firms the tendency is in that direction.

Figure 10.2 expresses the same development in terms of shares. When
interpreting these figures it is important to note that SMEs' share of the
private employment base was 48.3 percent in the beginning of the period.
So the first observation here is that for both job gains and job losses, the
SME shares are well above their share of the employment base. As mentioned in the introduction, this accords with a large number of studies
that have been carried out in a number of countries in the last couple of
decades. As SMEs are overrepresented also for job losses, the results in
a sense suggest that employment is more volatile in SMEs than in large
firms. It is not true, however, as some authors seem to suggest (Davis et
al., 1993; 1996a; 1996b), that on the basis of this kind of data one can
infer that individual jobs in SMEs are more uncertain or shorter in duration than are large firm jobs. This is so because job changes that cancel
out during an individual analysis year are not reflected in the data, and
neither is, e.g., an exchange of 20 secretaries for 20 computer programmers (Davidsson, 1995a; Davis et al., 1993; 1996a; 1996b). It may still
be true that SME jobs are more uncertain jobs, but that conclusion needs
empirical evidence of a different kind.

A second observation from Figure 10.2 is that in each individual year,
SMEs' share of job gains exceeds their share of job losses. The converse
is true for large firms. While both SMEs and large firms experienced net
job losses during the 1990–93 recession period, the SME share of net job
losses stayed at 29 percent, i.e., a much smaller figure than their share of
the employment base.

Relatively little of a cyclical pattern emerges in Figure 10.2. This
differs from US results, where dramatic differences in SME employment
creation shares have been reported for different phases of the business
cycle (Kirchhoff and Phillips, 1988; Kirchhoff and Greene, 1995). In
Sweden during this particular period, the shares are comparable for the
1990–93 recession and the economically brighter years that preceded and
followed that period. The only more notable difference is SMEs' smaller
share of job losses in 1990, the first recession year.

This last result is also one of the main observations from Figure 10.3.
The spark for the recession, so to speak, was the dramatic increase (>30
percent) in large firm job losses in 1990. SME job losses also increased
that year, but not at all as dramatically. From 1991 and onwards, SMEs
and large firms display very similar development patterns for job losses.
In 1994 both categories were back on 1989 levels or lower. However,
SME job losses never reached the same extremes, relatively to 1989, as
did large firm job losses.

SMEs and large firms followed very similar patterns for job gains from 1989 through 1992. For both categories the figures drop at a rate that increases year by year until in 1992 they are little more than 70 percent of the 1989 figures. As already observed the two categories follow differential development paths during 1993 and 1994, with SME figures rising earlier and more sharply than large firm figures. While SMEs exceeded index 100 in 1994, large firms were still below 90.

All in all, our results suggest that SMEs were heavily overrepresented as gross and net job creators during the 1990–93 recession period. As this holds true also for the years before and after the recession there is little support in these data for the notion that SMEs' relative role as job creators is markedly different in different phases of the business cycle. There were, however, temporal differences between large and smaller firms in terms of when trend shifts occurred and the relative strength of these shifts.

5   Results Concerning Job Creation Among SMEs in Different Industry Sectors

Figures 10.4 through 10.7 display results for SMEs' shares of job creation over the years within different industry sub-sectors. Taken together, the four sectors sum up to the entire "private sector" analyzed previously. Three different shares are displayed for each year in each figure. First, there is the SME share of (initial) job stock. The development of this share is interesting in its own right, since it shows the trend of structural (size-wise) shift over time. It is imperative, however, to understand that the development of the SME share of the job stock is not solely the result of job gains and losses. Reclassification of firms that grow beyond, or shrink below, the 200 employee cutoff also affects the development of this share (Davidsson, 1994; 1995b; Davis et al., 1993; 1996a; 1996b). In addition, transfer into and out of the "private sector" affects the figures. Therefore, the development of the SME share of the employment base does not show where new jobs originate.

The two remaining shares, i.e., those referring to job gains and losses, are our real focus of interest. Comparison between one of these and the SME job stock share shows whether SMEs are over- or under-represented in job gains and losses. Direct contrasting of the SME gains and losses shares shows the group's net job creation performance. If the share of job gains is larger than the share of job losses, this means that SMEs perform relatively "better" as net job creators than large firms, and vice versa. As large firms' shares are merely the mirror image of the SME shares (Figure 10.2) they were left out in order to simplify the exhibits.

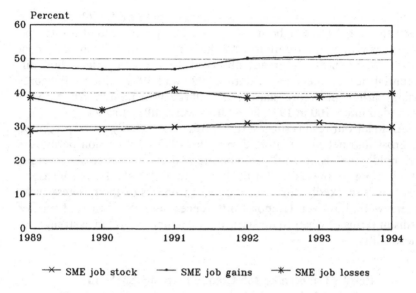

Figure 10.4. SME Job Shares, Manufacturing

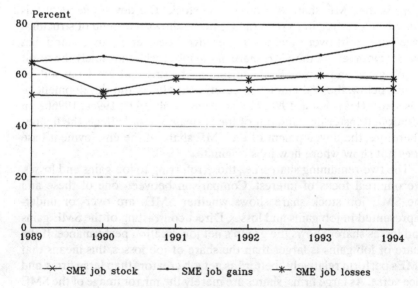

Figure 10.5. SME Job Shares, Professional Services

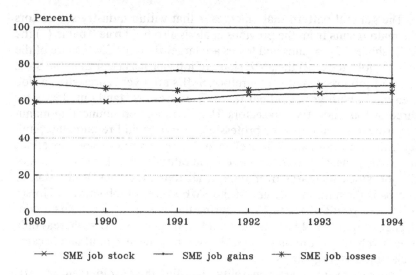

Figure 10.6. SME Job Shares, Retail/Hospitality

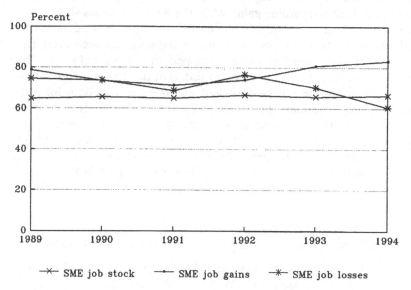

Figure 10.7. SME Job Shares, Miscellaneous

298 Per Davidsson, Leif Lindmark and Christer Olofsson

The general pattern that emerges is that within industry sub-sectors the main results from the previous analysis also hold true. That is, (1) the SME shares of job gains and losses are larger than the SME share of the existing job stock, (2) the SME share of job gains is larger than the SME share of job losses, and (3) therefore, SMEs are over-represented as job creators in both gross and net terms. These results stand out clearly for three of four industry sub-sectors. They are most pronounced in manufacturing, but hold also for professional services and retailing/hospitality. The rather awkward "miscellaneous" group shows some deviations from this general pattern. Another generality is that the SME share of the job stock increases over time in all four industries. While this, of course, is the natural outcome of the SME shares of job gains and losses it is also a result of the fact that during the deep recession years a non-negligible number of large firms shrank and became SMEs whereas only a relatively modest number of SMEs outgrew the size limit and became reclassified as large firms.

There seems to be less generality regarding the development of SME job gains and losses shares over different business cycle conditions. In manufacturing, both the gains and the losses shares turned downwards as the economy turned downwards, and rose again towards the end of the period. In retailing/hospitality the pattern is similar to manufacturing for job losses, while the job gain share shows the opposite pattern, first rising and then declining. The miscellaneous group is instead similar to manufacturing regarding gains, while the SME job losses share oscillates over time. In professional services the gains share started out stable and rose towards the end of the period as the economy recovered. The losses share in the same sector first dropped, then remained stable. The four sub-sectors thus display as many different patterns as any stochastic process would be expected to yield, and there is little basis for generalizing interpretations. The most striking finding that holds true for all industries is instead that despite very considerable macroeconomic fluctuation there are no really dramatic fluctuations in the SME shares of job gains and losses. The only exception to that is the sharp drop for the SME job losses share in the "miscellaneous" category in 1994, which can be traced to major cutbacks among large construction companies in that year.

6   Results Concerning the Components of SME Job Creation

Figures 10.8–10.13 give another more detailed picture of SME job creation during the studied period. While we no longer make a distinction between industry sub-sectors within the private sector, different forms

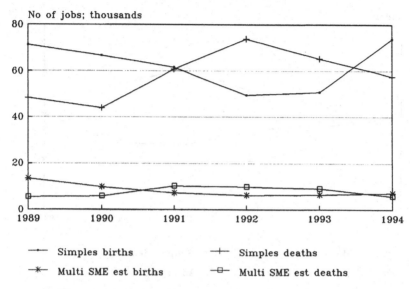

Figure 10.8. SME Birth/Death Job Volatility

of job dynamics and different types of SME establishments are separated. SME Tops and SME Branches have here been combined in a
"Multi-establishment SME" category, but separated from "SME
Simples," i.e., single-establishment small firms. The reader should be
reminded that the data concern establishment level, not firm level
changes. That is, we know that the job changes displayed here occurred
in establishments that were part of small firms. It is not necessarily the
case that, e.g., job losses from multi-establishment SME deaths are associated with the death of entire small or medium-sized firms, but only with
the closing down of establishments within such firms.

Figure 10.8 displays job gains and losses that result from the birth and
death of different types of SME establishments. The figure shows clearly
that birth and death job change data for SMEs are dominated by the
development of Simples. The reason for this is the large number of
Simples; they also dominate the SME employment base. Taken one by
one, most of them are very small and insignificant indeed.

Judging from Figure 10.8 establishments in Simples and multi-
establishment SMEs seem to have developed in a similar fashion during
the period studied. Birth job gains declined in 1990 for both categories,
and they both produced a net deficit during 1991–93. However, for
Simples the death job losses did not rise until 1991. Figure 10.9, which

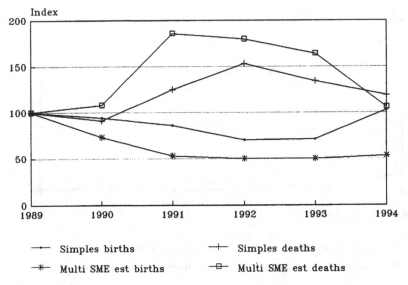

Figure 10.9. SME Birth/Death Job Volatility

displays each category's development relative to its own 1989 figures, reveals that Simples birth job gains fell less, and Simples death job losses increased less, than did the corresponding figures for multi-establishment SMEs. In 1994 it was still the case that little more than half as many jobs were created via multi-establishment SME births as was the case in 1989.

This relatively favorable development of Simples is apparent also when expansions and contractions are analyzed. These data are displayed in Figures 10.10 and 10.11. Again, it should be kept in mind that "Multi-establishment SME expansion" does not necessarily mean that a SME (firm) expanded; other establishments within the same SME may have declined. As establishment and firm is the same in the case of Simples, firm level interpretation is unproblematic for that category.

Simples dominate the data also as regards expansion and contraction job changes, although not so heavily as was the case with birth- and death-related job changes. Figure 10.10 reveals that Simples expansion job gains continued to increase in 1990, contributing to the fact that the category did not experience an expansions over contractions job deficit until 1991. For multi-establishment SMEs, contraction job losses already outnumbered expansion job gains in 1990. Otherwise, the two categories' development patterns look similar.

This is confirmed by Figure 10.11 as regards expansions. A substantial

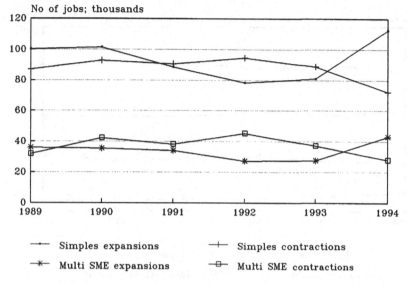

Figure 10.10. SME Expansions/Contractions Job Volatility

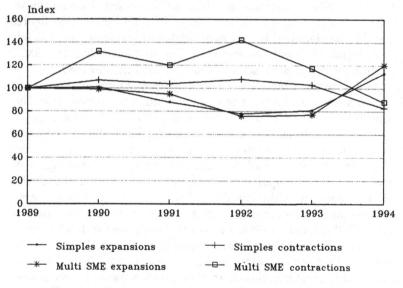

Figure 10.11. SME Expansions/Contractions Job Volatility

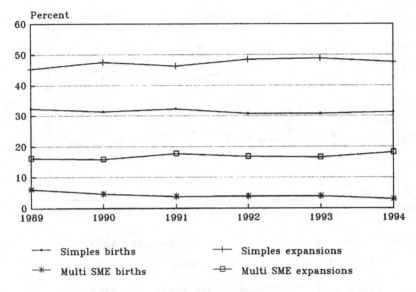

Percent

        —•— Simples births   —+— Simples expansions

        —*— Multi SME births   —□— Multi SME expansions

Figure 10.12. Shares of SME Job Gains

difference emerges as regards contraction job losses. These did not rise much at all for Simples despite the deep recession. For multi-establishment SMEs, contraction job losses increased dramatically in 1990. In 1992, they peaked at a level 40 percent above the 1989 figure. In fact, this development is strikingly similar to that found for LE job losses in Figure 10.3, with the exception that multi-establishment SME contraction job losses were actually lower in 1994 than in 1989.

Let us now turn to Figure 10.12, which displays in terms of shares how the constituent parts of SME gross job creation develop over time. The first observation here is that over time differences in shares are, again, rather small considering the dramatic trend shifts in the economy at large. A tentative generalization for Simples would be that the birth share is somewhat lower, and the expansion share somewhat higher in the recession years compared with the beginning and the end of the period. For multi-establishment SMEs the births share dropped sharply in the beginning of the recession, never to recover. In fact, this share is the lowest, 3.0 percent, in 1994. This is to be compared with 6.1 percent in 1989. The expansion share fluctuates and rises with the 1994 recovery.

Figure 10.13 displays corresponding shares of SME job losses. The fluctuations are greater in this chart, giving some support for the notion that also among SMEs, it is more the job loss fluctuations than the job

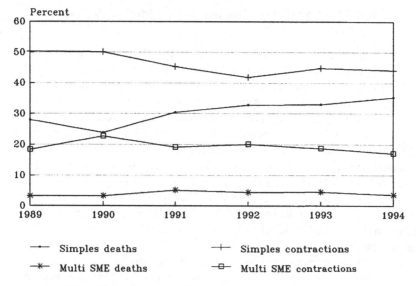

Figure 10.13. Shares of SME Job Losses

gains fluctuations that determine the net changes over time. However, it is quite natural that the Simples contractions share declines and the Simples death share rises during the course of this deep recession. When a very small firm starts to shrink, it does not take many years before it reaches the zero level. The multi-establishment death share rises during the recession and declines in the recovery.

In summary, the data displayed in Figures 10.8–10.13 suggest that it was not the somewhat larger, multi-establishment SMEs that kept up SME employment and job creation during the recession. Multi-establishment SMEs' development was similar to, and compares only marginally favorably to, that of large firms. Rather, it was primarily the development among the many very small, single-site firms that made the SME sector come out relatively better as job creators than large firms. Given the relative lack of resources such small firms must suffer from, this result may appear surprising and perhaps also a bit alarming. One might justifiably wonder what direction the economy takes when firms that according to all that we have learnt cannot be the most efficient producers are the main providers of new jobs. We will revert to this issue in the Discussion section. Let us first turn to another important issue: is it at all true that SMEs are over-represented as job creators, or have we been misled by methodological flaws?

7   Is the High SME Job Creation Share a Methodological
      Artifact?

In our computations of job gains and losses, the changes are assigned to
the size category the establishment belonged to at the beginning of each
analysis year. Davis et al. (1993; 1996a; 1996b) have pointed out that this
may bias the results in favor of small firm job creation. The reason is that
if a firm randomly fluctuates across the chosen size boundary, all the contraction losses will be attributed to large firms, while all job gains are
attributed to smaller firms. Davis et al. (1993; 1996a; 1996b) label this
phenomenon "the regression fallacy." Their reasoning is part of a rather
active debate on truth and reality as regards small firm job creation (cf.
Baldwin and Picot, 1995; Carree and Klomp, 1996; Davidsson, 1994;
1995b; Gallagher and Robson, 1995; ENSR, 1995; Haltiwanger, 1995;
Harrison, 1994a; 1994b; Kirchhoff and Greene, 1995; Storey, 1994; 1995;
van der Hoeven et al., 1994).

In a separate paper (Davidsson et al., 1996b) we have estimated the
influence of the "regression fallacy" on our results. This was accom-
plished by keeping track of all establishments that form part of firms that
cross the size boundary as a result of organic growth or decline, merger,
spin-out/buy-out, etc. The job *changes* that occurred in such establishments were then split equally between the size classes involved – SMEs
(<200 employees) and large firms – instead of being attributed solely to
the base-year category. The job *stock* that is transferred is not an issue
for the "regression fallacy." Our data permit such calculations, but only
for the economy as a whole, i.e., including primary industries and the
public sector. As the public sector is large and heavily dominated by large
organizations, SMEs' share of the employment base is smaller in such an
analysis, or approximately 33 percent. Likewise, SMEs' share of job
changes is also smaller.

The result as regards expansion job gains for the 1989–94 period is
that the correction brings down the (annual average) SME share of
expansion job gains from 45.7 to 45.0 percent. This represents a small
share of SMEs' extent of over-representation as gross job creators. The
same is true for correcting the contraction side; SMEs' share rises from
36.7 to 37.2 percent. After correcting for "regression fallacy," the SME
share of expansion job gains still exceeds their share of the employment
base by more than 11 percentage points. SMEs' share of expansion job
gains exceeds their share of contraction job losses by almost 8 percentage points. Correcting for the "regression fallacy" thus amounts to correcting for fractions of percentages. Qualitatively the results are
unaffected.

8 Discussion

Our analysis has established that during the deep 1990–93 recession in Sweden, as well as in the years immediately preceding and following that period, SMEs were a very important source of new jobs in Sweden. In both gross and net terms SMEs as a group fared better as job creators than did large firms. Nonetheless, SMEs also experienced net losses of jobs during the recession years. It was further established that the result that SMEs are over-represented as job creators is not due to the "regression fallacy." Correcting for this methodological flaw had minuscule effect on the results. Further, with minor exceptions the preceding conclusion holds true across industries.

The results do not indicate that SMEs' role in job creation is radically different under recession conditions and under boom or more normal economic conditions. If anything, there appears to be during this period a trend-wise increase in SMEs' shares of both job changes and the employment base across fluctuating macroeconomic conditions. Some temporal differences in the business cycle pattern were detected, however, when SMEs' development was compared to that of larger firms. Firstly, SMEs lagged (employment-wise) in the downturn. Secondly, the upswing started earlier and was more forceful among SMEs.

It is hard to imagine that both of those differences can be regarded as generally true for smaller and larger firms' roles in job creation over business cycles. One way to interpret why this pattern evolved in this particular case is as follows: Towards the end of the boom of the late 1980s, large corporations experienced cost problems that served as an incentive to become more efficient. That is, they kept up or even increased production without increasing their number of employees. Demand was still high, and the labor- and SME-intensive retail and consumer services industries kept employment up. SME employment continued to grow for various reasons; trend-wise increasing birth rates were one, and large firms' outsourcing strategies that transferred production to small subcontractors and professional services firms were another.

Eventually a crisis broke out in the financial sector, paralleled with increasing budget deficits in the government sector. This led to uncertainty and decreasing consumer confidence, which hurt the many SMEs that rely solely on domestic household demand. Therefore employment also declined sharply among SMEs. The recession was definitely there. It was further deepened because of declining international demand, especially since the public sector could no longer serve as a cushion. Rather, for the first time in many years employment also shrank in that sector. However, even amidst the deepest crisis many small firms were started or kept alive because of lack of alternative employment, even if they were not very profitable. Therefore, employment among SMEs never dropped as dramatically as did large firm employment.

When positive signs finally emerged, primarily in terms of success for the large exporters, consumer confidence resurged and the domestic-market dependent SMEs experienced (somewhat) better times again. Despite increased demand large firms did not need more personnel because of technological, organizational, and strategic changes that made them more efficient or less oriented towards internal growth. However, the fraction of SMEs that are direct suppliers of parts and services to large, exporting corporations found work for additional employees. Finally, policy measures aiming at reducing unemployment through increased new firm formation may have contributed to the dramatic increase in SME employment in 1994.

It was primarily the development among the many very small, single-site SMEs (Simples) that made SMEs relatively better than large firms as job creators during the recession. Multi-establishment SMEs followed a pattern more akin to that of large firms. This should be carefully considered when policy measures are discussed. It would have completely different implications if it were rapidly growing, highly advanced small firms that dominated the SME employment creation data.

A large proportion of those employed in small, single-establishment firms are owner–operators, partners, or family members. One possible reason why this category of firm appears relatively resistant to the onset of a deep recession is that they are much more downwards flexible in terms of the remuneration they pay their "employees" than are larger firms that pay more or less fixed salaries and wages. Especially when alternative employment is difficult to find, owner–operators are likely to hang on to their business activities for extended periods even if profitability is very low. Also, in terms of their type of business activities these tiny businesses are likely to be more flexible than somewhat larger firms. While the latter have a more clearly defined business mission that they follow, the operators of the smallest firms may take on any task that generates an income, as long as they possess the necessary skills.

Our analysis thus suggests that across industry sectors and different business cycle conditions SMEs are very important for job creation. In addition, our analyses of the relationship between SME dynamics and regional economic well-being suggest that the effect is positive or, at worst, neutral (Davidsson et al., 1994a; 1994b; 1995b; 1995c; 1996c). So the hypothesis that increased importance of SMEs is a sign of economic stagnation or decline has no support in our data. Similar evidence from country comparisons has been provided by Thurik (1995).

However, in 1994, which was an extremely good year in terms of SME net job creation, their net contribution of jobs was about 70,000. It would take about ten such years in a row to bring down current unemployment figures. This we know will not happen. In addition, the fact that it was very small firms – arguably subsistence firms – that made the SME sector perform relatively well during the deep recession gives reason to doubt that small and new firms will lead our way to a prosperous future.

Therefore, the SME sector as we have learnt to know it will not solve the current unemployment problem. In order to achieve that, radically new patterns of business dynamics are needed. This would probably require political decisions that permit the opening up of entirely new sectors of economic activity, and incentives for further increased creation and growth of new firms as well as incentives for large firms more aggressively to try to realize the full commercial potential of viable ideas that originate in small, innovative firms that may lack the resources needed for rapid and successful diffusion of their new products.

References

Aiginger, K. and G. Tichy, 1991, "Small Firms and the Merger Mania," *Small Business Economics*, 3, 83–102.
Baldwin, J. and G. Picot, 1995, "Employment Generation by Small Producers in the Canadian Manufacturing Sector," *Small Business Economics*, 7, 317–331.
Birch, D., 1979, *The Job Generation Process.* Final Report to Economic Development Administration. Cambridge, MA: MIT Program on Neighborhood and Regional Change.
Braunerhjelm, P. and B. Carlsson, "Industry Structure, Entrepreneurship and the Macroeconomy: A Comparison of Ohio and Sweden, 1975–1995" (in this volume).
Carree, M. and L. Klomp, 1996, "Small Business and Job Creation: A Comment," *Small Business Economics*, 8, 317–322.
Davidsson, P., 1994, "Small Firms as Job Creators – Myth or Fact?" Paper presented at *RENT XIII Conference*, Tampere, Nov. 1994.
Davidsson, P., 1995a, "SMEs and Job Creation in Sweden." Manuscript prepared for the OECD secretariat/Working Party on SMEs/the Ad Hoc Group on SME statistics.
Davidsson, P., 1995b, "Small Firms: Has Their Role as Job Creators Been Exaggerated?" Paper presented at *ICSB 40th World Conference*, Sydney, June 1995.
Davidsson, P., L. Lindmark and C. Olofsson, 1993, *Business Dynamics in the Swedish Economy: A Regional Perspective.* Report submitted to the EC Commission.

308   **Per Davidsson, Leif Lindmark and Christer Olofsson**

Davidsson, P., L. Lindmark and C. Olofsson, 1994a, *Dynamiken i svenskt näringsliv* (Business Dynamics in Sweden). Lund: Studentlitteratur.
Davidsson, P., L. Lindmark and C. Olofsson, 1994b, "New Firm Formation and Regional Development in Sweden," *Regional Studies*, 28 (4), 395–410.
Davidsson, P., L. Lindmark and C. Olofsson, 1995a, "The Trend Towards Smaller Scale During the 1980's: Empirical Evidence from Sweden." Paper presented at *ICSB's 40th World Conference*, Sydney, June 1995.
Davidsson, P., L. Lindmark and C. Olofsson, 1995b, "Small Firms, Business Dynamics and Differential Development of Economic Well-being," *Small Business Economics*, 7, 301–315.
Davidsson, P., L. Lindmark and C. Olofsson, 1995c, "Smallness, Newness, and Regional Development." Paper presented at *OECD High-level Workshop on SMEs, Innovation and Employment*, Washington D.C.
Davidsson, P., L. Lindmark and C. Olofsson, 1996a, *Näringslivsdynamik under 90-talet* (Business Dynamics in the '90s). Stockholm: NUTEK.
Davidsson, P., L. Lindmark and C. Olofsson, 1996b, "The Extent of Overestimation in Small Firm Job Creation – an Empirical Examination of the Regression Bias." Paper presented at *ICSB's 41st World Conference*, Stockholm, June 16–19 (forthcoming in *Small Business Economics*).
Davidsson, P., L. Lindmark and C. Olofsson, 1996c, "SMEs, Business Dynamics, and Economic Development During a Recession." Paper presented at the *ENDEC World Conference on Entrepreneurship*, Singapore, Dec. 6–8.
Davis, S.J., J. Haltiwanger and S. Schuh, 1993, Small Business and Job Creation: Dissecting the Myth and Reassessing the Facts, *Working Paper* No. 4492, Cambridge, MA: National Bureau of Economic Research.
Davis, S.J., J. Haltiwanger and S. Schuh, 1996a, *Job Creation and Destruction*. Boston: The MIT Press.
Davis, S.J., J. Haltiwanger and S. Schuh, 1996b, "Small Business and Job Creation: Dissecting the Myth and Reassessing the Facts," *Small Business Economics*, 8, 297–315.
Eberts, R.W. and E.B. Montgomery, 1994, "Employment creation and destruction: an analytical review." *Economic Review* (Federal Reserve Bank of Cleveland).
ENSR, 1994, *The European Observatory for SMEs, Second Annual Report*. Zoetermeer: EIM Small Business Research and Consultancy/European Network for SME Research.
ENSR, 1995, *The European Observatory for SMEs, Third Annual Report*. Zoetermeer: EIM Small Business Research and Consultancy/European Network for SME Research.
Fumagalli, A. and G. Mussati, 1993, "Italian Industrial Dynamics from the 1970s to the 1980s: Some Reflections on the Entrepreneurial Activity," *Entrepreneurship and Regional Development*, 5, 25–37.
Gallagher, C. and G. Robson, 1995, "Small Business and Job Creation – an Even Further Dissection of the Davis, Haltiwanger and Schuh Working Paper." *International Small Business Journal*, 13, 64–67.
Haltiwanger, J., 1995, "Small Business and Job Creation in the US: What Do We Know?" Paper presented at *OECD High-level Workshop on SMEs, Innovation and Employment*, Washington D.C.
Haltiwanger, J., "Job Creation and Destruction by Employer Size and Age: Cyclical Dynamics" (in this volume).

Harrison, B., 1994a, "The Small Firms Myth," *California Management Review*, Spring, 142–158.

Harrison, B., 1994b, *Lean and Mean: The Changing Landscape of Corporate Power in the Age of Flexibility.* New York: Basic Books.

Kirchhoff, B. and P. Greene, 1995, "Response to the Renewed Attacks on the Small Business Job Creation Hypothesis." Paper presented at *Babson College Entrepreneurship Research Conference*, London, April 1995.

Kirchhoff, B. and B. Phillips, 1988, "The Effect of Firm Formation and Growth on Job Creation in the United States," *Journal of Business Venturing*, 3, 261–272.

Loveman, G. and W. Sengenberger, 1991, "The Re-Emergence of Small Scale Production: An International Comparison." *Small Business Economics*, 3, 1–37.

OECD, 1987, "The Process of Job Creation and Job Destruction," *Employment Outlook*, 97–220.

Reynolds, P.D. and W.R. Maki, 1990. *Business Volatility and Economic Growth.* Final project report submitted to the US Small Business Administration.

Spilling, O.,1995, "Do Small Firms Create Jobs?" Paper presented at the *6th ENDEC World Conference on Entrepreneurship*, Shanghai, Dec. 1995.

Storey, D., 1994, *Understanding the Small Business Sector.* London: Routledge.

Storey, D., 1995, "Job Creation in SMEs" (mimeo; Warwick Business School).

Storey, D. and S. Johnson, 1987, *Small and Medium-Sized Enterprises and Employment Creation in the EEC Countries: Summary Report.* EC Commission, Programme of Research and Actions on the Development of the Labour Market, Study No. 85/407.

Thurik, R., 1995, "Small Firms, Large Firms and Economic Growth." Paper presented at *OECD High-level Workshop on SMEs, Innovation and Employment*, Washington D.C.

Van der Hoeven, W., A. Kleijnweg and W. Visser, 1994, "Job Creation in SMEs – an Assessment of the Importance of Size Distribution and Regression Fallacies" (mimeo; EIM, Zoetermeer).

CHAPTER 11

Job Flows of Firms in Traditional Services

Luuk Klomp and Roy Thurik

1 Introduction

Unemployment is the dominant problem of the European Union. In 1994, the unemployment rate, as a percentage of the labour force, in the Union was 10.6, while this rate was 6.7 in the United States and 2.5 in Japan. Unemployment is threatening for those involved. European unemployment is persistent: more than 40 percent of those unemployed in Europe are unemployed for more than a year. This percentage is 11 percent in the United States and 15 percent in Japan. Also, the youth (less than 25 years) unemployment in Europe (21 percent) is much higher than in the United States (13 percent) and in Japan (5 percent) (see OECD, 1994a). This makes unemployment threatening for European society as a whole.

"Small business has to save us" is a slogan often heard from European politicians and representatives of social and institutional groups. They fear a further rise of the already unacceptably high level of unemployment caused by the sheer endless series of efficiency and cost-cutting operations of the public and large business sectors. They seek salvation through the residual sector, the small business sector. They hope that unemployment can be fought and that macro employment growth can be accelerated by promoting smallness. Whether this hope is justified remains to be established from job flow studies.

Recent studies report high rates of gross job creation and gross job destruction regardless of the observed period or country. Average annual rates of gross job reallocation – defined as the sum of gross job creation and gross job destruction – in a wide range between 15 and 35 percent are found in the literature (see OECD, 1994b, ch. 3, for a review of the international evidence). Together with the magnitude of gross job real-location numerous studies – starting with Birch (1981) – have found that small firms have a stronger contribution to the creation of jobs than one might expect from their employment share. In other words, these studies

310

report that gross job creation rates of small firms exceed those of large firms. However, gross job destruction rates are also higher for small firms than for large ones. The obvious question is whether the net job creation rate – defined as the difference between gross job creation and gross job destruction – depends on firm size. If net job creation rates decrease with firm size, then the hope of representatives of national governments that stimulating the small business sector will favour macro economic employment growth is justified.

In this chapter we study job flows for traditional service industries. This study makes four contributions to the existing literature: Firstly, job creation and job destruction are broken down by firm size and firm age in our analysis. This allows us to distinguish between age and size effects on net and gross reallocation of jobs. This distinction between size and age effects is extremely important for the understanding of the contribution of small businesses to aggregate employment growth. The impact of firm age on aggregate employment figures has been largely overlooked in the empirical literature on job flows.[1] As far as we know the present study is the first analyzing the effects of firm size and firm age simultaneously.

Secondly, this study expands our knowledge on the heterogeneity of firms in terms of job creation and destruction, analyzing size and age effects both separately and simultaneously. If small and young firms outperform their large and old counterparts systematically in terms of net and gross creation, then we would observe a degree of homogeneity in the job creation and job destruction patterns within age and size groups. In other words, simultaneous job creation and destruction rates would be expected to be relatively small within such groups. The impact of the age variable in the homogeneity of job flow rates provides an indication of the relevance of the theories of Jovanovic (1982) and Ericson and Pakes (1995) to industry dynamics, because the importance of learning and selection effects among firms of different ages is stressed in these theories.

Thirdly, this study helps shed light on the question whether the well documented patterns of job creation and job destruction in the manufacturing sector are significantly different from those in the underresearched service industries. The gross job studies in the empirical literature are mainly concerned with manufacturing industries. See, for instance, Davis and Haltiwanger (1992; 1995), Ritter (1993), Broersma and Gautier (1995) and Konings (1995a; 1995b). Davis, Haltiwanger and Schuh (1996), for example, admit that their findings are restricted to manufacturing and recommend giving priority to the development of longitudinal firm level data sets for the service industries.[2] Gross job

312   Luuk Klomp and Roy Thurik

flow patterns in these industries may differ from those in manufacturing because the minor influence or even absence of scale economies in large parts of the service industries provides small firms with a relatively strong position in such industries. It is observed, indeed, that the proportion of small firms in services is systematically higher than in manufacturing.

Finally, by analyzing data from a mid-size European economy like the Netherlands, this study adds to the country by country comparison of job flows. It is instrumental for our understanding of whether country specific institutions are important in determining the movements and magnitudes of job creation and job destruction.

Section 2 is devoted to providing some definitions of gross job flows and basic facts. The heterogeneity of firms in terms of gross job creation, destruction and reallocation is analyzed in Section 3. The patterns of job creation and destruction by firm size and age are dealt with in Section 4. Finally, a summary and conclusions are given in Section 5.

2   Definitions of Gross Job Flows and Some Basic Facts

Before discussing some basic but essential properties of our rich data material, we have to deal with some definitions. We define our measures of job flows according to the Organization for Economic Cooperation and Development (OECD) (1987) and Dunne, Roberts and Samuelson (1989). This enables us to create an international context of our results. The definitions of job flows due to the birth (or entry), expansion, contraction and death (or exit) of firms between year $t - 1$ and year t are as follows:

B_t = employment (measured in full-time equivalents) in year t of all firms that first appear in the data set in year t

E_t = employment in year t minus employment in year $t - 1$ of all firms that expand or do not change employment between year $t - 1$ and year t

C_t = employment in year $t - 1$ minus employment in year t of all firms that contract between year $t - 1$ and year t

D_t = employment in year $t - 1$ of all firms that were in operation in year $t - 1$ but are not recorded in year t

Gross job creation (JC_t) and gross job destruction (JD_t) between year $t - 1$ and year t are defined as

$$JC_t = \left(\frac{B_t}{L_{t-1}} + \frac{E_t}{L_{t-1}} \right) \times 100\% \qquad (1)$$

and

$$JD_t = \left(\frac{C_t}{L_{t-1}} + \frac{D_t}{L_{t-1}} \right) \times 100\% \qquad (2)$$

respectively, where L_{t-1} is employment in all firms that are in operation in year $t - 1$.[3] The sum of JC_t and JD_t is a measure of gross job reallocation rate between year $t - 1$ and year t:

$$GROSS_t = JC_t + JD_t \qquad (3)$$

while JC_t minus JD_t is a measure of net job reallocation rate between year $t - 1$ and year t:

$$NET_t = JC_t - JD_t \qquad (4)$$

Firm level data are available for the Dutch hospitality and retail industries for the period 1985–1988. They stem from a yearly survey of Statistics Netherlands, called "Statistics of Man-Years and Gross Wages." The survey covers all firms employing paid labour. All four yearly data sets contain, for each firm, the number of employees, the first year of registration, the municipality of settlement, a four digit code (called SBI) of its main industry, the legal form and a firm identifier.[4]

Some basic facts on gross job flows in Dutch service industries are presented in Tables 11.1 and 11.2. Job creation, job destruction, gross job reallocation and net job reallocation rates for the retail and hospitality industries are given for three consecutive years in Table 11.1. Despite its simplicity many conclusions can be drawn from this table. Table 11.2 contains data at three and four digit industry level and deals with the heterogeneity question. It shows whether the net employment growth displayed in Table 11.1 appears in all three and four digit industries and whether firms within these industries are heterogeneous, i.e., whether simultaneous job creation and destruction is observed within these industries.

Let us start discussing four aspects of Table 11.1. Firstly, we observe substantial simultaneous job creation and destruction in both service industries. The gross job reallocation rates are over 20 percent for the retail trade and even over 30 percent for the hospitality industries. These percentages fall in the range of 20–39 percent, which is reported in OECD (1994b) for the service industries in 9 member countries. Furthermore, it is found in OECD (1994b) that, on average, gross rates in services are higher than those in manufacturing. A possible explanation is the high proportion of small and (probably) young firms in service industries where jobs are less stable than in their large counterparts. This explanation is consistent with the high gross rates for the hospitality

Table 11.1. *Job Flow Rates for the Years 1986–1988*

| | Year | | |
	1986	1987	1988
Retail trade			
Job creation	18.75	13.04	13.02
% due to birth[1]	24.48	33.97	30.80
expansion	75.52	66.03	69.20
Job destruction	13.70	8.98	10.59
% due to death[1]	67.08	48.11	54.58
contraction	32.92	51.89	45.42
GROSS	32.45	22.02	23.61
NET	5.05	4.07	2.43
Hospitality Industries			
Job creation	19.11	17.30	20.19
% due to birth[1]	34.33	39.36	42.60
expansion	65.67	60.64	57.40
Job destruction	15.20	13.66	15.25
% due to death[1]	35.92	35.58	52.79
contraction	64.08	64.42	47.21
GROSS	34.31	30.96	35.44
NET	3.92	3.63	4.94

[1] We emphasize that the turnover of firms – i.e., birth and death – is overestimated in the data set. This holds for small non-incorporated firms in particular, because firms are recorded only in years in which a paid employee is employed.

industry, which is the sector with the smallest average firm size in the Netherlands.

Secondly, the magnitude of job creation and destruction implies that a substantial worker reallocation is required to accommodate the job reallocation. The lower bound of worker reallocation – which is the maximum of job creation and job destruction – is about 13 and 17 percent of employment for the retail and hospitality industries, respectively.[5]

Thirdly, both job creation and job destruction rates are approximately equal in the hospitality industries for the three years. This is also the case

Table 11.2. *Job Flow Rates by Industries, Size-Weighted Averages[1]*

SBI	Industry	Job Creation	Job Destruction	Gross	Net
65/66	*Retail trade (total)*				
651	Meat, fish, poultry and dairy products	13.88	15.29	29.17	−1.41
652	Potatoes, fruit, vegetables, beverages, chocolate and tobacco	15.09	8.21	23.30	6.88
653	Pharmacies	13.50	13.43	26.93	0.07
654	Medical and orthopaedic goods, perfumery and toilet articles	13.94	11.37	25.31	2.57
655	Clothing	13.62	9.98	23.60	3.64
656	Textiles, wool, linen and dress materials	13.28	11.45	24.72	1.83
657	Footwear, leather goods and travel accessories	12.52	10.50	23.02	2.03
658	Floor covering and furnishing fabrics	12.54	10.79	23.32	1.75
659	Domestic decoration and electric household appliances	13.04	10.08	23.12	2.96
661	Household utensils and do-it-yourself materials	15.96	9.60	25.57	6.36
662	Cars, motor-cycles and bicycles	15.01	10.46	25.47	4.56
663	Gasfilling stations	15.57	12.62	28.19	2.94
664	Books, newspapers and magazines	16.70	15.11	31.82	1.59
665	Photographic and optical equipment, watches and jewelry	12.42	11.23	23.64	1.19
666	Flowers, plants and pets	17.60	12.61	30.21	4.98
667	Fuel oil, bottled gas, coal and wood	8.97	11.27	20.24	−2.29
668	Games and toys, sports goods, camping articles and caravans	19.62	13.16	32.79	6.46
669	Department stores and mail order houses	17.62	16.24	33.85	1.38
67	*Hospitality (total)*				
6711	Restaurants	15.78	12.03	27.81	3.75
6712	Cafeterias	21.34	14.88	36.22	6.46
6721	Cafes	22.46	16.50	38.96	5.95
6741	Hotels	13.12	8.13	21.25	4.99
6799	Remaining hospitality industries	26.25	25.64	51.89	0.61

Note: For the SBI code the "Standaard Bedrijfsindeling" of Statistics Netherlands (CBS) of 1974 is used.
[1] The job flow rates are size-weighted averages of the 1986–1988 period.

in the retail trade for the years 1987 and 1988, while higher job creation and destruction rates are observed for the year 1986. They are probably incidental and the result of mergers or take-overs in some particular industries.[6] We conclude that job flows in the period 1986–1988 are quite stable for both service industries. Although this period is too short to carry out a formal test of any hypothesis on cyclical patterns of job reallocation, we are inclined to conclude that there is no indication that job reallocation is countercyclic, i.e., that there is no negative correlation between the gross and the net rate. This conclusion supports the view in the literature (Boeri and Cramer, 1992), which interprets structural change in employment as a continuous process driven by small firms. A different view (Davis and Haltiwanger, 1992) is that structural change is concentrated in cyclical downturns. Evidence in Broersma and Gautier (1995) suggests that the first view is valid for small firms and the second view for large ones. Because small firms dominate services we expect that job flows in the retail and hospitality industries are indeed independent of the cycle. This expectation relaxes the limitation of the data that employment is only observed for the period 1985–1988.

Fourthly, the magnitude of job flows due to birth and death falls in the range reported in the OECD (1994b) for the service sectors of nine countries.[7] This result is an indication that the overestimation of job flows due to birth and death is limited, although we repeat that – particularly for small non-incorporated firms – the turnover of firms is overestimated in the data set.

Table 11.2 presents average job flow rates for three digit industries in the retail trade and for four digit industries in the hospitality sector.[8] It shows positive net reallocation rates in 16 out of 18 industries in the retail trade and in all 5 industries in the hospitality sector. All industries show substantial job creation and destruction rates. Job creation and job destruction rates range from 8.97 to 19.62 percent and from 8.21 to 16.24 percent for the retail trade and from 13.12 to 26.25 percent and from 8.13 to 25.64 percent for the hospitality industries, respectively. The importance of simultaneous job creation and destruction in the industries of Table 11.2 indicates the heterogeneity of firms within the industries. The absolute value of net job reallocation, i.e., net employment change, can be interpreted as the minimum amount of job reallocation required. Higher magnitudes of job creation and destruction in an industry would imply more heterogeneity within that industry; i.e., creation of jobs is observed in some firms, while job destruction takes place in other firms within that industry. We analyze the importance of heterogeneity in the next section.

3   The Heterogeneity of Firms

In this section we extend the analysis of firm heterogeneity including age and size effects. We investigate whether within narrowly defined groups of firms, e.g., young and small hotels, homogeneity in terms of job creation and job destruction is observed. The level of homogeneity is an important basis for public support of groups of firms that contribute strongly to employment growth.

We use a measure of firm heterogeneity according to the standard set out in Dunne, Roberts and Samuelson (1989). This measure has also been applied in Davis and Haltiwanger (1992), OECD (1994b), Boeri (1994) and Broersma and Gautier (1995). The job reallocation in excess of the absolute value of the net employment change (EXC) is the basis to measure heterogeneity within a group of firms. EXC for the entire sector is then defined as

$$EXC = \{GROSS - |NET|\} \times L/100 \tag{5}$$

where L is total sectoral employment.

The excess of job reallocation is decomposed into a component that represents excess job reallocation within groups of firms ($WITHIN$) and into a component that represents excess job reallocation between groups of firms ($BETWEEN$). The decomposition and the within-group and between-group employment shifts are defined in equations (6)–(8).

$$EXC = WITHIN + BETWEEN \tag{6}$$

$$WITHIN = \sum_i [(GROSS_i - |NET_i|) \times L_i/100] \tag{7}$$

$$BETWEEN = \sum_i [|NET_i| \times L_i/100] - |NET| \times L/100 \tag{8}$$

In case firms within a group are homogeneous, simultaneous job creation and job destruction is relatively unimportant within these groups, resulting in a low value of $WITHIN$ and in a high value of $BETWEEN$. If we express the values of $WITHIN$ and $BETWEEN$ as a percentage of EXC, we obtain a measure of heterogeneity of firms within groups. Table 11.3 reports the results for the retail and hospitality sectors for the 1986–1988 period.

Our data set of firms is broken down according to size, age, three or four digit industries and combinations of these three variables. The results are provided in Table 11.3. The choice for three or four digit industries is that products and services are assumed to be generally homogeneous within these industries. If there were systematic differences between job creation and destruction processes on the one hand and firm size on the other hand, we would observe relatively high employment shifts between size groups and low employment shifts within size groups. Finally, the age variable is included in Table 11.3 because the theories of Jovanovic (1982) and Ericson and Pakes (1995) on industry dynamics

Table 11.3. *Heterogeneity of Firms: Percentage of Excess Job Reallocation (EXC) Due to Between-Group Employment Shifts*

	Average values for the period 1986-1988				
Group type	Age	Size	Age and Size	3/4 digit industries[1]	All[2]
Number of groups	4	5	20	18/5	360/100[3]
Retail trade	6.21	7.54	17.93	0.89	26.25
Hospitality sector	23.29	16.34	25.81	0.00	28.74

[1] The retail trade is divided into 18 three digit industries; the hospitality sector is divided into 5 four digit industries.
[2] Based on a grouping of firms by age, size and the three or four digit industries simultaneously.
[3] Six of 360 and 1 of 100 groups are empty in the retail and hospitality industries, respectively.

stress the importance of learning and selection effects among firms of different ages.

We draw three conclusions from Table 11.3. Firstly, three digit industries in the retail trade and four digit industries in the hospitality sector are very heterogeneous; i.e., for both sectors less than 1 percent of the excess job reallocation is due to between-group employment shifts. Secondly, even if firms are broken down by size, age and three or four digit industry simultaneously, the resulting within-group employment shifts are still about three times higher than the between-group employment shifts. This indicates that job reallocation is a firm level phenomenon rather than a sectoral or even a national one. We conclude that our results – like those of Dunne, Roberts and Samuelson (1989), Davis and Haltiwanger (1992) and Boeri (1994) – are in line with theories that predict firm heterogeneity (see Davis and Haltiwanger, 1992; Boeri, 1994 for a discussion of theories that stress the heterogeneity at the firm level).

Thirdly, the age and size variables are relatively important to measure the homogeneity of firms. This holds particularly for the hospitality sector, where the between-group employment shift based on four age classes accounts for about 81 percent of the between-group employment shift due to the grouping of all variables simultaneously.

The obvious question now is whether this heterogeneity remains at lower aggregation levels. An analysis similar to that reported in Table 11.3 shows that even within three and four digit industries the heterogeneity of firms remains high; i.e., if the excess job reallocation is broken down by size and age simultaneously, the so-called within-shifts are higher than the between-shifts. Moreover, the between-group employment shift based on age is higher than that based on size in 15 out of 18 three digit industries in retail trade and in all 5 four digit industries in the hospitality sector.

4   Job Creation and Destruction Rates by Firm Size and Age

We analyze the effects of firm size and age on job flows in this section. This yields the opportunity to evaluate the debated proposition of the job creation prowess of small firms. Moreover, we compare job creation and destruction rates of firms of different sizes, holding age fixed. These results provide information whether any positive relation between net job creation and small firms is merely the result of firm age. Finally, job creation and destruction rates that are higher for young firms than for older ones would support theories on industry dynamics based on learning processes of firms (Jovanovic, 1982; Ericson and Pakes, 1995). Successful young firms will grow rapidly, implying high job creation rates, while unsuccessful young ones are likely to exit, implying high job destruction rates.

Five size classes[9] and four age classes are created to analyze job flows. The results are displayed in Table 11.4. The job creation rates are lower than the job destruction rates for the retail trade (10.52 versus 11.04 percent) and for the hospitality industries (10.60 versus 14.16 percent). At first sight these percentages conflict with the results in Table 11.1, where positive net job reallocation rates – i.e., job creation rates minus job destruction rates – are reported. The reason for the differences between Tables 11.1 and 11.4 is the use of (base-year) size and age for individual firms in Table 11.4. As a consequence, firms that enter the market are excluded from Table 11.4 because (base-year) size and age are not defined for entrants.[10]

Gross job reallocation rates – i.e., the sum of job creation and destruction rates – are the highest for the smallest, youngest firms for the retail as well as the hospitality industries. The highest gross job reallocation rates are observed in the first size class, but they are remarkably stable for the other size classes for the retail and the hospitality sector. The same holds with regard to age for the retail trade. Gross job reallocation rates substantially decrease with the maturity of firms for the hospitality industries.[11]

Another result from Table 11.4 is that the job creation rate exceeds that of job destruction for young firms in both sectors. The net job real-

Table 11.4. *Annual Job Creation (JC) and Job Destruction (JD) Rates by Firm Size and Age for the 1986–1988 Period*

Retail Industries

JC
JD

			Size (number of employees)			
	1 - 3	3 - 6	6 - 10	10 - 20	20+	total
Age (years)						
1-2	30.37	24.04	25.37	15.73	16.18	20.62
	21.57	19.49	20.61	18.97	14.75	17.40
3-5	14.94	11.61	11.11	20.38	5.60	9.16
	19.84	14.27	13.95	14.02	8.81	11.77
6-10	10.89	9.17	8.63	9.40	16.55	11.78
	16.68	11.14	10.50	12.14	10.17	12.32
11+	8.21	6.93	6.61	6.02	12.06	9.66
	15.24	9.99	9.03	9.35	9.47	10.08
total	11.69	8.57	7.95	8.32	11.75	10.52
	16.78	11.05	10.07	10.62	9.73	11.04

Hospitality Industries

JC
JD

			Size (number of employees)			
	1 - 3	3 - 6	6 - 10	10 - 20	20+	total
Age (years)						
1-2	32.16	23.79	19.96	21.21	19.97	25.74
	25.22	21.35	19.03	22.77	11.62	21.29
3-5	15.25	17.50	9.61	9.83	—[1]	14.25
	21.74	13.83	16.63	14.13	—	17.31
6-10	12.44	10.81	10.13	9.47	7.24	10.19
	17.76	12.85	12.62	12.36	21.16	16.23
11+	10.57	8.70	7.91	6.96	7.30	7.96
	14.66	10.84	9.41	7.78	12.24	11.42
total	14.92	12.27	9.63	8.85	7.70	10.60
	18.58	12.89	12.10	10.69	14.03	14.16

[1] In this class we observe strong expansions and contractions or even exits in some firms for one year that are reversed in the next year. Because this observed high gross job reallocation rate may have a legal background rather than an economic interpretation, we exclude job creation and destruction rates in this class.

location rates of young firms are the highest for small firms. But the smallest firms in the other age classes do not reach higher than average net job reallocation rates. One may conclude that there is no distinct job creation prowess of small firms in the retail and hospitality sectors. On the contrary, the net job reallocation rate increases with firm size in the retail trade. However, there is some job creation prowess of young firms – i.e., net job reallocation rates are positive for young firms – while Table 11.4 reports negative net job reallocation rates for both sectors as a whole. The net job reallocation rate is generally independent of firm age for firms older than 2 years in the hospitality sector and for firms older than 5 years in the retail sector. A possible explanation is that many firms remain small in the retail and hospitality industries because of the limited or even negligible importance of scale economies in the service industries. This would imply that experience in the sense used by Jovanovic (1982) is obtained relatively quickly in the life-cycle of firms. Alternatively, entrepreneurs simply may not wish their business to grow for various reasons.

5 Summary and Conclusions

This chapter deals with the analysis of job flows. A new and elaborate data set is used for the hospitality and retail industries in the Netherlands for the period 1985–1988. We analyze the effects of firm size and age on the creation and destruction of jobs. The relationship between firm size and the net job reallocation rate – defined as the difference between gross job creation and gross job destruction – indicates whether small firms outperform their larger counterparts in terms of the net creation of jobs. This outperformance could be a guideline for policy measures aiming at the high unemployment rates experienced by most European countries. Moreover, we compare the job reallocation between small and large firms, controlling for age. This is done to investigate whether any positive relation between net job creation and small firms is merely the result of differences in firm age. It is well known that young firms are usually small. Finally, we investigate the impact of age on job flows. If young firms have to learn about their efficiency and cost levels – as is assumed in Jovanovic (1982) – it is expected that job flows decrease with firm age; i.e., young, successful firms will grow rapidly and young, unsuccessful firms are likely to exit, while this variation in job flows would decrease for more mature, stable firms.

On the whole, substantial simultaneous job creation and job destruction rates are established. The annual gross job reallocation rates are in excess of 20 percent for the retail trade and even in excess of 30 percent for the hospitality industries. The percentages – which are stable in the 1986–1988 period – fall in the range of 20–39 percent reported in OECD (1994b) for the service industries in 9 member countries. High magnitudes of job creation and job destruction are reported for three digit industries in the retail trade and for four digit industries in the hospitality industries. Simultaneous job creation and destruction within such industry implies severe heterogeneity: creation of jobs is observed in some firms, while job destruction takes place in other firms. Our results show that even firms of the same size and age within a three or four digit industry are not homogeneous in this respect. The conclusion must be that support is found for theories that try to explain firm heterogeneity.

The comparison of job flow rates for different size and age classes shows that gross job reallocation rates are highest for the smallest, youngest firms. Moreover, the highest gross job reallocation rates are observed for the smallest firms, but this rate is remarkably stable among the other size classes. The gross job reallocation rates are substantially higher for the youngest firms than for their elder counterparts. This implies that firms in the retail and hospitality industries learn from their own experience relatively quickly. This again is consistent with the small average firm size and the relatively simple production process observed in these service industries. The net job reallocation rates show that there is no job creation prowess of small firms in the retail and hospitality industries. On the contrary, the net job reallocation rate even increases with firm size in the retail trade. However, there is some job creation prowess of young firms. In other words, the net job reallocation rates are highest for the youngest firms in both sectors. The net job reallocation is generally independent of firm age in the three remaining age classes.

Small firms do not outperform their larger counterparts with respect to net job creation. In other words, the net job creation rates provide no justification to establish policy measures favouring small firms. Measures introduced to stimulate business start-up and to increase survival rates of young and small firms might be successful because high job reallocation rates are observed for these firms. The main determinants of new firm survival mentioned in EIM (1993) and in OECD (1994b) are relevant expert consultancy, formation of partnerships, easy access to information, managerial competence, sufficient marketing knowledge and adequate financial support. The success of policy measures stimulating entrepreneurship, business start-ups and their consequence for growth will probably be the object of much future research.

Job flows including their relation to firm size and age are examined in this chapter. However, some important topics remain to be investigated. We mention the quality of jobs and the wage level (see, for instance, Brown, Hamilton and Medoff [1990] for the analysis of these and other topics). Recently, significant attention has been given to the construction of longitudinal data sets (Hamermesh, 1993, ch. 11; Wagner, 1996; Davis and Haltiwanger, 1995). In our opinion the most important contribution is to be expected from the match of data on workers and jobs. Labour supply and demand aspects have to be connected in such a data set. Employer characteristics (like the level of education, gender and age of employees) can be related to firm characteristics (like geographic region, size and age). This would provide more in-depth insight into the process of job and worker reallocation.

Notes

We are very grateful to Statistics Netherlands, and especially to the main sections "Labour and Wages" and "Domestic Trade and Services", for providing the data and computational facilities. We thank Ad Abrahamse and Martin Carree for helpful comments and Hans Kuhbauch and Peter Spaans for technical support. We are obliged to David Audretsch, John Haltiwanger and other participants at the workshop on Entrepreneurship, SMEs, and the Macro Economy held in Jönköping on 13–15 June 1996 for valuable comments on an earlier version.

[1] An exception is Davis and Haltiwanger (1992). They find that, on average, job reallocation rates are substantially higher among young plants. Moreover, on average, young plants grow rapidly, while older plants shrink.

[2] In OECD (1994b, chapter 3) job flow rates are presented for the entire sector of service industries for nine member countries.

[3] The denominator in equation (2) $[L_{t-1}]$ is subject to a methodological discussion. Davis, Haltiwanger and Schuh (1996) and follow-up studies – for instance, Broersma and Gautier (1995) and Konings (1995a; 1995b) – claim that the use of $(L_{t-1} + L_t)/2$ should be preferred to that of L_{t-1} in equation (2). They propose to use $(L_{t-1} + L_t)/2$ instead of L_{t-1} to avoid the regression fallacy. Carree and Klomp (1996) emphasize that the correction for the "regression-to-the-mean" bias is to be preferred only if firms merely show *temporal changes* in the level of employment. In the case of *persistent* growth or decline initial size may be preferred to average size. We refer to Davis, Haltiwanger and Schuh (1996), Carree and Klomp (1996) and Klomp and Thurik (1996) for a detailed methodological discussion.

[4] Strengths and weaknesses of the data can be summarized as follows: A first and major strength is that the data cover all firms employing paid labour. This implies that small firms are also included. Such firms are important in service industries, where the proportion of small firms is higher than in manufacturing (see Carree and Thurik, 1991 for an analysis of firm-size distributions of two digit industries in the Dutch private sector for the 1978–1989 period). A second strength is that firm age – essential for our purposes – is known. This allows an analysis of the relationship between job flows and age and also the impact of age on the relationship between job flows and size. A third strength is that the data allow us to measure the number of (paid) employees in full-

time equivalents (fte). This is particularly important for service industries, where a substantial share of the labour force is employed on a part-time basis. A fourth strength is that job flows can be studied for (detailed) four digit business groups within the hospitality and retail industries.

Two limitations exist with regard to the study of job flows. First, the cyclical influence on job reallocation cannot be studied adequately, because data are available for the period 1985–1988 only. This gap is filled in Chapter 9 of this book by Haltiwanger, who investigates cyclical patterns of job creation by firm size and age. Second, the registration of entrants and exiters is not fully appropriate for our purpose. We define entrants in year t as those firms that appear in the data set in year t for the first time. Conversely, we define exiters in year t as those firms that are recorded in year $t - 1$ but not in year t. Unfortunately, these definitions of entry and exit result in an overestimation of the turnover of firms. This holds for small firms in particular. A situation may occur in which firms pay an employee in one year while in the subsequent or preceding year all the work is done by the self-employed owner/manager or his or her family members. In this chapter such firms are recognized as entrants or exiters, because only firms with paid employees are recorded.

5 Davis and Haltiwanger (1992) introduce an upper and a lower bound to relate job reallocation to worker reallocation. Worker reallocation is defined as the number of (full-time) employees whose place of employment or employment status differs between year $t - 1$ and year t. The upper bound equals the gross job reallocation, while the lower bound equals the maximum of job creation and job destruction.

6 The high job creation and destruction rates in the retail trade for the year 1986 are the result of substantial job flows in some large firms in industries 652, Potatoes, fruit, vegetables, beverages, chocolate and tobacco, and 669, Department stores and mail order houses, where some exits and major expansions of large firms are registered.

7 The only exception is the death rate in the retail trade for the year 1986. Probably this death rate is the result of some incidental mergers or take-overs of some large firms in 2 of 18 three digit industries.

8 We report job flows for four digit industries in the hospitality sector, because this sector is dominated by four four digit industries: restaurants, cafeterias, cafes and hotels. The other four digit groups are taken together in a group called "Remaining hospitality industries". The number of four digit industries in the retail trade is 66, which is too high to report in the table. Besides, we believe that the heterogeneity of the goods sold in the various four digit industries within a three digit industry is limited.

9 A difference occurs in the definitions of (employment) size for incorporated and non-incorporated firms. The reason for this difference is that for non-incorporated firms the owner is not listed on the pay-roll, while the (managing) director of an incorporated firm is. We assume that the efforts of unpaid workers for non-incorporated firms are represented by one full-time equivalent (fte). This assumption allows us to ascertain that more than one full-time employed person is at work in each non-incorporated firm. There are some incorporated firms where less than one full-time employed person is reported. We have to ignore these firms, because we are not interested in the specific properties of firms which are not open on a full-time basis. About 0.8 percent

of the total number of firms is removed by using this selection rule for the retail and hospitality industries.

[10] We also computed figures where firm size is defined as the average value of the 2 years. For new firms the first (base-) year size is set to zero, while this has been done for the second (end-) year for firms that exit the market. These alternative definitions do not change the general patterns in Table 11.4. Of course, this alternative definition shows an increase in job creation rates for small, young firms, but the same holds for job destruction rates of such firms. For the retail industries the net job reallocation rate is still the lowest for small firms and highest for large ones, while for the hospitality industries the net job reallocation rates for the smallest and for the largest firms are still lower than those in the three size classes in the middle.

[11] We do not report job creation and destruction rates for large firms in the second age class for the hospitality industries in Table 11.4. We observe strong expansions and contractions or even exits in some firms for the 1985–1986 period which are reversed in the next period. Because the observed high gross job reallocation rate may have a legal background rather than an economic meaning, we do not report job creation and destruction for this group.

References

Birch D.L., 1981, "Who Creates Jobs?" *The Public Interest*, 65, 3–14.

Boeri T., 1994, "Why Are Establishments So Heterogeneous?" *Small Business Economics*, 6, 409–420.

Boeri T. and U. Cramer, 1992, "Employment Growth, Incumbents and Entrants: Evidence from Germany," *International Journal of Industrial Organization*, 10, 545–565.

Broersma L. and P. Gautier, 1995, "Job Creation and Job Destruction by Small Firms: An Empirical Investigation for the Dutch Manufacturing Sector," *Research Memorandum 1995–1*, Vrije Universiteit, Amsterdam.

Brown C., J. Hamilton and J. Medoff, 1990, *Employers Large and Small*, Cambridge, Massachusetts: Harvard University Press.

Carree M. and L. Klomp, 1996, "Small Business and Job Creation: A Comment," *Small Business Economics*, 8, 317–322.

Carree M. and A.R. Thurik, 1991, "Recent Developments in the Dutch Firm-Size Distribution," *Small Business Economics*, 3, 261–268.

Davis S.J. and J. Haltiwanger, 1992, "Gross Job Creation, Gross Job Destruction, and Employment Reallocation," *Quarterly Journal of Economics*, 107, 819–863.

Davis S.J. and J. Haltiwanger, 1995, "Measuring Gross Worker and Job Flows," *NBER Working Paper 5133*.

Davis S.J., J. Haltiwanger and S. Schuh, 1996, "Small Business and Job Creation: Dissecting the Myth and Reassessing the Facts," *Small Business Economics*, 8, 297–315.

Dunne T., M.J. Roberts and L. Samuelson, 1989, "Plant Turnover and Gross Employment Flows in the U.S. Manufacturing Sector," *Journal of Labour Economics*, 7, 48–71.

EIM, 1993, *The European Observatory for SMEs*, Zoetermeer, The Netherlands.

326   **Luuk Klomp and Roy Thurik**

Ericson R. and A. Pakes, 1995, "Markov-Perfect Industry Dynamics: A Framework for Empirical Work," *Review of Economic Studies*, 62, 53–82.
Hamermesh D.S., 1993, *Labour Demand*, Princeton, New Jersey: Princeton University Press.
Jovanovic B., 1982, "Selection and the Evolution of Industry," *Econometrica*, 50, 649–670.
Klomp L. and A.R. Thurik, 1996, "Job Flows of Firms in Traditional Services," *Discussion Paper TI 96–131/6*, Tinbergen Institute, Amsterdam-Rotterdam, 23 pp.
Konings J., 1995a, "Job Creation and Job Destruction in the UK Manufacturing Sector," *Oxford Bulletin of Economics and Statistics*, 57, 5–24.
Konings J., 1995b, "Gross Job Flows and The Evolution of Size in U.K. Establishments," *Small Business Economics*, 7, 213–220.
OECD, 1987, *Employment Outlook*, Paris.
OECD, 1994a, *Jobs Study: Facts, Analysis, Strategies*, Paris.
OECD, 1994b, *Employment Outlook*, Paris.
Ritter J.A., 1993, "Measuring Labour Market Dynamics: Gross Flows of Workers and Jobs," *Federal Reserve Bank of St. Louis Review*, 75(6), 39–57.
Wagner J., 1996, "Firm Size, Firm Age and Job Duration," *Review of Industrial Organization*, 11, 201–210.

PART IV

Innovation, Productivity and Growth

CHAPTER 12

Innovation in UK SMEs: Causes and Consequences for Firm Failure and Acquisition

Andy Cosh, Alan Hughes and Eric Wood

1   Introduction

This chapter describes the extent and nature of innovative activity amongst small and medium-sized enterprises (SMEs) in the UK in the 1990s. It also provides an analysis of the way in which it is related to the past innovative activity of these firms, their past performance and competitive environment. We also model the relationships among innovative activity, business failure and acquisition, taking account of the firm's age, size and industry.

Our analysis makes use of a specially constructed longitudinal SME database compiled by the authors and their colleagues at the ESRC Centre for Business Research (CBR) and its predecessor, the Small Business Research Centre, at the University of Cambridge. Since 1990, the CBR has conducted three separate postal and telephone surveys covering a sample of over 2,000 SMEs in the UK. Taken together the surveys provide a wide range of information on innovation input and innovation output, together with a variety of other aspects of firm behaviour and performance over the decade up to 1995. The questions asked to elicit information on the extent and nature of innovative activity in our sample are shown in the Appendix.

The analysis which follows focuses on innovative outputs, in particular on the respondents' own identification of whether or not they have innovated and the extent to which their innovation was new only to their firm, or to all firms in their industry, or to all firms in general. Our chapter is therefore based on the "subject" approach to measuring innovation rather than the "object" approach (which focuses on the identification with hindsight of significant or major innovations based on expert

329

opinion or technical literature surveys). We then relate this "subject" based measure of innovative activity to other features of our sample businesses.

In the next section we present a description of our sample and of the surveys on which the empirical analysis is based. We also provide, using a mixture of probit and cross-tabulation techniques, a description of the variations in innovative activity within our sample across businesses grouped by size, age and industry. Given the paucity of systematic information on SME innovative activity in the UK at the firm level, this analysis is of interest in itself. It also enables us to compare the results emerging from the "subject" approach with those based on the "object" approach such as those for the UK from the Science Policy Research Unit (SPRU) database (Robson and Townsend, 1984) or the U.S. Small Business Administration (SBA) database (Acs and Audretsch, 1988) as well as with a recent "subject" based study of product innovation in manufacturing plants in the UK, Germany and Northern Ireland (Roper et al., 1996). In addition it provides the necessary background against which we subsequently analyse the links among innovation, survival and various aspects of business performance. This analysis is carried out in Section 3. There the role of innovation is examined in the light of a model originally proposed by Downie (1958) and developed by Metcalfe and Gibbons (1986) and Metcalfe (1994). Essentially, the model postulates a two-way relationship between innovation and growth and performance at the firm level. On the one hand, a firm's technological innovativeness in one period is a primary determinant of its performance in the next. On the other, a firm's performance is an important determinant of its future innovative effort. Poor performance is a spur to taking on the risk and uncertainty of innovation whilst past success may lead to the pursuit of more conservative policies. Such reasoning has been echoed by Nickell and Nicolitsas (1995), who model innovative activity as a response to business adversity in the presence of imperfect capital markets. It is also reflected in recent surveys of the empirical literature (Geroski, 1995; Wood, 1995).

The results of our analysis have implications both for the role that SMEs may play in the innovative performance of the economy as a whole, and for their role in the evolution of market structure. In the latter area the recent literature has emphasised the role of small firm innovative activity in overall industry performance (Acs and Audretsch, 1987; 1988; 1990; Audretsch, 1995; Geroski and Pomroy, 1990; Geroski, 1995). These implications are briefly discussed in the final section, which also provides summary conclusions.

2   The Surveys and Sample Characteristics

The first CBR postal survey of two thousand SMEs was conducted in 1991. It was designed to include approximately 1,000 manufacturing SMEs and 1,000 SMEs in business services. Data were obtained on a wide range of performance and internal and external characteristics of these businesses covering the period 1985–91. The report of this survey (SBRC, 1992) provided the first comprehensive view of the UK SME sector since the report by Bolton (1971). A specific section dealing with innovation asked firms to report major innovations under a number of headings, as well as to report on R&D inputs and employment. The respondents to the original survey were then re-surveyed in 1993. The objective of the second survey was to examine financing constraints facing UK SMEs and evaluate the extent to which these affected performance; it did not include questions concerning innovation activity. This produced 1,341 postal and fax responses.

A third survey of these firms, with a specific focus on the innovation process in the UK SME sector, was conducted in 1995. The results of this survey, based upon the European Commission Community Innovation Survey (CIS), provided substantially richer data on innovation than the 1991 survey. An important advantage of the third survey is that, unlike the first, it provides a measure of the novelty of an innovation. In addition to asking whether a firm had made product or process innovations, the 1995 survey enquired whether an innovation was simply new to the firm, or new to the firm's industry or new to all industries. It also included the full range of innovation input and output questions included in the CIS survey. The third survey obtained 1,001 responses. Of these, 694 firms completed the full postal questionnaire and 307 returned shorter questionnaires by fax or telephone. Our analysis in this paper focuses mostly on the innovation output provided by these firms. However, our analysis of firm survival is dependent only on innovation responses in the 1991 survey and thus includes all of the original 2,000 respondents. The precise questions asked in the 1991 and 1995 surveys are shown in the Appendix.

In both the second and third surveys, the CBR tracked down information on non-respondents from a wide variety of sources, thus providing information on firm failures in our sample. It was found that by 1995, 390 of the original sample of 2,000 firms had failed or were moribund (e.g., in receivership) and a further 219 had been acquired. A separate analysis of the characteristics of the 594 firms which were alive but did not respond has been carried out and shows no evidence for attrition bias which non-response may produce, at least in terms of size, industry, age or previous growth experience (Bullock et al., 1996).

As the 694 postal responses to the 1995 survey provide the most detailed information on innovation patterns, we focus entirely on those firms in this section. A full discussion of the 1991 and 1995 results may be found in SBRC (1992) and Cosh and Hughes (1996b), respectively. Table 12.1 shows a breakdown of the 694 firms, by size, age and sector. The breakdown of the SME sector by size is according to the standard European Commission definition, except that we have amalgamated the largest two size categories normally employed. Micro firms are defined as those employing between 1 and 9 employees, small firms as employing between 10 and 99 and medium-sized firms as employing between 100 and 499 employees. The 694 firms are drawn roughly equally from the manufacturing and business service sectors and roughly equal proportions were started before and after 1980. Interestingly we find that, whilst business services have a higher proportion of micro firms, it is manufacturing which has the higher proportion of newer firms.

Whilst it is widely accepted that size and age influence innovative activity at the firm level (Schumpeter, 1934), several different explanations have been offered. These do not always imply the same type of relationship between innovation and either size or age. Larger, more established firms, it is argued, have greater financial resources to devote to research and development, giving them a crucial advantage over smaller, newer firms in the area of innovation, particularly in innovation-intensive industries (Winter, 1984). On the other hand, smaller and younger firms are said to possess greater organisational flexibility, which implies better internal communication, closer relationships with suppliers and customers and less resistance to change from within the firm, thus conferring certain advantages on small younger firms in industries with rapid technological change (Mueller, 1988; Scherer, 1988). Clearly, the fact that the CBR database is restricted to SMEs limits our ability to contribute to this debate across the full size range. On the other hand it is unusual in enabling us to gain a detailed picture of variations in innovative activity within the SME sector based on a large sample of businesses in services as well as manufacturing.

The first three columns of Table 12.2 show a breakdown of innovation patterns by firm employment size within the CBR sample. The proportion of firms in each size group which report the introduction of innovations over the three years 1993–95 increases steadily with increasing firm size. This is true both for product and process innovations and for innovations which are new to the firm, new to the firm's industry and new to all industries. Chi-square tests were used to test the significance

Table 12.1. *Characteristics of 694 SMEs in the 1995 Postal Innovation Survey*

Number (%) of firms in each category[a]

	Micro	Small	Medium	All	Older	Newer
No. employees in 1990/ Year firm started	1-9	10-99	100-499		Pre-1980	Post-1980
	No (%)	No (%)	No (%)	No	No (%)	No (%)
All firms	138 (23)	344 (58)	114 (19)	694	295 (44)	378 (56)
Metals	2	20	8	34	12	21
Chemicals	4	16	7	33	11	22
Mechanical engineering	14	64	15	108	33	71
Electrical engineering	7	23	8	43	20	21
Food processing	1	8	5	15	3	12
Textiles, clothing, footwear	2	23	8	36	7	28
Timber and furniture	5	16	3	29	8	20
Paper and pulp	13	27	7	53	20	33
All manufacturing	48 (16)	197 (64)	61 (20)	351	114 (33)	228 (67)
Management consulting & advertising	44	76	29	178	95	80
Technical and professional consulting	27	49	14	110	58	46
Other business services	16	20	9	49	27	19
All business services	90 (31)	147 (51)	53 (18)	343	181 (55)	150 (45)

[a] In some cases, the sub-totals do not add up to the total shown. In the case of different firm size categories, this is because some firms from the original sample had outgrown their SME status and had more than 500 employees. In addition, some firms did not provide information on the number of employees. In the case of older and newer firms, some firms did not report the year in which they were started. For companies which fell in this category we were able to establish age by independent checks at Companies House; for the small number of our sample not reporting age and which were also partnerships or sole proprietorships this check was not possible and so it was not feasible to calculate their age.

Table 12.2. *Innovation Patterns by Firm Size*

Firm size group	Micro	Small	Medium	Prob (innov)= f(log size)[a]		Prob (innov)= f(log size)[b]	
No. of employees	1-9	10-99	100-499	β	T value	β	T value
% Firms in each size group reporting:							
Product innovations:							
New to firm	34**	54**	70**	0.24	6.25**	0.27	6.32**
New to own industry	14**	21**	32**	0.15	3.67**	0.19	4.05**
New to all industries	10**	14**	24**	0.14	3.07**	0.17	3.36**
Process innovations:							
New to firm	27**	48**	62**	0.26	6.71**	0.28	6.66**
New to own industry	7**	9**	25**	0.23	4.57**	0.25	4.54**
New to all industries	6**	6**	13**	0.15	2.59**	0.16	2.63**
Both product & process innovations:							
New to firm	10**	32**	52**	0.35	8.10**	0.36	7.95**
New to all industries	3**	3**	9**	0.14	2.14**	0.18	2.52**

Note: Chi^2 tests were used to examine whether the proportion of firms which reported a particular type of innovation was significantly different across the different firm size groups.
[a] Probits include no dummies.
[b] Probits include logarithm of age, and industry dummies (either for the industries shown in Table 12.1 or, in cases of non-convergence, simply for manufacturing/services).
** Significant at the 5 percent level (either Chi^2 test or t statistic). * Significant at the 10 percent level.

of the differences in the proportion of firms in each size group reporting a particular type of innovation. In all cases, these differences were significant at the 5 percent level. A further disaggregation of the smallest size class (not reported in the table) reveals that firms with fewer than

5 employees are rarely innovative. Firms with over 5 employees account for 100 percent of novel innovations and 80 percent of all innovations from micro manufacturing firms. The remaining columns of Table 12.2 show the results of probit analyses of the relationships between different types of innovation and firm size. The first set of probits report the effect of size on innovativeness without controlling for age and industry. In the second set, we control for age and industry. In all types of innovation, innovativeness increases significantly with firm size. However, the greater the novelty of innovation, the smaller the impact of size on innovativeness. The probit analysis reveals that the impact of size on innovativeness is not sensitive to controls for age and industry.

The proportion of firms in each size group introducing product innovations is higher than that introducing process innovations, independently of the novelty of the innovation. In each size class, a much smaller proportion of firms which report product or process innovations new to their firm judged that those innovations were either new to their industry or new to all industries.

It is interesting to compare these outcomes for our subject based survey with those arising from object based approaches. Our own calculations (see Table 12.3) based on the SPRU database suggest that of the group of SMEs in the UK introducing "major technological innovations" in the period 1980–83, slightly fewer than half were firms with 100 or

Table 12.3. *A Comparison of Innovation Patterns by Firm Size*[a]

Firm size group	Micro	Small	Medium	All SMEs	Number of firms
No. of employees	1-9	10-99	100-499	1-499	
CBR SME Innovation Survey 1995					
% Firms in each size group reporting:					
Either product or process innovations:					
New to firm	50.0**	70.6**	86.9**	**70.6**	**216**
New to all industries	16.7**	16.8**	31.1**	**19.6**	**60**

Table 12.3. *(cont.)*

% UK manufacturing SMEs in each size group					
All UK manufacturing SMEs excluding those with less than five employees[b]	37.4	55.7	6.9	100	72430
All innovative UK manufacturing SMEs[c]	29.2	61.4	9.4	100	46366
All UK manufacturing SMEs introducing novel innovations[d]	35.2	52.7	12.1	100	12856

SPRU Innovation Survey 1983

No. of SMEs in each size group introducing a "major innovation" in the period 1980-83	13	50	60	123	123
% of all SMEs introducing a "major innovation" in the period 1980-83 by size group	10.6	40.7	48.8	100	123

Sources: The innovation data come from the 1995 CBR innovation survey and the SPRU innovation survey. The SPRU data were made available by the Economic and Social Resume Council Data Archive and are used by permission. The Data Archive bears no responsibility for the analysis reported here.
Note: Chi[2] tests were used to examine whether the proportion of firms which reported a particular type of innovation was significantly different across the different firm size groups.
[a] Only manufacturing firms are included in this table as a result of availability of employment size class data for UK SME sector.
[b] Taken from the DTI (1996); firm data refer to 1994. The reason for excluding firms with fewer than five employees is that amongst micro firms in the 1995 survey, 100% of those with novel innovations and 80% of those with any type of innovation had 5 or more employees.
[c] Assumes that firms in each category introduce product or process innovations with the same likelihood as the corresponding firms in the CBR innovation survey.
[d] Assumes that firms in each category introduce novel innovations with the same likelihood as the corresponding firms in the CBR innovation survey.

more employees and approximately 11 percent had fewer than 10 employees. The former is roughly the same as the proportion reported in similar work for the US (Acs and Audretsch, 1991, p. 741). In contrast, the CBR innovation database suggests that just over 12 percent of SMEs with innovations new to all industries had 100 or more employees and over one third were micro firms. Both of these figures fall slightly when all SME innovators (both those with novel innovations and those with diffusion innovations) are considered, rather than focusing exclusively on novel innovators. The majority of both novel and diffusion innovators amongst manufacturing SMEs are small firms (those with 10 to 99 employees). It should be noted that Table 12.3 shows the proportion of innovating firms, not the proportion of innovations, within each size group. If, as is likely, the number of innovations per innovative firm increases with firm size, larger SMEs would account for a higher proportion of SME innovations than SME innovators.

Our results suggest that the object approach used in those studies underestimates the proportion of innovative SMEs which are small compared to the subject approach. Our subject approach implies that, despite the small proportion of micro SMEs likely to believe themselves to be pioneer innovators, their numerical significance in the economy as a whole means micro firms are likely to introduce more such innovations as well as diffusion innovations than medium-sized firms. Also, the majority of innovators in the SME sector are likely to be small firms. It has to be recognised, however, that the object approach has the advantage of hindsight and identifies innovations which have in a sense made the grade. The subject approach is inevitably more contemporaneous and will include some innovations which in the course of time will be proved uncommercial. The subject approach is, therefore, more likely to reflect the seedbed role of the SME sector as a generator of novel innovations and experiments compared to the object approach.

Table 12.4 shows innovation patterns in the SME sector by firm age. The first two columns indicate the proportion of firms in different age groups which reported innovations. The differences in the proportion of firms reporting innovations between older and newer firms are small and not significant. The probit analyses using age as a continuous variable (reported in column 3) suggest a positive relationship. Column 5 shows however that this result reflects an aggregation bias arising from ignoring size and industry effects. Once these are allowed for, the probit analysis reveals that increasing age tends to reduce innovation and that this effect is statistically significant for product innovations new to the firm and for firms carrying out both product and process innovations new to all industries.

Table 12.5 shows in bold type the innovation patterns for the manufacturing and business service sectors separately. The proportion of firms introducing process innovations is virtually identical, though a marginally higher proportion of manufacturing process innovations were new

Table 12.4. *Innovation Patterns by Firm Age*

Age group	Older	Newer	Prob (innov)= f (log age)[a]		Prob (innov)= f (log age)[b]	
Year firm began trading	Pre-1980	1980+	β	T value	β	T value
% Firms in each size group reporting:						
Product innovations:						
New to firm	52	54	-0.00	0.07	-0.18	2.48**
New to own industry	20	20	0.04	0.56	-0.10	1.27
New to all industries	14	14	0.02	0.31	-0.11	1.19
Process innovations:						
New to firm	49	42	0.12	1.99**	-0.02	0.34
New to own industry	11	11	0.27	0.50	-0.13	1.37
New to all industries	7	6	-0.00	0.01	-0.15	1.41
Both product & process innovations:						
New to firm	34	28	0.14	2.18**	-0.07	1.00
New to all industries	4	4	-0.11	0.94	-0.25	1.99**

Note: Chi² tests were used to examine whether the proportion of firms which reported a particular type of innovation was significantly different across the different firm age groups.
[a] Probits include no dummies.
[b] Probits include logarithm of size, and industry dummies (either for the industries shown in Table 12.1 or, in cases of non-convergence, simply for manufacturing/business services).
** Significant at the 5 percent level (either Chi² or *t* statistic). * Significant at the 10 percent level.

to the firm's own industry than in business services. The proportion of manufacturing firms reporting the introduction of product innovations was higher than for business service firms, as was the proportion of these which were new to the firm's own industry or to all. There is a significant difference between manufacturing and the business service sectors in the proportion of firms reporting product innovations new to the firm. The proportion of firms reporting both product and process innovations new to the firm are also significantly higher in manufacturing. This may reflect an implicit bias against innovation reporting in service firms since the CIS definition of innovation emphasises technological aspects. Thus our 1991 survey, which separately identified innovation in products or services, in production processes, in work practices or work force organisation and in administrative and office systems and which is not subject to this potential bias, shows similar major innovation rates in products (SBRC, 1992).

Table 12.5 also shows innovation patterns across a more detailed breakdown of the manufacturing and business service sectors. Over 80 percent of electrical engineering firms reported product innovations; at least half of these reported that their innovations were new to their industry or all industries. Around 60 percent of chemical, mechanical engineering and metals firms reported product innovations, and roughly 40 percent of these firms reported that their innovations were new to their industry or all industries. In the food, textile, timber and furniture and paper industries, fewer than 15 percent of firms reported product innovations new to their own or all industries.

The chemical and metals industries are the most innovative in the area of process innovations. Over 50 percent of firms in these industries reported process innovations. Over 20 percent of chemicals firms reported process innovations new to their own industry or all industries, while the corresponding figure for metals was 15 percent. The combination of product and process innovations is most important in the chemicals industry with well over 50 percent of firms reporting the introduction of both novel product and novel process innovations.

Within the business services sector, the most innovative sector is technical and professional services. Nearly 60 percent of firms in this industry reported product innovations and one third of these were new to the firm's industry or all industries. Around 40 percent of advertising and management consultancy service and other business service firms reported product innovations, and roughly 40 percent of these were new to the firm's own industry, all industries or both.

These results are consistent with those found by other studies (Robson and Townsend, 1984; Acs and Audretsch, 1988, both of which use an

Table 12.5. Innovation Patterns by Sector and Industry

Sector	Metals	Chemi	Mechanic engin.	Electri engin.	Food	Textile & clothing	Timber & furnit	Paper & pulp	All manufact	Manage consulting	Technical consulting	Oth business services	All business services
Number of firms	34	33	108	43	15	36	29	53	351	178	110	49	343
% Firms in each sector reporting:													
Product innovations:													
New to firm	62**	73**	61**	84**	60**	39**	48**	40**	58**	40**	59**	39**	46**
New to own industry	24**	30**	26**	40**	13**	14**	10**	13**	23	15**	20**	18**	17
New to all industries	18**	27**	17**	28**	7**	6**	3**	9**	15	11**	15**	12**	13
Process innovations:													
New to firm	65	61	42	49	33	42	38	42	46	47	46	37	46
New to own industry	15	21	14	12	13	11	14	2	12	8	10	10	9
New to all industries	12**	18**	7**	5**	7**	8**	3**	2**	7	6**	6**	10**	6

Both product & process innovation:													
New to firm	44**	55**	32**	44**	33**	17**	24**	30**	35**	25**	35**	20**	27**
New to all industries	6**	12**	4**	5**	7**	0**	0**	0**	4	3**	5**	6**	4

Note: Chi^2 tests were used to examine whether the proportion of firms which reported a particular type of innovation was significantly different across the different industries and sectors.
** Significant at the 5 percent level. * Significant at the 10 percent level.

"object based" approach, and Archibugi and Pianta, 1994). A common finding is that the most innovative manufacturing sectors are the engineering sectors, including electrical engineering, chemicals, mechanical engineering and metals. This suggests that subjective evaluations may be as reliable as the object approach in mapping industry relativities.

Table 12.6 reports the results of probit analyses of the relationship between broad industrial sector and innovativeness. Only in the cases of product innovations new to the firm and product innovations new to the firm's own industry is sector a significant determinant. Manufacturing firms are more likely than business service firms to report such product innovations.

We conclude this section by noting that firm size and industry are important determinants of a firm's innovative activity. However, innovation should also be seen as part of a dynamic competitive process within these sectors. To explore the role of innovation further requires an insight into the causes and consequences of innovation within a competitive model. The analysis that follows focuses on the broadest definition of innovation, including both novel and diffusion innovations. This approach provides an important insight into the importance to firms of innovative activities in general and highlights the fact that the significant role of technological change is not limited to novel or "major" innovations.

3   Innovation and the Competitive Process

In a pioneering analysis, Downie (1958) proposed a model of the competitive process based upon the interaction between firm performance and innovation. He suggested that there were two, partially offsetting, forces of change at work within an industry in a market economy. The "transfer mechanism" creates "a tendency for more efficient firms to grow . . . at the expense of less efficient firms" (p. 60). "If the transfer mechanism continued to be operated by an unchanged set of relative efficiencies the ultimate result could only be the concentration of the whole output of an industry in the hands of one, the most efficient, firm". Noting that we do not observe monopolies in all sectors, he argued that "there must therefore be some counter-force to the transfer mechanism" (pp. 60–61). This he termed the "innovation mechanism", and it results in a process "whereby relative efficiencies are changed" (p. 62), through the uneven distribution of discoveries and application of new, more efficient production techniques.

Within this model, relatively slow growth or decline follows a decline in relative efficiency, which in turn reflects a relative failure to innovate.

Table 12.6. *Probit Analysis of Innovation*
Patterns by Sector

Sector	Prob (innovating)= f(manufacturing)[a]		Prob (innovating)= f(manufacturing)[b]	
	β	t value	β	t value
% Firms in each sector reporting:				
Product innovations:				
New to firm	0.31	3.17**	0.30	2.98**
New to own industry	0.18	1.64	0.19	1.68*
New to all industries	0.13	1.11	0.15	1.17
Process innovations:				
New to firm	0.02	0.23	-0.07	0.67
New to own industry	0.15	1.20	0.10	0.70
New to all industries	0.03	0.22	-0.00	0.02
Both product & process innovation:				
New to firm	0.20	2.02**	0.13	1.16
New to all industries	-0.08	0.47	-0.08	0.44

[a] Probits include no dummies.
[b] Probits include logarithm of age and logarithm of size.
** Significant at the 5 percent level. * Significant at the 10 percent level.

In contrast with the array of innovative advantages usually attributed to
efficient larger firms (e.g., Nelson and Winter, 1978), Downie argued that
slow growing (and thus less efficient) firms did not necessarily have a
lower chance of success in innovation in the future. While acknowledg-
ing that less efficient slow-growing firms are likely to have less financial
resource to devote to innovative activity than more efficient, faster-
growing firms, Downie argued that "it seems highly probable that the
next advance in technique will be made by some other firm than the one

which, by means of the last advance, made itself into the most efficient in the industry" (p. 92). The reason for this is that more efficient firms will be less highly motivated to innovate than smaller less efficient firms. In addition to the pain of rethinking established habits and processes and the risk that innovation investment will be wasted, an efficient firm "will feel little immediate fear of being overtaken by others on a scale sufficient to threaten its position" (p. 90). While a less efficient firm may suffer from less intimate knowledge of the currently most efficient techniques, it will be "free from the distorting influence of the pride of creation" (p. 91). Another reason why less efficient firms may be the next to innovate is that technological advance may be faster than the replacement cycle. Most importantly, however, less efficient firms will be far more highly motivated to re-examine their existing methods and experiment with new ones. The transfer mechanism "threatens the inefficient firm with destruction, and I suggest that it is the efforts of such firms to avoid destruction which result in changes in the constellation of efficiencies" (p. 62).

Downie's model sought to predict and explain changes in industrial concentration in terms of the interplay between the transfer and innovation mechanisms. The model did not take account of the possibility of takeovers through which larger firms, which grew as a result of their past innovation success, acquire small firms with the best current innovations. Such takeover activity might affect the functioning of the transfer mechanism in two markedly different ways. Such takeovers may enable large firms which grew as a result of past innovative success to prevent the most innovative smaller firms from usurping their position, thereby obstructing the transfer mechanism. Alternatively, if smaller firms with innovative ideas lack the resources to market their ideas effectively, possibly as a result of imperfect capital markets, takeover may provide access to required resources and could enable them to grow relative to previous market leaders, thus to some extent promoting the transfer mechanism. In the latter, large firms play a second best role in filling the missing finance market left by imperfect capital markets (Hughes, 1992; Cosh and Hughes, 1994; Cosh and Hughes, 1996a). We return to this discussion in Section 5 when we analyse the impact of innovation on the probability of acquisition.

Relying on data for productivity as a proxy for a firm's innovativeness, Downie argued that there was empirical support for both the innovation and transfer mechanisms. In support of the innovation mechanism, Downie cited evidence from a sample of sixteen industries, in which productivity changes within firms in each industry were, in all cases, a negative function of the relative productivity at the start of the period. As evidence for the transfer mechanism, Downie maintained that the balance of evidence implied that the changes in relative firm sizes (measured by net output) within an industry were not random but were associated with relative efficiency, though he did acknowledge that changes in net output and productivity were only weakly correlated in his sixteen sample industries.

More recently, similar models to Downie's "innovation mechanism" have been tested using innovation data generated by SPRU. Nickell and Nicolitsas (1995), for example, modelled the introduction of new technology on the change in market share, change in profit per employee and change in the ratio of interest payments to cash flow. The Nickell and Nicolitsas results are consistent with the Downie hypothesis of an innovation mechanism since they observed a significant negative relationship between past change in profits per employee and the subsequent introduction of new technology.

There is also some evidence which implies the opposite, i.e., that current innovation performance is a positive function of past overall firm performance, which implies that there is persistence in both innovativeness and overall performance. Blundell et al. (1993), for example, observed that within industries, firms with larger market shares were more innovative than others. As Geroski (1995) argues, however, this work suffers from the serious problem that it only employs a partial sample of the SPRU innovation data, ignoring many small firm innovations which dominate the database. The view that this may have affected the direction of the relationship that Blundell et al. observed is supported by the findings of Geroski and Pomroy (1990), who demonstrated that the innovation activity captured in the SPRU innovation data as a whole appears to have had a deconcentrating effect, which is at odds with the notion of persistence in innovation and overall performance. In a second examination of the causality running from innovation to overall performance, using a partial sample of the SPRU innovation data, Geroski (1995) did not find any evidence of a significant relationship between innovation and either growth or profitability. This could be due to the fact that, as with Blundell et al. (1993), the sample excludes innovative small firms in the SPRU data.

In the following sections, we complement the preceding research on innovation in large firms by examining innovation and overall performance patterns in SMEs using the CBR panel database. In Section 4, we examine evidence on the "innovation mechanism", exploring data on the determinants of innovation in the 694 firms which responded to the most recent CBR survey. In Section 5, we ask whether innovation helps firms avoid destruction and evaluate its link with the likelihood of acquisition.

For this analysis, we use innovation data from the original CBR survey in 1991 and compare the subsequent survival of innovating and non-innovating firms.

4   The Determinants of Innovation

We examine evidence for an "innovation mechanism" by testing for a positive impact of past relative decline on innovation using a simple probit model shown in Table 12.7. The dependent variable measures whether or not the firm introduced either a product or process innovation in the period 1992–95. We express this as a function of past growth performance, past innovation activity and past competitive environment facing the firm, as well as size and age. We control for sectoral variation with industry dummies.

Regarding past growth performance, in keeping with the view that decline in market share motivates innovation, we use as our measure the proportional change in employment over the period 1990–93 relative to the industry average.[1] Lower relative efficiency is expected to increase the innovative effort and hence increase the probability that a firm will introduce an innovation in the next period.[2]

We evaluate the preceding hypothesis against competing alternative ones. Contrary to Downie's assertion, it could be argued that, through their intimate and possibly exclusive knowledge of leading edge technology acquired while making the last advance, technologically leading firms will have certain advantages over other firms and may be able to translate those into further innovative advances. To test this view, we include a firm's past innovation activity as an explanatory variable. Past innovation activity is measured by whether or not a firm introduced either a product or a process innovation in the 5 years 1986–91.[3]

Another possible view is that the spur to innovate arises directly from a firm's assessment of its competitive environment, rather than its subsequent realisation that it is losing market share. In other words, one may not observe poor performance to be a spur to innovation, because firms threatened by their competitor's development of a new product may be able to respond with an equivalently innovative product before they have started to lose market share. We use three indicators of the competitive environment to test this: the number of serious competitors in 1991, the extent to which firms perceived increasing competition over the 3 years 1988–91 to be a significant limitation on their ability to meet their business objectives and a dummy for whether or not a firm reported that any of its competitors was an overseas firm.

The results in Table 12.7 confirm the positive relationship between

Table 12.7. *The Impact of Past Performance and Environment on Subsequent Innovation Activity*

	Probability (product or process innovation 1992-95)	
	β	t value
Intercept	-0.042	(0.05)
Either product or process innovation 1986-91[a]	0.981	(4.22)**
Employment growth 1990-93 (cf. industry average)	-0.006	(0.15)
Log of number of serious competitors in 1991	-0.199	(1.64)
Increasing competition 1987-90[b]	-0.108	(1.22)
Dummy for overseas competition in 1991	1.119	(3.70)**
Log (employment size)	0.357	(3.25)**
Log (age)	-0.218	(1.22)
N	468	
Chi^2 goodness of fit test	(P = 0.451)	

Note: Probits include industry dummies.
[a] Roughly one third of respondents to the 1991 survey did not answer one or more of the questions regarding their innovation activity in the period 1986–91. Missing values were classified using multiple imputation techniques following Little and Rubin (1990). For an analysis of the sensitivity of the parameter estimates to alternative imputation schemes, see the Appendix.
[b] Respondents were asked to score the importance of various factors, one of which was "increasing competition", as a limitation on their ability to meet their business objectives. A score of 1 denoted that a factor was an "insignificant" limitation on their ability to meet their business objectives while a score of 4 denoted "very significant" and 5 "crucial".
** Significant at the 5 percent level. * Significant at the 10 percent level.

size and the propensity to innovate which we reported earlier. They do not, however, provide direct support for the proposition that poor growth performance relative to the industry average in the past provides a significant stimulus to innovate. The coefficient of employment growth in the period 1990–93 relative to the industry average, though signed as expected, is not significantly different from zero.

Nor does increasing competition or the number of serious competitors significantly spur on innovation. However, if a firm has overseas competitors it significantly increases the probability that it will innovate. Evaluated at sample medians, the results imply that firms which had overseas competitors in 1991 were more than 100 percent more likely than those which did not to have innovated in the three years 1992–95. This implies either that greater overseas competition encourages firms to innovate to maintain or increase their competitiveness or that firms that innovate are more likely to be in, or be moving into, markets characterised by international competition (Kitson and Wilkinson, 1996). The model controls for industry effects, so one might argue that the former explanation is more appropriate, even though the 2-digit level industry dummies may be too aggregated to remove all industry effects. Perhaps more important is the fact that we are relating innovation to a lagged overseas competition variable. If the hypothesis that the competitive environment motivates innovation is correct, then it suggests that overseas competition and domestic competition are qualitatively different and that overseas competitors provide a greater competitive incentive to innovate than do domestic competitors.

Another significant determinant of current innovation performance is a track record in innovation. Evaluated at sample medians, our results imply that firms which introduced an innovation in the period 1986–91 were nearly 100 percent more likely than firms which did not to innovate in the three years 1992–95 (the estimated coefficient of innovation in the period 1896–91 is not significantly different from 1). There appears to be considerable persistence in innovative activity in this sample of firms. The probability of the introduction of either a product or a process innovation in 1992–95 is greatly and significantly increased by the introduction of an innovation in the period 1986–91. This is not consistent with Downie's vision of past innovation failures attempting to catch up. The relative size of the coefficients suggests, however, that a track record in innovation is not as strong an influence on subsequent innovation activity as whether or not a firm has overseas competitors.

In Table 12.8, we examine a similar model, but this time for the probability of *planned future* innovation. Once again, the best predictors of future innovation are size, past innovative activity and presence or

Table 12.8. *The Impact of Current Performance and Environment on Plans to Innovate in Future*

	Probability (planned innovation 1995-97)	
	β	t value
Intercept	-2.413	(2.90)**
Either product or process innovation 1992-95	2.674	(9.26)**
Employment growth 1990-95 (cf. industry average)	0.133	(0.80)
Log of number of serious competitors in 1995	0.153	(1.31)
Increasing competition 1992-95[a]	-0.096	(0.79)
Dummy for overseas competition in 1995	1.273	(3.75)**
Log (size)	0.200	(2.03)**
Log (age)	0.009	(0.04)
N	483	
Chi² goodness of fit test	(P = 0.13)	

Note: Probits include industry dummies.
[a] Respondents were asked to score the importance of various factors, one of which was "increasing competition", as a limitation on their ability to meet their business objectives. A score of 1 denoted that a factor was an "insignificant" limitation on their ability to meet their business objectives while a score of 4 denoted "very significant" and 5 "crucial".
** Significant at the 5 percent level. * Significant at the 10 percent level.

absence of overseas competitors. Poor employment growth performance as before does not appear to increase the probability of plans for future innovation. In contrast with Table 12.7, however, the relative coefficients in Table 12.8 imply that a track record in innovation is a stronger influ-

ence than the existence of overseas competition on a firm's plans to innovate in future. This may imply that while most current innovators intend
to continue to innovate in future, those which do not have overseas competitors may be less likely to translate these intentions into actual innovations. This is also consistent with the hypothesis that competition
motivates innovation.

In conclusion we find larger firms which have overseas competitors
and have innovated are most likely to innovate in the next period. If their
employment growth performance is below the industry average, there
does not appear to be a significant change in their subsequent innovation activity, and the evidence for a powerful innovation mechanism is
therefore weak. It might be argued that this reflects not a lack of desire
to innovate as a way out of adversity, but a lack of resources to do so,
especially financial resources in imperfect capital markets (Nickell and
Nicolitsas, 1995). A separate analysis by the present authors reveals that
although financial constraints and the high cost of innovating are cited
as the main barrier to innovation by CBR sample firms as a whole, there
is no significant difference in the severity of these constraints as experienced by innovators and non-innovators, respectively. Differences in
access to market and technical information are more powerful discrim-
inators between these two groups (Cosh et al., 1996).

5   The Consequences of Innovation for Survival, Acquisition and "Failure"

In the previous section, we examined whether or not poor growth performance in the past motivates firms to innovate in the future. In this
section, we ask whether or not the introduction of an innovation in the
past increases the probability of firm survival, or, in Downie's terms,
enables a firm to "avoid destruction" (p. 62), by failure or loss of independence through acquisition. In other words, we are interested here in
the question of whether or not the evidence indicates that innovation is
indeed a good survival strategy.[4]

Table 12.9 shows the pattern of firm survival for innovating and non-
innovating firms in both manufacturing and business services. The category "failed or failing" includes all those firms which are confirmed as
having already failed, are in receivership, have had winding up orders
placed on them or are non-trading. Also included in this group are 19
firms which could not be traced after an exhaustive process of checking
telephone numbers and addresses, Companies House records and a
variety of electronic databases. In addition to analysing failed or failing
firms, we consider firms which were acquired between 1991 and 1995.

Table 12.9. *Consequences of Innovation Activity for Firm Survival*

	All firms 1991	Status of firm in 1995 (%)					
		Failed or failing		Acquired/ merged		Alive and independent	
Number of firms[a]							
Manufacturing	1050	171	(16.3%)	129	(12.3%)	750	(71.4%)
Business services	930	219	(23.5%)	90	(9.7%)	621	(66.8%)
Total	1980	390	(19.7%)	219	(11.1%)	1371	(69.2%)
% Reporting product innovation 1986-91[b]							
Manufacturing		49		70^{pq}		55	
Business services		50		69^{pq}		55	
Total		50		69^{pq}		55	
% Reporting process innovation 1986-91[b]							
Manufacturing		43		69^{pq}		57^p	
Business services		25		38		33	
Total		33		56^{pq}		46^p	

Note: Bonferroni one way ANOVA comparisons were used to test whether differences in the proportion of firms which reported a particular type of innovation were significant at the 5 percent level.
[a] Does not add up to 2028 as a result of missing industry data for 1991, and exclusion of firms which were acquired by 1991 or which employed more than 500 employees in 1991. Roughly one third of respondents to the 1991 survey did not answer one or more of the questions regarding their innovation activity in the period 1986–91. The figures in the table correspond with case 3 in Table 12.A1 in the Appendix.
[b] Each cell represents the proportion of firms with a particular status which reported a product or process innovation in the period 1986–91. Roughly one third of respondents to the 1991 survey did not answer one or more of the questions regarding their innovation activity in the period 1986–91. Missing values were classified using multiple imputation techniques following Little and Rubin (1990). For an analysis of the sensitivity of the parameter estimates to alternative imputation schemes, see the Appendix.
[p] Proportion of innovative firms significantly higher than for "failed or failing" firms.
[q] Proportion of innovative firms significantly higher than for "alive and independent" firms.

Table 12.9 indicates a somewhat higher failure rate for business service than for manufacturing firms, and vice versa, for acquisition rates. It also shows that product and process innovations appear to have different effects on firm survival in both sectors. The introduction of product innovations reduces the likelihood of firm failure by a smaller margin than the introduction of a process innovation. And the introduction of a product innovation increases the probability that a firm will be taken over by a greater margin than a process innovation.

Previous studies (Audretsch, 1991; 1995; Audretsch and Mahmood, 1995) have examined how the underlying technological regime in an industry influences the risk of exit confronting new establishments. The results indicate that the risk of exit tends to be higher in highly innovative environments. A limitation of this work is that it does not link the risk of exit to innovative activity at the firm level. Also, the innovation data refer predominantly to product innovations, largely ignoring the role of process innovations. As Audretsch and Mahmood (1995) noted, "More detailed longitudinal data sets need to be developed to link the technological and product strategies of individual businesses to their post-entry performance. Such data sets and analyses will surely yield worthwhile insights regarding the manner in which firms and industries evolve over time" (p. 102). The CBR data allow us to do just that and, in addition, provide the opportunity to analyse the role of process innovations in firm survival patterns.

Table 12.10 shows the results of a probit analysis of the effects of product and process innovation on firm survival. The analysis indicates that process innovation significantly reduces the probability of firm failure. Product innovation is a significant positive determinant of the probability of a firm's being acquired but has no impact on the probability of subsequent failure. Evaluated at sample medians, our results suggest that firms which introduced a process innovation in the five years 1986–91 were 22 percent less likely than those which did not to have failed by 1995 and those which introduced a product innovation in 1986–91 were 26 percent more likely than those which did not to have been acquired by 1995. Some caution is required in interpreting the latter result as it is sensitive to the approach taken to missing values for the innovation variables while the former is robust across different missing value schemes (see the Appendix). Older SMEs are significantly less likely to die or to be acquired and larger SMEs are significantly more likely to be the subject of a takeover. These results are broadly consistent with other studies of UK failure and survival (Cosh and Hughes, 1994; Storey et al., 1987) except that the size effect on failure is somewhat weaker.

Table 12.10. *Probit Results of Survival on Product and Process Innovation*

	Probability (failure 1991-95)[a]		Probability (takeover 1991-95)[b]	
	β	t value	β	t value
Intercept	-0.147	(0.59)	-1.205	(2.97)**
Product innovation 1986-91[c]	0.007	(0.08)	0.256	(2.48)**
Process innovation 1986-91[c]	-0.221	(2.53)**	-0.010	(0.09)
Log (size)	-0.008	(0.25)	0.285	(7.76)**
Log (age)	-0.212	(4.00)**	-0.331	(3.51)**
N[d]	1628		1481	
Chi² goodness of fit test	(P = 0.36)		(P = 0.36)	

Note: Probits include industry dummies.
[a] The sample for this probit includes "alive and independent" and "failed or failing" firms but excludes all acquired firms.
[b] The sample for this probit includes "alive and independent" firms and acquired firms but excludes "failed or failing" firms.
[c] Roughly one third of respondents to the 1991 survey did not answer one or more of the questions regarding their innovation activity in the period 1986–91. Missing values were classified using multiple imputation techniques following Little and Rubin (1990). For an analysis of the sensitivity of the parameter estimates to alternative imputation schemes, see the Appendix.
[d] Not all cases could be included as a result of missing age or employment data.
** Significant at the 5 percent level. * Significant at the 10 percent level.

The lower probability of process innovators' failing is entirely consistent with Downie's notion of a "transfer mechanism" whereby innovating firms outperform their non-innovating counterparts. Since survival appears not to be dependent on innovation in products, this implies that to increase survival chances, firms must innovate in the way in which products are produced and brought to the market. A direct comparison with the findings of Audretsch (1991; 1995) and Audretsch and Mahmood (1995) is not possible as our data provide information on innovation activity at the firm level whereas their data do not. It is interesting, however, to note that while their results point to a link between product innovation activity and firm survival, our result suggests that the role of product innovations may be less important than that of process innovations.

It is less clear, however, what implications the higher probability of product innovators' being acquired has in the context of the transfer mechanism. As noted, Downie's model did not take account of the effect of takeovers on the functioning of the transfer mechanism. The truncation of our sample at 500 employees is particularly relevant here, since the mergers and acquisitions literature shows that the acquirers of innovative SMEs are likely to be those larger firms excluded from our sample. Does the loss of independence for product innovating firms in some sense imply failure or can it be considered as a form of success? There does not appear to be a simple answer to this question. While it is true that limited resources in an innovative small firm might leave it vulnerable to takeover by a larger firm which perceives the market potential of the innovation and possesses the skills and resources to market the product effectively, it is also true that some innovative small firms deliberately seek takeover (ACOST, 1990; Murray, 1995). Whatever the precise motivational factors on the side of the small firm, the results are consistent with the idea that product innovation activity within the target firm is an important factor in the decision of the acquiring firm, and that acquisition may be an important exit route by which innovative entrepreneurs can capitalize on their past success by selling out the equity in their firm (Cosh and Hughes, 1994).

6   Conclusions

The subject-based approach to investigating innovation patterns within the SME sector, while confirming some results obtained using the object-based approach, provides interesting new insights into the innovation process. The two approaches appear to produce similar innovation patterns across different industries, with the highest innovation rates in the engineering industries. However, the two approaches suggest rather different patterns of innovation across different sizes of SMEs. In particular, the subject-based approach adopted here suggests that although the probability of innovation and firm size are positively related, micro manufacturing firms account for a considerably higher proportion of manufacturing SME innovators than do medium-sized firms, although the very smallest firms with fewer than 5 employees are significantly less likely to be innovators than those employing from 5 to 9 employees. The subject approach probably overstates the rate of "successful" innovation compared to the object approach, which is based more on hindsight. Our results are consistent with micro and small manufacturing firms' playing an important "seed-bed" role in technological change and industry evolution.

Turning to the model of the competitive process, our probit results do not provide direct support for the notion of an "innovation mechanism" in which adversity in terms of poor growth performance fosters innovative activity. Relative growth performance does not appear to be a significant determinant of innovation activity. It should be noted, however, that one cannot conclude on the basis of this finding that such an "innovation mechanism" is not active, since we have not modelled as fully as we might the nature of the financial constraints facing firms in adversity, though what evidence we have does not suggest a difference in financial constraints between innovating and non-innovating firms. Nevertheless, our findings are consistent with the hypothesis that adversity in the sense of the competitive environment motivates innovation. Firms which have overseas competitors are significantly more likely to introduce innovations.

Our evidence provides clear support for a strong floor to the "transfer mechanism" whereby innovating firms are less likely to fail than non-innovating firms. In contrast to previous evidence which suggests that firm failure is linked to product innovation activity, our results indicate that the probability of firm failure is significantly reduced by the introduction of process innovations but is not significantly influenced by the introduction of product innovations. However, firms which introduce product innovations are more likely to be acquired than non-innovators. If, as the results suggest, the decision of the acquiring firm is associated with product innovation activity within the target firm, with the acquiring firm seeing potential in the innovation to improve its own performance, then this is also consistent with a "transfer mechanism". Further analysis of the impact of innovation on export, turnover, employment and productivity growth will be the subject of future research.

Appendix: The Questionnaire Approach to Innovation and the Problem of Missing Values

Innovation Questions in the 1995 Survey

*In this section we would like you to tell us about your innovative activity. We are interested in innovation in products and processes which are **new to your firm**.*

*In answering the questions in this section, please count innovation as occurring when a new or changed product is introduced to the market (product innovation) or when a new or significantly improved production method is used commercially (process innovation), and when **changes** in knowledge or skills, routines, competence, equipment, or engineering practices are required to make the new product or to introduce the new process.*

*Please do **not** count as product innovation, changes which are purely aesthetic (such as changes in colour or decoration), or which simply involve product differentiation (that is minor design or presentation changes which differentiate the product while leaving it technically unchanged in construction or performance).*

B1   Has your firm introduced any innovations in products (goods or services) or processes during the last three years which were new to your firm? *(Please tick only **one** box in **each** row)*

	Yes	No
Products		
Processes		

If you ticked No for *both* products *and* processes please skip B2–B6 and move on to question B7.

B2   If you introduced a product innovation, was it, to the best of your knowledge, already in use in other firms either in (a) your industry or (b) other industries? If you made more than one product innovation please answer with respect to your most important product innovation. *(Please tick only **one** box in **each** row)*

Product innovation	Yes	No	Don't know
(a) In use in your industry			
(b) In use in other industries			

B3   If you introduced a process innovation was it, to the best of your knowledge, already in use in other firms either in (a) your industry or (b) other industries? If you made more than one process innovation please answer with respect to your most important process innovation. *(Please tick only **one** box in **each** row)*

Process innovation	Yes	No	Don't know
(a) In use in your industry			
(b) In use in other industries			

Innovation Question in the 1991 Survey

F1 Has your firm been successful in introducing any major innovations during the **last 5 years**? *tick as appropriate*

	Yes	No
In products or services		
In production processes		
In work practices, or workforce organisation		
In supply, storage or distribution systems		
In administration and office systems		

If YES, please give brief details

The Missing Value Problem for Innovation Data from the 1991 Survey

Of the 2,028 responses to the 1991 survey, 555 (27.4 percent) firms did not respond to the question regarding the introduction of product innovations and 769 (37.9 percent) did not respond to the process innovation question. A similar problem arose in the 1995 survey with question B1, but it was possible in this survey to deduce answers for most cases by referring to responses to questions B2 and B3. The resulting proportion of missing values for the innovation questions in the 1995 survey was only slightly above 1 percent.

In dealing with the missing values for the innovation questions in the 1991 survey, we adopt the approach of Little and Rubin (1990), who recommend multiple imputation. This technique involves considering the possible missing data mechanism in both data collection and data analysis and matching alternative imputation schemes to the likely missing data mechanisms. This results in multiple imputations for the missing values which can be used to reflect the uncertainty due to non-response.

There are various possible explanations for the missing data problem in the 1991 survey. The following is a list of possible missing data mechanisms for the innovation questions in the 1991 survey along with an appropriate approach for dealing with missing values:

1   There is no identifiable missing data mechanism and missing value cases are all excluded.
2   All missing values both for product and process innovation represent cases of non-innovation.
3   The missing values are the result of uncertainty due to insufficient preamble in the 1991 survey explaining precisely what was meant by innovation and what kinds of product/process improvements were not considered to represent an innovation. Missing values are classified as innovators or non-innovators using discriminant analysis. The probability of being assigned to either group is 50 percent. In practice, as a result the majority of missing value cases both for product and for process innovation are classified as non-innovators.
4   As in 3 above, but missing values are classified as innovators or non-innovators using discriminant analysis in which the probability of being assigned to either group is not 50 percent but according to the probability of actual respondents responding yes or no to a particular kind of innovation.
5   The missing values for process innovation are, in part, special because the wider set of options in the 1991 survey compared with the 1995 survey (see the questionnaires above) meant that many firms (particularly service firms) which would have answered yes to process innovation in 1991 had the question been phrased in the way it was in 1995, actually made no response to process innovation. For example, a respondent from

a service firm in which a new computing system had been installed read through all the options and seeing administration and office systems, decided that was more appropriate than production processes and so replied yes to the former and left the latter blank. Missing values are classified according to the following scheme. Firstly, only those firms which did not respond to the question on innovation with regard to any of the categories of production processes, work practices, or workforce organisation, supply, storage or distribution systems, administration and office systems were assigned a missing value for process innovation. Of the remaining cases, all firms replying in the affirmative to any of the above categories were entered as process innovators and all others as non-innovators. Secondly, for the remaining missing values, the cases were classified as innovators or non-innovators using discriminant analysis in which the probability of being assigned to either group is 50 percent.

6   As above, but non-respondents are classified as innovators or non-innovators using discriminant analysis in which the probability of being assigned to a group is not 50 percent but according to the probability of actual respondents reporting an innovation.

All the analysis in this chapter which uses the data for innovation in the 5 years 1986–91 is repeated in Table 12.A1 using these six alternative approaches to dealing with missing values. The estimates shown in bold are those shown in the analysis above, as these are considered to represent the most plausible explanation and provide the best results. The table indicates little variation in the estimates under the different assumptions. Only in the models for the probability of takeover does the significance of the estimates for innovation in the period 1986–91 differ across the six alternative approaches, with the estimate for product innovation being significant at the 5 percent level for three alternatives, at the 10 percent level under one alternative and insignificant in the others.

Table 12.A1. *The Impact of Missing Value Classification on Equation Estimates*

The allocation of missing values for the innovation variables 1986-91

Run number	1		2		3		4		5		6	
	x	y	x	y	x	y	x	y	x	y	x	y
Product innovation 1986-91	896	0	896	0	1125	0	1222	229	1125	229	1222	326
No product innovation 1986-91	577	0	1132	555	903	555	806	326	903	326	806	229
Totals	1473	0	2028	555	2028	555	2028	555	2028	555	2028	555
Process innovation 1986-91	622	0	622	0	900	0	725	278	1370	103	1502	880
No process innovation 1986-91	637	0	1406	769	1128	769	1303	491	658	666	526	-111*
Totals	1259	0	2028	769	2028	769	2028	769	2028	769	2028	769

Parameter estimates under alternative assumptions

Probability (product or process innovation 1992-95)

	β1	β2	β3	β4	β5	β6	Mean	Standard deviation
intercept	0.081	-0.016	-0.042	-0.071	-0.105	-0.147	-0.050	0.079
either product or process innovation 1986-91	0.855**	0.983**	0.981***	0.984**	1.03**	1.054**	0.981	0.069
employment growth 1990-93 (cf. industry average)	0.057	-0.008	-0.006	-0.006	-0.003	-0.004	0.000	0.026
log of number of serious competitors in 1991	-0.239	-0.209*	-0.199	-0.201	-0.196	-0.201*	-0.208	0.016
increasing competition 1987-90	-0.192	-0.112	-0.108	-0.106	-0.117	-0.105	-0.123	0.034
dummy for overseas competition	1.354**	1.150**	1.119**	1.142**	1.237**	1.242**	1.207	0.088
log (employment size)	0.436**	0.368**	0.357**	0.353**	0.355**	0.363**	0.372	0.032
log (age)	-0.114	-0.210	-0.218	-0.206	-0.246	-0.254	-0.208	0.050
N	269	468	468	468	468	468		
Chi^2 goodness of fit test	0.59	0.45	0.45	0.44	0.51	0.51		

Table 12.A1. *(cont.)*

Probability (failure 1991-95)

intercept	0.186	-0.152	**-0.147**	-0.129	-0.085	-0.051	-0.063	0.128
product innovation 1986-91	0.144	0.031	**0.007**	-0.026	0.023	0.051	0.038	0.058
process innovation 1986-91	-0.478**	-0.375**	**-0.221****	-0.205**	-0.252**	-0.323**	0.000	0.105
log (employment size)	-0.053	-0.012	**-0.008**	-0.007	0.000	-0.003	-0.014	0.020
log (age)	-0.149**	-0.202**	**-0.212****	-0.213**	-0.213**	-0.210**	-0.200	0.025
N	890	1628	1628	1628	1628	1628		
Chi² goodness of fit test	0.41	0.34	0.36	0.36	0.33	0.27		

Probability (takeover 1991-95)

intercept	-0.829	-1.169**	**-1.205****	-1.184**	-1.203**	-1.199**	-1.132	0.149
product innovation 1986-91	0.061	0.240**	**0.256****	0.175*	0.271**	0.151	0.192	0.080
process innovation 1986-91	0.051	-0.135	**-0.010**	0.006	-0.052	0.062	0.000	0.073
log (employment size)	0.330**	0.292**	**0.285****	0.289**	0.288**	0.287**	0.295	0.017
log (age)	-0.454**	-0.327**	**-0.331****	-0.333**	-0.330**	-0.335**	-0.352	0.050

	N	Chi² goodness of fit test
	811	0.09
	1482	0.34
	1482	0.36
	1482	0.32
	1482	0.37
	1482	0.31
	1482	

Notes: Probits include industry dummies. (x) All cases in the innovation variables 1986–91 including those which were assigned values.
(y) Numbers of cases which were assigned values.
+The reason why this number is negative is that several firms which reported that they had not introduced a process innovation in the 5 years 1986–91 reported that they had introduced innovations in work practices, or workforce organisation, supply, storage and distribution systems, or in administration and office systems.
** Significant at the 5 percent level. * Significant at the 10 percent level.

Notes

1 The reason for using changes in employment rather than in turnover as an indicator of growth was the smaller number of missing values for employment. Despite the high level of correlation between turnover and employment in our data, the use of employment data might introduce an interpretation problem as a decline in employment may be associated with a loss of market share, rising productivity growth or a combination of both.

2 It could be argued that if a firm is motivated to introduce an innovation by relatively poor growth performance in the past, the amount of effort that it can expend towards this end will be constrained by its financial position. To measure the strength of this effect, we included profit margin as an explanatory variable. It was in all cases insignificant. There are a significant minority of firms which did not provide data on profits so including profitability meant that a number of cases had to be excluded from the model. Given the missing values and the insignificance of profit margin, it was excluded from the model.

3 The parameter estimates shown in Table 12.7 use some imputed data for innovation activity in the period 1986–91. For details of the imputations and an analysis of the sensitivity of the parameter estimates to alternative imputation schemes, see the Appendix, where we show that the significance of the reported results is not generally sensitive to the imputation method chosen.

4 Clearly, the impact of innovation on productivity, export, turnover and employment growth performance is also of direct relevance to the concept of a "transfer mechanism". A preliminary analysis of the relationship between innovation and employment growth performance can be found in Cosh, Hughes and Wood (1996), who found a significant positive relationship between innovation and employment growth. A more detailed analysis of these relationships will be the subject of future work.

References

ACOST (Advisory Council On Science and Technology). 1990. *The Enterprise Challenge: Overcoming Barriers to Growth in Small firms*. HMSO. London.

Acs, Z.J. and Audretsch, D.B. 1987. Innovation, market structure, and firm size. *The Review of Economics and Statistics* 69:4:567–574.

Acs, Z.J. and Audretsch, D.B. 1988. Innovation in large and small firms. *American Economic Review* 78:678–690.

Acs, Z.J. and Audretsch, D.B. 1990. *Innovation and Small Firms*. MIT Press. Cambridge, Mass.

Acs, Z.J. and Audretsch, D.B. 1991. Innovation and size at the firm level. *Southern Economic Journal* 57:3:739–744.

Archibugi, D. and Pianta, M. 1994. *Background Paper*. OECD Workshop on Innovation, Patents and Technological Strategies. OECD. Paris. 8–9 December 1994.

Audretsch, D.B. 1991. New-firm survival and the technological regime. *Review of Economics and Statistics* 60:3:441–450.

Audretsch, D.B. 1995. *Innovation and Industry Evolution*. The MIT Press. Cambridge, Mass.

Audretsch, D.B. and Mahmood, T. 1995. New firm survival: New results using a hazard function. *Review of Economics and Statistics* 77:1:97–103.

Blundell, R., Griffith, R. and Van Reenen, J. 1993. Knowledge stocks, persistent innovation and market dominance: Evidence from a panel of British manufacturing firms. Institute for Fiscal Studies Working Paper, No W 93/19.

Bolton, J.E. 1971. *Report of the Committee of Inquiry on Small Firms*. Cmnd. 4811. HMSO. London.

Bullock, A., Duncan, J., and Wood, E. 1996. The survey method, sample attrition and the SME Panel Database, in *The Changing State of British Enterprise: Growth, Innovation and Competitive Advantage in Small and Medium Sized Firms 1986–95*. Ed. A. Cosh and A. Hughes. ESRC Centre of Business Research. University of Cambridge.

Cosh, A.D. and Hughes, A. 1994. Acquisition activity in the small business sector, in *Finance and the Small Firm*. Ed. A. Hughes and D.J. Storey. Routledge. London.

Cosh, A.D. and Hughes, A. 1995. *Failures, Acquisitions and Post Merger Success: The Comparative Characteristics of Large and Small Companies*. ESRC Centre for Business Research Working Paper No. 18. Department of Applied Economics. University of Cambridge.

Cosh, A.D. and Hughes, A. 1996a. International merger activity and the national regulation of mergers: A UK perspective. *Empirica* 23:3:279–302.

Cosh, A.D. and Hughes, A. 1996b. *The Changing State of British Enterprise: Growth, Innovation and Competitive Advantage in Small and Medium Sized Firms 1986–95*. ESRC Centre of Business Research. University of Cambridge.

Cosh, A.D., Hughes, A., and Wood, E. 1996. Innovation: Scale, objectives and constraints, in *The Changing State of British Enterprise: Growth, Innovation and Competitive Advantage in Small and Medium Sized Firms 1986–95*. Ed. A. Cosh and A. Hughes. ESRC Centre of Business Research. University of Cambridge.

Downie, J. 1958. *The Competitive Process*. Camelot Press. London.

DTI (Department of Trade and Industry). 1996. Small and medium sized enterprise (SME) statistics for the United Kingdom, 1994. Small Firms Statistics Unit.

Geroski, P.A. 1995. *Innovation and Competitive Advantage*. Economics Department Working Papers No. 159. Organisation for Economic Co-operation and Development.

Geroski, P.A. and Pomroy, R. 1990. Innovation and the evolution of market structure. *The Journal of Industrial Economics* 38:299–314.

Hughes, A. 1992. Competition policy and the competitive process: Europe in the 1990s. *Metroeconomica* 43:1–50.

Kitson, M. and Wilkinson, F. 1996. Markets and competition, in *The Changing State of British Enterprise: Growth, Innovation and Competitive Advantage in Small and Medium Sized Firms 1986–95*. Ed. A. Cosh and A. Hughes. ESRC Centre of Business Research. University of Cambridge.

Little, R. and Rubin, D. 1990. The analysis of social science data with missing values, in *Modern Methods of Data Analysis*. Ed. J. Fox and J. Long. Sage. London and New Delhi.

Metcalfe, J.S. 1994. Evolutionary economics and technology policy. *The Economic Journal* 104:931–944.

366   Andy Cosh, Alan Hughes and Eric Wood

Metcalfe, J.S. and Gibbons, M. 1986. Technological variety and the process of competition. *Economie Appliquée* 39:3:493–520.

Mueller, D.C. 1988. The corporate life-cycle, in *Internal Organisation, Efficiency and Profit*. Ed. S. Thompson and M. Wright. Phillip Allan. London.

Murray, G. 1995. *Six European Case Studies of Successfully-Exited, Venture Capital Finance European NTBFs*. Warwick Business School. Paper presented at High Technology Small Firms Conference. Manchester Business School, September.

Nelson, R.R. and Winter, S.G. 1978. Forces generating and limiting concentration under Schumpeterian competition. *The Bell Journal of Economics* 9:524–544.

Nickell, S. and Nicolitsas, D. 1995. *Does Doing Badly Encourage Management Innovation?* Paper prepared for the R&D, Innovation and Productivity Conference at the Institute of Fiscal Studies. 15–16 May 1995.

Robson, M. and Townsend, J. 1984. *Users Manual for ESRC Archive File on Innovations in Britain Since 1945: 1984 update*. Science Policy Research Unit. University of Sussex. Brighton.

Roper, S., Ashcroft, B., Love, J.H., Dunlop, S., Hofman, H. and Vogler-Ludwig, K. 1996. *Product Innovation and Development in UK, German and Irish Manufacturing*. Northern Ireland Research Centre. Belfast. Fraser of Allender Institute. Glasgow.

SBRC. 1992. *The State of British enterprise: Growth, Innovation and Competitive Advantage in Small and Medium Sized Firms*. Small Business Research Centre. University of Cambridge. Cambridge.

Scherer, F.M. 1988. Innovation and small firms. Testimony before the Subcommittee on Monopolies and Commercial Law. Committee of Judiciary. US House of Representatives. February 24.

Schumpeter, J.A. 1934. *The Theory of Economic Development*. Harvard University Press. Cambridge, Mass.

Storey, D.J., Keasey, K., Watson, R. and Wynarczyk, P. 1987. *The Performance of Small Firms*. Croom Helm. Beckenham.

Winter, S.G. 1984. Schumpetarian competition in alternative technological regimes. *Journal of Economic Behaviour and Organization* 5:287–320.

Wood, E. 1995. Small and large firms in the innovation process, in *Innovation: National Policies, Legal Perspectives and the Role of Small Firms*. Ed. A. Cosh and A. Hughes. ESRC Centre for Business Research. University of Cambridge.

CHAPTER 13

Productivity Growth and Firm
Size Distribution

Zoltan J. Acs, Randall Morck and Bernard Yeung

1   Introduction

A fundamental issue in economics is how to achieve productivity growth.
Given limited resources, productivity growth is the only way to sustain
and increase standards of living. In this chapter, we ask an empirical
question: Is productivity growth related to market share distribution by
firm size? Suppose we sort every establishment by its industry classification and by the range of its parent corporation's size. We record also
the establishment's number of employees. We then have a distribution
of share of establishments and employment by firm size in each industry. Are industries with greater productivity growth associated with a
greater market share of small firms or with a greater market share of
large firms?

It is surprising that the empirical question has never been raised
before. There are good reasons to expect that productivity growth is
related to the distribution of market share by firm size. Small and large
firms have different capabilities in introducing innovations and in adopting and commercializing innovations. They also make different contributions to productivity growth. We therefore would like to verify that
market share distribution by firm size is indeed related to productivity
growth and to identify which class of firms makes more contribution to
productivity growth, small or large firms? Answers to these questions
shed light on the relative importance of large and small firms in promoting productive growth. It is hoped, that they will also improve our
understanding of the innovation process, from advancing radical innovation to implementing it in production.

We carry out our empirical investigation using U.S. cross-sectional
industry data. We find that industries in which larger firms have a greater
market share have greater productivity growth; market share is defined

either as the share of employment or as the share of establishments. Moreover, total factor productivity growth also increases with growth in larger firms' market share. We check the possibility that our results are spurious because of variable measurement errors and missing variables and find that our results appear to be robust.

In the next section, we discuss the motivation of our empirical question. We present our data in Section 3 and results in Section 4. Section 5 reports our robustness check, followed by conclusions in Section 6.

2   Motivation

There has not been a debate on whether small or large firms are more important in generating productivity growth, and there should be. Productivity growth comes from using new ways to use inputs to generate better output. It involves both generation of new ideas and successful implementation of them. Small and large firms carry out these activities differently.

There is a popular perception that small firms are the engine of innovation. Recent experiences in emerging markets are startling: upstart small firms serve as an engine of growth while large state-owned firms drag growth. Although these observations are extreme and there are good explanations for them, smaller firms make undeniable contributions to productivity growth in these economies. Similarly, in many fast growing economies, e.g., Hong Kong, which have experienced phenomenal productivity growth, small firms have considerable market shares and are often alleged to be the generator of productivity growth. These observations suggest that smaller firms play an important role in generating productivity growth.

At the same time, it is well known that larger companies invest substantially more in creating and adopting innovation. Private R&D spending is in the main undertaken by large corporations. Also, large scale adoption and commercialization of innovation are usually undertaken by established large corporations. These efforts generate results. While smaller companies initiated the personal computer (PC) and microchip revolution, the larger IBM made major contributions to these industries' productivity growth via its investment in R&D, manufacturing and marketing. It is possibly the case that the current Intel and Microsoft are contributing more to productivity growth in their respective industries now than when they were younger and smaller.

It is convenient to assess the contribution of small and large firms to productivity growth via a Schumpeterian lens (Schumpeter, 1934; 1942). In a Schumpeterian world, individuals and firms driven by profit incentives come up with new products and more efficient production processes to displace old firms falling behind in efficiency and innovations. In the presence of competitive pressures, indigenous firms must adopt innovations and improve their overall efficiency in order to survive. Thus, productivity growth follows from the creation and commercialization of ideas and their resultant competitive pressures. We can assess the relative contributions of smaller and larger firms to productivity growth in these terms.

Arguments in Favor of Smaller Firms

Innovation is about having new ideas. It is motivated individuals, not firms, which are merely legal entities, who create ideas. We argue, as in Acs et al. (1997), that individuals in smaller firms have more incentives to innovate. Large corporations have agency problems and blurred property rights which reduce employees' incentive and frustrate their effort to innovate.

In large organizations employees often only have limited intellectual property rights. They have to share returns to their innovation with many other employees, even if their names are distinctly associated with an innovation, say in the form of patent ownership. In some corporations, employees have to sign explicit agreements to surrender property rights to their invention to the firm. The justification is that it is the corporation's investment and general resources that stimulate and facilitate the development of innovations.[1]

The stipulation to share the fruit of innovation with other employees also causes a free-riding problem: less motivated individuals can free ride on other people's innovative effort and results. Worse yet, individuals in a large corporation can improve their economic well-being via bureaucratic politics to capture more rents from another's innovation. The limited intellectual property rights, the partial reward to innovations, and the possibility of free-riding on another's effort reduce employees' incentive to innovate.

Incentive contracts may mitigate the agency-incentive problem, but they create other problems. To mitigate the agency problem, incentive contracts aim to provide a direct linkage between employment earnings and cash flow due to innovation results. These contracts therefore must link job compensation to earnings from old innovations. Such contracts, however, will first lead to inevitable bickering over who has made what contribution: that is, dispute on defining and sharing innovation results.

In addition, these incentive contracts lead to bureaucratic inertia and distortions which also discourage innovation efforts. These stem from employees' interest to protect cash flow generated by their old innovations. Past innovators in an organization push for refinement of their old ideas, rather than the pursuance of new ideas, because doing so will enhance their value within the corporation. Corporate leaders promoted to their positions as a result of their past innovations will explicitly direct corporate resources towards the refinement of their old ideas under the pretense of investing in ideas with a proven record. Other employees will also stifle the pursuit of new ideas that threaten the value of existing knowledge and routines which benefit them. Employees who cannot benefit considerably from a new change may also impose pressure to retard the change if they have to make substantial efforts to adopt to the change. Bureaucratic inertia and distortions can cause delay and may even stop the implementation of innovation.

In summary, larger corporations will tend not to be innovative and are slow to adopt radically new ideas.

Unattached individuals do not face the aforementioned distortions. In a social environment where individual property rights are reasonably well protected, unattached individuals would normally be able to reap the full benefit of their innovation. Individuals who possess an innovation and have enough financial means would enter the market whenever the expected benefits exceed the expected costs. They become small firm owners. Their small firms provide the innovations which stimulate productivity growth.

Note that our argument is not that individuals in existing smaller firms have better property rights protection than their counterparts in larger organizations. Rather, our argument is that unattached individuals are more innovative because they do not have the property rights and incentives problems that individuals in larger organizations face. Unattached individuals equipped with an innovation start a business, usually much smaller in scale than indigenous firms, to implement their innovation, and their smaller firms stimulate productivity growth.

Arguments in Favor of Larger Firms

While the property rights consideration suggests that smaller firms are more important contributors to productivity growth, there are several arguments which favor the opposite: (1) larger firms have a resource advantage, (2) larger firms have an advantage in entering markets, and (3) and larger firms reap more immediate benefits from innovations because of their larger scale and scope of operation.

Innovation is by definition information based; there is information asymmetry between an innovator and outsiders. Commercializing an innovation requires innovators' effort and intrinsic skills, which are not fully observable to outsiders. Thus, adverse-selection and moral-hazard problems make outside financing options both costly and limited. Internal financing is a necessity. However, individuals and small firms face a more severe financial constraint than large corporations which have more internal financial resources and more collateral assets to raise external funds. In particular, large firms with established market power can build up wealth to finance further innovations. This is an integral argument in Schumpeter (1942).

Adopting and commercializing innovations involve breaking down market entry barriers. Larger firms are more capable in breaking down entry barriers than individuals and smaller firms. They have more internal financial resources to construct large production capacity. This is often a credible signal for determined entry, necessary for breaking down entry barriers. They also have more resources to persevere in market share battles which entail expensive marketing, price cutting, and bidding for key personnel, suppliers, and distributors. Consequently, incumbent firms are more ready to yield market share to large entrants with abundant resources than to small entrants with only limited resources. This in turn implies that it is less costly for larger entrants than it is for smaller entrants to penetrate a market.

The third consideration is based on the well known internalization argument popular in the foreign direct investment literature (e.g., Morck and Yeung, 1991). Larger firms have secured larger scale and scope of operations. Thus, their innovation will have a greater scale and scope of immediate application, which should translate to higher and less risky financial rewards. There is then the possibility that the larger scale and scope of larger firms induce these firms to be more active in creating and adopting innovations (Mitchell et al., 1996).

In summary, there are arguments in favor of smaller firms' being main contributors to productivity growth – smaller firms are more likely to be equipped with innovative ideas while larger corporations have a more bureaucratic environment not conducive to creating and adopting innovations. There are also arguments in favor of larger firms' being main contributors to productivity growth – larger firms have a resource advantage, are more capable and likely to break entry barriers, and can capture more immediate returns to innovations. We therefore seek answers to the following empirical questions:

1 Is productivity growth significant related to the share of larger and smaller firms?
2 If yes, is greater productivity growth associated with greater presence of smaller firms or with greater presence of larger firms?

3   Data

The empirical questions call for relating productivity growth to firm size distribution, say by regressing productivity growth on market share of large and small firms. There are several ways to do so: (1) use cross-sectional industry level data within a country, (2) use cross-sectional country level data, and (3) use multiple country multiple industry level data, (4) use cross-sectional time series panel data of the specified varieties. This study is based on U.S. cross-sectional industry level data.

Extensive multiple country time series data are not readily available to us. We are able to find industry level measures of productivity and firm size distribution only for the U.S. However, the data limitation is not necessarily undesirable. Productivity growth is influenced by institutional environment (Olson, 1996), which in turn influences firm size distribution. There are no simple ways to capture the effect of institutional environment; such an attempt would be by itself a major theoretical and empirical undertaking. Regressing industry level productivity growth on the industry level firm size distribution using a single country's data, we suppress variations in macro institutional (e.g., political, governmental, legal) environment and thus identify in a conservative manner whether firm size distribution matters given the data-country's institutional environment. After similar regression analyses for other countries are conducted, we shall have a set of results which shed light on how the institutional environment and firm size distribution interactively affect productivity growth.

We are unfortunately not able to obtain time series data. Our regression results are based on only one year's worth of U.S. cross-sectional industry data. In Section 5, we shall discuss the implication of this data limitation on our research.

We draw on two data sources to form our data set. The first is the *NBER Manufacturing Productivity Database*, which is itself compiled by pooling various government data sources, e.g., *Census Bureau's Annual Survey of Manufactures* and *Census of Manufactures*. The data set contains information on inputs, output, and total factor productivity for 450 manufacturing industries (based on the 1972 4-digit level SIC classification codes 2000–3999). The *NBER* constructs this data by aggregating establishment observations by industry. From the database we retrieve our main dependent variable, "total factor productivity" (*tfp*), to measure productivity growth. This variable is defined as follows:

$$tfp = dy/y - (s_1 \times dx_1/x_1 + \cdots + s_5 \times dx_5/x_5)$$

where

dy/y = percent growth in output (real shipments)

dx_i/x_i = percent growth in factor input i

s_i = expenditures for each input/

average of t and $t - 1$ industry shipments

$x_1, \ldots, x_5$ = raw materials, production worker hours,

number of non-production employees, energy, capital

The second data set is the new census-based *Statistics of U.S. Business* (SUSB) from the U.S. Small Business Administration (SBA). The data in the file are classified by industries (based on the 1972 4-digit level SIC classification). It is our understanding that the data are compiled in the following way: First, all firms with over 250 employees are surveyed.[2] Second, establishments are then sorted into industries according to their own declared industry classification and into "size" classes according to their parent firms' number of employees. The size classes are coded 2, 3, 4, 5, 6, and 7; representing parent firm employment ranges of 1–4, 5–9, 10–19, 20–99, 100–499 and above 500, respectively. (Size class 1 represents "industry total.") Establishments whose parents cannot be identified are sorted into size class 2, which assumes the parent firm employs fewer than five persons.[3] Third, establishment level data are then summed within size class. The variables most useful to us are beginning of the year (which is defined as in March) "employment" and "number of establishments" in each parent firm size class. On the basis of these variables, we can obtain for each industry the "establishment share" and "employment share" of each parent firm size class. As well, we can use these shares to formulate a composite index for firm size distribution. We also retrieve from the data set "total establishment birth" (establishments newly put into operation) and "total establishment death" (establishments closed down) in each industry.[4]

We examine the consistency of the second set of data by checking that for each variable the industry total is equal to the sum by size class and that the end of the year data minus the beginning of the year data is equal to the reported annual change. For example, we check whether reported annual change in total industry employment is equal to the sum of reported change in employment by parent firm size classes. The data consistency check reveals that the 1990 and 1991 beginning of the year data and the reported annual changes in 1990 are reliable. (The data set has data from 1989 to 1991. We did not use data other than the 1990 and 1991 beginning of the year data because of concerns about data consistency.)

374   Zoltan J. Acs, Randall Morck and Bernard Yeung

Combining the two data sources, we have the required variables to examine how a U.S. industry's total factor productivity in 1991 is related to the 1990 employment and establishment share of large and small firms in the industry. A stylized representation of our empirical question is as follows:

$$TFP_{1991} = a + b_1 \times (\text{small firms' share})_{1990} +$$

$$b_2 \times (\text{large firms' share})_{1990}$$

$$TFP_{1991} = a + b_1 \times (\text{change in small firms' share})_{1990} +$$

$$b_2 \times (\text{change in large firms' share})_{1990}$$

The research questions are "Are b_1 and b_2 significant?" and "What are their signs?"

4   Results

Background Changes

It is useful to have a glimpse of the background changes in productivity and industry characteristics in U.S. manufacturing in 1991 before we start our main statistical analyses. We should also bear in mind from the outset that the second half of 1991 was the beginning of a recession in the U.S.

Tables 13.1A and 13.1B report descriptive statistics for "total factor productivity (tfp)," "employment," and "establishment count." In both tables, the top row of numbers are statistics for tfp. The second block of rows of numbers represents shares by parent firm size class. In Table 13.1A, share is defined as employment in a firm size class divided by industry total. In Table 13.1B, share is defined as establishment counts in a firm size class divided by industry total. The firm size classes are defined according to the range of parent firm employment: 1–4, 5–9, 10–19, 20–99, 100–499 and above 500. The third block of rows of numbers represents change in the shares.

Tables 13.1A and 13.1B first reveal that U.S. manufacturing industry on average experienced a decline in total factor productivity in 1991 by 1.07 percent: that is, average industry real shipments dropped by 1.07 percent after accounting for changes in factor inputs. (The median is −1.46 percent.) That is not unexpected given that 1991 was the beginning of a recession.

In addition, Tables 13.1A and 13.1B show that larger firms, whose parent firms have more than 500 employees, accounted for 57 percent of employment but only 22 percent of establishments (row 7 of both Tables 13.1A and 13.1B), which is inevitable given that larger firms usually have

Table 13.1A. *Simple Statistics of Total Factor Productivity, Employment Distribution, and the Change in Employment Distribution by Firm Size Class Data, 1991*

xi = employment in firm size class i / industry's total employment (beginning of the year)

$dxi = xi(t) - xi(t-1)$

class i = 2　3　4　5　6　7　1

parent empl. = 0-4, 5-9, 10-19, 20-99, 100-499, >500, total

Variable	N	Mean	Std Dev	Sum	Minimum	Q1	Q2	Q3	Maximum
TFP	450	-0.0107[a]	0.0537	-4.8221	-0.2075	-0.0401	-0.0146[a]	0.0148	0.2624
X_2	298	0.0139	0.0221	4.1490	0	0.0031	0.0074	0.0165	0.2540
X_3	301	0.0253	0.0284	7.6263	0.0007	0.0080	0.0163	0.0331	0.2225
X_4	322	0.0451	0.0433	14.5102	0.0019	0.0158	0.0316	0.0577	0.2416
X_5	338	0.1771	0.1158	59.8667	0.0054	0.0827	0.1606	0.2488	0.5393
X_6	345	0.2045	0.0934	70.5432	0.0072	0.1392	0.2013	0.2628	0.5749
X_7	361	0.5678	0.2393	204.9704	0.0000	0.3951	0.5907	0.7555	0.9928
DX_2	259	0.0013[a]	0.0027	0.3353	-0.0161	0.0001	0.0007[a]	0.0021	0.0136
DX_3	262	0.0022[a]	0.0048	0.5775	-0.0273	-0.0000	0.0013[a]	0.0040	0.0293
DX_4	298	0.0030[a]	0.0071	0.8845	-0.0253	-0.0007	0.0022[a]	0.0052	0.0337
DX_5	323	0.0026[a]	0.0175	0.8557	-0.0643	-0.0070	0.0014[c]	0.0096	0.0919
DX_6	326	-0.0008	0.0327	-0.2755	-0.1683	-0.0146	-0.0014	0.0132	0.2008
DX_7	346	-0.0068[a]	0.0286	-2.3384	-0.2030	-0.0186	-0.0037[a]	0.0055	0.1063

[a], [b], and [c] represent significance in 2-tail test at 1, 5, and 10% level, respectively.

Table 13.1B. *Simple Statistics of Total Factor Productivity, Establishment Count Distribution, and the Change in Establishment Count Distribution by Firm Size Class Data, 1991*

X_i = number of establishments in firm size class i / total number of establishments in the industry (beginning of the year)

dX_i = $x_i(t) - x_i(t-1)$

| class i = | 2 | 3 | 4 | 5 | 6 | 7 | 1 |

parent empl. = 0-4, 5-9, 10-19, 20-99, 100-499, >500, total

Variable	N	Mean	Std Dev	Sum	Minimum	Q1	Q2	Q3	Maximum
TFP	450	-0.0107[a]	0.0537	-4.8221	-0.2075	-0.0401	-0.0146[a]	0.0148	0.2624
X_2	393	0.2291	0.1179	90.020310	0	0.1414	0.2516	0.2916	0.7185
X_3	388	0.1224	0.0498	47.496632	0	0.0839	0.1238	0.1590	0.2453
X_4	386	0.1226	0.0441	47.340002	0.0088	0.0909	0.1280	0.1546	0.2609
X_5	391	0.2029	0.0728	79.324687	0	0.1556	0.2000	0.2509	0.4348
X_6	389	0.1085	0.0547	42.201792	0	0.0686	0.1026	0.1376	0.3243
X_7	392	0.2210	0.1807	86.616576	0	0.0862	0.1672	0.3162	0.8919
DX_2	392	0.0119[a]	0.0295	4.669175	-0.1167	-0.0007	0.0117[a]	0.0256	0.1920
DX_3	386	0.0035[a]	0.0253	1.343226	-0.1118	-0.0089	0.0034[a]	0.0175	0.1429
DX_4	386	0.0015	0.0236	0.580044	-0.1424	-0.0085	0.0023[b]	0.0131	0.0967
DX_5	391	-0.0054[a]	0.0238	-2.109785	-0.1103	-0.0179	-0.0074[a]	-0.0048	0.1231
DX_6	388	-0.0040[a]	0.0194	-1.553497	-0.1098	-0.0132	-0.0044[a]	0.0032	0.0978
DX_7	392	-0.0071[a]	0.0237	-2.801724	-0.1846	-0.0137	-0.0044[a]	0.0011	0.0968

a, b, and c represent significance in 2-tail test at 1, 5, and 10% level, respectively.

more large scale establishments. The larger firms in general experienced a decline in both employment and establishment share while the opposite is true for smaller firms (the third block of rows in both Tables 13.1A and 13.1B). The observation appears to be consistent with the conventional wisdom that small firm start-up is counter-cyclical. We do need to be cautious. Because of missing industry observations, certain biases may have been introduced into the data. Nevertheless, further results reported in the next two tables suggest that variations in employment and establishment share by firm classes are not driven purely by the 1991 recession.

We next examine the actual change in number of establishments by parent firm size class. The top panel in Table 13.1C reports statistics from the full sample. The middle and the bottom panels report, respectively, statistics from industries losing and gaining establishments. The table reveals that in 1991 U.S. manufacturing experienced a net increase in establishments; 119 industries lost establishments and 274 gained establishments. In the middle panel, we observe that larger firms accounted for about 20 percent of establishment shut-downs, roughly the same proportion as their share of establishments. However, the lower panel shows that in industries with a net creation of establishments, larger firms still on average closed down establishments while the smaller firms (size class 2 to 4) accounted for more than 100 percent of establishment creation. Hence, the results suggest that larger firms were on average closing down establishments, perhaps driven to do so by the upcoming recession, while smaller firms were the driving force in establishment creation.

Table 13.1D reports actual changes in employment in the data year. In the top panel, we report numbers from the full sample. Again, not unexpectedly, U.S. manufacturing lost employment: the second row of the first panel shows that total job loss was 626,706, which was about 4.29 percent of total manufacturing employment at the beginning of 1991. The numbers in the top panel suggest that larger firms were cutting jobs while smaller firms were creating jobs.

A closer look reveals a more complicated picture. We divide the sample into industries registering net job gains and net job losses; about 80 percent of industries experienced net job losses and 20 percent experienced net job gains. The statistics for the two subsamples are reported in the middle and bottom panels of Table 13.1C. The two panels reveal that larger firms in the main accounted for 70 percent of the job losses in the job-losing industries and 71 percent of the job gains in the job-gaining industries (from the "sum" column, the entry in row x_7 divided by the entry in row x_1, in both the middle and the bottom panels). In both subsamples, larger firms accounted for about 57 percent of

Table 13.1C. *Change in Number of Establishments by Firm Size Class, 1990–1991*

Y_i = *beginning number of establishments in firm size class i:1990*

class i =   2   3   4   5   6   7   1

parent empl. = 0-4, 5-9, 10-19, 20-99, 100-499, >500, total

Var.	N	Mean	Std Dev	Sum	Min.	Median	Max.
Full sample							
TFP	450	-0.0107[a]	0.0537	-4.822	-0.208	-0.015[a]	0.262
Y_1	393	15.178[a]	86.549	5965	-250	4[a]	1057
Y_2	392	14.337[a]	62.222	5620	-37	4[a]	972
Y_3	386	4.749[a]	22.013	1833	-87	2[a]	258
Y_4	386	2.632[a]	19.633	1016	-134	1[a]	288
Y_5	391	-3.325[a]	20.417	-1300	-111	-1[a]	289
Y_6	388	-1.722[a]	6.914	-668	-63	-1[a]	27
Y_7	392	-1.357[a]	9.097	-532	-35	-1[a]	116
Net change in industry establishment count < 0							
TFP	119	-0.012[b]	0.057	-1.368	-0.191	-0.014[a]	0.197
Y_1	119	-15.908[a]	33.013	-1893	-250	-5[a]	-1
Y_2	119	0.185	12.380	22	-37	-1	57
Y_3	117	-1.299	12.846	-152	-87	0	41
Y_4	116	-3.086[b]	15.041	-358	-134	-1[c]	19
Y_5	118	-6.034[a]	15.359	-712	-80	-1.5[a]	12
Y_6	116	-2.690[a]	6.152	-312	-25	-1.5[a]	12
Y_7	118	-3.212[a]	6.453	-379	-34	-1[a]	11
Net change in industry establishment count > 0							
TFP	274	-0.013[a]	0.049	-3.606	-0.208	-0.017[a]	0.262
Y_1	274	28.679[a]	98.390	7858	0	8[a]	1057
Y_2	273	20.505[a]	73.302	5598	-9	7[a]	972
Y_3	269	7.379[a]	24.531	1985	-24	3[a]	258
Y_4	270	5.089[a]	20.851	1374	-47	2[a]	288
Y_5	273	-2.154	22.173	-588	-111	-1[c]	289
Y_6	272	-1.309[a]	7.185	-356	-63	-0.5[a]	27
Y_7	274	-0.558	9.928	-153	-35	-1[a]	116

[a], [b], and [c] represent significance in 2-tail test at 1, 5, and 10% level, respectively.

employment. Hence, larger firms actually showed more employment volatility than smaller firms. They were certainly not cutting jobs across all industries as a response to recession.

Average *tfp* for job-gaining and job-losing industries and for

Table 13.1D. *Change in Employment by Firm Size Class, 1990–1991*

X_i = *beginning employment in firm size class i: 1990*

class i =   2   3   4   5   6   7   1

parent empl. = 0-4, 5-9, 10-19, 20-99, 100-499, >500, total

Var.	N	Mean	Std Dev	Sum	Min.	Median	Max.
Full sample							
TFP	450	-0.0107[a]	0.0537	-4.822	-0.208	-0.015[a]	0.262
X_1	376	-1666.77[c]	4065.5	-626706	-38028	-793[a]	17578
X_2	259	38.290[a]	157.138	9917	-114	13[a]	2012
X_3	267	39.603[a]	166.505	10574	-779	19[a]	1406
X_4	303	35.297[b]	295.419	10695	-1915	17[b]	3820
X_5	327	-227.636[a]	898.742	-74437	-4383	-92[a]	11130
X_6	332	-362.087[a]	906.75	-120213	-6105	-196[a]	3152
X_7	352	-1252.849[a]	3784.926	-441003	-38282	-535[a]	8304
Net industry level job change < 0							
TFP	302	-0.0143[a]	0.051	-4.318	-0.208	-0.175[a]	0.262
X_1	302	-2352.04[a]	4104.689	-710316	-38028	-1199[a]	-8
X_2	210	41.876[a]	170.679	8794	-114	14[a]	2012
X_3	218	42.849[a]	168.898	9341	-779	22[a]	1406
X_4	243	19.288	212.592	4687	-1915	17[b]	827
X_5	263	-322.300[a]	694.300	-84765	-4383	-134[a]	1439
X_6	267	-466.356[a]	930.361	-124517	-6105	-282[a]	3152
X_7	277	-1801.256[a]	4032.980	-498948	-38282	-846[a]	1282
Net industry level job change > 0							
TFP	74	-0.0100[c]	0.049	-0.74	-0.145	-0.013	0.163
X_1	74	1129.865[a]	2359.32	83610	10	478[a]	17578
X_2	49	22.918[b]	74.711	1123	-31	9[a]	495
X_3	44	25.455	164.706	1120	-162	3	1012
X_4	55	105.491	528.189	5802	-341	15	3820
X_5	60	170.350	1454.56	10221	-481	-18	11130
X_6	59	76.763	673.4	4529	-2312	34	2828
X_7	69	866.435[a]	1410.45	59784	-796	438[a]	8304

[a], [b], and [c] represent significance in 2-tail test at 1, 5, and 10% level, respectively.

establishment-gaining and establishment-losing industries is reported in the first row of the middle and bottom panels of both Tables 13.1C and 13.1D. These average *tfp*'s are not statistically significantly different from one another; they actually have very similar magnitude.

Therefore, the emerged picture is as follows: In our data year (1991) the U.S. manufacturing sector on average experienced negative total productivity growth, net job loss, and net closing down of establishments. There were no discernible differences in the *tfp* of expanding versus contracting industries when expansion and contraction were measured in terms of employment and establishment counts. Larger firms generally lost both employment and establishment share. However, while the trend was that larger firms were closing down establishments, they were even more of the driving force behind industry variations in employment – they accounted for more than their share of job creation in job-gaining industries and more than their share of job losses in job-losing industries.

Results

We now turn to the relationship between total factor productivity and distribution of employment and establishments by parent firm size class. We shall first report some simple correlations between total factor productivity and share of employment and establishment by parent firm size class.

In anticipation of subsequent regression analysis, we transform the total factor productivity measure from the NBER database in the following way:

$$ttfp = \log\{(tfp + 0.5)/[1 - (tfp + 0.5)]\}$$

The transformation is done to preserve the sign of the original *tfp* measure and to allow the transformed variable to span a greater domain than the original *tfp*.[5] The original *tfp* is roughly bounded within -0.25 and 0.25. In our regression, we do not want the independent variable to be bounded within such a narrow range.

Table 13.2A reports the simple correlation between *ttfp* (in 1991) and the employment shares of the six parent firm size classes (as indicated by beginning of 1991 data) and also between *ttfp* and the changes in these employment shares (defined as beginning of 1991 data − beginning of 1990 data). Table 13.2B reports the same simple correlation between *ttfp* and establishment shares and between *ttfp* and the changes in the establishment shares.

The top row in both tables shows that *ttfp* is positively correlated with larger firms' share (x_7) and with changes in larger firms' share (dx_7). While the correlations are not highly significant, they are significant at the 1-tail 10 percent level. The top row in both tables also shows that *ttfp* is negatively correlated with smaller firms' shares $(x_2, ... x_6)$ and also with changes in these smaller firms' shares $(dx_2, ... , dx_6)$. The correlations are

Table 13.2A. *Simple Correlation Between Total Factor Productivity and Employment Share, and the Change in Employment Share, by Firm Size Class, 1991*

	TFFP	X2	X3	X4	X5	X6	X7	DX2	DX3	DX4	DX5	DX6	DX7
TFFP Prob n	1.0000 0.0 450	-0.1326 0.022 298	-0.1429 0.013 301	-0.0885 0.113 322	-0.0972 0.074 338	0.0635 0.239 345	0.0696 0.187 361	-0.1403 0.024 259	-0.0544 0.381 262	-0.0317 0.586 298	0.0302 0.589 323	0.0179 0.748 326	0.0723 0.180 346
X2		1.0000 0.00 298	0.9307 0.000 286	0.7951 0.000 284	0.4569 0.000 287	0.0234 0.692 289	-0.6310 0.000 292	0.3018 0.000 259	0.3547 0.000 254	0.1976 0.001 269	-0.1617 0.007 278	-0.0290 0.631 277	-0.0065 0.912 286
X3			1.0000 0.000 301	0.9278 0.000 288	0.6467 0.000 293	0.0658 0.260 295	-0.7288 0.000 293	0.4045 0.000 256	0.3458 0.000 262	0.2350 0.000 274	-0.1353 0.023 284	-0.0494 0.410 281	-0.0136 0.818 288
X4				1.0000 0.000 322	0.7942 0.000 310	0.1550 0.006 311	-0.8152 0.000 313	0.3802 0.000 254	0.2247 0.000 255	0.3606 0.000 298	-0.1294 0.025 299	-0.0963 0.099 295	-0.0177 0.758 305
X5					1.0000 0.000 338	0.4899 0.000 325	-0.9458 0.000 332	0.3194 0.000 257	0.4133 0.000 257	0.2708 0.000 292	0.0926 0.097 323	-0.1106 0.052 309	-0.0875 0.117 323
X6						1.0000 0.000 345	-0.6757 0.000 336	0.0844 0.178 257	0.0967 0.121 259	0.1534 0.009 291	0.1185 0.036 314	0.1396 0.012 326	-0.2792 0.000 325
X7							1.0000 0.000 361	-0.4051 0.000 257	-0.3893 0.000 255	-0.3034 0.000 291	-0.0311 0.580 319	0.0073 0.897 317	0.1556 0.004 346
DX2								1.0000 0.000 259	0.2475 0.000 247	0.1891 0.003 247	0.0459 0.468 252	0.0119 0.851 252	-0.1716 0.006 253
DX3									1.0000 0.000 262	0.0153 0.809 251	0.0682 0.280 252	-0.0914 0.148 252	-0.1688 0.007 254
DX4										1.0000 0.000 298	-0.0040 0.947 285	-0.0044 0.942 282	-0.2438 0.000 286
DX5											1.0000 0.000 323	-0.2502 0.000 303	-0.3797 0.000 312
DX6												1.0000 0.000 326	-0.8006 0.000 308
DX7													1.0000 0.000 346

Table 13.2B. Simple Correlation Between Total Factor Productivity and Establishment Share, and the Change in Establishment Share, by Firm Size Class, 1991

	TFP	X₂	X₃	X₄	X₅	X₆	X₇	DX₂	DX₃	DX₄	DX₅	DX₆	DX₇
TFP	1.0000	-0.1292	-0.1136	-0.1570	0.0377	0.1618	0.0776	-0.0493	0.0739	-0.0946	0.0292	0.0477	0.0097
Prob	0.000	0.010	0.025	0.002	0.457	0.001	0.125	0.330	0.148	0.063	0.564	0.349	0.848
n	450	393	388	386	391	389	392	392	386	386	391	388	392
X₂		1.0000	0.6611	0.3136	-0.2123	-0.5897	-0.6852	0.2183	-0.1238	-0.0785	-0.1739	0.0179	0.0711
		0.00	0.000	0.000	0.000	0.000	0.000	0.000	0.015	0.124	0.001	0.725	0.160
		393	388	386	391	389	392	392	386	386	391	388	392
X₃			1.0000	0.5613	0.0185	-0.5712	-0.7205	-0.0491	0.2350	-0.1832	-0.1132	-0.0083	0.0956
			0.000	0.000	0.717	0.000	0.000	0.335	0.000	0.000	0.026	0.871	0.060
			388	385	386	385	387	387	386	385	386	384	387
X₄				1.0000	0.3997	-0.3872	-0.7016	0.0230	-0.1117	0.2610	-0.2531	-0.0071	0.0804
				0.000	0.000	0.000	0.000	0.653	0.029	0.000	0.000	0.890	0.115
				386	384	384	385	385	386	386	386	383	383
X₅					1.0000	0.2916	-0.4877	0.0384	0.0727	-0.0003	-0.0099	-0.1031	-0.0230
					0.000	0.000	0.000	0.450	0.155	0.995	0.845	0.043	0.651
					391	388	390	390	385	386	386	387	390
X₆						1.0000	0.2049	-0.0019	0.0971	-0.0176	0.0144	0.0869	-0.1660
						0.000	0.000	0.970	0.057	0.731	0.778	0.087	0.001
						389	389	391	384	384	391	387	391
X₇							1.0000	-0.1521	-0.0161	0.0473	0.2364	0.0043	-0.0138
							0.000	0.003	0.753	0.355	0.000	0.932	0.785
							392	391	385	385	390	388	392
DX₂								1.0000	-0.5243	-0.0834	-0.2685	-0.0676	-0.3074
								0.000	0.000	0.102	0.000	0.184	0.000
								392	386	385	390	388	391
DX₃									1.0000	-0.4165	0.0936	-0.0544	-0.0607
									0.000	0.000	0.067	0.288	0.235
									386	384	385	384	385
DX₄										1.0000	-0.3170	-0.1378	-0.0577
										0.000	0.000	0.007	0.259
										386	386	383	385
DX₅											1.0000	-0.2448	-0.2444
											0.000	0.000	0.000
											391	387	390
DX₆												1.0000	-0.3272
												0.000	0.000
												388	388
DX₇													1.0000
													0.000
													392

often significant at the 2-tail 5 percent level. Hence, the correlations suggest that industries dominated by smaller firms have lower total factor productivity.

To improve on the preliminary results, we regress $ttfp$ on the employment share (establishment share) of the parent firm size classes. We run a separate regression for the share of every class of parent size. Because of multicollinearity, we cannot enter the shares for all classes simultaneously.

Three independent variables are introduced in the multiple regressions. First, we include a lagged value of $ttfp$ ($ttfp_{t-1}$). Productivity growth may be serially correlated because it often takes time to adopt productivity improving technology fully.

Second, we include the log of value-added in $t - 1$ as another control variable (log(real value-added)$_{t-1}$, where real value-added = real shipment − real expenditures on raw materials). Larger industries are typically "older" and older industries' productivity expectedly grows more slowly. Also, it is generally the case that in macroeconomic studies large economies grow more slowly. An analogous treatment here is to introduce the lagged value of value-added into our regression.

Our third control variable is a capital intensity measure, K/L_{t-1} [(plant and equipment)/direct production worker-hours]$_{t-1}$. We introduce K/L_{t-1} as a control variable for several reasons. First, productivity growth may be capital-biased, which is likely the case in the U.S. Second, we are concerned that the total factor productivity measure may have a "rent" element. The tfp measure we use is calculated as the change in real value of shipments minus the sum of the product of the change in each factor input and its cost share (where the cost shares of inputs sum to 1). Part of this tfp measure may reflect "market power."[6] To capture the potential rent component in the tfp measure, we introduce K/L_{t-1}, since high capital intensity can serve as an entry barrier.

Table 13.3A reports the regression results when $ttfp$ is regressed on employment shares and changes in employment shares by parent firm size classes. Table 13.3B reports the results when $ttfp$ is regressed on establishment shares and on changes in establishment shares by parent firm size classes. Notice again that we run a separate regression for the share of every class of parent size. Because of multicollinearity, we cannot enter the shares for all classes simultaneously. Thus, each column in both Tables 13.3A and 13.3B represents an independent set of regressions. Columns with heading X_2 to X_7 represent, respectively, that the prime independent variable is the market share of parent firms whose employment is within 1–4, 5–9, 10–19, 20–99, 100–499, and above 500.

Table 13.3A. *Regressing Total Factor Productivity on Employment Proportion, and on the Change in Employment Proportion, by Firm Size Class, 1991*

Y: TTFP = log{(tfp + 0.5) / [1 - (tfp + 0.5)]}
X: x_i = employment in firm size class i industry's total employment (beginning of the year)
     dx_i = $x_i(t) - x_i(t-1)$
     K/L(t-1) = plant & equipment in millions of 1987 dollars / millions of actual production worker hours (in year t-1)
     lnvadd(t-1) = log(value added) in t-1

	x_2	x_3	x_4	x_5	x_6	x_7	dx_2	dx_3	dx_4	dx_5	dx_6	dx_7
No Control												
Coeff.	-1.102[b]	-0.880[b]	-0.376	-0.154[c]	0.135	0.056	-9.041[b]	-1.913	-0.811	0.319	0.108	0.482
t	(2.30)	(2.50)	(1.59)	(1.79)	(1.18)	(1.32)	(2.27)	(0.88)	(0.55)	(0.54)	(0.32)	(1.35)
d.f.	296	299	320	336	343	359	257	260	296	321	324	344
R-square	.0176	.020	.0078	.0095	.004	.0048	.0197	.003	.0010	.0009	.0003	.0052
Control = TTFP(t-1)												
Coeff.	-1.109[b]	-0.879[b]	-0.371	-0.146[c]	0.137	0.052	-9.025[b]	-1.956	-0.858	0.399	0.097	0.472
t	(2.31)	(2.48)	(1.56)	(1.68)	(1.19)	(1.24)	(2.26)	(0.89)	(0.58)	(0.67)	(0.29)	(1.32)
d.f.	295	298	319	335	342	358	256	259	295	320	323	343
R-square	.0179	.0204	.0095	.0114	.0042	.0073	.0198	.0034	.0024	.0047	.0018	.0078
Control = TTFP(t-1), K/L(t-1)												
Coeff.	-0.990[b]	-0.828[b]	-0.378	-0.143	0.176	0.037	-8.862[b]	-1.612	-0.833	0.391	0.097	0.448
t	(2.03)	(2.27)	(1.53)	(1.52)	(1.45)	(0.79)	(2.17)	(0.72)	(0.55)	(0.66)	(0.29)	(1.25)
d.f.	294	297	318	334	341	357	255	258	294	319	322	342
R-square	.0233	.0216	.0095	.0114	.0071	.0089	.0199	.0056	.0024	.0049	.0020	.0101
Control = TTFP(t-1), K/L(t-1), lnvadd(t-1)												
Coeff.	-1.036[b]	-0.872[b]	-0.395	-0.177[c]	0.106	0.057	-8.744[b]	-1.736	-0.955	0.272	0.091	0.500
t	(2.10)	(2.38)	(1.60)	(1.85)	(0.80)	(1.17)	(2.14)	(0.77)	(0.63)	(0.45)	(0.27)	(1.38)
d.f.	293	296	317	333	340	356	254	257	293	318	321	341
R-square	.0251	.0265	.0124	.0199	.0119	.0166	.0238	.0083	.0087	.0089	.0120	.0135

a, b, and c represent significance in 2-tail test at 1, 5, and 10% level, respectively.

Table 13.3B. Regressing Total Factor Productivity on Establishment Proportion, and on the Change in Establishment Proportion, by Firm Size Class, 1991

Y: $TTFP = \log\{(tfp + 0.5) / [1 - (tfp + 0.5)]\}$

X: x_i = establishment in firm size class i / industry's total establishment (beginning of the year)

$dx_i = x_i(t) - x_i(t-1)$

$K/L(t-1)$ = plant & equipment in millions of 1987 dollars / millions of actual production worker hours (in year $t-1$)

$lnvadd(t-1) = \log(\text{value added})$ in $t-1$

	x_2	x_3	x_4	x_5	x_6	x_7	dx_2	dx_3	dx_4	dx_5	dx_6	dx_7
No Control												
Coeff.	-0.2307[b]	-0.4824[b]	-0.7514[a]	0.1088	0.6211[a]	0.0904	-0.3519	0.6160	-0.8452[a]	0.2586	0.5156	0.0862
t	(2.575)	(2.246)	(3.115)	(0.744)	(3.226)	(1.538)	(0.975)	(1.451)	(1.862)	(0.577)	(0.937)	(0.192)
d.f.	391	386	384	389	387	390	390	384	384	389	386	390
R-square	.0167	.0129	.0246	.0014	.0262	.006	.0024	.0055	.0089	.0009	.0023	.0001
Control = TTFP(t-1)												
Coeff.	-0.2327[a]	-0.4825[b]	-0.7582[a]	0.1089	0.6215[a]	0.0913	-0.3852	0.6260	-0.8479[a]	0.2658	0.5150	0.0867
t	(2.588)	(2.244)	(3.126)	(0.743)	(3.221)	(1.547)	(1.038)	(1.460)	(1.863)	(0.584)	(0.934)	(0.193)
d.f.	390	385	383	388	386	389	389	383	383	388	385	389
R-square	.0169	.0129	.0249	.0014	.0262	.0061	.0028	.0055	.0090	.0009	.0023	.0001
Control = TTFP(t-1), K/L(t-1)												
Coeff.	-0.2046[b]	-0.4030[b]	-0.6732[b]	0.2440	0.6273[a]	0.0545	-0.3187	0.6694	-0.8398[c]	0.1923	0.4964	0.0041
t	(2.179)	(1.787)	(2.566)	(1.563)	(3.264)	(0.783)	(0.856)	(1.567)	(1.852)	(0.423)	(0.904)	(0.009)
d.f.	389	384	382	387	385	388	388	382	382	387	384	388
R-square	.0197	.0164	.0267	.0162	.0371	.0087	.0102	.0178	.0188	.0104	.0133	.0071
Control = TTFP(t-1), K/L(t-1), lnvadd(t-1)												
Coeff.	-0.2107[b]	-0.3831[c]	-0.6613[b]	0.2268	0.5920[a]	0.0638	-0.3723	0.7083[c]	-0.8295[c]	0.1802	0.5406	0.0085
t	(2.247)	(1.694)	(2.524)	(1.452)	(3.039)	(0.915)	(0.998)	(1.658)	(1.832)	(0.397)	(0.986)	(0.019)
d.f.	388	383	381	386	384	387	387	381	381	386	383	387
R-square	.0254	.0196	.0324	.0218	.0400	.0163	.0239	.0248		.0169	.0207	.0132

[a], [b], and [c] represent significance in 2-tail test at 1, 5, and 10% level, respectively.

Columns with heading dX_2 to dX_7, respectively, represent that the prime independent variable is the change in the share of parent firms whose employment is within 1–4, 5–9, 10–19, 20–99, 100–499, and above 500. For example, the first column in Table 13.3A marked X_2 represents the regression of *ttfp* on the employment share of parent firms having only 1 to 4 employees; the seventh column marked dX_2 represents the regression of *ttfp* on the change in the employment of share of parent firms having only 1 to 4 employees. In the top panel, *ttfp* is regressed on only the share variable. In the second panel, we add the lagged value of *ttfp* as another independent variable. In the third panel, we add the lagged value of K/L, and in the bottom we further include the lagged value of log(real value-added) in the regressions.

The results suggest that *tfp* is higher the greater the larger firms' share. The results in both Tables 13.3A and 13.3B show that smaller firms' shares attract negative and often significant coefficients. The changes in smaller firms' shares also attract negative coefficients but they are less significant. Larger firms' shares and the change in their shares both attract positive coefficients. They are occasionally significant at the 10 percent 1-tail level.

To save space, we do not report the coefficient of the control variables in Tables 13.3A and 13.3B. Two of the control variables, K/L_{t-1} and $ttfp_{t-1}$, are both positive as expected, but they are utterly insignificant. The remaining control variable, log(value added)$_{-1}$, is negative and occasionally marginally significant at the 10 percent level.

The preliminary results in Tables 13.2A, 13.2B, 13.3A and 13.3B highlight that factor productivity is indeed related to the distribution of market share to firm size classes. They suggest that industries whose larger firms capture a greater share of employment and establishments have greater total factor productivity.

We obtain the relationship between *tfp* and small and large firms' market share individually – there is an obvious "missing variable" problem as other firm size classes' shares are not represented. As we have stated earlier, it is not sensible to do a multiple regression incorporating all firm size classes' shares because they are very highly correlated (see the simple correlations in Table 13.2). One reasonable approach is to find a continuous variable that is a composition of all the firm size classes' shares. A candidate is "employment/establishment" in each industry. The variable can be expressed as

$$s_2 \times (L/est)_2 + \cdots + s_7 \times (L/est)_7$$

where

$(L/est)_2$ = employment/

number of establishments in parent firm size class i

$i = 2, \ldots, 7$ representing, respectively, that parent firm
employment is within 1–4, 5–9, 10–19, 20–99, 100–499
and above 500

s_i = number of establishments in parent firm size class i/
total number of establishments in the industry

Hence, "employment/establishment" of an industry is an
"establishment-share-weighted" average of each firm class's average
employment per establishment. Note that larger parent firms typically
have more employment per establishment.[7] Thus, the greater the establishment share of larger firms the higher the variable. The "employ-
ment/establishment" variable we actually use is the log of the ratio based
on the beginning of 1991 data. We also use the first difference of the variable (the beginning of 1991 data minus the beginning of 1990 data). We
call the two variables L/est and CHL/est.

L/est is by construction correlated with larger firms' establishment
share and CHL/est is correlated with changes in larger firms' establishment share. We need to verify that L/est is an acceptable composite variable of all firm size classes' employment shares. We find that L/est is
positively and very significantly correlated with the employment share
of firm size class 7 (parent firm employment exceeds 500) and is negatively and very significantly correlated with other firm size classes'
employment shares. Similarly, CHL/est is positively and very significantly
correlated with the change in the employment share of firm size class 7
while negatively and very significantly correlated with the changes in the
employment share of firm size classes 2 to 5.

Our empirical question is, How does tfp relate to L/est and CHL/est?
We regress ttfp on the two variables with and without the control variables, $ttfp_{t-1}$, K/L_{t-1}, and log(real value-added)$_{t-1}$. The results are
reported in Table 13.4. The "employment/establishment" variable (L/est)
has a positive coefficient significant at the 1 percent level in all specifications. Similarly, the change in "employment/establishment" (CHL/est)
has a positive coefficient significant at the 5 percent level. Again, the
control variables result in regression coefficients of the expected sign,
but only the lagged value of value-added attains a marginal level of
significance.

In summary, our empirical results suggest that total factor productiv-

388   Zoltan J. Acs, Randall Morck and Bernard Yeung

Table 13.4. *Regressing Total Factor Productivity on Industry Employment/Establishment, and on the Change in Industry Employment/Establishment, in 1991*

	4.1	4.2	4.3	4.4	4.5	4.6
constant	-0.1911[a] (3.667)	-0.1077 (1.450)	-0.0305[b] (2.111)	0.0218 (0.328)	-0.1657[a] (3.129)	-0.0734 (0.978)
L/EST	0.0330[a] (2.691)	0.0338[a] (2.592)	-	-	0.0325[a] (2.652)	0.0349[a] (2.662)
L/EST$_t$ -L/EST$_{t-1}$	-	-	0.3894[b] (2.405)	0.3520[b] (2.117)	0.3907[b] (2.433)	0.3797[b] (2.298)
Control Variables						
TTFP$_{t-1}$	-	-0.0259 (0.530)	-	-0.0392 (0.802)	-	-0.0260 (0.533)
K/L$_{t-1}$	-	0.0002 (1.154)	-	0.0003 (1.562)	-	0.0002 (0.937)
log(Value -added)$_{t-1}$	-	-0.0137 (1.500)	-	-0.0098 (1.088)	-	-0.0156[c] (1.695)
R-square	0.0188	0.0272	0.0152	0.0242	0.0335	0.0426
d.f.	379	376	374	371	373	370

t-statistics in parentheses
[a], [b], and [c] represent significance in 2-tail test at 1, 5, and 10% level, respectively.

ity varies with the market share distribution by firm size: the greater the market share of larger firms, the higher the industry's total factor productivity.

5   Robustness Check

In this section, we report some robustness checks of the results. Our first concern is whether L/est and CHL/est are picking up "rents" or are indeed indicating that industries with a greater market share or larger firms have higher total factor productivity. Recall that when we introduce the control variables, we point out that our total factor productivity measure may capture "rents" – industries with more market power may register a higher *tfp* not because they experience higher total factor productivity, but because the *tfp* calculation may include market power of the existing firms in the industry. The point then is that our dependent variable potentially is measured with error. Larger firms in industries with concentrated market power ought to have a large market share.

L/est and CHL/est may then be capturing the measurement error in the preceding regressions.

There is a way to examine the possibility. The basic format of our regression is

$$ttfp_t = b \times L/est_{t-1} \quad \text{(or} \quad b \times CHL/est_{t-1}) \tag{1}$$

Suppose that "rent" exists in our *tfp* variable and that in regression equation (1) L/est and CHL/est are indeed picking up the "rent" element. L/est and CHL/est should obtain a more positive regression coefficient in industries with more "rent." We can test whether L/est and CHL/est are merely picking up "rent" by changing the regression specification as follows:

$$ttfp_t = (b_0 + b_1 \times rent_{t-1}) \times L/est_{t-1}$$
$$[\text{or} \quad (b_0 + b_1 \times rent_{t-1}) \times CHL/est_{t-1}] \tag{2}$$

where "rent" is a proxy capturing the presence of measurement error in *tfp* as a result of market power. When the presence of "rent" is the only explanation of our previous results, b_0 should be zero and b_1 should be positive. We can reject a "rent" measurement error explanation when b_0 is statistically significantly positive.

We find two proxies for "rent." The first one is "sum of establishment birth and death/original number of establishment" $[(B + D)/est]_{t-1}$. In our data set, establishment birth represents a greenfield start-up while establishment death represents the closing down of an establishment. Thus, $[(B + D)/est]_{t-1}$ captures the extent to which an industry is contested and indicates low fixed costs in the industry. In other words, the higher $[(B + D)/est]_{t-1}$, the lower the "rent." We expect that if L/est and CHL/est are merely picking up rents, the cross-terms between $[(B + D)/est]_{t-1}$ and them (i.e., b_1) will be negative and significant while L/est and CHL/est themselves (i.e., b_0) will be insignificant.[8]

Another plausible variable to capture "rent" is capital intensity, K/L_{t-1}. Industries with higher capital intensity are likely to have a greater fixed cost component and thus more "rent." We expect that if L/est and CHL/est are merely picking up rents, the cross-terms between K/L_{t-1} and them (b_1) will be positive and significant while L/est and CHL/est themselves (b_0) will be insignificant.

The regression test results are reported in Table 13.5. We regress *ttfp* on L/est and its cross-terms with $[(B + D)/est]_{t-1}$ and with K/L_{t-1} (columns 1 and 2, respectively), on CHL/est and its cross-terms with $[(B + D)/est]_{t-1}$ and with K/L_{t-1} (columns 3 and 4, respectively), and then on both L/est and CHL/est and their cross-terms with $[(B + D)/est]_{t-1}$ and

Table 13.5. *Regressing Total Factor Productivity on Industry Employment/Establishment, on the Change in Industry Employment/Establishment, and on Their Cross-Terms with K/L_{t-1} and with [(Number of Establishment Birth + Death)/Original Number of Establishments]$_{t-1}$, 1991*

	(1)	(2)	(3)	(4)	(5)	(6)
with no control variables						
L/EST	0.0296^b (2.267)	0.0301^b (2.250)	-	-	0.0331^b (2.260)	0.0307^b (2.271)
x [(B + D)/ est]$_{t-1}$	0.0354 (0.755)	-	-	-	0.0103 (0.145)	-
x K/L$_{t-1}$	-	0.0001 (0.544)	-	-	-	0.0001 (0.328)
L/EST$_t$ -L/EST$_{t-1}$	-	-	0.7442^b (1.938)	0.4631^b (2.264)	0.8066^c (1.663)	0.3784^c (1.757)
x [(B + D)/ est]$_{t-1}$	-	-	-2.0610 (1.018)	-	-2.3642 (0.815)	-
x K/L$_{t-1}$	-	-	-	-0.0014 (0.590)	-	0.0001 (0.005)
R-square	0.0202	0.0195	0.0180	0.0162	0.0380	0.0338
d.f.	378	378	373	373	371	371
with control variables as in Table 13.4						
L/EST	0.0302^b (2.171)	0.0515^a (3.016)	-	-	0.0372^b (2.371)	0.0511^a (2.938)
x [(B + D)/ est]$_{t-1}$	0.0369 (0.782)	-	-	-	0.0015 (0.021)	-
x K/L$_{t-1}$	-	-0.0003 (1.600)	-	-	-	-0.0003 (1.424)
L/EST$_t$ -L/EST$_{t-1}$	-	-	0.6998^c (1.804)	0.3931^c (1.785)	0.8562^c (1.725)	0.3264 (1.478)
x [(B + D)/ est]$_{t-1}$	-	-	-2.0101 (0.992)	-	2.7355 (0.932)	-
x K/L$_{t-1}$	-	-	-	-0.0007 (0.285)	-	0.0006 (0.236)
R-square	0.0288	0.0338	0.0268	0.0244	0.0474	0.0478
d.f.	375	375	370	370	368	368

t-statistics in parentheses
a, b, and c represent significance in 2-tail test at 1, 5, and 10% level, respectively.

with K/L_{t-1} (columns 5 and 6, respectively). In the top panel we report regressions without any control variables and in the bottom panel we report regressions with all the control variables we used in Table 13.4 ($ttfp_{t-1}$, K/L_{t-1}, and log(value-added)$_{t-1}$). It turns out that the regression coefficients for the stand-alone L/est and CHL/est are always positive and significant, just as they are in Table 13.4. The regression coefficients for the cross-terms are never significant and sometimes they have a sign opposite to that expected by the "pure rent" hypothesis (the fourth entry in column 5 in the lower panel). In other words, we find that b_0 in equation 2 is positive and significant while b_1 is insignificantly different from zero. These results contradict the hypothesis that our L/est and CHL/est are picking up merely a measurement error due to the presence of "rents" in tfp.

Our results would be "cleaner" if computer related industries were taken out of our sample because these industries are known to have productivity trends very different from those of other industries. The industry classifications in our sample are reconciled with the classifications in 1972. We therefore match the 1972 SIC classifications and the latest SIC classifications to identify industries in our sample that may include computer related industries.[9] We exclude these industries from our sample and re-run the regressions as in Table 13.4. We indeed obtain more significant regression coefficients for L/est and CHL/est, which remain positive.

There is another potential problem in our main regression results reported in Table 13.4. Our data year is 1991, the beginning of a recession. We were advised that during the beginning of a recession, larger firms typically allowed a greater buildup of inventory than smaller firms. Larger firms might then seem to maintain their productivity while smaller firms did not. Our L/est and CHL/est may be picking up the phenomenon. To mitigate the problem, we include "change in real inventory" as another control variable in the regressions in Table 13.4. We indeed find that "change in real inventory" is positive and significant in the regression. However, the behavior of L/est and CHL/est remains the same as in Table 13.4 (they obtain positive and significant regression coefficients).

We question further how the data year, 1991, affects our results. We believe that by accident we might have picked a desirable year for our experiment. The recession in the early nineties began in 1991. Large and small firms react differently to a recession: the former usually contract by laying off workers while the latter are more prompt to close out small establishments. Hence, larger firms may have more idle capital than smaller firms during a recession. Thus industries with more large firms may be more likely to register *lower* total factor productivity than industries with more small firms. Our choice of data year biases against finding that industries with more large firms have a greater total factor productivity. Our results are then particularly noteworthy.

Zoltan J. Acs, Randall Morck and Bernard Yeung

Finally, we are concerned with a survival bias problem. Firms grow larger because they are better (Jovanovic, 1982). Industries with a greater share of larger firms may be industries with a greater share of better firms. Our results then suggest that better firms generate more productivity growth. The point, in our opinion, is not an objection to our finding. Rather, it addresses what the proper interpretation should be. We discuss our interpretation in the next section.

6   Discussion and Conclusion

In this chapter, we examine the relationship between productivity growth and market share distribution by firm size. Our results are based on a cross-sectional study of the U.S. manufacturing industry data in 1991. In the data year, the U.S. manufacturing sector on average experienced negative total factor productivity growth, job losses, and a net decline in the number of establishments. Against this background, we find that industry total factor productivity is associated with market share distribution by firm size, where market share is defined as employment share and/or establishment share. Industries in which larger firms have a greater market share have a higher total factor productivity growth.

Concerned with our data limitation, we examine the robustness of our result. We are first concerned whether our observation is spurious. We examine and eliminate one plausible explanation of our observation – our total factor productivity measure has a rent component and it is captured by our proxy for large firms' market share. Second, we are concerned whether our result is driven by macroeconomics. Our data year was the beginning of a recession. We introduce an additional independent variable, the change in inventory, in our regressions to check the possibility that larger firms are hoarding inventory at the beginning of a recession and thus register less decline in their productivity. We find that our results are unaffected. We also question how the choice of the first year of a recession cycle affects our results and conclude that it will actually bias against the possibility of finding our observation. While we are optimistic about the robustness of our observation, we still advocate caution and welcome closer scrutiny.

We should be very cautious in interpreting our results. Our results suggest that larger firms contribute more to productivity growth than smaller firms. Why? Would that be due to the Schumpeterian reason (Schumpeter, 1942), larger firms have more resources to adopt and implement innovations? Would that be a reflection of survival bias, larger firms are larger because they are better in the Jovanovic (1982) sense, and better firms contribute more to productivity growth? Note that the second explanation obviously offers absolutely no room for policy activism. Even the first explanation does not readily suggest any policy actions: firms are very capable in wasting subsidized resources instead of using them to increase productivity.

Our results also do not suggest that smaller firms do not make substantial contribution to productivity growth. Many radical and yet fruitful innovations are brought onto the marketplace by small firms. However, many more small firms are trivial start-ups which will eventually wither. Thence, the average contribution of smaller firms to productivity growth can appear trivial. Moreover, the contribution of radical innovations by truly innovative small firms will take time to manifest their influence on productivity.

In our opinion, there is likely a Schumpeterian transition story: small firms introduce radical innovations and large firms magnify the impact of the innovations. The large firms may be the formerly small and yet successful firms, or they are agile large firms successful in acquiring and adopting the innovations brought by small firms. The Schumpeterian transition story suggests that productivity growth is positively associated with the current market share of larger firms but is positively associated with the market share of smaller firms in the past. We therefore urge a follow-up of this study using cross-sectional time series data.

Notes

We are grateful for the helpful comments from the conference discussant, David Storey, and the conference participants, in particular, Paul Gompers and John Haltiwanger. We are also grateful to Beverly Burr, Gunter Dufey, Alec Levinson, Joanne Oxley, Elaine Reardon, and Laura Robinson for their helpful comments.
[1] Often, employees also have to sign an explicit agreement that they will refrain from being in a position that directly competes with their current employer within a certain time period after their departure. Hence, they cannot easily conceal an idea, resign from their job, and then use the idea to compete with their old employer.
[2] For a discussion of the SUSB data see Armington, 1997.
[3] We were told that these establishments inevitably had very "small" parents who even failed to file corporate income tax returns.
[4] Other variables are of limited use because there are too many missing values.
[5] It can be easily verified that $ttfp$ and tfp have the same sign and that $ttfp$ stretches from positive infinity to negative infinity as tfp varies from 0.5 to -0.5. The transformation is done to make our regressions conform more to the statistical assumptions in ordinary least squares (OLS). Regression results using

the original *tfp* as the dependent variable are qualitatively identical to what we are going to report here.

[6] It is easy to understand the formulae in the case of perfect competition and a homogeneous degree 1 production function. For simplicity, consider a two factor homogeneous degree 1 production function, $Q = f(x_1, x_2)$, where Q is output and x_1 and x_2 are factor inputs. With f_i's defined as partial derivatives, Q can be expressed as follows:

$$Q = f_1 \times x_1 + f_2 \times x_2$$

Taking total derivative, we obtain

$$dQ/Q = f_1 \times dx_1/Q + f_2 \times dx_2/Q + (df_1 \times x_1 + df_2 \times x_2)/Q$$

Assuming perfect competition, we obtain $p \times f_1 = W_1$ and $p \times f_2 = W_2$, where p is Q's price and W_i's are factor prices of x_i's. By substitution,

$$dQ/Q = (W_1 \times x_1/P \times Q) \times dx_1/x_1 + (W_2 \times x_2/P \times Q) \times$$
$$dx_2/x_2 + (df_1 \times x_1 + df_2 \times x_2)/Q$$
$$= (s_1 \times dx_1/x_1 + s_2 \times dx_2/x_2) + (df_1 \times x_1 + df_2 \times x_2)/Q$$

where

$$s_i's = W_i \times x_1/P \times Q, \text{ and the sum of all } s_i = 1$$

In the context of the above, *tfp* is $[dQ/Q - (s_1 \times dx_1/x_1 + s_2 \times dx_2/x_2)]$, which is exactly how *tfp* in the NBER tape is obtained.

However, if there is market power, $MR \times f_1 = W_1$ and $MR \times f_2 = W_2$, where MR is marginal revenue. Profit maximization implies that $MR = MC$ (marginal cost). By substitutions, $[dQ/Q - (s_1 \times dx_1/x_1 + s_2 \times dx_2/x_2)]$ is as follows:

$$(P/MC - 1) \times (s_1 \times dx_1/x_1 + s_2 \times dx_2/x_2)$$
$$+ (df_1 \times x_1 + df_2 \times x_2)/Q$$

Hence, a simple *tfp* calculation may have a "rent" component which is $(P/MC - 1) \times (s_1 \times dx_1/x_1 + s_2 \times dx_2/x_2)$. While it is possible to obtain *tfp* given the presence of market power and in the context of a general production function, we do not have the required data to do so.

[7] Indeed, the average employment per establishment increases monotonically with the size of parent firms. The average is, respectively, 1.90, 6.77, 13.76, 40.65, 120.53, and 320.25 (persons) for parent firm employment equal to 1–4, 5–9, 10–19, 20–99, 100–499, and above 500.

[8] The $[(B + D)/est]_{t-1}$ measure has its problems. A high establishment death rate may mean not just that there are low exit costs but that an industry is declining. A high establishment birth rate may mean not just that there are low entry costs but also that an industry is expanding. We therefore try several versions: we use $[(B + D)/est]_{t-1}$, B/est_{t-1}, and D/est_{t-1}. They all lead to qualitatively similar results. We opt to focus on using $[(B + D)/est]_{t-1}$ because the variable mitigates the problem of measuring industry expansion and decline.

[9] We find eight such industries: 3574, 3579, 3629, 3661, 3663, 3674, 3679, and 3699.

References

Acs, Zoltan J. and David Audretsch (1987), "Innovation, Market Structure, and Firm Size," *Review of Economics and Statistics*, Vol. 69 (4), November, 567–574.

Acs, Zoltan J. and David Audretsch (1988), "Innovation in Large and Small Firms: An Empirical Analysis," *American Economic Review*, Vol. 78 (4), September, 678–690.

Acs, Zoltan J. and David Audretsch (1989), "Small-Firm Entry in US Manufacturing," *Economica*, Vol. 56, 255–265.

Acs, Zoltan J., Randall Morck, Myles Shaver, and Bernard Yeung (1997), "The Internationalization of Small and Medium Size Firms: A Policy Perspective," *Small Business Economics*, 9(1), 7–20.

Armington, Catherine (1997), "Statistics of U.S. Business – Microdata and Tables of SBA/Census Data on Establishment Size, Office of Advocacy, U.S. Small Business Administration.

Cockburn, Iain and Rebecca Henderson (1995), Do Agency Costs Explain Variation in Innovative Performance," working paper, Massachusetts Institute of Technology, presented at the NBER IO Summer conference, Cambridge, Mass.

De Soto, Hernando (1989), *The Other Path*, Harper & Row Publishers, New York.

Evans, David S. and Boyan Jovanovic, (1989), "An Estimated Model of Entrepreneurial Choice under Liquidity Constraints," *Journal of Political Economy*, Vol. 97 (4), 808–827.

Holtz-Eakin, Douglas, David Joulfaian, and Harvey S. Rosen (1994a), "Entrepreneurial Decisions and Liquidity Constraints," *Rand Journal of Economics*, Vol. 25 (2), Summer, 334–347.

Holtz-Eakin, Douglas, David Joulfaian, and Harvey S. Rosen (1994b), "Sticking It Out: Entrepreneurial Survival and Liquidity Constraints," *Journal of Political Economy*, Vol. 102 (1), 53–75.

Jovanovic, Boyan (1982), "Selection and the Evolution of Industry," *Econometrica*, Vol. 50, 649–670.

King, Robert G. and Ross Levine (1993), "Finance and Growth: Schumpeter Might Be Right," *Quarterly Journal of Economics*, Vol. 108, August, 717–737.

Lenway, Stefanie, Randall Morck, and Bernard Yeung (1996), "Rent-Seeking, Protectionism and Innovation in the American Steel Industry," *Economic Journal*, 106, March, 410–421.

Mitchell, Will, Randall Morck, Myles Shaver, and Bernard Yeung (1996), "Causality Between International Expansion and Investment in Intangibles, with Implications for Financial Performance and Firm Survival," paper presented at the University of Illinois (Urbana-Champaign) CIBE Conference on Longitudinal Studies of Foreign Market Entry, April, 1996.

Morck, Randall and Bernard Yeung (1991), "Why Investors Value Multinationality," *Journal of Business*, Vol. 46 (2), 165–187.

Olson, Mancur Jr. (1996), "Distinguished Lecture on Economics in Government: Big Bills Left on the Sidewalk: Why Some Nations Are Rich, and Others Poor," *Journal of Economic Perspectives*, Vol. 10 (2), Spring, 3–24.

Schumpeter, Joseph A. (1934), *The Theory of Economic Development*, Cambridge, Mass: Harvard University Press.

Schumpeter, Joseph A. (1942), *Capitalism, Socialism and Democracy*, New York: Harper & Brothers.

Winter, Sidney (1984), "Schumpeterian Competition in Alternative Technologies Regimes," *Journal of Economic Behavior and Organization*, Vol. 5, 287–320.

Name Index

Subject Index

adverse selection: in venture capital market, 223–5
agency costs, 212, 215; in determining leverage, 218; in entrepreneurial firms, 217; reducing, 225
asset specificity: in Williamson's theory of the firm, 70–2
asymmetric information, 207, 223, 230–1

bounded rationality: in Williamson's theory of the firm, 70–2
business: as learning experiment, 163
business dynamic indices, 120–3
business failure: capital in analysis of, 20, 163–6; data sources for analysis of small-business failure, 166–8; human capital in analysis of, 20, 163–4, 172–7; model of small-firm failure, 168–71, 177–80

capital (*see also* human capital; venture capital): in analysis of small-business failure, 20, 163–6; factors in access to financial, 20; investors staging infusions of, 211–20
cash flow: to determine control right allocation, 222; incentive effects, 224; separation of allocation from control, 228; terminal, 224
clusters. *See* industry clusters
comparative advantage: in collecting and processing information, 51; of intermediator, 57; in ownership of resources, 54
competence: of firm owner, 52–5; of incumbent enterprises, 82; managerial, 73–4; of recruiters, 64
competition: dynamics of, 14–15
competitive advantage: sustainable, 52; trade-related information as source of, 56
contracts, venture capital, 226–9

coordination: role of firm in, 48–50
creative destruction (*see also* volatility): business turbulence and volatility as measure of, 119–23; causing economic growth, 103–8; related to economic growth, 98–101, 113; sources of, 108–13

data sources: analysis of economic growth in relation to business volatility, 98; analysis of job flows, 313; for analysis of relation of firm size to productivity growth, 372–4; analysis of role of SMEs in job creation, 287–91; for analysis of small-business failure, 163, 166–8; for analysis of small-firm short-run performance, 187–90; for analysis of UK small and medium-sized firms, 331–2; for creative destruction analysis, 116–17; missing values in innovation survey (1995), 355–63
debt, convertible: in venture capital financing, 225–7
diversity: of firms in industry, 65–6; new firms in generation of, 80; of shocks, 64
division of labor, 55–6

economic growth (*see also* productivity growth): caused by creative destruction, 103–8; creative destruction preceding, 101–3; creative destruction related to, 98–101, 113; measures of, 117–19; model of regional, 103–13; relation to productivity, 30; relation to turbulence and volatility, 17; role of small and medium-sized firms in, 5–12; sources of, 31
economic performance, macroeconomic (Ohio and Sweden: 1975–95), 138–43
economics, institutional, 70–2
economic shocks: effect on firms of persistent and transitory, 26, 47, 74; effect on job creation and destruction,

401

402   Subject Index

26; information about, 47; oil price and monetary shocks in five-variable VAR analysis of job flows, 257–81
economies of scale (*see also* minimum efficient scale [MES]): with integration, 63, 66; in production, 63
employer age. *See* firm age
employers: firms as, 55–6
employer size. *See* firm size
employment (*see also* job creation; job destruction; job growth; manufacturing sector): changes in distribution in Ohio and Sweden (1975–95), 143–5; changes in firms (1992–3), 23–6; job creation and destruction measures, 241; levels in small firms (1958–92), 8–11; Ohio and Sweden (1975–95), 138–43; small business share of (1958–77, 1958–92), 7, 9–10
entrepreneurial regime: innovating under, 84–5; likelihood of innovating under, 84–5; new entrants to, 16, 91; small firm innovation rate under, 86
entrepreneurs: ability to synthesize information, 75; as concept to explain the firm, 46–7; conditions for removal of, 228; detection of change in firm, 74; firms as, 82; in firms with venture capital, 215–20, 222–31; information synthesis in concept of, 46–7; learning of, 88–9; low- and high-ability, 224–6; new firms as, 82; in Oi's small-firm model, 190–1; role of, 15; in Schumpeter's analysis, 14–15; as social class, 45
evolution: learning role in business, 162
evolutionary theory: of firm, 80–6; of industry, 82–6; innovation in, 80

financial structure: of young microfirms, 20–1, 186–03
financing: convertible debt in venture capital, 225–7; public policy related to, 33–4; sources for large and small businesses, 18–21; of startup firms, 207–8; venture capital staged, 211–20
firm age: characteristics of UK small and medium-sized firms (1993–5), 332–3; job creation and destruction by (1986–8), 319–21; job flows rates by (1972, 1988), 242–3, 246–7*t*; role in job creation and destruction analysis, 241–3
firm growth: new, 83; in Sweden and Ohio, 145–6

firms (*see also* heterogeneity of firms; homogeneity of firms): achieving minimum efficient scale (MES), 83–5, 89; comparison of synthetic and ownership theories of, 68–70; concept of entrepreneur to explain, 46–7; as coordinator, 48; as decision-making unit, 48–9; definitions of, 48–50; distribution in Ohio and Sweden (1975–95), 143–6; as employers, 55–6; evolutionary theory of, 80–6; factors influencing creation of, 47; financing of startup, 207–8; four-factor theory of, 57–9; heterogeneity of Dutch, 315–16; as information-processing mechanism, 47; information used to control resources, 53; as intermediators, 56–7; likelihood of survival of new, 85; numbers in Ohio and Sweden (1975–95), 142; organizational structures of, 66; as organizations, 57–9; ownership theory of, 68–70; resource-based theories of, 72–4; role of innovative activity, 84–5; size of, 63–6; synthetic model of, 47, 65; synthetic theory of, 65–8, 72–4; theory of form selection, 82–6; as users of information, 50–2; variation in likelihood of survival, 87–8; venture capital for young, innovative, 206, 208; Williamson's theory of, 70–2
firms, large: in analysis of job creation during recession and recovery, 288–9; annual job changes (1989–94), 291–3; arguments in favor of, 370–1; financing share of, 18–20; incentives to innovate, 369–71; job gains and losses (1989–94), 291–5; job volatility index (1989–94), 293*f*, 294–5; response to cyclical change (1989–94), 291–4; role in innovative activity, 28–9; share of job gains and losses (1989–94), 292*f*, 294; share of private employment base (1989–94), 292*f*, 294
firms, new: cross-national analysis of births of, 112–13; growth of, 83; venture capital contributions (1969–95), 209–11
firms, small: characteristics of, 190–2; contributions to innovation, 368–9; in economic theory, 12–14; financial variables in model of survival of, 192–7; financing share of, 18–20; growth (1970s and 80s), 68; incentives to innovate in, 369–70; model of failure of, 171–2; model of survival, 197–202;